An Institutional Investor Publication it

MANAGED

FUTURES

Performance,
Evaluation and
Analysis of
Commodity Funds,
Pools and Accounts

Carl C. Peters, Editor

PROBUS PUBLISHING COMPANY
Chicago, Illinois
Cambridge, England

ISBN 1-55738-291-3

Printed in the United States of America

BB

2 3 4 5 6 7 8 9 0

To my wife, Nancy.

Carl C. Peters

Contents

Preface

This book presents a cohesive look at an emerging asset category that is being taken seriously by both individual and institutional investors—that of professionally managed investments using derivative instruments (futures, forward contracts, and options) in the commodity and financial markets. The attractiveness of these investments lies in their historically high returns, low to negative correlation with traditional investments in stocks and bonds, capability of acting as a hedge against inflation, and liquidity. This book examines the theoretical and methodological basis for performance, as well as historical performance itself. Included are the original works of various researchers in evaluating the performance of managed futures products—public commodity funds, private commodity pools, and individual managed accounts, as well as commodity trading advisors.

The first chapter gives a perspective and overview of this asset category, termed "managed futures," and lays out the important issues regarding performance. Chapters 2 and 3 are the first articles published on the use of futures—in this case passive portfolios of futures contracts—which showed their promise in diversifying portfolios and hedging against inflation. Chapter 4 is the first work on actively managed futures in combination with stock and bond portfolios. Authored by the late John Lintner of Harvard University, it showed how active management of commodity and financial futures produced significantly positive but substantially different patterns in returns from stocks and bonds. Furthermore, he showed how widely different patterns in returns could occur between managed futures accounts, and the potential they had for being combined into attractive investment alternatives. The remaining chapters investigate the performance of managed futures products in comparison to more traditional investments, in diversification of stock and bond portfolios, and as a hedge against inflation.

Every attempt has been made to preserve the exact wording and results of the works as they originally appeared. Minor modifications were necessary, however, in form and layout to maintain a consistancy within this book. In some instances the word "chapter" was substituted for "paper" or "article" in the original text; in no way is it intended to imply that the author was writing a chapter specifically for this book at the time the paper or article was written. Typos or errors in the original were left essentially uncorrected, unless in so doing the meaning was left unchanged.

I am grateful to the authors, journals, and organizations who gave their permission for these important works to be reproduced. A special word of thanks to both Al Orr and Frank Pusateri who initially saw the value in this project, and to the Managed Futures Trade Association for its encouragement. Thanks also to Morton Baratz and Leon Rose for their helpful suggestions during the preparation of the manuscript.

Finally, I would like to acknowledge the special efforts of the staff of Probus Publishing. Carol Klein went far beyond the call of duty in seeing that deadlines were met. This book would not have been possible without the foresight and encouragement of my editor.

Carl C. Peters, Ph.D.
A. O. Management Corporation
Pittsburgh, Pennsylvania

Introduction

The purpose of this book is to introduce the reader to managed futures in concept and application, and to review and summarize what has been found about performance. It is hoped that by developing an understanding of this new asset category and describing important research findings that a cohesive picture of the product will emerge that will be beneficial to both investors and researchers.

"Managed futures" refers to professionally managed investments in commodity and financial futures markets.* Management is accomplished through Commodity Trading Advisors (CTAs) who are registered with and regulated by the Commodity Futures Trading Commission (CFTC). Estimates put the 1991 level of investment in managed futures at over $25 billion, compared to less than $500 million in 1980.** While still small in comparison to stocks and bonds, the annual compounded growth rate of over 40% indicates a growing popularity and acceptance by investors. Managed futures have drawn the interest of both individual and institutional investors who are attracted by the potential of returns from non-traditional markets, diversification potential offered to traditional stock and bond portfolios, and the possibilities of hedging their portfolios against inflation.

This book contains, besides an introductory first chapter, numerous works of other authors who have addressed the subject of performance of managed futures products. The criteria for works to be used in this book include relevance of subject material and the presence of a review process in either preparation or presentation. Refereed academic journals obviously qualify. Also included are conference proceedings and professional presentations, on the assumption that the presenters accounted for the professional nature of their audience. Reports and working papers for sponsored research are likewise included if the sponsor was a recognized institution or program. Specifically excluded are newspaper and trade journal articles, editorials, or promotional material.

---

*Also included, but to a lesser extent, are cash and forward contracts, and options on futures.
**The Wall Street Journal, p. C12, August 27, 1990.

Chapter One

Managed Futures— A Performance Perspective

Carl C. Peters

This chapter begins with a description of the characteristics of futures, and managed futures investments. There are certain unique features such as margin, leverage and event sensitivity which are part of futures products that need to be understood in order to correctly interpret performance. The remaining part of this chapter addresses these following main issues of performance:

1. Performance as a stand-alone investment
2. Potential as a hedge against inflation
3. Correlation to stock and bond performance
4. Effectiveness in portfolio diversification

Description of Managed Futures Investments

A futures contract is an agreement to deliver or accept a specified quantity of a commodity (or financial instrument) at a predetermined price at a designated time in the future. Futures contracts exist for a number of diverse commodity and financial instrument groups. Included are the grains, livestock, foods and fibers, petroleum and related products, metals, currencies, interest rate instruments and indices for stocks and bonds. A buyer is said to have established a long position (i.e. agreed to accept delivery) and can profit if prices rise. A seller, on the other hand, has established a short position (i.e., agreed to deliver) and can profit if prices fall. For most

3

investors liquidation is done by selling or buying an equal number of contracts to offset their original positions. Because of the ease of entering or exiting, going long or short, relatively low costs per transaction, and liquidity of the futures markets, professional management generally consists of active buying and selling, frequently aided by technical analysis [Brorsen and Irwin (1985)] in an attempt to profit from both rising and falling prices.

Domestic futures markets operate under regulations of the Commodity Futures Trading Commission (CFTC), the commodities counterpart of the Securities Exchange Commission (SEC). Additionally, the National Futures Association (NFA) monitors, administers, and self-regulates the professional conduct and financial responsibility of its membership, as does the National Association of Security Dealers (NASD) for securities.

Futures investing involves putting up a "good faith" deposit (also called "margin") to ensure that an adverse price movement will be covered if a contract is liquidated at a loss. However, margin for futures investments is different from that required for stocks and bonds. Stocks margins constitute a partial payment for the stock, the remainder or debit balance is usually kept in a margin account as a debt upon which interest is charged. Commodity margins, on the other hand, are good-faith deposits to insure that adverse price movements are covered. Stock margin requirements fluctuate in a range of 50% to 90% of the stock purchased. Commodity margin requirements are usually only 5% to 10% of the face value of a contract. Whereas the purchaser of stock using a margin has to *pay* interest on the difference between his deposit and the value of the stock, the investor in commodities can *receive* interest on the money which is used as the "good-faith" deposit. It is common to use between 10% to 30% of investment funds to satisfy all margin requirements in managed futures accounts, with the remainder used as reserve. Since short-term instruments such as U. S. Treasury Bills can be used for margin, it is not uncommon for an account to be able to earn interest on its entire investment capital while being used for margin and reserve.

Managed futures investments fall into three broad categories each with their own cost structure and capital requirements: individual accounts, private pools and public commodity funds. Individual accounts generally have low costs and large minimum capital requirements. Public commodity funds, on the other hand, have higher costs but the lowest minimum investment requirements. Private commodity pools have generally the lowest costs, and investment minimums somewhere in between. These categorizations are not all inclusive, and exceptions do exist. There can, however, be substantive differences in performance for each, so their identities should be kept distinct.

An important issue to be considered when analyzing performance is the time period selected for analysis. The inflationary era of the late 1970s caused commodity prices to move upwards substantially. The decade of the 1980s, on the other hand, marked a return to lower inflation and relative price stability. To the extent that performance of managed futures products is related to price trends in commodity prices (a subject addressed by some of the research herein) and that inflation is detrimental to stock and bond investments, periods of high and low inflation can have a significant impact on relative performance. Figure 1-1 gives an overview of the time period analyzed for each of the research articles contained in this book.

Performance as a Stand-Alone Investment

Performance comparisons between investment alternatives necessarily include measures of both return and risk. Most researchers equate risk with variability of returns and its most popularized measure—standard deviation. The higher the standard deviation the larger the variability, and the lower the probability that the average rate of return will occur in any one period. Although standard deviation suffers from some shortcomings [See Strahm (1983), or Peters (1989)], it has found wide acceptance by both researchers and investors as a proxy for risk.

One measure of performance is the simple ratio of return-to-risk (typically the ratio of excess return [over and above the risk-free rate] to standard deviation—called the Sharpe Ratio). Maximizing these ratios (return-to-risk), while an intuitively appealing approach, does not take into account the investor's risk preferences [Reilly (1985)]. A proper and complete analysis would address the unique utility function of each investor. This of course is not possible except under the most general circumstances [See Fischmar and Peters (1990)], so we are left with simple comparisons of return and risk between alternatives. Table 1-1 summarizes the findings of researchers who compared managed futures as stand-alone investments to stocks, bonds and T-bills. Results appear to be mixed but do reflect a consistency when examined in detail.

Table 1-1 is organized by product groups—passive futures portfolios, commodity trading advisors, private commodity pools and public funds. Results for each author can be viewed by examining performance for various asset alternatives across each row in the table.

Without exception, all researchers found managed futures products to have higher variability (as measured by variance or standard deviation) than stocks, bonds or T-bills. The question then becomes whether returns

Figure 1-1   Studies, Products and Time Frames

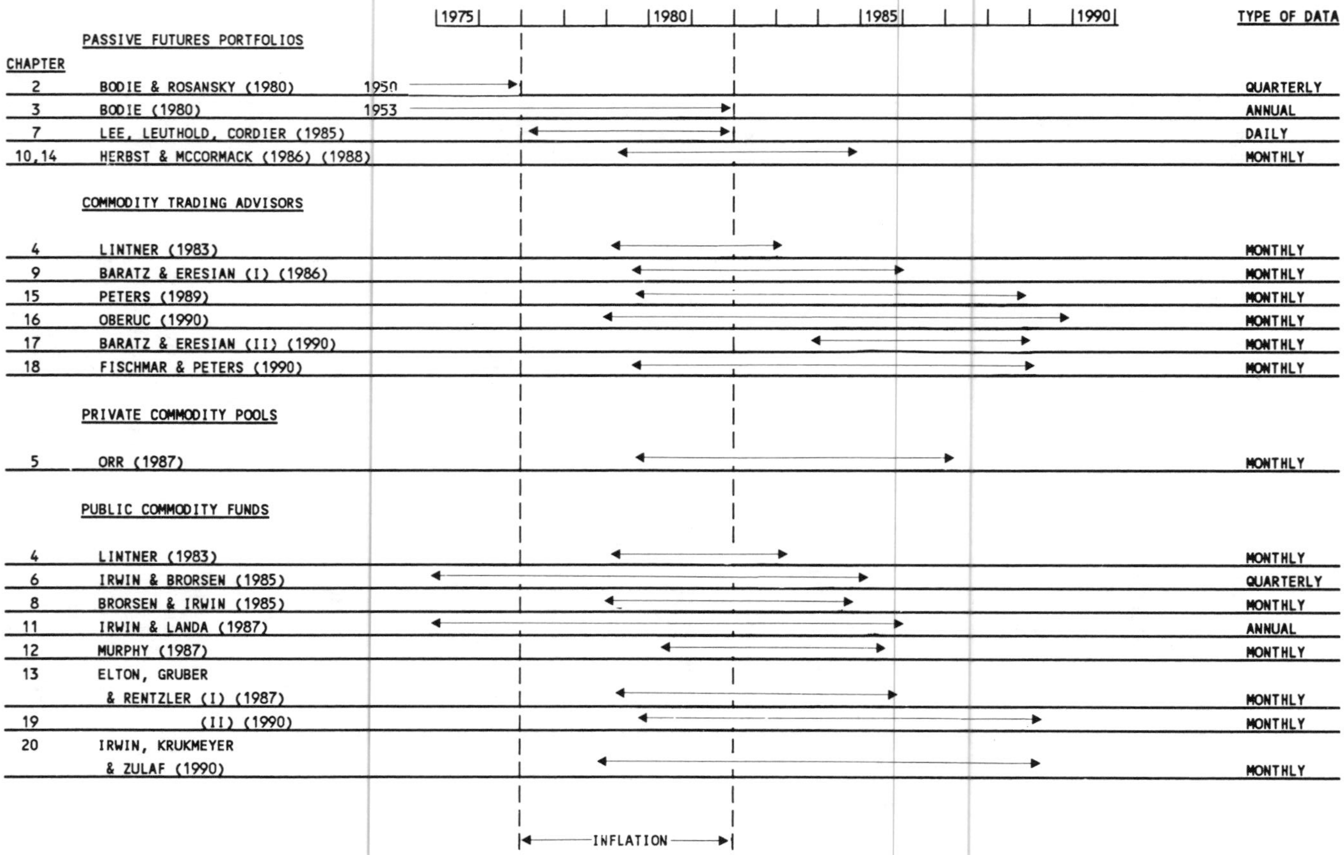

		1975					1980					1985					1990		TYPE OF DATA

CHAPTER

PASSIVE FUTURES PORTFOLIOS

Chapter	Study	Data
2	BODIE & ROSANSKY (1980) 1950	QUARTERLY
3	BODIE (1980) 1953	ANNUAL
7	LEE, LEUTHOLD, CORDIER (1985)	DAILY
10,14	HERBST & MCCORMACK (1986) (1988)	MONTHLY

COMMODITY TRADING ADVISORS

Chapter	Study	Data
4	LINTNER (1983)	MONTHLY
9	BARATZ & ERESIAN (I) (1986)	MONTHLY
15	PETERS (1989)	MONTHLY
16	OBERUC (1990)	MONTHLY
17	BARATZ & ERESIAN (II) (1990)	MONTHLY
18	FISCHMAR & PETERS (1990)	MONTHLY

PRIVATE COMMODITY POOLS

Chapter	Study	Data
5	ORR (1987)	MONTHLY

PUBLIC COMMODITY FUNDS

Chapter	Study	Data
4	LINTNER (1983)	MONTHLY
6	IRWIN & BRORSEN (1985)	QUARTERLY
8	BRORSEN & IRWIN (1985)	MONTHLY
11	IRWIN & LANDA (1987)	ANNUAL
12	MURPHY (1987)	MONTHLY
13	ELTON, GRUBER & RENTZLER (I) (1987)	MONTHLY
19	(II) (1990)	MONTHLY
20	IRWIN, KRUKMEYER & ZULAUF (1990)	MONTHLY

INFLATION

Table 1-1 Relative Performance as a Stand-Alone Investment

CHAPTER	PASSIVE FUTURES PORTFOLIOS	TIME PERIOD	DATA*	FUTURES RETURN	FUTURES STANDARD DEVIATION	FUTURES RATIO**	STOCKS RETURN	STOCKS STANDARD DEVIATION	STOCKS RATIO	BONDS RETURN	BONDS STANDARD DEVIATION	BONDS RATIO
2	BOOLE & ROSANSKY (1980)	1/50-12/76	A, M	13.83	22.43	.62	13.05	18.45	.69	2.84	6.53	.43
3	BOOLE (1980)	1/53-12/81	A, M	5.69***	17.36	.33	6.68	19.48	.34	-1.65	7.43	-.22
7	LEE, LEUTHOLD, CORDIER (1985)	1/78-12/81	A, D	N.A.	N.A.		N.A.	N.A.		N.A.	N.A.	
10,14	HERBST & MCCORMACK (1986)(1988)	1/80-12/84	A, M	N.A.	N.A.		N.A.	N.A.		N.A.	N.A.	
	COMMODITY TRADING ADVISORS											
4	LINTNER (1983)	7/79-12/82	A, M	2.72	12.36	.22	1.35	5.09	.27	.67	5.21	.13
9	BARATZ & ERESIAN (1) (1986)	1/80-12/85	A, M	2.75	12.85	.22	.91	4.27	.21	1.06	4.28	.25
15	PETERS (1989)	1/80-12/88	A, M	2.44	9.80	.25	1.37	4.82	.28	1.02	3.67	.28
16	OBERUC (1990)	3/79-12/89	A, A	18.2-27.9 (9)	31.1-33.8 (9)	.58-.82	11-23.6(9)	17.8-27.9 (9)	.62-.88	2.8-18 (9)	3.9-11.7 (9)	.72-1.61
17	BARATZ & ERESIAN (11) (1990)	1/86-12/88	A, M	.63-4.27 (1)	6.95-18.87 (1)	.19	1.29	5.49	.22	1.29	3.66	.35
18	FISCHMAR & PETERS (1990)	1/80-12/88	A, M	N.A.	N.A.		N.A.	N.A.		N.A.	N.A.	
	PRIVATE COMMODITY POOLS											
5	ORR (1987)	1/80-12/86	A, M	1.60	6.50	.25	.95	4.40	.22	1.45	4.00	.36
	PUBLIC COMMODITY FUNDS											
4	LINTNER (1983)	7/79-12/82	A, M	2.03	9.58	.21	1.35	5.00	.27	.67	5.21	.13
6	IRWIN & BROSEN (1985)	1/75-12/83	R, A	6.6	21.2	.31	8.3	14.9	.56	.4	15.6	.03
8	BROSEN & IRWIN (1985)	12/78-5/83	A, M	(10)	(10)	(10)	(10)	(10)	(10)	(10)	(10)	(10)
11	IRWIN & LANDA (1987)	1/75-12/85	R, A	9.9	22.9	.43	9.5	14.7	.65	2.9	16.3	.18
12	MURPHY (1987)	5/80-4/85	A, M	.81 (2), 2.31 (3)	5.92	.13-.39	1.38	4.13	.33	N.A.	N.A.	
13	ELTON, GRUBER & RENTZLER (1) (1987)	7/79-6/85	A, M	.07 (4)	11.30 (4)	0	.74	4.16	.18	.41	2.79	.15
	(11) (1990)	1/80-12/88	A, M	2.25 (5)	10.4 (6)	.22	16.88 (5)	4.91 (6)	3.03	11.40 (5)	4.17 (6)	2.73
19	IRWIN, KRUKEMYER	1/79-12/89	A, M	1.13 (7)	9.97 (7)	.11	1.47	4.65	.32	.97	4.02	.26
20	& ZULAUF (1992)	1/79-12/89	A, M	22.4-1.73			1.47	4.65	.0	.97	4.82	.24

Notes: *Type of Data (A = Actual, R = Real), Performance Time Frame (A = Annualized, M = Monthly)
**Ratio of Return to Standard Deviation
***Excess Return Only (Over and Above T-Bill Rate)

(1) Data for 25 individual CTAs was given. Ranges shown are the minimum—maximum for each category

(2) Net, after costs

(3) Gross, before costs

(4) Average monthly returns for annual holding periods

(5) Actual returns, annualized

(6) Monthly Standard Deviation

(7) Public Commodity Funds

(8) Institutional and Pension Commodity Products

(9) Oberuc analyzed hedged CTA returns for U.K., Germany, France, Switzerland

(10) Brorsen and Irwin applied stochastic dominance and found public futures funds superior for investors with higher risk tolerances, inferior for lower risk tolerance investors.

were high enough to justify this additional risk. Researchers found that returns for CTAs [Lintner (1983), Baratz and Eresian (1985, 1989), Oberuc (1990)] and private pools [Orr, (1985, 1987)] were indeed higher than stocks, bonds and T-bills. None of the research addressed the return-risk preferences of investors so the question if returns were high enough to overcome the increased variability remains unanswered.

Findings regarding public funds were somewhat different, however. Lintner (1983) found higher returns for public commodity funds than stocks, bonds and T-bills. Brorsen and Irwin (1985) and Irwin and Landa (1987) also drew the same conclusion regarding bonds and T-bills, but found returns approximately equal to stocks. Murphy (1986) found inferior returns compared to stocks and T-bills on a *net* basis, but higher returns on a *gross* basis (he did not examine bonds). Elton, Gruber and Rentzler (1987, 1990) found inferior returns compared to traditional investments. These differences in findings show a deterioration in *relative* performance between public commodity funds and traditional investments over time, coincidental with the transition from the inflationary times of the late 1970s to the period of relative economic stability of the 1980s. That public funds lost their return advantage, while CTA and private pools did not, reflects in part their higher cost structure. Murphy (1986) and Irwin, Krukmeyer and Zulaf (1992) showed how decreasing cost structures could have changed their conclusions regarding public funds.

Potential as a Hedge against Inflation

The likelihood that inflation can produce weakness in stock and bond markets probably needs no lengthy explanation. As prospects for inflation appear, interest rates rise, causing concerns that consumption and private domestic investment will fall, i.e., reduce aggregate demand for goods and services. The discounted present value of company earnings also drops and stocks in general become weak. On the other hand, inflation means a rise in prices. During inflation commodity prices generally trend upwards over time [Bodie (1983)]. Commodity trading advisors, whether technicians and fundamentalists, are generally trend-followers, so it is expected that they would exploit inflation-generated trends. Have managed futures outperformed stocks and bonds during such periods? Table 1-2 summarizes the results of several academic studies in this area.

The last column of Table 1-2 lists the conclusions of the authors in regard to effectiveness as a hedge against inflation.

Table 1-2 Correlation to Alternative Investments and Inflation

CHAPTER	PASSIVE FUTURES PORTFOLIOS	TIME PERIOD	DATA*	CORRELATION BETWEEN FUTURES AND		CORRELATION BETWEEN STOCKS AND BONDS	CORRELATION BETWEEN FUTURES AND INFLATION
				STOCKS	BONDS		
2	BODIE & ROSANSKY (1980)	1/50-12/76	A, A	-.24	-.16	-.10	+.58
3	BODIE (1980)	1/53-12/81	A, M	-.21	-.23	+.19	+.25
7	LEE, LEUTHOLD, CORDIER (1985)	1/78-12/81	A, D	INDEPENDENT (1)	N.A.	N.A.	N.A.
10,14	HERBST & MCCORMACK (1986) (1988)	1/80-12/84	A, M	N.A.	N.A.	N.A.	N.A.
	COMMODITY TRADING ADVISORS						
4	LINTNER (1983)	7/79-12/82	A, M	-.065	+.148	+.417	N.A.
9	BARATZ & ERESIAN (1) (1986)	1/80-12/85	A, M	-.029	-.114	+.377	N.A.
15	PETERS (1989)	1/80-12/88	A, M	-.081	-.109	+.310	N.A.
16	OBERUC (1990)	3/79-12/89	A, M	LOW TO NEGATIVE (2)	LOW TO NEGATIVE (2)	LOW TO POSITIVE (2)	N.A.
17	BARATZ & ERESIAN (11) (1990)	1/84-12/88	A, M	+.057	+.087	N.A.	N.A.
18	FISCHMAR & PETERS (1990)	1/80-12/88	A, M	N.A.	N.A.	N.A.	N.A.
	PRIVATE COMMODITY POOLS						
5	ORR (1987)	1/80-12/86	A, M	+.003	-.003	+.391	POSITIVE (3)
	PUBLIC COMMODITY FUNDS						
4	LINTNER (1983)	7/79-12/82	A, M	+.234	+.151	+.417	N.A.
6	IRWIN & BROKSEN (1985)	1/75-12/83	R, A	-.633	-.529	+.374	+.606
8	BROKSEN & IRWIN (1985)	12/78-5/83	A, M	N.A.	N.A.	N.A.	N.A.
11	IRWIN & LANDA (1987)	1/75-12/85	R, A	-.56	-.47	+.46	+.55
12	MURPHY (1987)	5/80-4/85	A, M	N.A.	N.A.	N.A.	N.A.
13	ELTON, GRUBER & RENTZLER (1) (1987)	7/79-6/85	A, M	-.121	-.003	N.A.	+.01
19	(11) (1990)	1/80-12/88		0	0	N.A.	-.03
20	IRWIN, KRUKEMEYER & ZULAF (1992)	1/79-12/89	A, M	+.086	+.054	N.A.	-.011

Notes: *Type of Data (A = Actual, R = Real), Performance Time Frame (A = Annualized, M = Monthly)
(1) Regression analysis was applied to daily data for returns from the commodity futures index (CFI) and S&P 500, with a variety of lead/lag relationships.
(2) Oberuc applied correlation analysis to CTAs and stock and bond returns from the United Kingdom, Germany, France and Switzerland.
(3) Orr showed that stocks and bonds were below and private commodity pools above their respective long-term trend lines during a period of higher inflation (1/80–6/83).

Bodie and Rosansky (1980) examined quarterly prices for 27 years, 1950–1976, for stocks, bonds, bills and a passive portfolio of all actively traded commodity futures. They found returns from futures positively correlated with inflation, but negatively correlated with stocks and bonds. Furthermore, they found that a hypothetical portfolio consisting of 60% stocks and 40% passive futures reduced variability of an all-stock portfolio without sacrificing return. In a follow-up study, Bodie (1983) examined annual prices for 29 years, 1953–1981, for stocks, bonds, bills and a passive portfolio of commodity futures. He found real rates of return for commodity futures again to be positively correlated with inflation, while stocks, bonds and bills were negatively correlated with inflation, but positively correlated with one another. These studies acknowledge the conservative approach of using a strict buy and hold strategy for futures, where the only hope for long term positive nominal rates of return was through unanticipated inflation, but point out that even a passive strategy produces some improvements to the overall portfolio.

The question of how well managed futures did, compared to a passive portfolio of futures during periods of inflation, was addressed in a study by Irwin and Landa (1987). They examined, among other things, the performance of stocks, bonds, bills, a passive portfolio of all actively traded commodity futures, and performance of futures funds during the period 1975–1985. Their study showed that managed futures far out-performed their passive counterpart during the inflationary era of 1977–1981, in addition to showing significantly better performance during the entire 1975–1985 period.

Orr (1985, 1987) analyzed return patterns and showed that stock and bond returns were below their long-term trendlines, and managed futures above, during the period of higher inflation of the early 1980s.

Generally, most researchers found managed futures to be an effective hedge against inflation. An exception was Elton, Gruber and Rentzler (1987, 1990), who found no indications of effectiveness. However, they used monthly data over a period which did not span a time of sustained inflation. They also used direct month-to-month comparisons and ignored possible lead-lag relationships between commodity prices and the measured rate of inflation. Other researchers who used quarterly or annual data and longer time frames reached opposite conclusions. The problems discussed above could account for these differences in findings.

Correlation with Stocks and Bonds

Before discussing correlation, an important first step is to define the needs of the investor. It is assumed that the investor already has a portfolio of traditional assets including stocks and bonds. His needs are to earn a return large enough to meet the requirements of the beneficiaries of his portfolio, and to control risk to the lowest possible levels. Risk is assumed to be portfolio return variability; the higher the variability the less likely that the average return will occur. Although this definition has its limitations and other measures may be more appropriate [Peters (1989)], [Fischmar and Peters (1990)], it has found wide use in modern portfolio management.

In the context of traditional modern portfolio theory [Markowitz (1959)] the objectives of the investor are first to use a portfolio on the so-called "efficient frontier,"[1] commensurate with his return/risk preferences, and second, to find ways to shift this efficient frontier towards more return and less risk. These objectives are illustrated in an example shown in Figure 1-2 using stock/bond portfolios with and without managed futures. A portfolio made up of stocks and bonds only (portfolio "A") can be improved by the addition of a third asset category (in this example, managed futures) if a favorable shift occurs in the efficient frontier as shown. The investor can reallocate units to achieve more return at the same risk (portfolio "B"), less risk for the same return (portfolio "C") or any combination in between.

Risk is measured by standard deviation. The higher the standard deviation, the greater the risk. The shift in efficient frontier upwards (more return) and to the left (less risk) is accomplished by adding new asset classes with the correct characteristics to the portfolio. Correlation is an important dimension of performance because of the role it plays quantitatively and qualitatively in determining if portfolio enhancement can occur through diversification. Elton, Gruber and Rentzler (1987) showed that a futures investment should be added to a portfolio if

$$\begin{bmatrix} \text{Sharpe Ratio of} \\ \text{Candidate Asset} \end{bmatrix} \geq \begin{bmatrix} \text{Correlation} \\ \text{Coefficient} \end{bmatrix} \times \begin{bmatrix} \text{Sharpe Ratio} \\ \text{of Portfolio} \end{bmatrix}$$

The Sharpe Ratio is defined as the ratio of excess return (beyond the risk-free rate) to standard deviation. If the correlation coefficient is zero the above condition reduces to

$$\begin{bmatrix} \text{Sharpe Ratio of} \\ \text{Candidate Asset} \end{bmatrix} \geq 0$$

which can only occur if the rate of return exceeds the risk-free rate.

Figure 1-2   Portfolio Return/Risk Relationships—Stocks and Bonds with Managed Futures

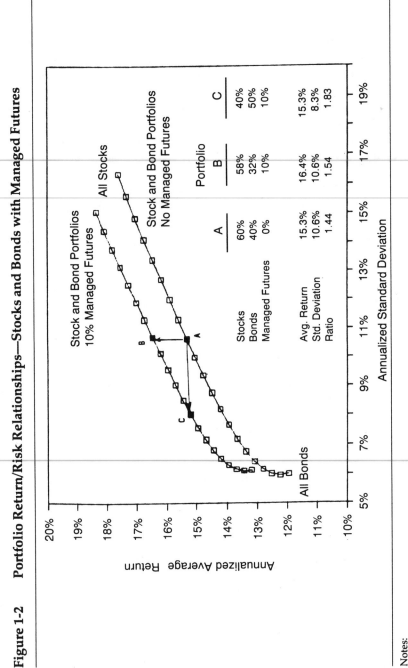

Notes:

1. The "efficient frontier" is defined mathematically as that combination of assets that have minimum combined variance at all possible levels of return.

2. Based on monthly returns during 1980–1989. Stocks are represented by the S&P 500 Index, bonds by the Shearson Lehman International Government Corporate Bond Index, and managed futures by the MAR Equal Weighted CTA Index.

Therefore, if there is no significant correlation, a managed futures invest-ment can enhance portfolio performance when its expected return is merely greater than the risk-free rate. And, all other things being the same, if correlation is negative the "hurdle" rate of return becomes even less. Thus the correlation coefficient is an important determinant of the effectiveness of any asset used for diversification.

There are a number of reasons to expect little correlation between man-aged futures and stocks and bonds. Conditions which are not favorable to stocks and bonds usually are favorable for managed futures. Inflation, deflation and times of economic and political uncertainty can cause major moves in the price of commodities. As an example, when inflation appeared during 1977–1981, the Consumer Price Index (CPI) rose over 60%. Futures funds averaged over 37% over the same five-year period [Irwin and Landa (1987)]. On the other hand, stocks averaged 14%, while bonds only broke even. Nearly all economic circumstances are reflected somewhere in the commodity markets, and it is probable that the diversity of these forces helps contribute to non-correlation between managed futures and stocks and bonds.

Another possible basis for non-correlation between managed futures and stocks and bonds is the diversity of the markets traded. There are at least 30 futures contracts on U. S., CFTC regulated exchanges which qualify for large scale trading.[2] Market categories include agriculturals (wheat, corn, soy-beans, soybean meal, and oil), livestock (hogs and cattle), foods and fibers (sugar, coffee, cotton, cocoa), petroleum products (crude oil, heating oil, unleaded gasoline), metals (silver, gold, platinum, copper), currencies (Brit-ish pound, German mark, Japanese yen, Swiss franc, Canadian dollar), interest rate instruments (U. S. Treasury Bonds, Bills, Notes, Eurodollar Deposits, Municipal Bond Index), and stock indices (S & P 500). The diver-sity of markets traded contribute to the non-correlated nature in perfor-mance between managed futures and stocks and bonds.

Yet another factor contributing to non-correlation is the structure of futures contracts themselves. When a position is taken in a futures contract it can be just as easily long (i.e., to profit from rising prices) or short (i.e., to profit from falling prices). There are no rules making it relatively more difficult to establish short as opposed to long positions as there are in the equity markets. If one has the ability to recognize trends, profits can be made either in rising or falling markets. The capability of profiting from declining markets can provide a significant degree of non-correlation in return pat-terns. A clear example of the difference between managed futures and other asset management styles is to consider active management in the debt and equity markets. Most traditional investing by institutions is to buy and hold in these markets, and to retreat to cash when weakness occurs. The Commodity Trading Advisor, on the other hand, can be long or short (or neutral). It is not difficult to see how the latter strategy could be non-correlated with the former.

Table 1-2 summarizes the results of research regarding correlation of managed futures to other investments. With few exceptions researchers have found no significant correlation between futures products and stocks or bonds. And in no case did the correlation approach that found between stocks and bonds themselves. Lintner (1983) found small positive correlation between funds and stocks, but improvements from diversification were still possible. Orr (1985, 1987) showed small positive correlation was present between pools and stocks or bonds during a period of low inflation, but the reverse was true during a period of higher inflation. Irwin and Landa (1987) showed small positive correlation between stocks and passive futures portfolios, but strong negative correlation between stocks and public commodity funds over the same time period. The remaining authors found no positive correlation, and some found evidence of significant negative correlation.

In summary, there is agreement that returns from managed futures products are independent or negatively correlated with those of stocks and bonds. Oberuc (1990) has extended these conclusions to include Eurostocks and Eurobonds as well.

Performance in Portfolio Diversification

The results of the preceding section show that futures products appear to have little positive correlation to stocks and bonds, making them promising candidates for portfolio diversification. Improvement in portfolio performance can occur whenever the efficient frontier is shifted upward (toward more return) and/or to the left (less risk). If this occurs the investor can reallocate his asset mix to include the diversifying investment and a mix of original assets in order to obtain larger return for the same risk, less risk for the same return, or a combination of both.

Table 1-3 summarizes research results regarding the question of diversification. With two exceptions, (both from the same authors), researchers found that futures products could have improved portfolio performance.

Bodie and Rosansky (1980), Bodie (1983), Herbst and McCormack (1986, 1988) and Irwin and Landa (1987) all examined passive futures investments in combination with stocks and/or bonds and concluded that enhancement would have occurred. Orr (1985, 1987) examined private pools in a similar

Table 1-3 Effectiveness in Portfolio Diversification

CHAPTER	PASSIVE FUTURES PORTFOLIOS	TIME PERIOD	DATA*	METHODOLOGY	RESULTS
2	BODIE & ROSANSKY (1980)	1/50-12/76	A, A	A PASSIVE (BUY & HOLD) FUTURES PORTFOLIO WAS ADDED TO AN ALL STOCK PORTFOLIO	EFFECTIVE**
3	BODIE (1980)	1/53-12/81	A, M	A PASSIVE (BUY & HOLD) FUTURES PORTFOLIO WAS ADDED TO PORTFOLIOS OF STOCKS, BONDS AND T-BILLS	EFFECTIVE
7	LEE, LEUTHOLD, CORDIER (1985)	1/78-12/81	A, D	N. A.	EFFECTIVE
10, 14	HERBST & McCORMACK (1986) (1988)	1/80-12/84	A, M	FUTURES CONTRACTS WERE RANDOMLY SUBSTITUTED FOR STOCKS IN PORTFOLIOS	EFFECTIVE
	COMMODITY TRADING ADVISORS				
4	LINTNER (1983)	7/79-12/82	A, M	PORTFOLIOS OF CTA'S WERE ADDED TO PORTFOLIOS OF STOCKS AND BONDS	EFFECTIVE
9	BARATZ & ERESIAN (1) (1986)	1/80-12/85	A, M	FOLLOW-UP TO LINTNER STUDY USING INDIVIDUAL AND PORTFOLIOS OF CTA'S	EFFECTIVE
15	PETERS (1989)	1/80-12/88	A, M	COMPOSITE PERFORMANCE OF A REPRESENTATIVE CTA WAS ADDED TO STOCK AND BOND PORTFOLIOS	EFFECTIVE
16	OBERUC (1990)	3/79-12/89	A, M	MANAGED FUTURES (MAR CTA INDEX) WAS ADDED TO EURO STOCK AND BOND PORTFOLIO (5)	EFFECTIVE
17	BARATZ & ERESIAN (11) (1990)	1/84-12/88	A, M	FOLLOW-UP TO 1986 STUDY BY SAME AUTHORS	EFFECTIVE
18	FISCHMAR & PETERS (1990)	1/80-12/88	A, M	THE EFFECT OF ADDING MANAGED FUTURES (MAR CTA INDEX) ANALYZED VIA COMPROMISE STOCHASTIC DOMINANCE	EFFECTIVE (1) (2)
	PRIVATE COMMODITY POOLS				
5	ORR (1987)	1/80-12/86	A, M	PRIVATE COMMODITY POOLS (MAR POOLS INDEX) WAS ADDED TO STOCK AND BOND PORTFOLIOS	EFFECTIVE
	PUBLIC COMMODITY FUNDS				
4	LINTNER (1983)	7/79-12/82	A, M	PORTFOLIOS OF PUBLIC COMMODITY FUNDS WERE ADDED TO STOCK AND BOND PORTFOLIOS	EFFECTIVE
6	IRWIN & BRORSEN (1985)	1/75-12/83	R, A	PUBLIC COMMODITY FUNDS WERE ADDED TO PORTFOLIOS CONSISTING OF STOCKS, BONDS AND T-BILLS	EFFECTIVE
8	BRORSEN & IRWIN (1985)	12/78-5/83	A, M	N. A.	
11	IRWIN & LANDA (1987)	1/75-12/85	R, A	PUBLIC COMMODITY FUNDS WERE ADDED TO PORTFOLIOS CONSISTING OF STOCKS, BONDS, T-BILLS, GOLD, REAL ESTATE	EFFECTIVE
12	MURPHY (1987)	5/80-4/85	A, M	STATISTICAL SIGNIFICANCE OF ALPHA AND BETA (3) OF TECHNICAL COMMODITY FUNDS IN PORTFOLIOS	MIXED
13	ELTON, GRUBER & RENTZLER (1) (1987)	7/79-6/85	A, M	PORTFOLIO BREAKEVEN ANALYSIS WAS PERFORMED ON PUBLIC COMMODITY FUNDS	NOT EFFECTIVE
19	(11) (1990)	1/80-12/88	A, M	FOLLOW-UP TO 1987 STUDY BY SAME AUTHORS	NOT EFFECTIVE
20	IRWIN, KRUKEMEYER & ZULAF (1990)	1/79-12/89	A, M	REPLICATION OF TECHNIQUES USED BY ELTON, GRUBER, RENTZLER ON PUBLIC COMMODITY FUNDS	MIXED (4)
		1/79-12/89	A, M	REPLICATION OF TECHNIQUES USED BY ELTON, GRUBER, RENTZLER ON INSTITUTIONAL FUNDS	EFFECTIVE

Notes: *Type of Data (A = Actual, R = Real), Performance Time Frame (A = Annualized, M = Monthly)
**"Effective" means that the efficient frontier was shifted to the left (less risk), upward (more return) or both

(1) Conditions were derived showing that minimum thresholds of managed futures were necessary for improvement to occur
(2) The probability of loss was lowered at every possible level of expected return
(3) Alpha is defined as above market returns; Beta is contribution to portfolio risk.
(4) Marginally effective for the period 1979–1989. Not effective for the subperiods 1982–1989 or 1985–89.
(5) Oberuc studied diversification potential for stock and bond portfolios in the U.K., Germany, France and Switzerland.

manner, with the same conclusions. Lintner (1983), Baratz and Eresian (1985, 1989), Fischmar and Peters (1990) and Oberuc (1990) found that CTA performance would likewise have improved performance of stock and bond (and cash) portfolios.

The results for public commodity funds were not as clear. Lintner (1983), and Irwin and Brorsen (1985) found that improvement could occur by using public commodity funds for diversification. However, Murphy (1987) found that portfolio enhancement depended on costs associated with public commodity funds; improvement did occur when using returns on a *gross* basis (before costs) but not on a *net* basis (after costs). Elton, Gruber and Rentzler (1987) concluded that public commodity funds were not attractive additions to portfolios of stocks and bonds. While Elton, Gruber and Rentzler (1990) drew the same conclusion, they also found that public commodity funds with general partners with above average performance in prior funds produced significantly better returns with new products— enough so to have qualified them as attractive diversification assets for stock and bond portfolios. Irwin, Krukmeyer and Zulaf (1992) showed that public commodity fund performance, when adjusted to reflect institutional level costs and fees, justified their inclusion in stock and bond portfolios.

Summary

The purpose of this book was to review and summarize the findings of various researchers regarding the performance of managed futures. Performance was measured along the following lines:

1. As a stand-alone investment.
2. As a hedge against inflation.
3. Correlation with returns of traditional investments.
4. As a diversifying asset in stock and bond portfolios.

Results were categorized by type (Passive Futures Portfolios, Commodity Trading Advisors, Private Commodity Pools and Public Commodity Funds), and time period analyzed. Table 1-4 summarizes the studies along these lines, and also shows an overview of conclusions.

Regarding stand-alone performance, results were mixed. Table 1-1 showed that all types of managed futures products had higher variability than stocks or bonds (passive futures had comparable variability). Returns were also higher than stocks and bonds for CTAs and Private Commodity Pools, but results for Public Commodity funds were mixed. Studies which

Table 1-4   Summary of Performance Results

CHAPTER		TIME PERIOD	DATA*	AS A STAND-ALONE INVESTMENT COMPARED** TO		CORRELATION WITH		EFFECTIVENESS IN PORTFOLIO DIVERSIFICATION
				STOCKS	BONDS	STOCKS & BONDS	INFLATION	
PASSIVE FUTURES PORTFOLIOS								
2	BODIE & ROSANSKY (1980)	1/50-12/76	A. A	COMPARABLE	BETTER	NEGATIVE	POSITIVE	EFFECTIVE
3	BODIE (1980)	1/53-12/81	A. M	COMPARABLE	BETTER	NEGATIVE	POSITIVE	EFFECTIVE
7	LEE, LEUTHOLD, CORDIER (1985)	1/78-12/81	A. D	N. A.	N. A.	INDEPENDENT	N. A.	N. A.
10,14	HERBST & MCCORMACK (1986)	1/80-12/84	A. M	N. A.	N. A.	N. A.	N. A.	EFFECTIVE
COMMODITY TRADING ADVISORS								
4	LINTNER (1983)	7/79-12/82	A. M	WORSE	BETTER	LOW	N. A.	EFFECTIVE
9	BARATZ & ERESIAN (1) (1986)	1/80-12/85	A. M	COMPARABLE	WORSE	SLIGHTLY NEGATIVE	N. A.	EFFECTIVE
15	PETERS (1989)	1/80-12/88	A. M	COMPARABLE	COMPARABLE	SLIGHTLY NEGATIVE	N. A.	EFFECTIVE
16	OBERUC (1990)	3/79-12/89	A. M	COMPARABLE (1)	COMPARABLE (1)	LOW TO NEGATIVE	N. A.	EFFECTIVE
17	BARATZ & ERESIAN (1) (1990)	1/84-12/88	A. M	COMPARABLE	WORSE	SLIGHTLY POSITIVE	N. A.	EFFECTIVE
18	FISCHMAR & PETERS (1990)	1/80-12/88	A. M	N. A.	N. A.	N. A.	N. A.	EFFECTIVE
PRIVATE COMMODITY POOLS								
5	ORR (1987)	1/80-12/86	A. M	COMPARABLE	WORSE	NONE	POSITIVE	EFFECTIVE
PUBLIC COMMODITY FUNDS								
4	LINTNER (1983)	7/79-12/82	A. M	WORSE	BETTER	SLIGHTLY POSITIVE	N. A.	EFFECTIVE
6	IRWIN & BROREN (1985)	1/75-12/83	R. A	WORSE	BETTER	NEGATIVE	POSITIVE	EFFECTIVE
8	BROREN & IRWIN (1985)	12/78-5/83	A. M	MIXED (6)	MIXED (6)	N. A.	N. A.	N. A.
11	IRWIN & LANDA (1987)	1/75-12/85	R. A	WORSE	BETTER	NEGATIVE	POSITIVE	EFFECTIVE
12	MURPHY (1987)	5/80-4/85	A. M	MIXED (2)	N. A.	N. A.	N. A.	MIXED (2)
13	ELTON, GRUBER & RENTZLER (1) (1987)	7/79-6/85	A. M	WORSE	WORSE	SLIGHTLY NEGATIVE	NONE	NOT EFFECTIVE
	(1) (1990)	1/80-12/88	A. M	WORSE	WORSE	ZERO (5)	NONE	NOT EFFECTIVE
19	IRWIN, KRUKEMYER & ZULAF (1990)	1/79-12/89	A. M	WORSE (3)	WORSE (3)	SLIGHTLY POSITIVE	NONE	MIXED (7)
20		1/79-12/89	A. M	COMPARABLE (4)	BETTER (4)	N. A.	N. A.	EFFECTIVE (4)

Notes: *Type of Data (A = Actual, R = Real), Performance Time Frame (A = Annualized, M = Monthly)
   **Comparison is made between futures and stocks or bonds, i.e., "better" mean futures were better, etc.

(1) Oberuc studied hedged CTA performance and stocks, bonds and cash for the U.K., Germany, France and Switzerland.
(2) Worse on a net (after cost) basis, better on a gross basis
(3) Public commodity funds
(4) Pro forma using institutional fees
(5) Overall conclusion based on previous studies
(6) Better for higher risk tolerant investors, otherwise worse
(7) Marginally effective during 1979–1989, not effective for smaller sub-periods

were conducted earlier in the 1980s tended to show funds having better returns, while those completed later (after taking into account more of the bull market of the 1980s) showed a deterioration in relative performance compared to stocks and bonds.

All studies were unanimous in their findings that futures products had no significant positive correlation to stocks or bonds. Many found no correlation and some found significantly negative correlation. These conclusions are particularly noteworthy when considering futures products for diversifying stock and bond portfolios.

Of the eight studies that examined the performance of futures products as a hedge against inflation, five found confirming evidence. The distinguishing characteristic of four of these studies is that they covered periods of sustained inflation and used longer time frames of measurement (i.e., quarterly or annual data). The fifth study, Orr (1987), specifically looked at performance around long-term trendlines. In contrast, the remaining three studies neither completely spanned inflationary periods, nor used long time frames. Short-term, month-to-month comparisons were made without attempting to test for lead-lag relationships.

Finally, the large majority of the authors found futures products effective in diversifying stock and bond portfolios. An area of disagreement occurred in public commodity funds products; however, it was shown that conclusions were very sensitive to cost structures and time period analyzed. In summary, the weight of academic evidence seems to conclude that futures products have clearly no correlation with stocks and bonds and offer potentially attractive benefits in diversifying stock and bond portfolios. Research as well as methodological considerations also argue strongly for inflation hedging effectiveness. Performance as a stand-alone investment appears to be mixed, depending on the product and time period analyzed.

It should be noted that managed futures have now just completed their first full decade, and as such are still in relative infancy compared to stocks and bonds. We should be cautioned that inferences are being drawn from data that is relatively short in duration, and for economic conditions that may not be representative of the long term. The findings of the authorities produced herein have yet to stand the most rigorous test—time.

Endnotes

1.   The "efficient frontier" is defined mathematically as that combination of assets that have minimum combined variance at all possible levels of return.

2. Additionally, there are a growing number of futures contracts traded on foreign futures exchanges as well as cash and forward contracts in currencies which can have significant liquidity.

Bibliography

Baratz, Morton S. and Eresian, Warren. "The Role of Managed Futures Accounts in an Investment Portfolio." *MAR Conference on Futures Money Management,* January, 1990.

Baratz, Morton S. and Eresian, Warren. "The Role of Managed Futures Accounts in an Investment Portfolio." *MAR Mid-Year Conference on Futures Money Management,* July, 1986; Chicago, Illinois.

Bodie, Zvi. "Commodity Futures as a Hedge against Inflation." *The Journal of Portfolio Management,* Spring, 1983.

Bodie, Zvi and Rosansky, Victor. "Risk and Return in Commodity Futures." *Financial Analysts Journal,* May–June, 1980.

Brorsen, B. Wade and Irwin, Scott H. "Examination of Commodity Fund Performance." *Review of Research in the Futures Markets,* Vol. 4, 1985.

Elton, Edwin J., Gruber, Martin J., and Rentzler, Joel C. "The Performance of Publicly Offered Commodity Funds." *Financial Analysts Journal,* July–August 1990.

Elton, Edwin J., Gruber, Martin J., and Rentzler, Joel C. "Professionally Managed, Publicly Traded Commodity Funds." *Journal of Business,* Vol. 60, No. 2, 1987.

Fischmar, Daniel and Peters, Carl C. "Portfolio of Stocks, Bonds and Managed Futures Using Compromise Stochastic Dominance." *The Journal of Futures Markets,* Vol. II, No. 3, June, 1991.

Herbst, Anthony F. and McCormack, Joseph P. "A Further Examination of the Risk-Return Characteristics of Portfolios Combining Commodity Futures Contracts with Common Stocks." *Working Paper Series, Center for the Study of Futures Markets,* Columbia University, February, 1988.

Herbst, Anthony F. and McCormack, Joseph P. "An Examination of the Risk-Return Characteristics of Portfolios Combining Commodity Futures Contracts with Common Stocks." *Working Paper Series, Center for the Study of Futures Markets,* Columbia University, January, 1986.

Irwin, Scott and Brorsen, B. Wade. "Public Futures Funds." *The Journal of Futures Markets,* Vol. 5, No. 2, 1985.

Irwin, Scott and Landa, Diego. "Real Estate, Futures, and Gold as Portfolio Assets." *The Journal of Portfolio Management,* Fall, 1987.

Irwin, Scott H., Krukmeyer, Terry, and Zulauf, Carl R. "The Investment Performance of Public Commodity Pools over 1979–1989," submitted to *The Journal of Futures Markets,* and accepted for publication, 1992.

Lee, Chung F., Leuthold, Raymond, and Cordier, Jean. "The Stock Market and Commodities Futures Market: Diversification and Arbitrage Potential." *Financial Analysts Journal,* July–August 1985.

Lintner, John. "The Potential Role of Managed Commodity—Financial Futures Accounts (and / or Funds) in Portfolios of Stocks and Bonds." *Presented at the Annual Conference of the Financial Analysts Federation,* May, 1983; Toronto, Canada.

Markowitz, H. *Portfolio Selection: Efficient Diversification of Investments.* New York: Wiley, 1959.

Murphy, J. Austin. "Futures Fund Performance: A Test of the Effectiveness of Technical Analysis." *The Journal of Futures Markets,* Vol. 6, No. 2, 1986.

Oberuc, Richard E. "How to Diversify Portfolios of Euro-stocks and bonds with hedged U. S. Managed Futures." First International Conference on Futures Money Management, May 4, 1990; Geneva, Switzerland.

Orr, Almer. "John Lintner and the Theory of Portfolio Management." *Presented at the Sixth Annual Managed Accounts Reports Conference,* February, 1985; Chicago, Illinois (Revised, 1987).

Peters, Carl C. "A Comparative Analysis of Portfolio Diversification Criteria using Managed Futures." *Proceedings of the Fourth Annual Convention of the Pennsylvania Economic Association,* May, 1989.

Peters, Carl C. "New Perspectives on Portfolio Risk Management." *Presented at the 10th Annual MAR Conference on Futures Money Management,* January, 1989; Scottsdale, Arizona.

Strahm, N. "Preference Space Evaluation of Trading System Performance." *Journal of the Futures Markets,* 3(3), 1983.

Chapter Two

Management Summary

Title: "Risk and Return in Commodity Futures"

Publication: *Financial Analysts Journal,* May–June 1980

Authors: Zvi Bodie, Associate Professor, Boston University
              Victor Rosansky, doctoral student, Boston University

Data: Quarterly prices for 27 years, 1950–1976, for commodity futures, long-term Government Bonds, U.S. Treasury Bills and common stocks.

Methodology: A "benchmark" portfolio of commodity futures, consisting of all liquid futures during the period of this study, was created. No active management was considered, only a buy-and-hold strategy was used, with roll-overs as necessary as contracts expired.

         Returns from the commodity futures portfolio were analyzed in comparison to returns from long-term Government Bonds, U.S. Treasury Bills and common stocks.

Results: Average annual returns were about the same from the futures portfolio (13.83%) as for common stocks (13.05%), and both far out-performed bonds (2.84%), Bills (3.63%) and the rate of inflation (3.43%). Standard deviations for futures and stocks were also about equal. However, the pattern in returns between the two were quite different, with futures showing substantially less downside risk. The same conclusions held when returns were adjusted for inflation.

         Futures returns were significantly negatively correlated with stocks (r=−.24) and bonds (r=−.10), and positively correlated with inflation (r=+.58).

         A hypothetical portfolio consisting of 60% common stocks and 40% futures reduced return variability of an all stock portfolio by one-third, without sacrificing return.

continued

Comments: This study was the first at showing the desirable features of commodity futures in portfolio diversification. The authors concluded that commodity futures were "naturally" negatively correlated with stocks and bonds, and were good inflation hedges. The long-term nature of the study also revealed that downside risk may be less for a futures portfolio than for stocks or bonds. Transactions costs were excluded.

Risk and Return in Commodity Futures*

Zvi Bodie
Victor I. Rosansky

Summary

How do returns on commodity futures compare with returns on common stocks? The authors found that, over the period 1950 to 1976, the mean return on their benchmark portfolio of commodity futures was about the same as the mean return on common stocks. On the other hand, the futures tended to do well in years when the stocks were doing badly, and vice versa. By switching from an all-stock portfolio to one invested 60% in stocks and 40% in futures, an investor could have reduced his return variability by one-third without sacrificing any of his return.

Furthermore, the commodity futures proved to be very good inflation hedges. Four of their best years coincided with four of the seven years of the highest acceleration in inflation. While the dispersion of the real returns on the commodity futures portfolio was smaller than the dispersion of its nominal returns, the reverse was true for both stocks and bonds.

The mean rates of return and variabilities of the 23 individual commodities in the authors' sample were distributed over a wide range. But only one commodity—eggs—had a negative rate of return for the 27-year period.

The authors thank John Aber, Fischer Black, Fred Graver, Alex Kane and Franco Modigliani for their helpful comments.
*This paper was published in the *Financial Analysts Journal*, May–June, 1980. Reprinted with permission.

Hardly any of the individual commodities (other than the obvious cases such as hogs and pork bellies) showed significant correlation with each other.

Introduction

This chapter provides a comprehensive analysis of the rates of return on commodity futures contracts traded in the United States from 1950 to 1976 and compares them to the rates of return earned on stocks and bonds over that same period. We hope that the results reported here will serve as a benchmark against which commodity futures mutual funds and computerized trading programs can compare themselves, in much the same way that common stock performance is compared with the Standard & Poor's 500.

To date, most of the published research on commodity futures has focused on the issue of market efficiency.[1] Many researchers have tested the validity of the normal backwardation hypothesis, according to which a commodity's futures price tends to be a downward biased estimate of its spot price in the cash market at the contract's maturity date. The theory maintains that, on balance, there is an excess of short hedgers who wish to avoid the risk of downward commodity price movements and are therefore willing to sell their goods at a price lower than the spot price expected to prevail at maturity in order to induce speculators to take up the slack in the long side of the market. In effect, the hedgers offer speculators an insurance premium for their services. The results reported in this article shed some additional light on the backwardation issue.

The Study

Our study encompassed all major commodities traded in futures markets in the United States from December 1949 to December 1976. We calculated quarterly series for each of 23 individual commodity futures using two alternative definitions of rate of return. According to our first definition, rate of return was computed simply as the percentage change in the futures price over the three-month holding period. The second definition, however, is probably of greater interest to commodity fund managers and their clients; it takes into account the interest they could have earned by posting Treasury bills as margin. We explain the rationale behind this procedure in some detail in the appendix.

Both series were generated by assuming a buy-and-hold strategy whereby contracts for the different commodities were entered into at quarterly intervals, held for three months and then liquidated. In order to obtain non-overlapping holding periods, we chose the last trading days of February, May, August and November as our buying and liquidating dates.[2] In order to examine the normal backwardation issue, we chose for each commodity the futures contract that expired as close as possible to three months from the date of purchase. For example, we would purchase the December wheat contract on the last trading day in August of any year and liquidate it on the last trading day in November of that year.

Table 2-1 presents the delivery months actually used for each of the quarterly trading dates; in most cases, a contract expiring in exactly three months was available, but in some cases it was necessary to use contracts that expired at later dates. In February of any year, for instance, no June contract for the grains existed, so we used the July contract and liquidated it at the end of May. At the end of each holding period, the contract price was thus essentially equal to the spot price of the commodity; our buy-and-hold strategy produced positive returns if—and only if—the futures price was a downward-biased estimate of the spot price three months ahead.

We also calculated the rates of return on a "benchmark" portfolio of commodity futures. For these calculations, we used the arithmetic mean of the individual commodity rates of return in each quarter, which implies that the portfolio consisted of equal dollar amounts invested in each commodity. The number of commodities in our benchmark portfolio increased over the 27-year period of our study. In 1950, there were ten actively traded commodities; as new commodities began to trade on organized exchanges, we added them to the portfolio. By December of 1976, our portfolio contained 23 commodities.

Benchmark Portfolio Results

Table 2-2 compares the year-end indexes of cumulative wealth relatives for commodity futures with those for common stocks, long-term U.S. government bonds, one-month Treasury bills and the level of consumer prices over the 1950–76 period. The cumulative wealth relative indexes show how much one dollar invested in each asset category at the end of 1949 would have grown by the end of each of the 27 subsequent years, assuming all earnings were reinvested at the end of each quarter. The commodity futures series is calculated using the measure of return that includes the interest earned on Treasury bills posted as margin (R2). The third column of Table 2-2 lists the

Table 2-1   Trading Dates

| Commodity | Last Trading Day of | | | | Price Data Start Last Day of |
	February	May	August	November	
Wheat	July	Sept.	Dec.	March	Nov. 1949
Corn	July	Sept.	Dec.	March	Nov. 1949
Oats	July	Sept.	Dec.	March	Nov. 1949
Soybeans	July	Sept.	Jan.	March	Nov. 1949
Soybean Oil	July	Sept.	Dec.	March	Nov. 1949
Soybean Meal	July	Sept.	Dec.	March	Nov. 1949
Broilers	July	Sept.	Jan.	March	Aug. 1968
Plywood	July	Sept.	Jan.	March	Feb. 1970
Potatoes	Nov.	Nov.	Jan.[a] March	March	Nov. 1949
Platinum	July	Oct.	Jan.	April	Feb. 1964
Wool	July	Oct.	Dec.	March	Nov. 1949
Cotton	July	Oct.	Dec.	March	Nov. 1949
Orange Juice	July	Sept.	Jan.	March	Nov. 1966
Propane	Sept.[b] July	Sept	Dec.	May	May 1968
Cocoa	July	Sept.	Dec.	March	Feb. 1953
Silver	June[c] July	Sept.	Dec.	March	Aug. 1963
Copper	June[d]	Sept.	Dec.	March	Aug. 1953
Cattle	June	Oct.	Dec.	April	Nov. 1964
Hogs	June	Oct.	Dec.	April	Feb. 1966
Pork Bellies	July	Feb.	Feb.	March	Feb. 1964
Eggs	Sept.[e] June	Sept.	Dec.	Sept.[f] April	Nov. 1949
Lumber	July[g] June	Sept.	Jan.	March	Nov. 1969
Sugar	July	Oct.[h]	Jan.[h,a] March	May[h]	Feb. 1953

The commodity futures contracts used and the exchanges on which they are traded are: wheat, corn, oats, soybeans, soybean oil crude, soybean meal, iced broilers and plywood (*Chicago Board of Trade*); Maine potatoes and platinum (*N.Y. Mercantile Exchange*); wool grease, cotton #2, frozen concentrated orange juice and propane (M.B.)(*N.Y. Cotton Exchange*); cocoa (*N.Y. Cocoa Exchange*); silver and copper (*Commodity Exchange Inc.*); midwestern live cattle, live hogs, frozen pork bellies, shell eggs and lumber (*Chicago Mercantile Exchange*); sugar (world, bulk)(*N.Y. Coffee and Sugar Exchange*).

a. For both potatoes and sugar, the January contract was frequently not traded. In those cases, the price of the March contract was used.

b. A July propane contract became available in February 1971.

c. Starting on February 1968, the June silver contract disappears and is replaced with July silver.

d. Starting in February 1958, we take the price of July copper.

e. Starting in February 1968, a July egg contract became available and in March 1969 a June contract.

f. Starting in November 1968, an April egg contract became available.

g. A June lumber contract became available in February 1971.

h. In the years 1953–56 the contract months for sugar changed frequently. Although March and July contracts were usually available, September and January contracts frequently were not.

Sources: Data for the period 1949–52 are from the U.S. Department of Agriculture, Commodity Exchange Authority annual publication, *Commodity Futures Statistics*. All other data were taken from *The Journal of Commerce*.

Table 2-2   Index of Year-End Cumulative Wealth Relatives, 1949–76

Year	Common Stocks	Commodity Futures	Number of Commodities	Long-Term Government Bonds	U.S. Treasury Bills	Consumer Price Index
1949	1.000	1.000	—	1.000	1.000	1.000
1950	1.317	1.526	10	1.000	1.012	1.058
1951	1.633	1.934	10	0.961	1.027	1.121
1952	1.933	1.910	10	0.972	1.044	1.131
1953	1.914	1.789	10	1.007	1.063	1.137
1954	2.922	2.056	13	1.080	1.073	1.132
1955	3.844	1.957	13	1.066	1.089	1.136
1956	4.096	2.246	13	1.006	1.116	1.168
1957	3.654	2.193	13	1.081	1.151	1.204
1958	5.239	2.164	13	1.016	1.169	1.225
1959	5.865	2.176	13	0.993	1.203	1.244
1960	5.892	2.174	13	1.129	1.235	1.262
1961	7.477	2.208	13	1.140	1.262	1.270
1962	6.824	2.227	13	1.219	1.296	1.286
1963	8.380	2.735	13	1.233	1.337	1.307
1964	9.762	3.067	14	1.277	1.383	1.322
1965	10.977	3.393	16	1.286	1.438	1.348
1966	9.872	3.890	17	1.333	1.506	1.393
1967	12.239	4.050	19	1.210	1.570	1.436
1968	13.593	4.101	19	1.207	1.651	1.503
1969	12.437	4.955	21	1.146	1.760	1.595
1970	12.935	5.550	22	1.285	1.877	1.683
1971	14.787	5.734	23	1.454	1.957	1.739
1972	17.592	7.666	23	1.537	2.032	1.799
1973	15.013	15.450	23	1.520	2.174	1.957
1974	11.037	20.389	23	1.586	2.347	2.196
1975	15.144	19.571	23	1.732	2.483	2.350
1976	18.754	22.065	23	2.022	2.609	2.463

number of different commodities included in the commodity benchmark portfolio in each year. The other series were obtained from Ibbotson and Sinquefield.[3]

Table 2-3 offers essentially the same information as Table 2-2, but in the form of year-by-year annual rates of return for each type of investment instrument, and the proportional change in the Consumer Price Index. Table 2-4 presents the important summary measures of the frequency distributions of the nominal rates of return reported in Table 2-3, as well as the real (inflation-adjusted) rates of return and the rates of return in risk premium form.

The annual return data in Tables 2-2 through 2-4 provide several striking comparisons. Perhaps the most remarkable is between commodity futures and common stocks. The means and standard deviations for these two categories (reported in Table 2-4) are almost equal. The mean nominal

Table 2-3   Year-by-Year Rates of Return, 1950–76

Year	Common Stocks	Commodity Futures	Long-Term Government Bonds	U.S. Treasury Bills	Rate of Inflation
1950	31.71	52.61	0.06	1.20	5.79
1951	24.02	26.71	−3.94	1.49	5.87
1952	18.37	−1.22	1.16	1.66	0.88
1953	−0.99	−6.32	3.63	1.82	0.62
1954	52.62	14.88	7.19	0.86	−0.50
1955	31.56	−4.79	−1.30	1.57	0.37
1956	6.56	14.75	−5.59	2.46	2.86
1957	−10.78	−2.34	7.45	3.14	3.02
1958	43.36	−1.33	−6.10	1.54	1.76
1959	11.95	0.54	−2.26	2.95	1.50
1960	0.47	−0.09	13.78	2.66	1.48
1961	26.89	1.55	0.97	2.13	0.67
1962	−8.73	0.87	6.89	2.73	1.22
1963	22.80	22.84	1.21	3.12	1.65
1964	16.48	12.13	3.51	3.54	1.19
1965	12.45	10.62	0.71	3.93	1.92
1966	−10.06	14.65	3.65	4.76	3.35
1967	23.98	4.13	−9.19	4.21	3.04
1968	11.06	1.24	−0.26	5.21	4.72
1969	−8.50	20.84	−5.08	6.58	6.11
1970	4.01	11.99	12.10	6.53	5.49
1971	14.31	3.31	13.23	4.39	3.36
1972	18.98	33.71	5.68	3.84	3.41
1973	−14.66	101.54	−1.11	6.93	8.80
1974	−26.48	31.96	4.35	8.00	12.20
1975	37.20	−4.01	9.19	5.80	7.01
1976	23.84	12.75	16.75	5.08	4.81

returns are 13.83 and 13.05% per year and the standard deviations are 22.43 and 18.95% per year for commodity futures and stocks, respectively.

On the other hand, the frequency distribution of commodity futures returns is considerably more positively skewed than that of stocks. Table 2-4 shows that the commodities had both a higher maximum and a higher minimum annual return. Since the largest annual loss on commodity futures was 6.32%, the large standard deviation of the distribution of returns is indicative more of "upside potential" than of "downside risk." If we adopt as a heuristic measure of downside risk both the frequency of incurring a loss and the size of the average loss, commodity futures look like a less risky investment than common stocks. Although both stocks and commodities had negative nominal returns in only seven of the 27 years, the mean annual loss on stocks was 11.46%, as opposed to 2.87% for the benchmark futures portfolio.

Commodity futures also seem to have outperformed long-term U.S. government bonds—not only in average profitability, but also in downside protection. The average nominal return on bonds was 2.84%, versus 13.83%

Table 2-4   Annual Rates of Return on Alternative Investments, 1950–76

Series	Mean	Standard Deviation	Standard Error	No. of Years Returns Are Negative	Mean Annual Loss[a]	Highest Annual Return (Year)	Lowest Annual Return (Year)
A. Nominal Returns							
(per cent per year)							
Common Stocks	13.05	18.95	3.65	7	11.46	52.62 (1954)	−26.48 (1974)
Commodity Futures with Treasury Bills	13.83	22.43	4.32	7	2.87	101.54 (1973)	−6.32 (1953)
Long-Term Government Bonds	2.84	6.53	1.26	9	3.86	16.75 (1976)	−9.19 (1967)
U.S. Treasury Bills	3.63	1.95	0.38	0		8.00 (1974)	0.86 (1954)
Rate of Inflation	3.43	2.90	0.56	1		12.20 (1974)	−0.50 (1954)
B. Real Returns[b]							
(per cent per year)							
Common Stocks	9.58	19.65	3.78	9	13.11	53.37 (1954)	−34.79 (1974)
Commodity Futures with Treasury Bills	9.81	19.44	3.74	11	3.64	85.24 (1973)	−10.30 (1975)
Long-Term Government Bonds	−0.51	6.81	1.31	13	6.55	12.11 (1960)	−11.90 (1967)
U.S. Treasury Bills	0.22	1.80	0.35	7	2.41	2.32 (1964)	−4.39 (1950)
C. Excess Returns[c]							
(per cent per year)							
Common Stocks	9.42	20.12	3.87	9	13.21	51.76 (1954)	−34.48 (1974)
Commodity Futures	9.77	21.39	4.12	13	3.91	91.59 (1973)	−10.05 (1975)
Long-Term Government Bonds	−0.79	6.43	1.24	17	4.73	11.67 (1976)	−13.40 (1967)

a. The mean annual loss is defined as the sum of the annual losses (negative rates of return) divided by the number of years in which losses occurred.

b. The real rate of return, R_r is defined by:

$$1 + R_r = \frac{1 + R_n}{1 + i},$$

where R_n is the nominal rate of return and i is the rate of inflation as measured by the proportional change in the Consumer Price Index.

c. The excess return is the difference between the nominal rate of return and the Treasury bill rate.

for futures, while the average annual losses were 3.86 and 2.87%, respectively. The data further suggest that commodity futures proved a very effective hedge against inflation. The early 1950s, the late 1960s and the early 1970s, which were the years of highest inflation during our 27-year sample period, were also the best years for our commodity futures portfolio. On the other hand, the annual rates of return in Table 2-3 confirm previously documented evidence that common stocks were a poor inflation hedge during the 1950–76 period.[4]

Table 2-4 indicates that the standard deviation of the *real* rates of return on commodity futures is smaller than the standard deviation of their *nominal* rates of return, whereas the opposite is true for stocks and bonds. The covariance of the nominal rate of return on futures with the rate of inflation is positive and exceeds half the variance of the rate of inflation, whereas the nominal rates of return on stocks and bonds are negatively correlated with inflation.[5] Table 2-5 presents the correlation coefficients between the rates of return for the various assets and inflation. Table 2-6 displays the seven best years and the seven worst years for both common stocks and commodity futures, and compares them with the seven years of the greatest acceleration in the rate of inflation. Four of the seven years of the greatest acceleration of inflation coincided with four of the best years for commodity futures (1950, 1969, 1973 and 1974); none of the best years for common stocks coincided with the years of most rapidly accelerating inflation. On the other hand, stocks had four of their worst years in four of the seven years of the greatest acceleration of inflation (1966, 1969, 1973 and 1974); futures had none. Table 2-6 suggests that commodity futures tended to do well when stocks were doing badly, and vice versa. The negative correlation coefficients between futures and stocks reported in Table 2-5 support this conclusion. Since the mean rates of return on futures and stocks are about the same (13% per year), an investor could have reduced his risk without lowering his mean return by diversifying his portfolio through mixing stocks with futures.

To quantify the effect of this type of diversification, we calculated the series of annual nominal rates of return on hypothetical portfolios consisting of stocks and commodity futures. Table 2-7 presents the results. The first column gives the nominal rates of return on a pure stock portfolio, the second column the rates on a portfolio invested 80% in stocks and 20% in commodity futures (with Treasury bills posted as margin), and so on until the last column, which represents a pure commodity futures portfolio. The bottom two rows of the table present the means and standard deviations of the rates of return on each portfolio. As one moves along the bottom row from the first to the last column, the standard deviation declines to a minimum of 12.68% per year when stocks are 60% of the portfolio, and then rises steadily. By switching from an all-stock portfolio to a portfolio invested 60% in stocks and 40% in commodity futures, an investor could have reduced his standard deviation by one-third without sacrificing any of his mean rate of return.

Table 2-5   Correlation Matrix of Annual Rates of Return, 1950–76

		Commodity Futures	Long-Term Government Bonds	Treasury Bills	Inflation
A.	Nominal Returns				
	Common Stocks	−0.24	−0.10	−0.57	−0.43
	Commodity Futures		−0.16	0.34	0.58
	Long-Term Government Bonds			0.20	0.03
	Treasury Bills				0.76
B.	Real Returns				
	Common Stocks	−0.25	0.14	0.18	−0.54
	Commodity Futures		−0.36	−0.48	0.48
	Long-Term Government Bonds			0.46	−0.38
	Treasury Bills				−0.75
C.	Excess Returns				
	Common Stocks	−0.20	0.08	—	−0.48
	Commodity Futures		−0.26	—	0.52
	Long-Term Government Bonds			—	−0.20

Table 2-6   Commodity Futures vs. Common Stocks As Inflation Hedges

Seven Years of Greatest Acceleration in Inflation*	Commodity Futures		Common Stocks	
	Best Seven Years	Worst Seven Years	Best Seven Years	Worst Seven Years
1950	1950	1952	1954	1953
1956	1951	1953	1958	1957
1966	1963	1955	1961	1962
1968	1969	1957	1963	1966
1969	1972	1958	1967	1969
1973	1973	1960	1972	1973
1974	1974	1975	1975	1974

*Acceleration of inflation is measured as the increase in the rate of inflation over the previous year's rate.

**Table 2-7   Nominal Rates of Return on Selected Common Stock—
Commodity Futures Portfolios, 1950–76**

| Year | Proportion of Portfolio Invested in Stocks | | | | | |
	100%	80%	60%	40%	20%	0
1950	31.71%	35.89%	40.07%	44.25%	48.43%	52.61%
1951	24.2	24.56	25.10	25.64	26.17	26.71
1952	18.37	14.45	10.53	6.62	2.70	−1.22
1953	−0.99	−2.06	−3.12	−4.19	−5.26	−6.32
1954	52.62	45.07	37.52	29.98	22.43	14.88
1955	31.56	24.29	17.02	9.75	2.48	−4.79
1956	6.56	8.20	9.84	11.47	13.11	14.75
1957	−10.78	−9.09	−7.40	−5.72	−4.03	−2.34
1958	43.36	34.42	25.48	16.55	7.61	−1.33
1959	11.95	9.67	7.39	5.11	2.82	0.54
1960	0.47	0.36	0.24	0.13	0.02	−0.09
1961	26.89	21.82	16.75	11.68	6.62	1.55
1962	−8.73	−6.81	−4.89	−2.97	−1.05	0.87
1963	22.80	22.81	22.81	22.82	22.83	22.84
1964	16.48	15.61	14.75	13.87	13.00	12.13 ·
1965	12.45	12.08	11.72	11.35	10.99	10.62
1966	−10.06	−5.12	−0.18	4.76	9.71	14.65
1967	23.98	20.01	16.04	12.07	8.10	4.13
1968	11.06	9.10	7.13	5.17	3.20	1.24
1969	−8.50	−2.63	3.24	9.11	14.98	20.84
1970	4.01	5.61	7.20	8.80	10.39	11.99
1971	14.31	12.11	9.91	7.71	5.51	3.31
1972	18.98	21.93	24.87	27.82	30.76	33.71
1973	−14.66	8.53	31.82	55.06	78.30	101.54
1974	−26.48	−14.79	−3.10	8.58	20.27	31.96
1975	37.20	28.96	20.72	12.47	4.23	−4.01
1976	23.84	21.62	19.40	17.18	14.96	12.75
Mean	13.05	13.21	13.36	13.52	13.67	13.83
Standard Deviation	18.95	14.74	12.68	13.77	17.43	22.43

Backwardation

The positive mean excess rate of return on the benchmark commodity futures portfolio seems to lend support to the normal backwardation hypothesis. This conclusion contradicts Dusak's study of three commodity futures (wheat, corn and soybeans) returns over the period 1952 to 1967.[6] To check the consistency of our data against hers, we restricted our sample to the same three commodities and the same time period she used; we found that the average excess returns in this subset of data are indeed close to zero. To us, however, it seems preferable to rely on the results of our larger sample of 23 commodities over the longer period 1950 to 1976.

We also tried to check whether our findings are consistent with the capital asset pricing model (CAPM).[7] According to the simple form of the CAPM, the mean excess rate of return on a security should equal its beta times the mean excess rate of return on the market portfolio. We followed standard practice and took the Standard and Poor's 500 as a proxy for the market portfolio. Since the mean excess rate of return on the S&P 500 was 9.42% per year during our 27-year sample period, while the mean excess rate of return on the benchmark commodity futures portfolio was 9.77% per year, the beta of commodity futures should be roughly equal to one.

A simple least squares regression of the excess rate of return on commodity futures, CMD, against the excess rate of return on the S&P 500, STK, gave us the following results:

CMD = 12.286 – 0.261 STK,
standard error of beta = 0.203.

Using a t-test, we can reject the null hypothesis that the "true" beta is one at any reasonable level of statistical significance.

Individual Commodities Results

Table 2-8 presents summary statistics of the distributions of annual rates of return on the 23 individual commodity futures studied. These are excess returns—i.e., they exclude the interest earned on the Treasury bills posted as margin. The most striking fact about these results is that only one of the 23 commodities—eggs—had a negative mean rate of return during the 27-year period. And even that negative mean is relatively small in absolute terms. The variability of the returns on the individual commodities, as measured by either their standard deviations or the range between the highest and the lowest annual returns, is large. Propane, the most variable commodity, has a staggering 202.088% per year standard deviation. This figure should be viewed with some caution, however, because it—as well as propane's high mean return of 68.26%—owes a great deal to the 559.21% return of 1973, the year in which the OPEC cartel quadrupled the price of crude oil.

The last column of Table 2-8 shows the beta coefficients derived from ordinary least squares time series regressions of the excess return on each commodity against the excess return on the S&P 500. Most are negative despite the fact that the corresponding means are positive. Figure A plots the mean excess return against beta for all 23 commodities. There does not seem to be any pattern in Figure A that resembles the upward sloping Security Market Line predicted by the CAPM.

When we ran a cross-section regression on mean excess return against beta we got the following results:

Table 2-8   Distribution of Annual Rates of Return on 23 Commodity Futures Contracts (percent per year), 1950–76

Commodity	Arithmetic Mean	Std. Dev.	Std. Error	Highest Annual Return (year)	Lowest Annual Return (year)	Number of Observations	Beta (s.e. of beta)
Wheat	3.181	30.745	5.917	112.970 (1973)	−37.971 (1976)	27	−0.370 (0.296)
Corn	2.130	26.310	5.063	101.586 (1973)	−26.055 (1955)	27	−0.429 (0.247)
Oats	1.681	19.492	3.751	56.603 (1950)	−27.443 (1955)	27	0.000 (0.194)
Soybeans	13.576	32.318	6.220	131.590 (1973)	−40.484 (1975)	27	−0.266 (0.317)
Soybean Oil	25.839	57.672	11.099	212.674 (1973)	−27.605 (1975)	27	−0.650 (0.558)
Soybean Meal	11.870	35.599	6.851	101.801 (1973)	−61.686 (1974)	27	0.239 (0.351)
Broilers	13.065	39.202	13.860	75.209 (1974)	−46.239 (1975)	8	−1.692 (0.395)
Plywood	17.968	39.962	16.314	94.595 (1972)	−19.031 (1973)	6	0.660 (0.937)
Potatoes	6.905	42.111	8.104	125.048 (1973)	−73.296 (1953)	27	−0.610 (0.400)
Platinum	0.641	25.185	7.594	47.584 (1967)	−38.524 (1970)	11	0.221 (0.411)
Wool	7.436	36.955	7.12	126.905 (1972)	−45.486 (1974)	27	0.307 (0.362)
Cotton	8.937	36.236	6.974	163.244 (1973)	−41.175 (1974)	27	−0.015 (0.360)
Orange Juice	2.515	31.771	10.047	74.538 (1971)	−32.298 (1976)	10	0.117 (0.557)
Propane	68.260	202.088	71.449	559.206 (1973)	−48.201 (1974)	8	−3.851 (3.788)
Cocoa	15.713	54.630	11.391	197.469 (1976)	−37.538 (1955)	23	−0.291 (0.589)
Silver	3.587	25.622	7.106	48.504 (1967)	−25.614 (1971)	13	−0.272 (0.375)
Copper	19.785	47.205	9.843	130.135 (1973)	−32.194 (1957)	23	0.005 (0.492)
Cattle	7.362	21.609	6.238	40.991 (1975)	−28.370 (1976)	12	0.365 (0.319)
Hogs	13.280	36.617	11.579	77.564 (1969)	−35.462 (1974)	10	−0.148 (0.641)
Pork Bellies	16.098	39.324	11.352	103.916 (1965)	−28.979 (1976)	12	−0.062 (0.618)
Egg	−4.741	27.898	5.369	56.425 (1969)	−47.156 (1971)	27	−0.293 (0.271)
Lumber	13.070	34.667	13.101	57.685 (1973)	−28.157 (1970)	7	−0.131 (0.768)
Sugar	25.404	116.215	24.232	492.009 (1974)	−71.799 (1975)	23	−2.403 (1.146)

CMD = 8.183 − 11.009 beta,
standard error of slope coefficient = 2.067.

The negative slope coefficient is inconsistent with the CAPM. And even when we excluded propane, which is the extreme outlier in the upper left corner of Figure 2-1, we still got a regression line with a negative slope:

CMD = 9.134 − 4.259,
standard error of slope coefficient = 2.520

Figure 2-1   Security Market Line for Commodity Futures

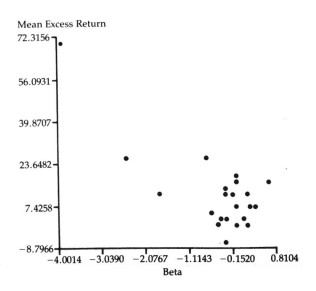

The fourth column of Table 2-8 shows the highest annual return for each commodity and the year in which it occurred. It indicates that 1973 was a banner year for many commodity futures. To what extent are the positive mean excess returns reported in the table due to just this one extraordinary good year? To answer this question, we recomputed all the statistics reported in Table 2-8 excluding 1973.

Table 2-9 reports the results. Table 2-9 shows that the mean annual rate of return on propane futures drops dramatically, from 68.26 to –1.88%. Almost all the other individual commodity means fall also. The mean excess return on the benchmark portfolio declines from the 9.77% reported in Table 2-4 to 6.62%.

Finally, Table 2-10 shows the correlation coefficients between the excess rates of return on the 23 commodity futures. As one would expect, the correlations between related commodities, such as hogs and pork bellies or soybeans, soybean oil and soybean meal, are the highest. Table 2-10 has some surprises, however—most notably, the relatively high correlations between potatoes and lumber (0.69) and potatoes and silver (0.49).

Table 2-9   Distributions of Annual Rates of Return on 23 Commodity Futures Contracts (percent per year), 1950–76 excluding 1973

Commodity	Mean	Std. Dev.	Std. Error	Number of Observations	Highest	Lowest
Wheat	-1.04	21.96	4.31	26	69.23	-37.97
Corn	-1.70	17.58	3.45	26	34.27	-26.06
Oats	1.25	19.74	3.87	26	56.60	-27.44
Soybeans	9.04	22.53	4.41	26	83.60	-40.48
Soybean Oil	18.66	44.83	8.79	26	182.23	-27.61
Soybean Meal	8.41	31.34	6.15	26	57.95	-61.69
Broilers	7.06	38.16	14.42	7	75.21	-46.24
Plywood	25.37	39.82	17.81	5	94.60	-2.28
Potatoes	2.36	35.56	6.97	26	90.93	-73.30
Platinum	0.67	26.55	8.40	10	47.58	-38.52
Wool	5.25	35.86	7.03	26	126.91	-45.50
Cotton	3.00	19.40	3.81	26	46.93	-41.98
Orange Juice	0.71	33.15	11.05	9	74.54	-32.30
Propane	-1.88	41.67	15.75	7	80.57	-48.20
Cocoa	12.38	53.47	11.40	22	197.47	-37.54
Silver	0.05	23.22	6.70	12	48.50	-25.61
Copper	14.77	41.57	8.86	22	129.98	-32.19
Cattle	7.94	22.57	6.80	11	40.99	-28.37
Hogs	7.66	33.96	11.32	9	77.56	-35.46
Pork Bellies	13.84	40.42	12.19	11	103.92	-28.98
Eggs	-4.69	28.45	5.58	26	56.43	-47.16
Lumber	5.63	31.26	12.76	6	55.63	-28.16
Sugar	24.59	118.88	25.35	22	492.01	-71.80
Benchmark Portfolio (without Treasury bills)	6.62	14.06	2.76	26	51.13	-10.05

Table 2-10 Matrix of Correlation Coefficients of Quarterly Rates of Return for 23 Commodity Futures, 1950–76

	Wheat	Corn	Oats	Soybeans	Soybean Oil	Soybean Meal	Broilers	Plywood	Potatoes	Platinum	Wool	Cotton
Wheat		0.65	0.52	0.29	0.41	0.23	0.20	0.11	0.25	0.22	0.08	0.54
Corn			0.70	0.67	0.52	0.43	0.44	0.16	0.26	0.17	0.16	0.39
Oats				0.38	0.35	0.23	0.03	0.44	0.21	0.25	0.09	0.20
Soybeans					0.54	0.66	0.60	0.03	0.17	0.05	0.42	0.27
Soybean Oil						0.21	0.26	0.01	0.27	0.30	0.19	0.22
Soybean Meal							0.28	0.08	0.15	−0.01	0.36	0.26
Broilers								0.09	0.07	0.09	0.38	0.17
Plywood									0.31	0.56	0.27	−0.29
Potatoes										0.43	0.08	0.26
Platinum											0.10	0.08
Wool												0.32

	Orange Juice	Propane	Cocoa	Silver	Copper	Cattle	Hogs	Pork Bellies	Eggs	Lumber	Sugar	Benchmark Portfolio
Wheat	0.19	0.22	0.10	0.22	0.09	0.21	0.45	0.50	0.11	0.24	0.30	0.61
Corn	0.11	0.34	0.28	0.23	0.06	0.30	0.45	0.44	0.23	0.03	0.38	0.78
Oats	0.18	0.01	0.19	0.30	−0.07	0.32	0.30	0.36	0.05	0.04	0.38	0.61
Soybeans	−0.02	0.41	0.28	0.13	0.06	0.27	0.36	0.25	0.17	0.01	0.22	0.71
Soybean Oil	−0.08	0.24	0.14	0.40	0.29	0.10	0.21	0.15	0.28	0.19	0.32	0.65
Soybean Meal	0.01	0.38	0.12	0.17	0.06	0.24	0.37	0.13	0.07	0.06	−0.01	0.52
Broilers	0.10	0.11	0.13	0.07	0.12	0.23	0.39	0.43	0.25	0.10	0.31	0.51
Plywood	0.18	−0.29	−0.14	0.46	0.09	0.29	0.28	0.27	0.08	0.45	0.27	0.32
Potatoes	−0.02	−0.12	−0.01	0.49	0.10	0.06	0.17	0.10	0.07	0.69	0.02	0.45
Platinum	0.22	−0.19	0.14	0.74	0.24	−0.01	0.20	0.17	0.18	0.51	0.16	0.44
Wool	−0.19	0.15	0.18	0.19	0.17	0.34	0.38	0.34	−0.04	0.31	−0.01	0.43
Cotton	0.13	0.30	0.14	0.05	0.12	0.21	0.40	0.31	−0.11	0.25	−0.11	0.48
Orange Juice		0.21	−0.27	−0.01	0.07	0.13	0.29	0.12	−0.08	0.09	0.05	0.20
Propane			0.10	−0.13	0.23	−0.11	0.17	−0.04	0.06	−0.28	−0.20	0.31
Cocoa				0.17	0.01	−0.20	−0.10	0.07	0.18	−0.10	0.20	0.34
Silver					0.31	−0.02	0.15	0.06	0.01	0.57	0.39	0.54
Copper						0.04	0.20		0.05	0.46	−0.02	0.29
Cattle							0.66	0.50	0.28	0.10	0.08	0.35
Hogs								0.83	0.25	0.15	0.13	0.63
Pork Bellies										0.02	0.20	0.54
Eggs										0.17	0.05	0.28
Lumber											0.15	0.38
Sugar												0.48

Conclusion

The mean rate of return on a well diversified portfolio of commodity futures contracts over the 27-year period 1950–76 was well in excess of the average risk-free rate. In fact, both the mean and variance of the return on our futures portfolio were close to the mean and variance of the return on the Standard & Poor's 500 common stock portfolio. Moreover, the futures portfolio had a more positively skewed return distribution than the stock portfolio and served as a far better hedge against inflation.

The distributions of returns on the individual commodity futures contracts by and large conform to that of the benchmark portfolio. Most are positively skewed with a positive mean excess return, although their variances are considerably greater than the portfolio's variance.

An important implication of our results is that the market portfolio of common stocks as represented by the Standard & Poor's 500 did not offer the minimum variance for the given mean return during the period 1950–76. By combining the Standard & Poor's 500 with our commodity futures portfolio, however, an investor could have achieved a reduction in variance with no concomitant decline in mean return.

The fact that the mean excess rates of return on commodity futures contracts are positive lends support to the normal backwardation hypothesis. On the other hand, the relation between these means and the corresponding beta coefficients appears to be inconsistent with the conventional form of the capital asset pricing model.

Appendix

An investment in a futures contract differs in an important way from most other investments. The investor in stocks or bonds has to pay for his securities at the time of purchase, either by using his own money or by borrowing a portion of the purchase price from a brokerage house. This borrowed money is commonly called "margin." In studies of rates of return on common stocks or bonds, the one-period rate of return is almost always calculated as:

$$R_t = \frac{(P_{t+1} + D_t)}{P_t} - 1, \tag{1}$$

where P_t and P_{t+1} are the starting and ending market prices of the security and D_t is the cash payout to the investor during the period. R_t is therefore the unlevered rate of return—i.e., the return to a hypothetical investor who purchased the security with his own funds.

Commodity contracts present the investor with a somewhat different situation. The contract itself is an agreement between a buyer and a seller: The buyer agrees to accept delivery of a specified amount and quantity of a commodity at a specified maturity date for a specified futures price; the seller agrees to make delivery in accordance with these specifications. Both the buyer and the seller can transfer their obligations to another party before the maturity date of the contract. That is, the buyer can liquidate his position by selling out to another buyer, and the initial seller can buy a contract from another seller. In actuality, delivery is made on only about one percent of the contracts initiated during the trading period.

A commodity contract is a viable instrument of intent. To legalize the agreement, and to provide some assurance of the financial ability of the buyer and seller to make good their losses, the commodity exchanges set a "performance bond"—commonly called the "m" The margin in futures trading thus differs significantly from the margin in stock or bond trading.

Margins in commodity markets are relatively low, usually seven to 10% of the value of the contract being traded. This factor has enabled investors to enjoy considerable leverage. For example, if an investor buys a contract of soybeans (5,000 bushels) at a futures price of four dollars per bushel, putting up $2,000 as margin, a 10% increase or decline in price will produce a profit or loss of $2,000, excluding a small transaction commission. If one uses the margin money as the initial investment in calculating R_t, then the rate of return is either plus or minus 100%, and the leverage factor is 10.

To compare the measured rates of return on commodity futures with the published unlevered rates of return on stocks and bonds, we adopted two alternative conventions. The first simply takes as the rate of return the proportional change in the futures price:

$$R_{1t} = \frac{P_{t+1} - P_t}{P_t}, \tag{2}$$

where P_t is the futures price at the start of quarter t. According to this definition, the rate of return on the soybean contract in the above example would be 10%. Equation 2 assumes that the investor posts a 100% margin and earns no interest on it.

But commodity exchanges permit the posting of Treasury bills as a performance bond in lieu of cash. Clearly, any rational investor would choose to post Treasury bills as margin, since he could earn the interest on them. Our second measure of the rate of return on an investment in commodity futures, therefore, includes this interest.

Applying our second measure of return, however, involves a minor complication. In practice, all commodity contracts are settled at the end of each business day. This means that after trading ends, the individual's account is credited or debited, depending whether the commodity contract increased or decreased in value from the previous day's close. If his account is credited with additional equity, he can immediately remove and pocket the excess. On the other hand, if his contract has decreased in value over the day, then he may be required to add equity to his account immediately in order to keep the minimum required margin balance. This procedure of daily settlement complicates the inclusion in the rate of return of the interest earned on the Treasury bills. While we know that futures prices—hence the equity in an account—do fluctuate daily, we attempted to circumvent this problem by taking the average equity in the account during the three-month holding period and computing the Treasury bill interest earned on that amount using the 90-day rate prevailing at the start of the period. Our second measure of the rate of return on a futures contract is therefore:

$$R_{2t} = \frac{1}{P_t}\left[(P_{t+1} - P_t) + R_{ft}\left(\frac{P_1 + P_{t+1}}{2}\right)\right], \tag{3}$$

where P_t is the futures price and R_{ft} the 90-day Treasury bill rate at the start of quarter t. Note that if P_{t+1} is close in value to P_t, R_{2t} will be approximately equal to the sum of the proportional change in the futures price and the 90-day Treasury bill rate:

$$R_{2t} \approx R_{1t} + R_{ft}. \tag{4}$$

There is an alternative, and perhaps more intuitively appealing, way to explain the derivation of R_{2t}. When an investor takes a long position in a futures contract, he promises to pay the current futures price at the end of the investment period rather than at the beginning. But this is equivalent to paying the present value of the current futures price—$P_t/(1+R_{ft})$—at the beginning of the period. In that case, the rate of return would be measured as:

$$R_{2t} = \frac{P_{t+1}(1 + R_{ft})}{P_t} - 1,$$

or equivalently:

$$R_{2t} = (1 + R_{1t})(1 + R_{ft}) - 1. \tag{5}$$

which is approximately equal to $R_{1t} + R_{ft}$.

To summarize, one can compare rates of return on commodity futures with rates of return on stocks and bonds in two ways. One can either compare the simple rate of return on commodities futures, R_{1t}, with the "risk premium" on stocks and bonds (the return in excess of the 90-day Treasury bill rate) or the rate of return including the interest earned on Treasury bills, R_{2t}, with the rate of return on stocks or bonds as conventionally measured. We used both measures for our study.

Endnotes

1. The most recent articles in this vein are by Katherine Dusak ("Futures Trading and Investor Returns: An Investigation of Commodity Market Risk Premiums," Journal of Political Economy, November/December 1973) and Thomas Cargill and Gordon C. Rausser ("Temporal Price Behavior in Commodity Futures Markets," Journal of Finance, September 1975).

2. We chose these particular starting dates because they provided the maximum number of futures contracts expiring at the end of our three-month holding periods.

3. Roger Ibbotson and Rex A. Sinquefield. *Stocks, Bonds, Bills and Inflation: The Past (1926–1976) and The Future (1977–2000)* (Charlottesville, VA: Financial Analysts Research Foundation, 1977).

4. See Zvi Bodie. "Common Stocks as a Hedge Against Inflation," *Journal of Finance,* May 1976.

5. The variance of the real rate of return on a security equals the variance of its nominal rate plus the variance of the rate of inflation minus twice the covariance between the security's nominal rate of return and the rate of inflation. If the covariance with inflation is negative, then the variance of the real rate of return must be greater than the variance of the nominal rate. If, however, the covariance is positive, then the variance of the security's real rate of return will exceed the variance of its nominal rate if and only if that covariance exceeds half the variance of the rate of inflation. The covariance between the nominal rate of return on futures and the rate of inflation is found by multiplying the correlation coefficient in Table 2-5 by the product of the standard deviations in Table 2-4: cov = 0.58 × 22.43 × 2.90 = 37.73. The number exceeds half the variance of inflation, which is 4.21.

6. Dusak, "Futures Trading and Investor Returns."

7. For an exposition of the capital asset pricing model, and a review of the tests performed to test it, see Michael C. Jensen "Capital Markets: Theory and Evidence," *Bell Journal of Economics and Management Science,* Autumn 1972.

Chapter Three

Management Summary

Title: "Commodity Futures as a Hedge against Inflation"

Publisher: *The Journal of Portfolio Management*, Spring 1983

Author: Zvi Bodie, Associate Professor, Boston University

Data: Annual prices for 29 years, 1953–1981, for commodity futures, 30-day U.S. Treasury Bills, 20-year U.S. Treasury Bonds and the S&P 500.

Methodology: As in his prior study, Bodie constructed a "well-diversified" portfolio of commodity futures consisting of liquid futures contracts. No active management was considered. Only a buy-and-hold strategy was used, with roll-overs as necessary as contracts expired.

    Futures were analyzed in the context of a "portfolio overlay," where margin for the futures component came from U.S. Treasury Bills. As such the effect of futures was *incremental* to the basic allocation to stocks, bonds and bills. This differs from the approach used by most other authors who used the traditional *substitution* techniques of modern portfolio theory.

    Real rates of return from the commodity futures portfolio were analyzed in comparison to Government Bonds, U.S. Treasury Bills and the S&P 500.

Results: The futures portfolio tended to do well "precisely" in those years when inflation was high.

    Real rates of return (adjusted for inflation) for bills, bonds and stocks were all negatively correlated with inflation, and all positively correlated with one another. Commodity futures, on the other hand, were positively correlated with the rate of inflation and negatively correlated with the others.

    The author applied this data to the construction of a hypothetical portfolio consisting first of bonds, bills and stocks and secondly to include commodity futures as well. The result was that at any level of risk, a higher mean rate of return was achieved by using futures.

continued

Comments: The study acknowledges the conservative approach of using strict buy-and-hold strategy for futures. It was pointed out that under such a strategy the only hope for long-term, positive return is through unanticipated increases in spot prices of the underlying commodities, i.e., unanticipated inflation. In doing his portfolio analysis, Bodie made the very conservative assumption that long-term, real rates of return from futures would be between 0% and 2%. (His study showed the real returns to be 5.69% for the 29 years analyzed). A favorable shift to the efficient frontier occurred from the use of futures.

Commodity Futures as a Hedge against Inflation*

They permit a significant improvement in the risk-return tradeoff.

Zvi Bodie

The purpose of this chapter is to explore how investors can use commodity futures contracts as a supplement to more conventional investments to improve the risk-return tradeoff in an inflationary environment. Admittedly, the economic raison d'etre of existing commodity futures markets is to provide a way of hedging risks of unanticipated changes in the prices of basic agricultural and industrial commodities, while investors are typically concerned with the real value of their income and wealth measured in terms of final consumption goods and services. Nevertheless, commodity futures markets can offer substantial hedging opportunities to the general investor as well as to the commodity specialist.

The chapter is organized as follows. I will first discuss why real or inflation-adjusted rates of return and their uncertainty ought to be the main concern of investors. I will present an analytical framework for formulating investment strategy, will examine the historical record of real rates of return on four asset categories: stocks, bonds, bills and commodity futures, and

I wish to thank my colleague, Alex Kane, and my research assistant, Michael Rouse, for their valuable help in preparing this chapter.
*The Journal of Portfolio Management, Spring 1983. Reprinted with permission.

will then demonstrate how the use of commodity futures can improve the risk-return tradeoff.

Why Real Investment Returns and Their Uncertainty Matter

With respect to the individual investor, i.e., the household, there can be little doubt that the dollar value of its investment portfolio is not what counts, but, rather, its real value in terms of purchasing power. Consequently, households will be concerned about the real or inflation-adjusted rate of return rather than the nominal rate of return on their investments.

If the future rate of inflation were known with certainty, it would make no difference whether investors were making their investment decisions on the basis of real or nominal rates of return, because the expected real rate of return on any asset would just be the nominal rate less the known inflation rate, and its real risk would be the same as its nominal risk. When inflation is unpredictable, however, a guaranteed nominal rate of return may be a highly uncertain one in real terms. As inflation becomes more uncertain, conventional private pension plans and contractual savings schemes offering a money-fixed stream of benefits, and conventional bonds and mortgages offering a fixed nominal rate of return become riskier and less attractive to investors.

What about institutional investors? The survival and success of institutional investors depend upon providing households with the kind of financial assets that households want to hold. As households become more and more interested in real rates of return, institutional investors must respond by offering new products and adjusting their investment policies accordingly. For example, if a life insurance company is offering a money-fixed savings plan to a household, then it can hedge simply by investing the funds it receives from households in long-term bonds and other assets that offer a guaranteed nominal rate of return. On the other hand, as households begin to demand innovative products that offer some kind of purchasing power guarantee, life insurance companies and other institutional investors must change their hedging strategies to compensate for the changed nature of their liabilities. Ultimately, if households are concerned about real rates of return, then financial institutions will be too.

The Analytical Framework

The analytical framework underlying the investment strategies I will present in this chapter is known as mean-variance analysis, and it goes back 30 years to the pioneering work by Harry Markowitz.[1] The basic premise underlying this approach is that the investor is risk averse: Given a choice between two investments offering the same mean (or average) rate of return, the investor would always choose the one that has less risk. Risk in the context of this analysis is identified with the unpredictability or uncertainty of achieving a given expected rate of return and is measured by its variance or standard deviation.

The investor's decision process falls into two stages. The first stage involves the computation of the risk-return opportunities; the second involves the choice of the most appropriate risk-return combination. In stage one, the investor starts by finding the minimum-risk strategy, determines the mean rate of return associated with it, and then seeks to derive other portfolios that offer higher and higher means with the least possible risk. The result of this part of the process is a tradeoff curve showing the terms-of-trade between risk and expected return.[2]

The inputs needed to generate the tradeoff curve are the means and standard deviations of the real rates of return on the assets being considered for inclusion in the portfolio and the correlations among them. In the following section, we examine what these parameters have been over the past 28 years and discuss our assumptions about their current values.

Inflation and Investment Returns: The Historical Record

Table 3-1 contains the historical record of real pre-tax rates of return on bills, bonds, stocks, and commodity futures for the period 1953 through 1981. The measure of the price level that was used in adjusting these rates of return was the Bureau of Labor Statistics' Consumer Price Index.

The first column in Table 3-1 is the real rate of return on a policy of "rolling over" 30-day Treasury bills and is representative of the rate of return on money-market instruments. This is by far the least volatile series, with a standard deviation of only 1.68%, because short-term interest rates have tended to follow closely movements in the rate of inflation over this period.

Table 3-1   Annual Real Rates of Return 1953-1981 (percent per year)

Year	(1) Bills	(2) Bonds	(3) Stocks	(4) Commodity Futures	Rate of Inflation (5) CPI
1953	1.19	2.99	–1.60	–3.48	0.62
1954	1.37	7.73	53.39	13.23	–0.50
1955	1.20	–1.66	31.08	–7.63	.37
1956	–0.39	–8.22	3.60	12.38	2.86
1957	0.12	4.30	–13.40	–5.04	3.02
1958	0.22	–7.72	40.88	–3.47	1.76
1959	1.43	–3.70	10.30	–2.84	1.50
1960	1.16	12.12	–1.00	–3.93	1.48
1961	1.45	0.30	26.05	.022	0.67
1062	1.50	5.60	–9.83	–2.40	1.22
1963	1.45	–0.43	20.81	16.32	1.65
1964	2.32	2.29	15.11	4.54	1.19
1965	1.97	–1.18	10.33	5.13	1.92
1966	1.36	–0.29	–12.98	9.70	3.35
1967	1.34	–11.87	20.32	–.064	3.04
1968	0.47	–4.76	6.05	–3.18	4.72
1969	0.44	–10.55	–13.77	12.20	6.11
1970	0.99	6.27	–1.40	–1.62	5.49
1971	1.00	9.55	10.59	–1.65	3.36
1972	0.42	2.20	15.06	29.35	3.41
1973	–1.72	–9.11	–21.56	72.69	8.80
1974	–3.74	–7.0	–34.47	17.97	12.20
1975	–1.13	2.04	28.21	–10.03	7.01
1976	0.26	11.39	18.16	5.30	4.81
1977	–1.55	–6.92	–13.07	4.90	6.77
1978	–1.83	–7.34	–2.42	18.60	9.03
1979	–2.59	–12.82	4.53	15.91	13.31
1980	–1.79	–15.80	17.44	5.25	12.41
1981	4.35	–8.47	–12.68	–33.08	8.90
Mean	0.37	–1.65	6.68	5.69	4.50
Standard Deviation	1.68	7.43	19.48	17.36	3.86

Correlation Coefficients:

	Bonds	Stocks	Commodity Futures	Inflation (CPI)
Bills	.430	.252	–.312	–.673
Bonds		.187	–.230	–.579
Stocks			–.210	–.467
Commodity Futures				.247

Note: The real returns were calculated according to the formula:

$$\text{Real rate of return} = 100 \times \left(\frac{1 + \text{nominal rate of return}}{1 + \text{rate of inflation}} - 1 \right)$$

using the CPI inflation rate.

Sources: The data on 1 month bills, 20 year bonds, and stocks are from Ibbotson and Sinquefield, *Stocks, Bonds, Bills and Inflation,* Financial Analysts Research Foundation.

The Commodity futures series was derived from price data in *The Wall Street Journal* using a method explained in the text.

The data on the CPI are from the U.S. Department of Labor.

Of course, this is not a coincidence. All market-determined interest rates contain an "inflation premium," which reflects expectations about the declining purchasing power of the money borrowed over the life of the loan. As the rate of inflation has increased in recent years, so too has the inflation premium built into interest rates. While long-term as well as short-term interest rates contain such a premium, conventional long-term bonds lock the investor into the current interest rate for the life of the bond. If long-term interest rates on new bonds subsequently rise as a result of unexpected inflation, the funds already locked in can be released only by selling the bonds on the secondary market at a price well below their face value. If, however, an investor buys only short-term bonds with an average maturity of about 30 days, then the interest rate earned will lag behind changes in the inflation rate by at most one month.

The problem with money-market instruments is their low rate of return. Over the last 29 years, the average pre-tax, inflation-adjusted rate of return on money-market instruments has been close to zero. In the most recent six-year period, that return has actually been negative. Perhaps the most likely scenario for the future is that inflation-adjusted returns will hover around zero, i.e., the interest rate will be about equal to the rate of inflation.

Column 2 presents the real rate of return an investor would have earned by investing in U.S. Treasury bonds with a 20-year maturity. The assumption underlying this series is that the investor bought a 20-year bond at the beginning of each year and sold it at the end. The return therefore includes both coupon interest and capital gains or losses. As the relatively low mean and high standard deviation indicate, the past 28 years was a bad period for the investor in long-term bonds. Capital losses caused by unanticipated increases in interest rates tended to more than cancel the coupon yield over this period.

It would probably be a mistake to assume that the mean real rate of return on long-term government bonds in the future is going to be the −1.65% per year that it was over the 1953 to 1981 period. A more reasonable approach to estimating the *ex ante* mean real rate would be to take the yield to maturity on long-term government bonds and subtract an estimate of the mean rate of inflation expected to prevail over the next 20 years. When we do this, we find a mean real rate of return on U.S. Treasury bonds of 3% per year.

Column 3 in Table 3-1 presents the real rate of return on the Standard and Poor's Composite Index of common stocks, which is a value-weighted stock portfolio of 500 large corporations in the United States. The return includes dividends and capital gains. The mean real rate over our sample period was 6.68% per year, which we will round off to 7.0% per year in our computations of the tradeoff curve.

Table 3-2   List of Commodity Futures Contracts Included in the Portfolio

Commodity	Year in which it first entered the portfolio
Wheat	1953
Corn	1953
Oats	1953
Soybeans	1953
Soybean Oil	1953
Soybean Meal	1953
Potatoes	1953
Wool	1953
Cotton	1953
Eggs	1953
Cocoa	1953
Copper	1953
Sugar	1953
Silver	1963
Cattle	1964
Platinum	1964
Pork Bellies	1964
Hogs	1966
Orange Juice	1966
Broilers	1968
Lumber	1969
Plywood	1970

Finally, let us focus our attention on column 4 in Table 3-1, which presents the annual rate of return one would have earned on a well-diversified portfolio of commodity futures contracts over the 1953 to 1981 period. The rate of return on a futures contract reflects the proportional change in the futures price over the holding period. The series was generated by assuming a "buy-and-hold" strategy whereby contracts were entered into at quarterly intervals, held for three months, and then liquidated. The number of commodities included varies over the period and depends primarily on the availability of reliable price data. Table 3-2 presents a full list of commodities and the year in which each was first added to the portfolio. The number was initially 13 in 1953; it increased to 22 in 1970, but subsequently declined to 18 by 1981. The portfolio was assumed to consist of equal dollar amounts invested in each commodity contract.

The rates of return for commodity futures listed in column 4 of Table 3-1 require an interpretation that is different from the real rates in columns 1 through 3. When investors take a long position in a futures contract, they do not buy it in the sense that they would buy a stock or bond or the physical commodity itself; rather, they agree to purchase the commodity for a specified price at a certain point in the future. The commodities exchange, which acts as an intermediary, requires all parties to a futures contract to post bond called "margin" to guarantee performance.[3] Investors are permitted to post Treasury bills, on which they continue to earn the interest, so the funds used as margin are therefore not strictly speaking an investment in commodity futures. The rates of return reported in column 4 should, therefore, be interpreted as the addition to the total investment portfolio rate of return the investor would have earned in each year on a position in commodity futures with a face value equal to the total investment in other assets.

In order for a buy-and-hold strategy in the futures market to be profitable, it is not enough for spot prices to be rising; they must rise by more than was anticipated in the futures price at the time the contract was entered into. On average, one might expect the spot price forecasts implicit in futures prices to be right and would therefore expect the mean rate of return on futures contracts to be zero.[4] More important for our purposes, however, futures contracts will yield a positive rate of return when there are *unanticipated* increases in spot prices, and it is this feature that makes them valuable as an inflation hedge.

A comparison of columns 4 and 5 in Table 3-1 shows that our buy-and-hold investment strategy in commodity futures tended to do well precisely in those years when the rate of inflation was high. We are probably safe in assuming that much of the increase in the CPI in those years was unanticipated. The mean rate of return on our well-diversified commodity futures portfolio during the entire 1953 to 1981 period was 5.69% per year, a strikingly large number, indicating that the period as a whole was probably one of unanticipated inflation.

The glaring exception is the year 1981, in which one would have lost 33% on our buy-and-hold strategy in commodity futures. In one sense, 1981 is not an exception: The 8.9% rate of inflation during the year, although still relatively high by historical standards, was considerably lower than the forecasts of most experts at the beginning of the year. It would probably be correct to say, therefore, that 1981 was a year of unanticipated deceleration in the rate of inflation. Just as we expect unanticipated acceleration in the rate of inflation to be associated with positive rates of return on a buy-and-hold strategy in commodity futures, so we should expect unanticipated deceleration in inflation to be associated with negative rates of return on futures. Of course, investors who had foreseen the deceleration in inflation ahead of time could have made a large positive rate of return by going short in commodity futures, but doing so would have had to be classified as speculating on one's own forecast of inflation, rather than hedging against inflation.

It is not at all clear what mean value we should assume for the rate of return on commodity futures in computing the tradeoff curve for the future. For this reason, we will assume two alternative values for this parameter, zero and 2% per year, and we will trace the consequences of each.

The other parameters that play a crucial role in determining the shape of the tradeoff curve are the correlation coefficients presented at the bottom of Table 3-1. Perhaps the most significant thing to notice is that the real rates of return on bills, bonds, and stocks are all negatively correlated with inflation and all positively correlated with one another. Commodity futures, on the other hand, are positively correlated with the rate of inflation and negatively correlated with the real rates of return on the other major asset categories. Therefore, they can serve to reduce the risk associated with any portfolio containing them.

Before proceeding to our presentation of the risk-return tradeoff curves, let us summarize the assumptions that we are making about the key parameters relating to the real rates of return on bills, bonds, stocks, and commodity futures and the interrelationships among them. With regard to the means, we assume zero on bills, 3% on bonds, 7% on stocks, and two alternative values on commodity futures: zero and 2%. With regard to the standard deviations and correlations, we assume the ones reported in Table 3-1.

The Risk-Return Tradeoff

The purpose of this section of the chapter is to show how commodity futures can improve the risk-return tradeoff faced by a tax-exempt investor. We will first consider what the tradeoff curve looks like when the set of asset choices is restricted to stocks, bonds, and bills and will then compare that to the tradeoff curve with commodity futures included.

Table 3-3   Risk-Return Tradeoff Curve: Stocks, Bills and Bonds

Point	Mean	Standard Deviation	Slope	Stocks	Bonds	Bills
				Portfolio Proportions		
A	0%	1.68%		0	0	1.00
			.88			
B	1	2.81		.06	.20	.74
			.60			
C	2	4.47		.12	.40	.48
			.56			
D	3	6.24		.17	.60	.23
			.55			
E	4	8.06		.25	.75	0
			.33			
F	5	11.06		.50	.50	0
			.25			
G	6	15.07		.75	.25	0
			.23			
H	7	19.48		1.00	0	0

Assumptions about real rates of return:

	Bills	Bonds	Stocks
Mean	0%	3%	7%
Standard Deviation	1.68%	7.43%	19.48%

Correlations:

Bonds	.430	
Stocks	.252	.187

Table 3-3 and Figure 3-1 contain all of the information relevant to the first of these two curves. Each row of the table corresponds to a point on the curve, starting from the minimum-risk point (A) with a mean real rate of return of zero and a standard deviation of 1.68% to the maximum return point (H) with a mean of 7% and a standard deviation of 19.48%. The last three columns of the table show the portfolio proportions corresponding to each point on the curve. These are the portfolio proportions that will produce the given mean real rate of return with minimum risk, and we find them by using an optimization procedure originally developed by Markowitz.[5] In our analysis, we have ruled out short sales or the purchase of securities on margin.

Figure 3-1   Risk-Return Tradeoff Curve: Stocks, Bonds, Bills

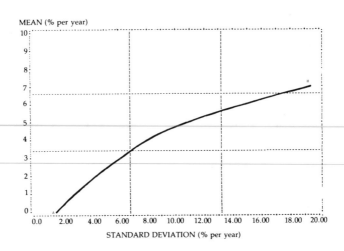

Figure 3-2   Probability Distributions of Portfolio Rates of Return

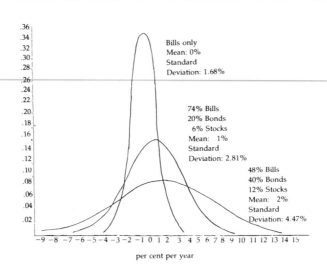

In order to provide a clearer picture of the meaning of a movement along the risk-return tradeoff curve, I have graphed in Figure 3-2 three probability distributions, corresponding to the first three points on the tradeoff curve in Figure 3-1. I based them on the assumption that the distribution of the real rates of return on the portfolios is normal, i.e., a "bell-shaped" curve. The first corresponds to the portfolio consisting of bills only, which has a mean of zero and a standard deviation of 1.68%. The second corresponds to the portfolio that has 74% invested in bills, 20% in bonds and 6% in stocks, with a mean real rate of return of 1% per year and a standard deviation of 2.81%. The third corresponds to a portfolio that has 48% invested in bills, 40% in bonds and 12% in stocks with a mean of 2% per year and a standard deviation of 4.47%. As the mean goes up, the bell-shaped curve shifts to the right and becomes more flat or stretched out, indicating greater upside potential but also greater downside risk.

Now we are ready to introduce commodity futures contracts into the portfolio. Remember that we are not actually using up any of our funds when we take a position in commodity futures; the funds are invested in stocks, bonds and bills. We are simply taking a position that has a face value equal to some specified proportion of the total amount invested in these other assets. The only restriction on the portfolio imposed by the futures contracts is that we must have an amount invested in bills equal to at least 10% of the position in commodity futures, to serve as margin.

The results with commodity futures included appear in Table 3-4 and Figure 3-3. Note that the minimum-risk strategy is still to invest 100% of our funds in bills, but it is now optimal to hedge that investment with a small position in the well-diversified commodity futures portfolio by taking a long position with a face value equal to 5% of the investment in bills. Under our assumption that the mean rate of return on commodity futures is zero, the mean real rate of return on the portfolio will remain unaffected, but there will be a reduction in standard deviation. Comparing curves 1 and 2 in Figure 3-3, we see that, for any mean real rate of return, introducing the right amount of commodity futures contracts into the portfolio enables us to reduce the standard deviation. It shifts the tradeoff curve to the left. The reduction in standard deviation is .24% at the minimum-risk end of the curve, increases to .32% in the middle, and then declines to .21% at the other end.

If we look at the last four columns in Table 3-4 and compare them with the last three columns of Table 3-3, we see that the addition of commodity futures contracts does not change the portfolio proportions of stocks, bonds, and bills by much. The major effect is that bills do not disappear entirely from the portfolio when we move to high mean real rates of return, because

Table 3-4   Risk-Return Tradeoff: Stocks, Bonds, Bills, and
            Commodity Futures

Mean	Standard Deviation	Slope	Portfolio Proportions			
			Stocks	Bonds	Bills	Commodity Futures
0%	1.44%		0	0	1.00	.05
		.91				
1	2.54		.06	.19	.75	.07
		.61				
2	4.18		.12	.39	.49	.09
		.57				
3	5.93		.18	.58	.24	.11
		.55				
4	7.74		.26	.73	.01	.13
		.33				
5	10.79		.51	.48	.01	.14
		.25				
6	14.86		.76	.23	.01	.15
		.22				
7	19.48		1.00	0	0	

Assumptions about real rates of return:

	Bills	Bonds	Stocks	Commodity Futures
Mean	0%	3.0%	7.0%	0%
Standard Deviation	1.68%	7.43%	19.48%	17.36%

Correlations:

	Bills	Bonds	Stocks
Bonds	.430		
Stocks	.252	.187	
Commodity Futures	−.312	−.230	−.210

we need bills to serve as margin on the commodity futures contracts. We also see that, as we move to higher mean real rates of return and the investment in stocks goes up, the size of the relative position in commodity futures increases steadily, although it never exceeds 15% of the total value of the investment portfolio.

Figure 3-3   Risk-Return Tradeoff Curves

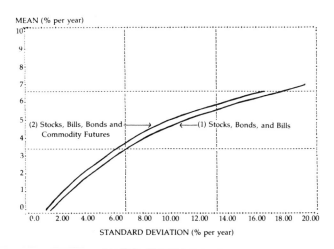

Figure 3-4   Risk-Return Tradeoff Curves

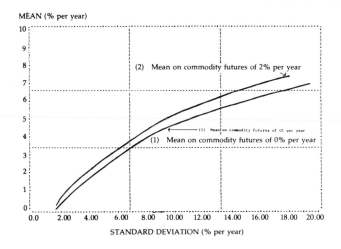

Table 3-5   Effect of Increased Mean Rate of Return on Commodity
             Futures to 2% Per Year

		Portfolio Proportions			
Mean	Standard Deviation	Stocks	Bonds	Bills	Commodity Futures
0.1%	1.44%	0	0	1.00	.05
1.0	2.31	.05	.15	.80	.09
2	3.81	.11	.33	.56	.13
3	5.45	.16	.52	.32	.16
4	7.12	.21	.70	.09	.20
5	9.23	.37	.70	.03	.30
6	12.40	.57	.39	.04	.43
7	16.05	.77	.18	.05	.55

What is the effect on the tradeoff curve of assuming a positive mean rate of return on commodity futures? Table 3-5 and Figure 3-4 present the results of assuming a 2% per year mean rate. Perhaps the best way to describe the effect is as an upward shift of the entire curve. At any level of risk, we can achieve a higher mean real rate of return, with the gain being larger the higher the level of risk. Even the minimum-risk portfolio now has a positive mean rate of return of .1% per year. It now becomes possible to attain a 7% mean real rate of return with a standard deviation of only 16.05% instead of 19.48%, by holding a portfolio consisting of 77% stocks, 18% bonds, 5% bills, and a position in commodity futures equal to 55% of the portfolio's value.

Summary and Conclusion

The objective of this paper has been to explore how a tax-exempt investor can use a passive buy-and-hold investment strategy in a diverse basket of commodity futures contracts as a supplement to common stocks, bonds, and bills to improve the risk-return tradeoff in an inflationary environment. We made the argument that such a broad-based position in commodity futures would tend to do well when there is unanticipated inflation, because commodity prices and consumer prices tend to move together. The evidence of the period from 1953 through 1981 seems to support this hypothesis. The evidence also suggests that the returns on stocks, bonds, and bills were negatively affected by inflation.

Using the historical correlations between the returns on these four categories of investments and making plausible assumptions about their mean rates of return, we then derived the pre-tax, real risk-return tradeoff curve facing an investor. By comparing the curve derived with commodity futures to the one without, we demonstrated that there was a substantial gain from including commodities.

Endnotes

1. See H. Markowitz, "Portfolio Selection," *Journal of Finance*, Volume 7 Number 1, March 1952.

2. For a discussion of how to choose the optimal point on the tradeoff curve, see Z. Bodie, "Hedging Against Inflation," *Sloan Management Review*, Fall 1979.

3. Margins on commodity futures contracts are typically low, ranging from 7% to 10% of the face value of the contract. For more detail about the commodity futures series, see Z. Bodie and V. Rosansky, "Risk and Return in Commodity Futures," *Financial Analysts Journal*, May/June 1980.

4. There is a good deal of controversy in the economics literature on this point. For further discussion and references see Bodie and Rosansky, op. cit.

5. The optimization procedure is described in Markowitz, op. cit.

Chapter Four

Management Summary

Title: "The Potential Role of Managed Commodity-Financial
                  Futures Accounts (and/or Funds) in Portfolios of Stocks
                  and Bonds"

Presentation: Annual Conference of the Financial Analysts Federation,
                  May 1983

Author: John Lintner, Professor, Harvard University

Data: Monthly prices and returns for 42 months, from July 1979,
                  through December, 1982, for fifteen futures-account
                  managers' composite performance, eight publicly offered
                  commodity funds, averages of all stocks listed on the New
                  York and American Stock Exchanges, the Salomon Broth-
                  ers high grade corporate bond index, U.S. Treasury Bills,
                  and Consumer Price Index.

Methodology: Managed futures returns from trading advisors and public
                  funds were analyzed in comparison to stocks, bonds and
                  bills, both on an actual and real (adjusted for inflation)
                  basis. As opposed to the earlier studies of Bodie, Lintner
                  used the performance of actively managed accounts.

Results: The ratio of return to risk (standard deviation) was higher
                  for a substantial fraction of trading advisors and public
                  funds than for stock, bond and standard bond portfolios.
                  A portfolio of equally weighted managed accounts, and
                  equally weighted futures funds similarly outperformed
                  stock and bond portfolios on a return/risk ratio basis.
                  Even stronger results were obtained by allocating funds
                  selectively among different managers (or among different
                  funds). As Lintner stated "Indeed, the improvement from
                  holding efficiently selected portfolios of managed ac-
                  counts or funds is so large and the correlations between
                  the returns on futures portfolios and those on the stock and
                  bond portfolios so surprisingly low (sometimes even neg-
                  ative) that the return/risk tradeoffs provided by aug-
                  continued

mented portfolios...clearly demonstrate tradeoffs available from portfolios of stocks alone (or portfolios of stocks and bonds). Moreover, they do so by very considerable margins."

Lintner went on to state that portfolios of stocks and/or bonds diversified with managed futures showed substantially less risk at every possible level of expected return than portfolios of stocks and/or bonds alone. These results are true for both actual returns and returns adjusted for inflation.

Comments: This landmark study was the first conducted using research from managed futures, as opposed to the buy-and-hold strategy used earlier by Bodie. The data base of 42 months is a fragile basis for making long-term extrapolations. Lintner acknowledged this and stated "although specific numbers may change, it is much less likely that the basis general interrelations will be greatly (or rapidly) altered—in particular the critical findings of low inter-correlations between portfolios of futures accounts and stocks and bonds are very likely to persist strongly in the future. And, in that event, all the general conclusions of this study will prove to be solid and robust."

The Potential Role of Managed Commodity-Financial Futures Accounts (and/or Funds) in Portfolios of Stocks and Bonds*

John Lintner

Diversification can substantially reduce the risks involved in portfolio returns and provide superior returns relative to the risks incurred. This basic insight was well understood by prudent and successful investment managers long before the advent of Markowitz and Modern Portfolio Theory. Investors, trust officers, and institutional portfolio managers for many decades have diversified their holdings of stocks across different companies and industry groups—and they have limited their maximum investment in any one company—in order to avoid having all their eggs in one basket, subject to all the risks of that one basket. They realized the very real possibility that unanticipated adverse developments could seriously reduce

*Paper presented at the Annual Conference of the Financial Analysts Federation, Royal York Hotel, Toronto, Canada, May 16, 1983. Shortly after this paper was presented Dr. Lintner died. When an author delivers a paper at a conference he normally reserves the right to revise the work after hearing the comments of his colleagues. His work is reproduced herein with the understanding that it may not have been Dr. Lintner's final word on the subject.

This paper has benefited from helpful discussions with Andre Perold and the use of his efficient programs for computing minimum variance portfolios. Patrick O'Connor and Ram Willner provided fine programming assistance.

63

the returns on any one security below the return they anticipated. But they also recognized from experience that such adverse outcomes (relative to their expectations) on any particular stock would probably have a much smaller (and possibly even no) effect on the returns on others. They also recognized that unanticipated adverse developments affecting some securities were likely to be offset by equally unanticipated good fortune and favorable surprises (relative to their expectations) on others. They allowed for the sea-tides which would raise or lower the returns on almost all their stocks in forming their judgments of the expected returns on the individual stocks in their portfolios. They then held diversified portfolios of stocks in order to use the law of averages and very substantially reduce the *net* impact on their *portfolio* returns of the unanticipated developments which would cause the returns actually realized on individual stocks to deviate (favorably or unfavorably) from their expectations.

On such intuitive and rather general grounds as these, most investment managers[1] have traditionally broadened the diversification of their portfolios by also including a substantial fraction of bonds, along with their stocks, in their overall investment position. While both bond and stock returns respond to changes in interest rates, they do so in different degrees, and stocks also respond to unanticipated changes in earnings and dividends which affect bond returns much less directly. Over the last decade or so, many major institutional investors have broadened the diversification of their portfolios still further by investing modest fractions of their assets in the direct ownership of real estate, and even in such other nontraditional outlets as diversified holdings of oil-well exploration pools and venture capital companies.

The managers of these large institutional investment portfolios must have diversified within their stock portfolios (and diversified further by adding bonds and some other types of investments) because they believed that the resulting broader portfolios would give them (on the basis of their own assessments and judgments) a *combination* of expected returns and overall risks which they preferred to any of the risk-return combinations available from any less diversified portfolios. Since these managers are all, as we say, risk-averse—they are always seeking higher returns, but avoid taking risks unless they think they are going to be adequately compensated for doing so—they must have believed that the resulting broader and more diversified portfolios would *either reduce* the overall risks involved in getting any given expected portfolio return, *or increase* the expected portfolio return attainable from bearing any given level of risk on their overall portfolio.[2] From either perspective, the diversification was undertaken in order to improve the tradeoffs of the expected returns and the overall risks of their combined portfolios of risk assets. In modern terminology, the diversification was believed to shift the efficient frontier of portfolio returns and portfolio risks upward and/or to the left when returns are plotted vertically and risks horizontally.

Over the years, most investment managers have undoubtedly made all or most of their decisions on the appropriate allocation of the funds in their portfolios—and their decisions on whether to add a new security or a new class of investments to their portfolios—largely on the basis of their information and assessments of the prospects and risks of the particular securities or groups of assets, and their usually rather intuitive judgments regarding the benefits of more or less diversification (or different patterns of diversification) in their portfolios. The great contribution of Modern Portfolio Theory, based on Markowitz' pioneering work in the 1950s,[3] is not to displace the judgment and responsibility of the investment manager, but rather to provide a rigorous framework for determining what the best allocation of funds invested in individually risky assets will be *if* the responsible manager decides that he wants to allocate his funds on the basis of a *given* set of judgments and assessments.[4] It has provided valuable insights into what assessments need to be made, how they interact with each other, and the relative importance of the different characteristics of a security being considered for a portfolio. In particular, it has rigorously established that *every* risk-averse investor—regardless of the degree of his risk-aversion— should add at least some investment in a new security (or group of new securities) to whatever portfolio he already holds *if* doing so will improve the return-risk tradeoff of that portfolio in the precise sense stated in the preceding paragraph.

This condition *will* be satisfied *if* (but *only if* [5]) a simple regression of the returns on the candidate security (or securities) against the returns on the existing portfolio shows a positive intercept or constant term—i.e., *if* it provides a higher risk-adjusted return than that provided by the existing portfolio. But while this condition is exact, it is not very informative regarding the particular characteristics of the candidate securities which will enable them to meet the test in any particular situation. A strictly equivalent but much more intuitively informative test is the following:[6]

> The risk and return characteristics of any given candidate security (or group of securities) will improve the risk-return tradeoff provided by *any* existing portfolio *if* and *only* if the *ratio* of the expected rate of return of the candidate(s) divided by the standard deviation of their returns is larger than the *product* of (a) the corresponding ratio assessed for the existing portfolio with (b) the

correlation between the returns on the candidate(s) and the returns on the existing portfolio.

Moreover, this test is still valid when the nominal returns or securities and portfolios are redefined as excess returns (over the short-term rates available each period) or as real returns (over inflation rates each period).

Purpose and Organization of Chapter. The purpose of the present chapter is to explore whether investments in managed accounts of trading advisors in the commodity and financial futures markets, and/or publicly traded futures funds, have shown risk and return characteristics which would make them a desirable means of further diversification for portfolios of stock and bond investments. As previously explained, they will be desirable supplements to more conventional stock and bond portfolios *provided* they improve the reward-risk tradeoffs for the overall portfolios by shifting the efficient frontier of portfolio returns and portfolio risks upward and/or to the left when returns are plotted vertically and risks horizontally. The body of the paper uses the rigorous but intuitively informative "reward/risk ratio" and "degree of intercorrelation" test described earlier. Since some investment managers are primarily concerned with nominal holding period returns as such—while others are more concerned with excess returns over short-term investment alternatives, and still others with real returns after allowing for inflation—all three measures of returns and risks will be examined.

To build up our analysis in an orderly progression from the raw data to our final conclusions, Section I will review the returns and the risk characteristics of the pooled accounts of leading trading advisors and of publicly offered funds, each manager or public fund considered separately. As a benchmark for our comparisons, the returns and risks of a well-diversified portfolio of common stocks and of a diversified portfolio of corporate bonds will be noted. Since many investors hold a basic portfolio invested roughly 60% in stocks and 40% in bonds, the returns and risks of a 60:40 stock-bond portfolio is also included. The following section analyzes the potential improvements in reward/risk ratios which have been available from holding diversified futures portfolios using a group of account managers or investing in several public funds. Section III then goes on to examine whether the addition of such a diversified sub-portfolio of investments with futures-account managers, or investments in futures funds, would have improved the risk/return performance of stock portfolios or the performance of combined stock and bond portfolios, using the tests previously described.

Preview and Summary of Our Findings and Conclusions. As would have been expected, the managed futures accounts and futures funds are shown to be investments with high risks but also high expected returns. It turns out that the return/risk ratios of a substantial fraction of the futures-managers and funds are higher than those on diversified stock (or stock and bond) portfolios. Moreover, a considerably larger fraction have shown higher ratios when the comparison is made with excess returns or real returns.[7]

The return/risk ratio of a separate portfolio with equal dollar investments in the hands of each of the fifteen futures-account managers in our sample (or equal dollars invested in each of the eight futures funds) would also have been substantially larger than that shown by a well-diversified portfolio of common stocks—and the ratio for portfolios of corporate stocks is in turn substantially larger than that for portfolios of corporate bonds.

Since several of these futures managers (or funds) have shown considerably higher return/risk ratios than this evenly spread composite of managers (or futures funds)—*and* since the intercorrelations between the return experience of these various "high ratio" managers or funds turn out to have been rather moderate—there are very large *additional* benefits obtainable by spreading the funds to be dedicated to futures investments selectively ("efficiently") among different managers (or diversifying selectively across different funds). This is shown by the impressive improvements in the return/risk ratios produced by this kind of optimizing and selective diversification. Equivalently, it is shown by the large reductions in the risks required to obtain any given expected rate of return on the funds invested in managed commodity-financial futures or in publicly offered funds.

Indeed, the improvements from holding efficiently selected portfolios of managed accounts or funds are so large—*and* the correlations between the returns on the futures-portfolios and those on the stock and bond portfolios are so surprisingly low (sometimes even negative)—that the return/risk tradeoffs provided by *augmented portfolios,* consisting partly of funds invested with appropriate groups of futures managers (or funds) combined with funds invested in portfolios stocks alone (or in mixed portfolios of stocks and bonds), clearly dominate the tradeoffs available from portfolios of stocks alone (or from portfolios of stocks and bonds). Moreover, they do so by very considerable margins.

The combined portfolios of stocks (or stocks and bonds) *after* including judicious investments in appropriately selected sub-portfolios of investments in managed futures accounts (or funds) show substantially less risk at every possible level of expected return than portfolios of stocks (or stocks and bonds) alone. This is the essence of the "potential role" of managed futures accounts (or funds) as a supplement to stock and bond portfolios suggested in the title of this chapter.

Finally, *all* the above conclusions continue to hold when returns are measured in real as well as in nominal terms, and *also* when returns are adjusted for the risk-free rate on treasury bills.

The data used. Our statistical analysis is based on two sets of data. The *first* is a file of the monthly returns shown in the available composite account performance reports filed by 15 futures-accounts managers with the CFTC, and the S.E.C., covering the 42 months beginning with July 1979 and ending with December 1982. We had access to these reports as filed by 32 of the largest account managers, but several had only been in business for a short period of time and several of the others provided only quarterly data over all or substantial parts of their record. Because of the substantial volatility in these accounts and markets, we believed we should have access to at least 40 "data points" in order to get reasonably good measures of the stochastic characteristics of any manager's performance. We also believed it would be desirable to use the most recent period of sufficient length available, in part because of the difficult times many of the managers experienced in late 1979 and again in 1982. The 15 series used include all those for which we had data which meet these two conditions.

The monthly rate of return reported to the CFTC is the percentage of beginning equity represented by the sum of all profits or losses taken on all positions closed within the month, plus the net profit or loss on all positions open at the end of the month, and plus interest earned on all T-bills held in lieu of margin deposits and other income on short investments of investors' equity not actively committed to futures positions, *less* all brokerage commissions, operating expenses, and management fees and bonuses. This official calculation of the rate of return based on beginning equity will obviously overstate the true rate of profit (or loss) when net new funds have been added to the accounts during the month—and correspondingly understate the rate of profit (or loss) when funds on balance have been withdrawn from the accounts during the month. One of the managers in our sample only entered additions or withdrawals on the last day of each month, so no adjustment was required. The monthly rate of return for the other 14 managers was adjusted on the assumption that the net additions or withdrawals reported during the month were evenly spread over 22 trading days in the month.[8] Even though this adjusted figure is still only an approximation for individual months for particular managers,[9] this adjustment should provide quite accurate estimates of the means, standard deviations, and intercorrelations over the 42 monthly returns as a whole (which are the critical statistics in our analysis). All our work and tables reported below are based on these adjusted returns. [We did, however, recalculate the risk/reward ratios and correlations using the "raw" (unadjusted) monthly rate of return on the CFTC basis; all of our substantive conclusions are robust with or without this adjustment.]

The data for each of the 15 futures-account managers represent the *composite* performance on all their accounts as given in their performance reports required by the CFTC. There is scattered evidence that the performance of smaller accounts on average tends to be somewhat less favorable than that on larger accounts,[10] and readers can bear this in mind in interpreting the implications of our results for their individual situation.

The *second set of data* on managed futures accounts used in this study is a file of the monthly changes in the net asset value of eight publicly offered commodity funds over the same 42 months, July 1979 through December 1982. The data were compiled from public reports by Jay Klopfenstein of Norwood Securities in Chicago and Frank S. Pusatri in New York and reported in Managed Account Reports, Columbia, MD. The number of these publicly offered funds has been increasing rapidly over the last two or three years, but for reasons explained above, we confined our analysis to the eight funds having an adequately long record of performance for our purposes.

We will analyze these two sets of data separately and in parallel. Each is of interest in its own right. A further reason for not merging the two records is that some of the performance records of managers in the first set include the assets of the publicly offered funds under their management along with their other individual accounts.

Our data on the returns available over the same period on a well diversified portfolio of *common stocks* are the weighted averages of the monthly holding period returns (including dividends) on all stocks with returns available listed on the NYSE and the AMEX, as reported on the tapes of the Chicago Center for Research in Security Prices. For the performance of corporate *bond portfolios,* we used the monthly total returns (including coupons) on Salomon Brothers' high grade corporate bond index. The monthly rates of return on Treasury Bills were computed from the Federal Reserve Bulletin, and the monthly inflation rate was based on the Consumers Price Index.

I.Overall Returns and Risk Performance of Managed Commodity-Financial Accounts and Publicly Offered Funds.

There is no question that even professionally managed futures accounts and funds involve substantial risks—as all prospectuses assert, often in italics or capital letters. The data in the first part of Table I.M(a) show that the standard deviations of the monthly holding period returns on the corporate accounts render the management of fifteen leading futures-account management companies ranged from 4.65% to 21.71%. The pooled accounts under each management has a maximum loss (in some one of the 42 months from July 1979 to the end of 1982) which ranged from a mere 9.5% to as much as 38%. The *average* the maximum loss in any month over the 15 managers was 23%, and the average of the standard deviations of monthly returns was 12.36%.

Correspondingly, from Table I.F(a) the standard deviations of the monthly returns on the shares of the eight publicly offered funds ranged from 6.5% to over 13% per month. Over this 42 month period, the greatest loss in any one month ranged from 11.0% for holders of one of the funds to over 44% for holders of another fund. The *average* of the maximum loss in any month over the eight funds was over 18%, and the average standard deviation of the monthly returns over these funds was 9.58%.

For perspective, these risks of loss in managed futures accounts or funds should be compared with those on the well-diversified portfolios of common stocks and corporate bonds shown in Section C of the same Tables. The monthly standard deviations of the monthly returns on 15 managed accounts ranged from one to over four times the 5.0% monthly standard deviation on stocks and the 4.3% s.d. on a 60:40 stock-bond portfolio; the s.d. for the eight futures funds ranged from 1.2 times to about 3 times as large as those on traditional stock and bond portfolios. The *average* of the maximum loss (for any one month) for the 15 managers (20.6%), and for the eight funds (18%), were respectively 1.91 and 1.69 times the 10.77% maximum loss on stocks in any month—and 2.67 and 2.36 times the 7.71% maximum loss on a 60:40 combined portfolio of stocks and bonds.

For the reader's convenience, all these comparisons of the risk and loss experience of managers and futures funds are brought together in Section A of Summary Table 4-1. To this point, we have been discussing the risks and losses incurred by investors in the managed accounts or funds, without any adjustment for inflation or the returns on alternative "safe" investments. The other two sections of this Summary Table show that both the absolute and the comparative risk experience of futures managers and funds is very much the same when returns are measured after deducting the "opportunity cost" of the foregone returns on "safe" investments in T-bills—and also when they are measured in "real" terms after subtracting the current (CPI) monthly inflation rate.

But while investments in managed futures accounts and publicly offered futures funds generally involve very high risks, the evidence is equally strong that many of the managers and funds have provided very high average returns. The data in Table I.M(a) shows that 13 of the 15 managers over the period July 1979 through the end of 1982 provided *average* monthly rates of return (in spite of their loss-months) which were larger than the average monthly return on diversified portfolios of either stocks or bonds (or mixtures of the two). Correspondingly, Table I.F(a) shows that six of the eight funds provided larger average monthly returns than diversified port-folios of stocks, and seven of the eight showed higher average returns than corporate bond portfolios over these 42 months. One of the managers produced pooled returns for his clients over six times that produced by average stock portfolios over the same period, and one of the public funds had returns over *three* times that of average stock portfolios (and over six times that of portfolios restricted to corporate bonds). Similarly, favorable comparisons are shown in Tables I.M(b) and (c), and I.F(b) and (c), when returns are measured net of T-bill yields or inflation rates.

These high returns provided by many of the managers and funds raise the question of whether they have been high enough to justify the risks incurred, which we have already seen also to be high. The first step in the analysis of this issue is to consider the reward/risk ratios provided by each manager or fund, and compare them with those which have been available on stocks and bonds. The data in Summary Table 2 show that these re-ward/risk ratios for different managers and funds covered a rather wide range. In terms of "raw" returns (Part A), the average ratio over the 15 managers of 0.21 was about 80% of that for stocks alone (or mixed portfolios of stocks and bonds), but over half-again as high as for portfolios of bonds alone. In Parts B and C, adjustments are made for foregone earnings on T-bills and for inflation. Here the comparisons are much more favorable. The average manager (or fund) provided an "Excess return/risk" ratio about *four* times as large as that provided by a 60:40 mixed portfolio of bonds and stocks—and provided a "real return/risk" ratio roughly twice that of the stock-bond portfolio. It is also worth noting that while the "raw return/risk" ratios of only six of 15 managers (and only three of eight funds) were larger than that for the mixed stock-bond portfolio, 13 managers (and six of the eight funds) had larger "excess return/risk" ratios—and 12 of the 15 managers (and five of the eight funds) provided larger "real return/risk" ratios than mixed stock-bond portfolios.

II. Potential Improvements in Risk/Reward Ratios from Diversifying Investments Among Futures Managers (or Futures Funds).

As indicated in the introduction, when returns are imperfectly correlated with each other, diversification can substantially reduce the risks involved in producing any given expected rate of portfolio return, and thereby substantially improve the reward/risk ratio available. This general principle is well illustrated (as are others) by the data included in the "B" Sections of the six larger Tables at the end of the chapter. Consider Table I.M(a) covering the experience of 15 managers, using returns with no adjustment for inflation on T-bills. The first line shows the results of an *undiscriminating* ("broadside") *diversification* which assumes that equal fractions of the total funds to be invested in managed futures accounts are placed in bonds of each of the 15 managers. This pooled investment would have shown an average monthly *return* of 2.72%, which is just the unweighted average of the returns of the separate managers. But note that the *maximum loss* in any one of the 42 months would have been –9.77%—which is *substantially less than half the average* (–20.59%) of the maximum losses of the 15 managers. In part, this reflects the fact that the different managers had their big loss months at different times. More fundamentally, this reflects the fact that the average correlation between the monthly returns of each manager with those of every other manager was only 0.285.[11] The fact that this average correlation among the monthly returns of different managers is so relatively low also explains the fact that the *standard deviation* of the returns on this evenly spread futures investment is only 7.35%—very substantially less than the average (12.36%) of the σs of the fifteen managers considered separately.[12] This reduction in the standard deviation of the returns on this evenly spread "Portfolio of Managers" in turn means that its reward/risk ratio (0.372) is correspondingly higher than the *average* (0.210) of the μ/σ ratios of the 15 managers considered separately.

So far, these results simply illustrate the well-known general principle stated in our introductory paragraph that when different investment returns have low intercorrelations with each other, the law of averages comes into play and substantial reductions in the portfolio risks—and substantial improvements in expected returns relative to the risk incurred—can be obtained by even a rather naive "broadside" diversification over different investments. In the present instance, the improvements have come simply from spreading funds evenly over the accounts of different managers.

But not all these 15 managers have equally attractive performance records. Several have shown reward/risk ratios[13] substantially larger than the average of the group (0.210), and two have shown ratios actually higher than the pooled accounts of the 15 managers (0.372). Taken together with the fact that the intercorrelations between the returns of different managers are relatively low or moderate, this suggests that *a selectively diversified portfolio, efficiently allocating funds among fewer* (but still several) *managers,* could *match* the expected monthly *returns* (2.72%) of the "broadside" equally allocated portfolio *while substantially reducing the portfolio risk.* The second line of section B in Table I.M(a) shows that this is indeed possible. The computer was programmed to find the allocation of funds over any subset of managers which would reproduce the 2.723% expected return but which would *minimize the standard deviation* associated with this return. The result is a portfolio which optimally allocates the funds targeted for futures investments over only seven of the 15 managers.[14] The expected return is the same (2.723%) as that provided by the broadside diversification, but the standard deviation of the returns on this efficiently diversified portfolio have been reduced to 4.987%—about two-thirds the risk involved in the undiscriminating diversification over all 15 managers. Correspondingly, with the same expected returns, the efficiently allocated portfolio over seven managers has a reward/risk ratio of 0.546, which is 47% *greater* than that (0.372) of the indiscriminating 15-manager portfolio.

This part of our work is brought together in Section A.a of the Summary Table 4-3. It will be observed that the efficient portfolio of selected managers just described produces a reward/risk ratio that is about *double* that on a well-diversified portfolio of common stocks, and more than twice that on a 60:40 portfolio of stocks and corporate bonds.

Section A.b of the Summary Table shows that very much the same benefits are realized when investors diversify however discrimately over the eight publicly offered futures funds—and that the *additional benefits* from diversifying among fewer funds on a selective and efficient basis are also similar in magnitude.[15] Sections B and C then show that the benefits of diversification *per se*—and the *additional* benefits of optimal selective diversification— are equally dramatic when the returns (and risks) in question are measured by "excess returns" (over T-bills) or in "real" terms after adjusting for inflation.

The third line in Section B of Table I.M(a) shows that if investors were wanting to allocate their funds among managers to incur the smallest possible risks on their sub-portfolio of futures investments, the standard deviation on their monthly returns could be reduced to 3.574%. *No* other allocation of funds among managers could produce a lower risk level. But the "risk-minimization" strategy would involve accepting expected monthly returns on managed futures investments of "only" 0.947%. (Even this is not much below the 1.076% expected return on a 60:40 mixed portfolio of stocks and bonds). But the second and third lines in Section B are both risk-minimizing ("efficient") portfolios to attain the indicated expected rates of return. Together, they tell us that *if* investors want to reduce their risks on funds put in the hands of futures-account managers from a standard deviation of 4.99% to 3.57% (the minimum attainable), they *must* at the same time be willing to accept a reduction in their expected returns from 2.72% to 0.95%. These two combination of expected return and (minimized) risk define two points on the "efficient frontier" for investments with future-account managers.

These are, of course, intermediate (as well as still higher) combinations of expected return and the minimum risk consistent with each return. The other four lines in Section B identify four such additional points on the efficient frontier for these investments. As an illustration, suppose an investor wanted and expected a return of 2.00%. Section A shows that he *could* get this expected return by putting all his futures account under the management of M7—but the standard deviation around this return would be a lofty 14.25% per month. The line for M7 in Section B shows that *if* he optimally allocated his accounts over a group of managers, he could have the *same expected return* with standard deviation of only 4.12%—less than *three-tenths* as large. Other entries in the lower part of Section B in all the tables tell the same story, varying only in degree of gain in risk reduction.

A good picture is said to be worth a thousand words. The expected returns along with the standard deviations of the returns provided by the 15 individual managers are plotted as heavy dots in Chart 1 on the next page. The heavy dots along the *solid line* show the risks involved in the *optimally allocated* portfolio of futures accounts with managers which would have *minimized the risk* of producing the *same return* as each manager produced. The horizontal distance from each heavy dot to the *solid* line on the left show the risk-reducing potential of efficient diversification among futures-account managers. With the single exception of M11 at the extreme upper right of the graph,[16] the risk-reductions (at *every* level of return) available from using the "efficiently selected and allocated portfolio-of-managers" approach are very impressive. The solid line itself defines the *efficient frontier* of the minimal sacrifices in expected returns which must be accepted if given reductions in risks are desired on the investment monies to be invested in futures-accounts managed by appropriate subsets of these 15 managers.

(We come to the *dashed* line further to the left in a moment). Every investor and every manager will have his own preference and his own feelings about how much more (minimized) risk he is willing to bear in order to get a little more expected (but uncertain) yield. The efficient frontier merely defines the best attainable set of choices he has among different combinations of the returns and risks he faces, so far as money to be invested with futures-account managers. *Where* he choose to sit along the best attainable frontier is purely a question of his own choice, given the trade-offs he faces.

These principles and these qualitative conclusions are *completely general*. They are illustrated again in Chart 2 which shows the efficient frontiers available to (presumably individual) investors choosing how to allocate some "futures money" among the eight publicly offered futures funds for which we have as much as 42 months data. Again, we see the large horizontal gains in risk reduction from using a selected portfolio of funds to gain a given expected return. Indeed, in one respect, Chart 2 (and the associated underlying data in the tables) is even more dramatic then Chart 1: four of the eight funds had a *lower* average return (and *very* much greater risks) than the minimum variance portfolio of funds![17]

III. The Effects on Risks and Returns of Adding Diversified Subportfolios of Investments with Futures-Account Managers (or Publicly Offered Futures Funds) to Portfolios of Common Stocks and/or Bonds.

To this point, we have considered only the improved tradeoffs between risks and returns which are available from the optimal diversification (over different managers or different publicly-offered futures funds) of the investment monies targeted for investment in the futures markets. But a glance at Chart 1 shows that the efficient frontier of futures investments with account-managers would provide the same average return as our very comprehensive portfolio of common stocks (or a 60:40 mixture of stocks and corporate bonds) with considerably less risk. Similarly, Chart 2 shows that even the minimum variance (and hence minimum return) portfolio of public future funds had a substantially higher expected return *and* somewhat less risk than either our diversified portfolio of stocks *or* our high-grade corporate bond portfolio.

These observations strongly imply that using at least moderate investments in such optimized sub-portfolios of futures investments *as a supplement* to the traditional common stock (or stock and bond) portfolios would produce *augmented portfolios* with much more favorable reward/risk tradeoffs than those provided by stock portfolios alone (or mixed stock and bond portfolios). In other words, the combined portfolios including futures investments will provide a higher return for *any* given acceptable level of risk—or equivalently, a lower level of risk associated with *any* given targeted expected rate of return—than can be provided by a portfolio of stocks alone (or by any mixed portfolio restricted to stocks and bonds). Risk-averse investors *always* prefer the portfolio combination which will give more return for the same risk, or the one which will reduce the risks involved in getting any given return—and this is accomplished by adding funds in diversified combinations of futures-account managers (or publicly traded funds) to the traditional stock and bond portfolios.

The improvements in the return/risk tradeoffs made available by combining properly selected combinations of futures investments with traditional stock and bond portfolios are dramatically shown by the (*dashed-line*) efficient frontiers shown in Charts 1 and 2. The efficient frontier of the *augmented portfolios* of futures and stocks and bonds lie substantially to the left (lower risk) and/or above (higher return for same risk) the attainable frontier with futures alone (the solid line), or those attainable from different combinations of stocks and bonds alone. (In order not to complicate the graph, the latter was not drawn in. The reader can find the x's denoting the STK, the BD, and the mixed 60:40 SB portfolio. The efficient frontier for various mixtures of stocks and bonds in a portfolio is essentially the curve (bending left) through these three points.[18]

The essential reason why the efficient frontier for the augmented portfolios of stocks and bonds and futures lies to the left (and above) that for portfolios of futures alone or portfolios of stocks and bonds alone is brought out by the elements of the *test* of whether a given candidate group of investments will improve the reward/risk performance of any existing portfolio, which was stated in the introduction, *the* candidate investment will always improve the performance of the existing portfolio whenever *its* (μ/σ) ratio is *larger than the product* of (a) the correlation of its returns with those of the existing portfolios with (b) the (μ/σ) ratio of the existing portfolio. The needed data are brought together in Table 4. The most striking aspect of this exhibit is the remarkably *low correlations* between an optimized portfolio of futures-account managers and portfolios of *either* stocks or bonds (or both). Although somewhat higher, the correlations of portfolios of public futures funds with stocks and bonds are still relatively low.

As a result of these low correlations, the portfolio of Ms passes the test as a desirable investment to be added to an existing bond portfolio and/or to a mixed stock and bond portfolio. Moreover, this is true whether the investment manager is concerned with rates of return *per se*, or with "excess" returns over bills, or with real returns after inflation. (To illustrate with the least favorable case, the M's (μ/σ) ratio of excess returns (on its minimum risk portfolio)[19] is only 0.009, but this is still nearly double the test statistics for stock portfolios of 0.059 × 0.082 = 0.0048—and it is nearly three times the test statistic of mixed S&B portfolios of 0.104 × 0.032 = 0.0033.) The results of the test are equally favorable to adding a selected portfolio of public futures funds to existing stock and/or bond portfolios, as may readily be confirmed.

Conclusions

The overall conclusions of our analysis were summarized—in ordinary language, but without filling in numbers—in the preview and summary section and need not be repeated here (except by reference). The numerical analysis supporting these conclusions have been supplied in the ensuing text, tables and charts. It should be apparent that certain very basic general principles and relationships have been at work throughout. But while all the general principles and all the *qualitative* conclusions we have stated have universal applicability and validity, the particular numerical results we have given defend on the particular data we have used. We have been conservative in restricting ourselves to futures funds or futures management companies which had at least 42 months of recent data to work with. But the period from July 1979 through its end of 1982 may not be a fully adequate basis for forming numerical assessments of the future levels of returns and risks. Responsible portfolio managers will want to (and should) use all their other information and judgments in forming their assessments of these matters for the relevant future periods with which they are concerned. But although the specific numbers may change, it is much less likely that the basic general interrelations will be greatly (or rapidly) altered—in particular the critical finding of the *low* intercorrelations between portfolios of futures accounts and stocks and bonds are very likely to persist strongly into the future. And, in that event, all the general conclusions of this study will prove to be solid and robust.

Table I.M(a)   Average Monthly Returns and Risks (Overall Performance of Fifteen Account Managers)

	Average Monthly Return (μ)	Standard Deviation of Return (σ)	Return-Risk Ratio (μ/σ)	Avg. Correl. with the 14 Other Mgrs.	Largest Loss in Any Month	Highest Return in Any Month	Months of Gain/Loss
A. Data for Individual Managers:							
M1	2.734%	11.693%	0.234	0.206	−15.61%	40.58%	26/16
M2	1.434%	12.350%	0.116	0.369	−20.62%	47.44%	21/21
M3	1.424%	5.945%	0.240	0.282	−13.14%	18.15%	20/22
M4	2.107%	15.751%	0.134	0.266	−34.33%	53.67%	20/22
M5	1.458%	9.178%	0.159	0.355	−16.79%	27.71%	24/18
M6	3.586%	9.905%	0.362	0.156	−13.06%	26.49%	24/18
M7	1.999%	14.247%	0.140	0.279	−22.01%	58.13%	23/19
M8	3.589%	14.213%	0.253	0.380	−12.61%	69.93%	24/18
M9	2.311%	11.647%	0.198	0.331	−18.10%	33.39%	22/20
M10	3.813%	13.293%	0.287	0.313	−20.52%	48.00%	26/16
M11	8.420%	21.709%	0.388	0.242	−30.26%	87.04%	27/15
M12	2.940%	8.881%	0.331	0.370	−15.71%	24.70%	27/15
M13	0.940%	16.820%	0.015	0.203	−37.96%	54.14%	19/23
M14	4.981%	15.097%	0.330	0.421	−28.67%	42.64%	27/15
M15	−0.206%	4.651%	−0.044	0.064	−9.52%	10.05%	19/23
Avg. of Columns:	2.723%	12.359%	0.210	0.285	−20.59%	42.80%	23.3/18.7

Table continues

Table I.M(a)   Continued

	Average Monthly Return (μ)	Standard Deviation of Return (σ)	Return-Risk Ratio (μ/σ)	Avg. Correl. with the 14 Other Mgrs.	Largest Loss in Any Month	Highest Return in Any Month	Months of Gain/ Loss
B. Data for Portfolios of Managers:							
a. Amts. M1–15	2.723%	7.315%	0.372		−9.77%	23.38%	25/17
. PTF (same μ):	2.723%	4.987%	0.546		−5.84%	13.28%	28/14
b. Risk PTF:	0.947%	3.574%	0.265		−6.09%	9.84%	22/20
. PTF for μ of M3:	1.424%	3.683%	0.387		−5.13%	9.78%	27/15
. PTF for μ of M7:	1.424%	4.116%	0.486		−4.64%	11.20%	27/15
. PTF for μ of M12:	2.940%	5.297%	0.555		−6.24%	13.90%	29/13
. PTF for μ of M14:	4.981%	9.214%	0.541		−9.53%	25.14%	29/13
C. Portfolios of Stocks, Bonds, or Bills:							
STK	1.351%	4.999%	0.270		−10.77%	12.57%	25/17
BD	0.665%	5.207%	0.128		− 8.90%	14.19%	22/29
S&B	1.076%	4.306%	0.249		− 7.71%	10.69%	25/17
BILL	0.935%	0.193%	4.845		− 0.57%	1.27%	42/0

Table I.M(b)   Average Monthly Excess[1] Returns and Risks (Overall Performance of Fifteen Account Managers)

	Average Monthly Excess Return (μ)	Standard Deviation of Excess Return (σ)	Excess Return-Risk Ratio (μ/σ)	Largest Loss in Any Month	Highest Return in Any Month	Months of Gain/Loss
A. Data for Individual Managers:						
M1	1.799%	11.661%	0.154	-16.65%	39.63%	26/16
M2	0.499%	12.304%	0.041	-21.69%	46.25%	20/22
M3	0.489%	6.007%	0.081	-14.06%	17.36%	18/24
M4	1.172%	15.752%	0.063	-35.03%	52.72%	17/25
M5	0.523%	9.178%	0.057	-17.71%	26.76%	22/20
M6	2.651%	9.862%	0.269	-14.06%	25.31%	23/19
M7	1.064%	14.218%	0.075	-22.58%	56.92%	22/20
M8	2.654%	14.194%	0.187	-13.25%	68.98%	26/16
M9	1.376%	11.696%	0.118	-19.00%	32.75%	26/16
M10	2.878%	13.259%	0.217	-21.14%	47.19%	26/16
M11	7.485%	21.688%	0.345	-30.88%	86.08%	26/16
M12	2.005%	8.851%	0.227	-16.68%	23.54%	25/17
M13	-0.688%	16.816%	-0.041	-39.04%	53.50%	16/26
M14	4.046%	15.106%	0.268	-29.73%	41.69%	27/15
M15	-1.141%	4.638%	-0.246	-10.26%	9.19%	17/25
Avg. of columns:	1.787%	12.348%	0.121	-21.45%	41.86%	21.8/20

See Note

Table continues

Table I.M(b) Continued

	Average Monthly Excess Return (μ)	Standard Deviation of Excess Return (σ)	Excess Return-Risk Ratio (μ/σ)	Largest Loss in Any Month	Highest Return in Any Month	Months of Gain/Loss
B. Data for Portfolios of Managers:						
Equal Amts. M1–15	1.787%	7.294%	0.245	−10.67%	22.43%	23/19
Eff. PTF (same m)	1.787%	4.954%	0.361	−6.53%	12.22%	28/14
Min. Risk PTF:	0.032%	3.570%	0.009	−6.72%	8.97%	19/23
Eff. PTF for μ of M3:	0.489%	3.671%	0.133	−6.04%	8.93%	23/19
Eff. PTF for μ of M7:	1.064%	4.090%	0.260	−5.76%	10.12%	27/15
Eff. PTF for μ of M12:	2.005%	5.271%	0.380	−6.97%	12.81%	27/15
Eff. PTF for μ of M14:	4.046%	9.181%	0.441	−10.18%	24.35%	29/13
C. Portfolios of Stocks and Bonds:						
STK	0.416%	5.099%	0.082	−11.96%	11.87%	23/19
BD	−0.270%	5.243%	−0.052	−9.83%	13.15%	18/23
S&B	9.141%	4.393%	0.032	−8.63%	9.99%	20/22

1 Monthly returns less bills, and standard deviations of the excess returns.

NOTE: The average correlations of the returns of each manager with those of the others are the same as those given in Table I.M(a).

Table I.M(c)   Average Monthly Real[1] Returns and Risks (Overall Performance of Fifteen Account Managers)

	Average Monthly Real Return (μ)	Standard Deviation of Real Return (σ)	Real Return-Risk Ratio (μ/σ)	Largest Real Loss in Any Month	Highest Real Return in Any Month	Months of Gain/ Loss
A. Data for Individual Managers:						
M1	2.016%	11.558%	0.174	−16.73%	39.15%	26/16
M2	0.716%	12.217%	0.059	−20.84%	46.01%	20/22
M3	0.606%	5.931%	0.119	−14.03%	17.06%	20/22
M4	1.389%	15.695%	0.088	−34.54%	52.23%	18/24
M5	0.740%	9.075%	0.082	−17.60%	26.28%	22/20
M6	2.900%	9.837%	0.295	−12.96%	25.06%	23/19
M7	1.284%	14.265%	0.090	−23.11%	57.27%	22/20
M8	2.872%	14.096%	0.204	−12.52%	68.50%	24/18
M9	1.593%	11.700%	0.136	−18.65%	33.31%	20/22
M10	3.095%	13.151%	0.235	−20.80%	46.96%	26/16
M11	7.702%	21.645%	0.356	−30.53%	85.98%	27/15
M12	2.222%	8 .880%	0.250	−16.06%	23.84%	25/17
M13	−0.471%	16.960%	−0.028	−38.87%	54.06%	17/25
M14	4.265%	14.960%	0.285	−28.88%	41.20%	26/16
M15	−0.924%	4.777%	−0.193	−10.58%	9.77%	17/25
Avg. of columns	2.005%	12.311%	0.143	−21.12%	41.78%	22.2/19.8

See Note

Table continues

Table I.M(c) Continued

	Average Monthly Excess Return (μ)	Standard Deviation of Excess Return (σ)	Excess Return-Risk Ratio (μ/σ)	Largest Loss in Any Month	Highest Return in Any Month	Months of Gain/Loss
B. Data for Portfolios of Managers:						
Equal Amts. of M1–15:	2.005%	7.223%	0.278	-10.32%	21.94%	24/18
Eff. PTF (same μ):	2.005%	4.851%	0.413	- 6.51%	12.21%	28/14
Min Risk PTF:	0.337%	3.578%	0.094	- 6.79%	9.54%	21/21
Eff. PTF for μ of M3	0.706%	3.669%	0.192	- 6.11%	9.56%	25/17
Eff. PTF for μ of M7	1.284%	4.050%	0.317	- 5.50%	10.09%	26/16
Eff. PTF for μ of M12	2.222%	5.157%	0.431	-6.92%	12.80%	28/14
Eff. PTF for μ of M14	4.265%	9.055%	0.471	- 9.79%	24.10%	29/13
C. Portfolios of Stocks, Bonds, or Bills:						
STK	0.633%	5.188%	0.124	-12.21%	12.36%	24/18
BD	-0.0534%	5.352%	-0.010	- 9.80%	13.07%	20/22
S&D	0.358%	4.458%	0.080	- 8.60%	10.48%	19/23
BILL	0.217%	0.409%	0.531	- 0.53%	1.11%	42/0

1 Monthly "raw" or nominal returns less the monthly percentage change in the CPI.

Table I.F(a)   Average Monthly Returns and Risks (Eight Publicly Offered Futures Funds)

	Average Monthly Return (μ)	Standard Deviation of Return (σ)	Return-Risk Ratio (μ/σ)	Avg. Correl. with the 14 Other Mgrs.	Largest Loss in Any Month	Highest Return in Any Month	Months of Gain/ Loss
A. Data for Individual Funds:							
F1	2.695%	9.632%	0.278	0.484	−14.205	25.20%	15/27
F2	1.360%	11.775%	0.115	0.478	−18.00%	36.40%	12/30
F3	0.907%	11.986%	0.076	0.484	−18.10%	37.30%	10/32
F4	1.998%	13.366%	0.149	−0.133	−44.10%	30.80%	15/27
F5	3.393%	6.539%	0.519	0.505	−11.00%	22.30%	18/24
F6	1.421%	7.275%	0.195	0.550	−13.60%	17.20%	15/27
F7	0.245%	8.182%	0.030	0.360	−15.10%	20.40%	18/24
F8	4.188%	7.892%	0.531	0.400	−11.20%	28.60%	15/27
Avg. of columns:	2.026%	9.581%	0.237	0.390	−18.16%	27.28%	14.0/28
B. Data for Portfolios of Funds:							
Equals Amts. F1–8:	2.026%	6.252%	0.324		−7.70%	21.40%	25/17
Eff. PTF (same μ):	2.026%	5.026%	0.403		−6.13%	19.74%	29/13
Min. Risk PTF:	2.009%	5.017%	0.401		−6.15%	19.72%	29/13
Eff. PTF for μ of F1:	2.695%	5.177%	0.521		−5.84%	20.55%	30/12
Eff. PTF for μ of F5:	3.393%	5.696%	0.596		−7.05%	21.04%	28/14

Table continues

Table I.F(a)   Continued

C. Performance of Stocks, Bonds or Bills:

	Average Monthly Return (μ)	Standard Deviation of Return (σ)	Return-Risk Ratio (μ/σ)	Avg. Correl. with the 14 Other Mgrs.	Largest Loss in Any Month	Highest Return in Any Month	Months of Gain/ Loss
STK	1.351%	4.999%	0.270		−10.77%	12.57%	25/17
BD	0.665%	5.207%	0.128		−8.90%	14.19%	22/20
S&B	1.076%	4.306%	0.250		−7.71%	10.69%	25/17
BILLS	0.935%	0.193%	4.845		−0.57%	1.27%	42/0

Table I.F(b) Average Monthly Excess[1] Returns and Risks (Eight Publicly Offered Futures Funds)

	Average Monthly Excess Return (μ)	Standard Deviation of Excess Return (σ)	Excess Return-Risk Ratio (μ/σ)	Largest Loss in Any Month	Highest Return in Any Month	Months of Gain/ Loss
A. Data for Individual Funds:						
F1	1.760%	9.610%	0.183	−15.06%	24.34%	15/27
F2	0.424%	11.817%	0.036	−19.17%	35.75%	10/32
F3	−0.028%	12.041%	−0.002	−19.27%	36.65%	9/33
F4	1.063%	13.434%	0.079	−45.31%	29.87%	10/32
F5	2.458%	6.502%	0.378	−11.90%	21.35%	15/27
F6	0.486%	7.252%	0.067	−14.25%	16.25%	14/28
F7	−0.690%	8.174%	−0.084	−16.03%	19.45%	12/30
F8	3.253%	7.857%	0.414	−12.06%	27.65%	15/27
Avg. of columns:	1.091%	9.586%	0.134	19.13%	26.41%	12.5/29.5
B. Data for Portfolios of Funds:						
Equal Amts. of F1–8*	1.091%	6.274%	0.174	−8.60%	20.45%	25/17
Min. Risk PTF:	1.097%	5.038%	0.218	−7.03%	18.79%	24/18
Eff. PTF for μ of F1:	1.760%	5.181%	0.340	−6.82%	19.59%	26/16
Eff. PTF for μ of F5:	2.458%	5.695%	0.432	−8.06%	20.12%	27/15

See Note

Table continues

Table I.F(b)   Continued

C. Performance of Stock and Bond Portfolios:

	Average Monthly Excess Return (μ)	Standard Deviation of Excess Return (σ)	Excess Return-Risk Ratio (μ/σ)	Largest Loss in Any Month	Highest Return in Any Month	Months of Gain/ Loss
STK	0.416%	5.099%	0.082	–11.96%	11.87%	23/19
BD	–0.270%	5.243%	–0.052	–9.83%	13.15%	18/24
S&B	0.141%	4.393%	0.032	–8.63%	9.99%	20/22

1 Monthly returns less bills, and standard deviation of the excess returns.

* Since the minimum risk PTF has a *larger* return than the "Equal Amts. of F1-8," there is no interest in the Efficient portfolio with the *same* (lower) return.

NOTE: The average correlations of the returns of each manager with those of the others are the same as those given in Table 1.F(a).

Table I.F(c)   Average Monthly Real[1] Returns and Risks (Overall Performance of Eight Publicly Offered Funds)

	Average Monthly Real Return (μ)	Standard Deviation of Monthly Real Return (σ)	Real Return-Risk Ratio (μ/σ)	Largest Real Loss in Any Month	Highest Real Return in Any Month	Months of Gain/Loss
A. Data for Individual Funds:						
F1	1.977%	9.639%	0.205	-14.49%	24.91%	15/27
F2	0.642%	11.771%	0.055	-18.81%	36.32%	11/31
F3	0.189%	11.987%	0.016	-18.91%	37.22%	10/32
F4	1.280%	13.356%	0.096	-44.96%	29.87%	13/29
F5	2.675%	6.442%	0.415	-11.55%	20.87%	15/27
F6	0.703%	7.250%	0.097	-13.43%	16.52%	14/28
F7	-0.473%	8.122%	-0.058	-16.03%	18.97%	12/30
F8	3.470%	7.769%	0.447	-11.49%	27.55%	15/27
Avg. of columns:	1.308%	9.542%	0.159	-18.71%	26.53%	13.1/28.9
B. Data for Portfolio of Funds:						
Equal Amts. F1|8:*	1.308%	6.205%	0.211	-8.25%	19.97%	24/18
Min. Risk PTF:	1.330%	4.930%	0.270	-6.45%	18.35%	26/16
Eff. PTF for μ of F1:	1.977%	5.060%	0.391	-6.37%	19.13%	27/15
Eff. PTF for μ of F5:	2.675%	5.587%	0.479	-7.60%	19.61%	27/15

See Note

Table continues

Table I.F(c) Continued

	Average Monthly Real Return (μ)	Standard Deviation of Monthly Real Return (σ)	Real Return-Risk Ratio (μ/σ)	Largest Real Loss in Any Month	Highest Real Return in Any Month	Months of Gain/Loss
C. Performance of Stocks, Bonds, or Bills:						
STK	0.633%	5.118%	0.124	-12.21%	12.36%	24/18
BD	-0.0534%	5.352%	-0.010	-9.80%	13.07%	20/22
S&B	0.358%	4.458%	0.080	-8.60%	10.48%	19/23
BILL	0.217%	0.409%	0.531	-0.53%	1.11%	42/0

1 Monthly "raw" or nominal returns less the monthly percentage change in the CPI.

*Since the minimum risk PIF has a *larger* return than the "Equal Amts. of F1–8," there is no interest in the Efficient portfolio with the *same* (lower) return.

NOTE: The average correlations of the returns of each manager with those of the others are the same as those given in Table 1.F(a).

Summary Table 1 Relative Risk and Loss Experience, 7/79 – 12/82
Managed Futures Accounts and Public Futures Funds and Stocks and Bonds*

A. Using Actual Monthly Returns

	Range	Average	Ratio Avg. to STK	Ratio Avg. to 60:40 S&B
Fifteen Managers				
s.d. of monthly returns	4.65% – 21.71%	12.36%	2.47	2.87
Max. loss any one month	9.52% – 37.96%	20.59%	1.91	2.67
Eight Public Funds				
s.d. of monthly returns	6.54% – 13.37%	9.58%	1.92	2.22
Max. loss any one month	11.00% – 44.10%	18.16%	1.69	2.36

Portfolios of Stocks or Bonds or a 60:40 Mixed Portfolio of S&B:

	Stocks	Bonds	Mixed Pft S&B
s.d. of monthly returns	5.00%	5.21%	4.31%
Max. loss any one month	10.77%	8.80%	7.71%

B. Using "Excess" Returns (Subtracting T-bill yields):

	Range	Average	Ratio Avg. to STK	Ratio Avg. to 60:40 S&B
Fifteen Managers				
s.d. of monthly returns	4.64% – 21.69%	12.35%	2.42	2.81
Max. loss any one month	10.26% – 39.04%	21.45%	1.79	2.49

Table continues

*Data from Tables I.M(a)–(c) and I.F(a) – (c) at end of paper.

	Range	Average	Ratio Avg. to STK	Ratio Avg. to 60:40 S&B
Eight Public Funds				
s.d. of monthly return	6.50% – 13.43%	9.59%	1.88	2.18
Max. loss any one month	11.90% – 45.31%	19.13%	1.60	2.22

Portfolios of Stocks or Bonds or a 60:40 Mixed Portfolio of S&B:

	Stocks	Bonds	Mixed Pft S&B
s.d. of monthly returns	5.10%	5.24%	4.39%
Max. loss any one month	11.96%	9.83%	8.63%

C. Using "Real" Returns (Subtracting CPI):

	Range	Average	Ratio Avg. to STK	Ratio Avg. to 60:40 S&B
Fifteen Managers				
s.d. of monthly returns	4.78% – 21.65%	12.31%	2.40	2.76
Max. loss any one month	10.58% – 38.87%	21.12%	1.73	2.46
Eight Public Funds				
s.d. of monthly returns	6.44% – 13.36%	9.54%	1.86	2.14
Max. loss any one month	11.49% – 44.96%	18.71%	1.53	2.18

Portfolios of Stocks or Bonds or a 60:40 Mixed Portfolio of S&B:

	Stocks	Bonds	Mixed Pft S&B
s.d. of monthly returns	5.12%	5.35%	4.46%
Max. loss any one month	12.21%	9.80%	8.60%

*Data from Tables 1.M(a) – (c) and 1.F(a) – (c) at end of chapter

Summary Table 2   Relative Reward/Risk Ratios*

Managed Futures Accounts and Public Futures Funds and Stocks and Bonds

A. Using Actual Monthly Returns:

	Range		Avg.	Ratio Avg. to STK	Ratio Avg. to Bonds	Ratio Avg. to S&B
Fifteen Managers	-0.04 – 0.39		0.210	0.78	1.64	0.84
Eight Futures Funds:	0.03 – 0.53		0.237	0.88	1.85	0.95
Diversified Stock Ptf.:		0.270				
Diversifed Bond Ptf.:		0.128				
60:40 Stock and Bonds		0.250				

B. Using "Excess" Returns (Over T-bills):

	Range		Avg.	Ratio Avg. to STK	Ratio Avg. to Bonds	Ratio Avg. to S&B
Fifteen Managers	-0.25 – 0.345		.121	1.48	**	3.78
Eight Futures Funds:	-0/08 – 0.378		.134	1.63	**	4.19
Diversified Stock Ptf.:		0.082				
Diversified Bond Ptf.:		-0.052				
60:40 Stock and Bonds		0.032				

C. Using "Real" Returns (After CPI Inflation):

	Range		Avg.	Ratio Avg. to STK	Ratio Avg. to Bonds	Ratio Avg. to S&B
Fifteen Managers	-0.193 – 0.476		.143	1.153	**	1.788
Eight Futures Funds:	-0.058 – 0.415		.159	1.282	**	1.988
Diversified Stock Ptf.:		0.124				
Diversifed Bond Ptf.:		-0.010				
60:40 Stock and Bonds		0.080				

*Data from Tables I.M(a) – (c) and I.F(a) – (c) at end of chapter.

**Not Applicable

Summary Table 3   Relative Reward/Risk Ratios (μ/σ) Available with Diversification over Futures Managers or Funds*

A. Using Actual Monthly Returns:

	This (μ/σ):	Ratio to Stock's (μ/σ):	Ratio to Bond's (μ/σ):	Ratio to (S&B)'s (μ/σ):
a. Fifteen Managers:				
***MEMO: Ave. of 15 (μ/σ) ratios:	0.210	0.78	1.64	0.84
Pft. of Equal Amts. in M1–M5:	0.372	1.38	2.91	1.49
Eff. Ptf. (with same expected return):	0.546	2.02	4.26	2.19
Min. Risk Ptf.:	0.265	0.98	2.07	1.06
b. Eight Future Funds:				
***MEMO: Ave. of 8 (μ/σ) ratios:	0.237	0.88	1.85	0.95
Pft. of Equal Amts. in F1–8:	0.324	1.20	2.53	1.30
Eff. Ptf. (with same expected return):	0.403	1.49	3.15	1.61
Min. Risk Ptf.:	0.401	1.49	3.13	1.60
B. Using "Excess" Returns (over T-bills):				
a. Fifteen Managers:				
***MEMO: Ave. of 15 (μ/σ) ratios:	0.121	1.48	**	3.78
Pft. of Equal Amts. in M1–15:	0.245	2.99	**	7.66
Eff. Ptf. (with same expected return):	0.361	4.40	**	11.28
Min. Risk Ptf.:	0.009	0.11	**	0.28
b. Eight Futures Fund:				
***MEMO: Ave. of 8 (μ/σ) ratios:	0.134	1.63	**	4.19
Pft. of Equal Amts. in F1–8:	0.174	2.12	**	5.44
Min. Risk Ptf.:	0.218	2.66	**	6.81
C. Using "Real" Returns (after CPI inflation):				
a. Fifteen Managers:				
***MEMO: Ave. of 15 (μ/σ) ratios:	0.143	1.15	**	1.79
Pft. of Equal Amts. in M1–15:	0.278	2.24	**	3.48
Eff. Ptf. (with same expected return):	0.413	3.33	**	5.16
Min. Risk Ptf.:	0.094	0.76	**	1.18
b. Eight Futures Bonds:				
***MEMO: Ave. of 8 (μ/σ) ratios:	0.159	1.28	**	1.99
Pft. of Equal Amts. in F1–8:	0.211	1.70	**	2.64
Min. Risk Ptf.:	0.270	2.18	**	3.38

*Data from Tables I.M(a)–(c) and I.F(a)–(c) at end of chapter.
**Not applicable
***Data from Summary Table 2

Table 4 Reward/Risk Rations (μ/σ) and Intercorrelations
Five Alternate Sub-portfolios of Managed Futures, Stocks and Bonds

A. Using Actual Monthly Returns:

	(μ/σ)	M	F	Stk.	Bds.	S&B
				Intercorrelations		
Min. Risk Ptf. of Ms:	0.265	1.000				
Min. Risk Ptf. of Fs	0.401	0.637	1.000			
All NYSE & AMEX Stocks:	0.270	-0.065	0.234	1.000		
Salomon Hi-grade Corporates:	0.128	0.148	0.151	0.417	1.000	
60:40 Mixture, Stk & Bds:	0.249	0.116	-0.024	0.898	0.774	1.000

B. Using "Excess Returns" (Over T-Bills):

Min. Risk Ptf. of Ms:	0.009	1.000				
Min. Risk Ptf. of Fs:	0.218	0.652	1.000			
All NYSE & AMEX Stocks:	0.082	0.059	0.250	1.000		
Salomon Hi-grade Corporates:	-0.052	0.130	-0.017	0.408	1.000	
60:40 Mixture, Stk & Bds:	0.032	0.104	0.167	0.899	0.767	1.000

C. Using "Real Returns" (After CPI Inflation):

Min. Risk Ptf. of Ms:	0.094	1.000				
Min. Risk Ptf. of Fs:	0.270	0.770	1.000			
All NYSE & AMEX Stocks:	0.124	0.012	0.233	1.000		
Salomon Hi-grade Corporates:	-0.010	-0.134	-0.017	0.446	1.000	
60:40 Mixture, Stk & Bds:	0.080	-0.056	0.153	0.903	0.787	1.000

Chart 4-1   Overall Performance—Fifteen Futures-Account Managers and Stocks, Bonds and Bills (7/79 – 12/82) (Percent per Month)

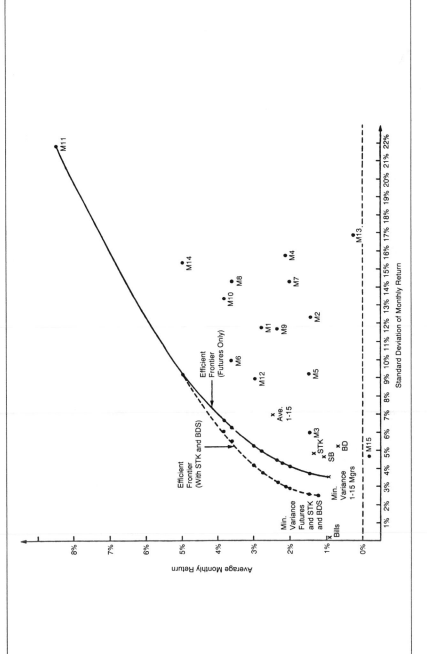

Chart 4-2   Overall Performance—Eight Publicly Offered Future Funds (and Stocks, Bonds and Bills) (7/79 – 12/82) (Percent per Month)

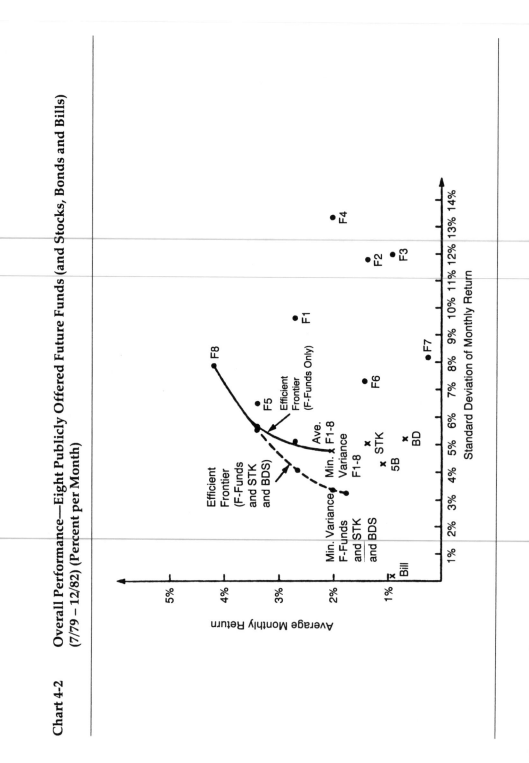

Endnotes

1. Except, of course, managers of specialized mutual funds.

2. Either of these seemingly alternative possibilities clearly implies the other. If the broader portfolio satisfies one of the conditions, it necessarily satisfies the other along the relevant upper portion of the efficient frontier when portfolio returns are plotted on the vertical axis and portfolio risks horizontally.

3. Harry M. Markowitz, "Portfolio Selection," *Journal of Finance*, March 1952, pp. 77–91, and Portfolio Selection: Efficient Diversification of Investments (New York: John Wiley & Sons, 1959).

4. Correspondingly, it provides him a rigorous basis for determining how much different his best allocation would be if, instead, he were to believe (and act upon) a different set of assessments.

5. This statement is rigorously true whenever the investment manager is willing to rely on the statistical relationships shown by past data in forming his assessments of the relevant future relationships between the risks and returns over the set of securities in question. As a theoretical proposition, it is equally true with respect to whatever set of modified or adjusted set of assessments the manager wishes to use on the basis of his own best judgment, relying on his experience and any other information he may have which indicates that the future relationships between securities will differ in some particular ways from the historical patterns. It is recognized, however, the interrelationships among the security risks and returns underlying this "regression test" are quite complex and it is difficult to apply this test when managers want to make their decisions on the basis of judgmental assessments which differ very much from historical patterns. In the latter case, the alternative (but mathematically equivalent) formulation given in the immediately following text will probably be more intuitively appealing and reliable.

6. For readers who like symbols, the condition stated in the text for a favorable shift in the efficient frontier due to the addition of some at least modest investment in the candidate security (or securities) is simply

$$\theta_i > \rho_{ip}\, \theta_p$$

where $\theta_i = \bar{r}_i/\sigma_i$ and $\theta_p = \bar{r}_p/\sigma_p$

and ρ_{ip} is the simple correlation between $\tilde{r}_i$ and $\tilde{r}_p$, while $\bar{r}_i$ and $\bar{r}_p$ are the expected rates of return on the candidate(s) for the portfolio and on the existing portfolio, respectively, and σ_i and σ_p are their corresponding standard deviations of return.

Interested readers can consult Appendix A for a rigorous proof of the equivalence of this test and the presumably well-known "positive intercept" test. (This appendix is not included, but is available on request to the author.)

7.   The fractions having higher return/risk ratios is also considerably larger in each case when the comparison is made with the ratios provided by a portfolio of corporate bonds.

Excess returns are computed as the actual return less the return on T-bills, and real returns are measured by actual returns less the inflation rate shown by the CPI in the given month.

8.   Let E be the beginning equity and P the net monthly profit defined by the CFTC. The monthly rate of return on the CFTC basis is R = P/E. Let A be the net additions and withdrawals during the month, and R* be the adjusted monthly rate of return allowing for additions and withdrawals. We assume (a) the A is spread evenly over the 22 trading days of the month, and (b) that simple interest is an adequate approximation within the month—i.e., that the funds added on the X'th day will earn at a rate of R*/22 per day for the (22-X) days it was in the account. We then have:

$$P = R* \left[E + \frac{A}{22} \left(\frac{21}{22} + \frac{20}{22} + \cdots + \frac{1}{22} \right) \right]$$

$$= R* \left[E + \frac{A}{22} \left(\frac{1}{22} \right) \left(\frac{22 * 21}{2} \right) \right]$$

$$= R* E \left[1 + \frac{A}{E} \left(\frac{21}{44} \right) \right]$$

$$R* = \frac{P}{E(1 + .477\, A/E)}$$

which is the formula used.

9.   This adjustment was the best we could make in the absence of more detailed information on the actual amount added or withdrawn each day of each month for each of the 14 managers.

10. There was not enough data to pursue this line of analysis in the present study.

11. The average correlation of the returns of any one manager with the returns of each of the fourteen others ranged from a low of .064 to a high of .421.

12. The latter are given in the second column of the A section of the total just above.

13. See the third column at the top of Table I.M(a).

14. Three of the managers (M3, M6, M15) would each be handling over 20% of the funds, M1 would have 13.5%, M11 8% with small amounts (3.6% and 2.3%) to M12 and M4.
   We might observe that the only intercorrelations which count in these allocations are those with the other funds in the efficient portfolio—the intercorrelations, risks and returns of the others rule them out of the final optimal portfolio.

15. They also come about for exactly the same reasons. Section A of Table I.F(a) shows that three of the eight public funds have a higher (μ/σ) ratio than the average (0.237), and two are higher than that of the "equal amounts" portfolio (0.324). The average inter-fund correlation is 0.391 (higher than that for managers but still moderate). The optimal portfolio for the second line of section B uses 5 of the 8 funds—23.8% in F4, 28.6% in F5, 12.5% in F6, 27.1% in F7 but only 8.0% in F8. The allocation to F8 is surprisingly low in spite of its high and (μ/σ) ratio because of intercorrelations, and the surprisingly high allocation to F4 arises from its negative average intercorrelation with the returns on the other funds.

16. Since all other managers show lower expected returns, any investor wanting as high an expected monthly return as the 8.42% provided by M11 must accept the 21.71% monthly standard deviation involved. But it should be noted that because of the low correlations of the M11 return with those of other managers (knowing the full set of returns on the other managers would explain only 5.9% of the variance of the M11 return), combined with its high average returns, M11 forms an important part of the optimal portfolios of managers all along the efficient frontier.

17. F4 vividly illustrates the importance of correlations in determining optional portfolios. The average return on F4 was slightly less than that on the minimum variance portfolio of funds, and its standard deviation

(13.37%) was 2.7 times as large as that on the minimum variance portfolio of funds. But since its average correlation with the seven other funds was negative (–0.133), it represents 23.8% of that minimal variance portfolio of funds.

18. In fact the minimum variance (most leftward) point on this curve would a 46–54% mixture using the stock-bond performance of the 42 months 7/79 through 12/82.

19. Note that the M's (μ/σ) ratio is larger on all other efficient portfolios.

Chapter Five

Management Summary

Title: "John Lintner and the Theory of Portfolio Management"

Presentation: Sixth Annual Managed Account Reports Conference, February, 1985. (Revised February, 1987)

Author: Almer H. Orr, III, President, A. O. Management Corporation

Data: Monthly prices and returns for 7 years, 1980-1986, for the Managed Account Reports (MAR) Futures Pool index, S&P 500, and Salomon Brothers High-Grade Corporate Bond Index.

Methodology: The MAR Futures Pool Index was analyzed in comparison to returns from the S&P 500 and Salomon Bond Index. Frequency distributions for each were discussed as was return-risk performances. Risk was measured by standard deviation in returns.

    Portfolios of stocks, bonds, and managed futures were constructed and performance compared on a return-risk basis.

    Correlation between stocks, bonds and managed futures were calculated. Relative performance of stocks, bonds and managed futures were examined with respect to performance during times of inflation.

Results: It was found that during the time period of the study the Futures Pool Index, an index of performance of public commodity pools, had significantly higher average monthly returns than stocks and bonds, along with a corresponding higher standard deviation. The return-risk ratio was higher than stocks, but lower than bonds.

    Diversifying stock and bond portfolios with managed futures had the effect of reducing risk for a given return, or increasing return at a given level of risk. A mix of 20% managed futures in stock, bond and stock-bond portfolios was identified as effective for diversification.

    Managed futures were found to have low or negative correlation with stocks and bonds.

continued

Comments: Orr's study confirmed some of Lintner's earlier findings using approximately twice as much data. Whereas Lintner used individual trading advisors and public commodity funds, Orr used an index of public commodity pools. Both arrived at essentially the same conclusions: because of relatively high returns and low or negative correlation with stocks and bonds, managed futures were an attractive means of portfolio diversification.

Orr concluded with an important comment on another aspect of managed futures which sets it apart from more traditional methods of diversification such as real estate—that of liquidity. "I am familiar with no easily liquidated investment other than managed futures which, while generating positive rewards over time, lowers the volatility of more traditional investments to any significant degree."

John Lintner and the Theory of Portfolio Management

Almer H. Orr, III

Futures money management is a field that was in its infancy seven years ago and practically did not exist 12 years ago. Today (1986) it is estimated that approximately $3 billion is under management, and the amount continues to grow. The most obvious reason is that professional commodity futures trading advisors have earned significant profits for their clients, especially in the inflationary early 1980s. During this period, the historical idea that stocks were the ideal hedge against inflation was found to be entirely wanting, and the professionally managed commodity futures account emerged to fill the void. Thus, another reason for investing in managed futures arose: a managed futures account proved to be one of the most reliable and most liquid ways to protect one's portfolio against the ravages of inflation.

As performance records grew longer and longer, people also discovered that managed futures performed independently of stocks and bonds to such an obvious degree that a new use was found: improving the reward/risk tradeoff in diversified investment portfolios. In a paper presented by the late Dr. John Lintner of Harvard University at the annual conference of the Financial Analysts Federation, May 16, 1983, the conclusions reached were startling in their power, particularly from so preeminent an authority as Dr. Lintner. His study, entitled "The Potential Role of Managed Commodity

Futures Accounts in Portfolios of Stock and Bonds," concluded that including efficiently selected portfolios of managed futures accounts with stock and bond portfolios "showed substantially less risk at every possible level of expected return than portfolios of stocks (or stocks and bonds) alone." Further, the study found that the correlations between the returns on futures portfolios and stock and bond portfolios were exceedingly low, at times negative, leading Dr. Lintner to conclude that "the improvements from holding efficiently selected portfolios of managed accounts or funds are so large...that the return/risk tradeoffs provided by augmented portfolios...clearly dominate the tradeoffs available from portfolios of stocks alone. Moreover, they do so by very considerable margins."

Dr. Lintner was one of the original contributors to the development of modern portfolio theory in the early 1950s and is well recognized by the investment community. Unfortunately, he was killed in an automobile accident shortly after he delivered his paper and was unable to revise and expand his work. His data was limited to the period from mid-1979 through the end of 1982, a short period for statistical analysis, as he acknowledged.

Dr. Lintner's paper was divided into three main parts, the first part being an examination of the tradeoffs between return and risk, the second, a description of ways of combining the advisors in order to lower risk, and the third, the most important, an analysis of the effects of adding managed futures to stock and bond portfolios. We will try to update and communicate the basics of Dr. Lintner's message by illustrating his findings with charts and graphs from data available to us. Although we believe Dr. Lintner's second section covering the combining of trading advisors is important, we have chosen to bypass it leaving others to address this subject. In the final section, we have undertaken to illustrate why managed futures blend so well with other types of investments. Some of the data presented and the examples used represent a departure from Dr. Lintner's work and serve to illuminate his conclusions from a slightly different point of view.

We have drawn comparisons of profit and volatility among stocks, bonds and managed futures for the seven-year period from January 1980 through December 1986. To represent stocks we chose the month-end closing price of the S&P 500 Index with dividends reinvested monthly. To represent bonds we chose the monthly close of the Salomon Brothers High-Grade Corporate Bond Index which includes interest earned. And to represent managed futures we selected the Managed Accounts Reports Futures Pools Index (FPI). In our opinion the severe competitive pressures being exerted on the futures industry to lower commission and advisors' fees over the past two years have reduced the costs of new funds significantly. We believe that this reduction is permanent (particularly for institutional and large investors, those for whom Dr. Lintner's study is of the greatest interest). The performance of the MAR Futures Pools Index has been higher than the MAR Futures Funds Index over time mostly because the Funds Index has been primarily composed of public funds sold when rates and fees were higher. As more new funds come to market with lower fees and older funds suffer redemptions, the performance of the two indexes should converge. It is our feeling that the S&P 500, the Salomon Brothers High-Grade Corporate Bond Index and the MAR Futurues Pools Index provide good representations of stocks, bonds and managed futures.

Examining Return and Risk

Dr. Lintner chose to view risk as the likelihood that a given expected return on a portfolio would not be achieved. He approached his study by exploring ways of minimizing this possibility. We in the commodity money management industry tend to view risk more as the "risk of losing one's capital," or, the possibility that one might lose more of his capital than he planned (extreme examples are the risk of ruin and the risk of catastrophic loss).

To measure risk, Dr. Lintner used the standard deviation of the monthly returns. The standard deviation is a measure of the variability of a group of numbers. The rationale behind its use is that the more variable the monthly returns of a particular investment are, the greater the possibility of future unacceptable loss. The less variable the monthly returns, on the other hand, the more likely the expected return would be achieved and the greater the likelihood of riding out an adverse period in order to be able to participate in the next profitable period. Using the standard deviation of the monthly returns provides us with a means of comparing different investments or investment strategies and, through optimization techniques, can allow us to structure investment portfolios with improved return/risk properties. An important aspect of using the standard deviation is that extreme monthly returns (both larger gains and losses) are much more heavily weighted than smaller returns. To attempt to minimize the standard deviation of monthly returns is to try to bring all the returns as close as possible to the average. In this process the more extreme returns are reduced as much as possible, a much desired aim from an investor's point of view.

Figure 5-1, three histograms, shows the number of monthly occurrences of each return for the S&P, the Bond Index and the FPI over the seven-year period of our study. In each figure the solid vertical lines rise from the point of the average return and the dashed vertical lines from –1 and +1 standard

Figure 5-1   Frequency Distributions of Monthly Returns for Stocks, Bonds and Managaed Commodities

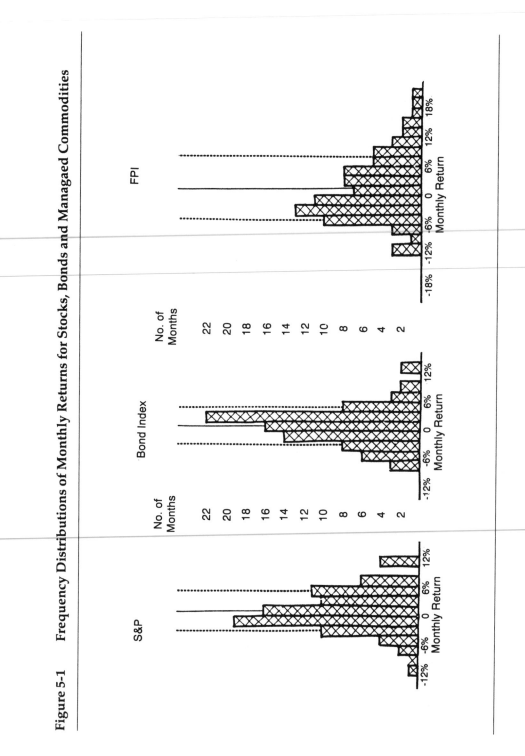

Figure 5-2   Return vs. Risk of Stocks, Bonds and FPI
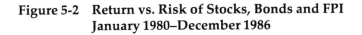
January 1980–December 1986

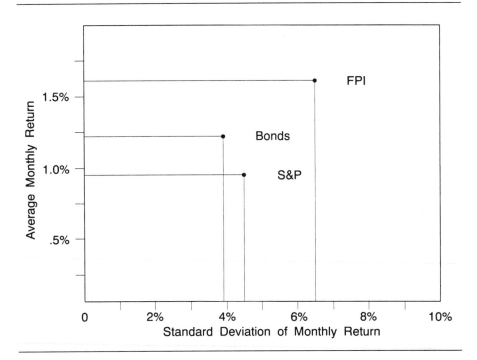

deviations. Clearly the monthly returns for the FPI are more spread out, as are the lines representing –1 and +1 deviations.

Let us go one step further. Figure 5-2 is a chart commonly used to illustrate the tradeoff between reward and risk. The vertical scale is the average monthly return; the horizontal scale, the standard deviation of the monthly returns. The three points were generated from the data used to make up the previous histogram. The most desirable place to have a point is in the upper left where the monthly return is the highest and the standard deviation of the returns is the lowest. More points will be added to Figure 5-2 later to examine the benefits to be gained by generating portfolios of various combinations of stocks, bonds and managed futures.

One investment tool commonly used as a measure of reward and risk is the Sharpe ratio. Essentially, it is the return divided by the standard deviation of the returns—the vertical value of Figure 5-2 divided by the horizontal value for each data point. In actual use it is the annualized return divided by the standard deviation of the monthly returns, annualized. As originally

designed, the Sharpe ratio subtracted the rate of return of a risk-free investment (Treasury bills) to allow comparisons across varying types of investments, over different time periods and under different economic climates.
In our industry we generally ignore the riskless rate of return because we
are usually comparing returns of only managed futures over like time
periods. A number of problems exist with using the Sharpe ratio as the only
measure of reward/risk (for example, it is of little value when examining
loss periods). For A. O. Management's internal research we evaluate potential trading systems by seperating the ratio's numerator (reward) from the
denominator (risk) and examining them separately. Having in mind what
level of return we wish to maintain over a given period, we then explore
ways to lower the standard deviation of the monthly returns, thus smooth-
ing our performance.

Another approach to measuring risk is to examine the way money is lost.
Our view is that it is less important how clients earn profits (under the
assumption that they will profit over time); it is more important how they
give back their profits. Since it is inevitable that some profits will be returned
from time to time, gradual erosion is preferable to a rapid decline. Again,
for our internal research, we have developed a measure which considers
only the loss periods when performing a calculation similar to that of the
Sharpe ratio. In addition, a string of successive loss periods uninterrupted
by a profit period is treated as a single loss period. These two variations on
the Sharpe ratio are suggested for you who care to do in-depth evaluations
of trading advisors' performance records. In the case of managed futures,
the rewards can be so great that they more than compensate for the increased
risk. Dr. Lintner, in fact, concluded that "...while investments in managed
futures accounts and publicly offered futures funds generally involve very
high risks, the evidence is equally strong that many of the managers and
funds have provided very high average returns." His comparison of managed futures with stocks and bonds led him to conclude that from a re-
ward/risk point of view, managed futures compare favorably.

The Role of Managed Futures in Stock and Bond Portfolios

In the final section of his paper Dr. Lintner dealt with combining different
types of investments. He explored the return/risk characteristics of stock
and bond portfolios that included managed futures and concluded:

"Indeed, the improvements from holding efficiently selected portfolios of managed accounts or funds are so large—*and* the corre-

lations between the returns of the futures portfolios and those on the stock and bond portfolios are so surprisingly low (sometimes even negative)—that the return/risk tradeoffs provided by *augmented portfolios*, consisting partly of funds invested with appropriate groups of futures managers (or funds) combined with funds invested in portfolios of stocks alone (or in mixed portfolios of stocks and bonds), clearly dominate the tradeoffs available from portfolios of stocks (or from portfolios of stocks and bonds). Moreover, they do so by very considerable margins.

The combined portfolios of stocks (or stocks and bonds)...show substantially less risk at every possible level of expected return than portfolios of stocks (or stocks and bonds alone). This is the essence of the "potential role" of managed futures accounts (or funds) as a supplement to stock and bond portfolios suggested in the title of this paper."

Dr. Lintner's message is clear: Managed futures accounts are different from other investments, and they have a definite place in a properly diversified portfolio.

Figure 5-3 depicts the monthly performance of three portfolios—the first comprised entirely of the Managed Accounts Reports Futures Pools Index (solid line), the second comprised of the S&P 500 (dotted line), and the third comprised of the Salomon Brothers High-Grade Corporate Bond Index (dashed line). No attempt has been made to adjust the data for inflation; although important, this subject is outside the scope of this paper.

For those acquainted with the futures money management industry, the graph does not reveal any surprises. Over time managed futures have earned returns comparable to stocks and bonds on both reward and reward/risk bases. During the earlier years, when inflation was the highest, the low correlation between the FPI and the other two indexes is apparent. This is one of Dr. Lintner's main points and will become even more obvious as we go on.

Figures 5-4A – 5-4C show the effects of combining various stock and bond portfolios with managed futures. Figure 5-4A is a combination of 80% S&P 500 and 20% futures, Figure 5-4B combines 80% bonds and 20% futures, and Figure 5-4C mixes 40% S&P 500, 40% bonds and 20% futures. Although we chose to add only 20% futures, a prudent number as we will see later, the dampening effect on volatility, particularly in the earlier years, is clear. Also noteworthy is the effect that managed futures had on the bond portfolio, especially through June 1982, the end of the ten-year bear market for bonds. As many investors learned the hard way, bonds provided no hedge against

Figure 5-3   Monthly Values of Stock, Bond and Futures Portfolios

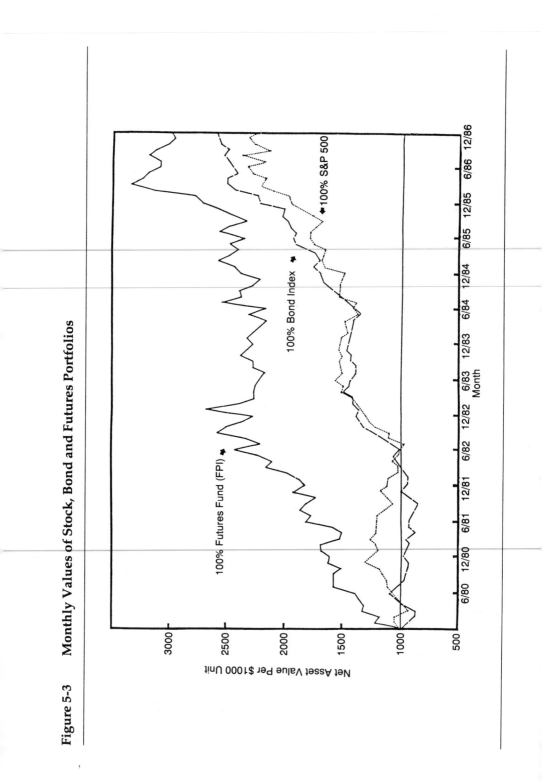

**Figure 5-4   Monthly Values of Stocks, Bond and Mixed
Portfolios With and Without Futures**

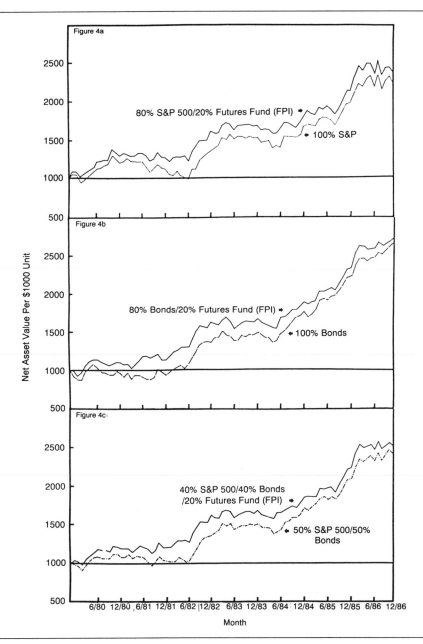

**Figure 5-5   Return vs. Risk of Stocks, Bonds, FPI and Combined
Portfolios (January 1980 – December 1986)**

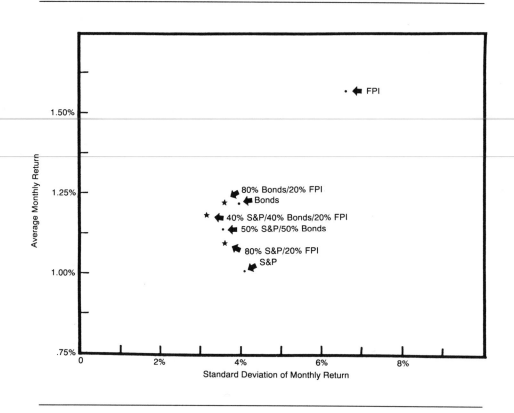

inflation. The addition of stocks, the supposed "inflation-hedge" investment, improved the portfolio's performance but did little to lower the
portfolio's volatility, particularly in the highly inflationary era prior to 1983.
Had there been more data on the performance of commodity money managers prior to 1980, the case for managed futures as the best hedge against
inflation would be even clearer.

We can underscore Dr. Lintner's main point here by noting that in each
case the inclusion of managed futures both improved the bottom-line profit
and lowered volatility. Let us examine in greater detail the role of managed
futures in the overall investment picture. Figure 5-5 is simply a blown up
version of Figure 5-2 with the returns and the standard deviations plotted

for the combined portfolios shown in Figures 5-4A-C. The points represent-ing the combined portfolios show a clear improvement, particularly in risk.

One can sense the source of excitement communicated so clearly in Dr. Lintner's words. For someone who had been searching for 30 years for ways to lower the risk in investment portfolios (raise reward/risk) and had become accustomed to miniscule improvements, to suddenly find a way to make a major step at once must have been powerful. One wonders if Dr. Lintner had yet digested the full magnitude of his discovery before he died.

What is it that causes the portfolios augumented with no more than 20% managed futures to perform so much better than portfolios without man-aged futures? An examination of Table 5-1 reveals that over the entire period studied, while the price changes of stocks and bonds have a measured degree of positive correlation, neither bonds nor stocks appear to have any correlation with managed futures. As will be commented on further in connection with Tables 5-1B and 5-1C, the correlations for the first half of our study period, the 3-1/2-year period January 1980–June 1983, a time of significantly higher inflation, reveal a negative relationship between the S&P and the FPI.

Being aware that the generally rising trend of the stocks, bonds and managed futures over the period studied was causing our correlations to be positive, we decided to study just the movements of each around its trendl-ine. A regression line over the entire period was calculated for each and was used to represent its trend. Next, the percentage difference between each monthly index value and its corresponding regression line value was calcu-lated and then plotted in Figures 5-6A and 5-6B. In effect, we took a time series, put a trendline through it, and then tilted it down until it was horizontal.

In the early, high-inflation years, the results are startling. For most of that period, managed futures and stocks and bonds were on the opposite sides of their trendlines. Even more startling is the closeness of the mid-1981 point at which each crossed its trendline and how each remained on the opposite side of its respective line after that. After 1983, when inflation had settled down to a more reasonable level, stocks, bonds and futures generally began to move in concert. The different relationships between futures and stocks and bonds in the first and the second half of our study period illustrate two points: (1) During the second time period when raw material commodity futures were generally flat, commodity trading advisors shifted their em-phasis to futures where they could earn profits—interest rates, currencies and stock indices—those closely related to the stock and bond markets, and (2) during the earlier period when raw material inflation was at its height, Dr. Lintner's observed negative correlation between futures and stocks and

Table 5-1   Correlations among Stocks, Bonds and Commodity Funds (FPI)

a. January 1980–December 1986

	S & P	Bonds
Bonds	.391	
FPI	.003	−.003

b. January 1980–June 1983

	S & P	Bonds
Bonds	.355	
FPI	−.036	−.125

c. July 1983–December 1986

	S & P	Bonds
Bonds	.485	
FPI	.143	.223

Figure 5-6   Deviation From Trendline of Stocks vs. FPI and Bonds vs. FPI

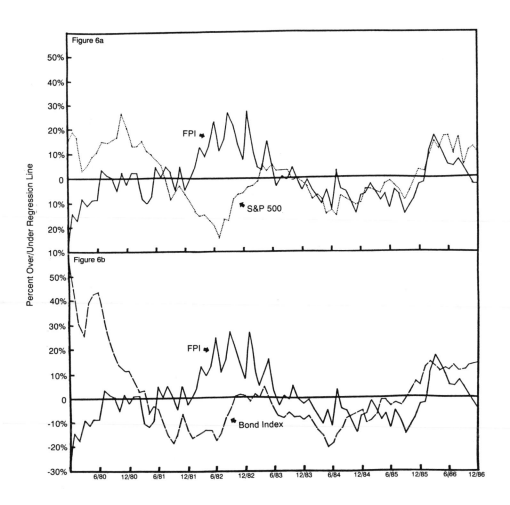

bonds was quite clear. With the addition of 1985's and 1986's results, evidence now indicates that, not only do managed futures protect against high inflation (and deflation), they also earn profits when inflation is a relatively minor problem. Figure 5-7, similar to Figures 5-6A and 5-6B reveals how closely stocks and bonds tracked each other over the entire seven-year period.

Table 5-2 shows the percentage of months that the three pairs of investments were on opposite sides of their trendlines. Similar to Table 5-1, the calculations were made for the entire seven-year period and for the 3-1/2-year period January 1980–June 1983, and 3-1/2-year period July 1983–December 1986.

Tables 5-2, 5-2A and 5-2B clearly reveal what Figures 5-6A and 5-6B show visually—during the early, high inflationary years, when stocks and bonds were on one side of their trendlines, managed futures were on the other. Particularly in high inflation periods, managed futures take over when stocks and bonds are flat or down. Figure 5-8 plots the Sharpe ratios on the vertical axis for various portfolios combining stocks, bonds and managed futures on the horizontal axis. The high points marked by the small vertical ticks reveal the portfolio combinations which generate the optimal reward/risk levels over the 1980–1986 time period.

Figure 5-8 reveals that the optimum mix of managed futures in stock, bond, and stock and bond portfolios is approximately 20%.

I am familiar with no easily liquidated investment other than managed futures which, while generating positive rewards over time, lowers the volatility of more traditional investments to any significant degree. This is the reason portfolios augumented by just 20% of managed futures show such an improvement from a reward/risk standpoint over those lacking futures. To restate what Dr. Lintner phrased so well, "Indeed, the improvements from holding efficiently selected portfolios of managed accounts or funds are so large...that the return/risk tradeoffs provided by augmented portfolios...clearly dominate the tradeoffs available from portfolios of stocks alone. Moreover, they do so by very considerable margins."

Figure 5-7   Deviation from Trendline of Stocks and Bonds

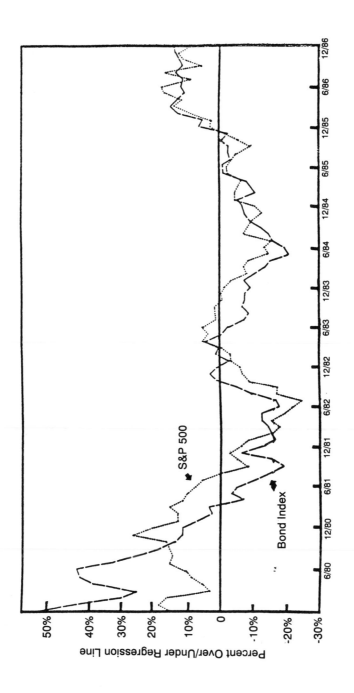

Table 5-2   Percentage of Months with Returns on Opposite Sides of Trendlines

a. January 1980–December 1986

	S & P	Bonds
Bonds	16%	
FPI	43%	42%

b. January 1980–June 1983

	S & P	Bonds
Bonds	23%	
FPI	70%	63%

c. July 1983–December 1986

	S & P	Bonds
Bonds	10%	
FPI	17%	21%

**Figure 5-8   Sharpe Ratio of Stocks and Bond Portfolios Combined With
Varying Percentages of Managed Futures**

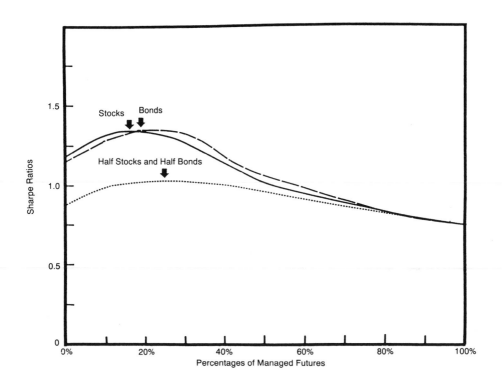

Chapter Six

Management Summary

Title: "Public Futures Funds"

Publication: *The Journal of Futures Markets*, 1985. Vol. 5, No. 2

Authors: Scott H. Irwin, doctoral student, Purdue University
B. Wade Brorsen, Assistant Professor, Purdue University

Data: Quarterly returns for the 40 quarter period 1975.1–1984.1 for public futures funds, stocks, bonds, Treasury bills, and the Consumer Price Index. Fund fees and costs were also part of the data base.

Methodology: The purpose of this study was to present aggregated information on returns, costs, and concentrations of public futures funds, as well as to analyze the role of these funds in financial asset portfolios.

Returns were compared on an annual basis for funds, stocks and bonds. Futures funds were analyzed in combination with stock and bond portfolios.

Results: Futures funds showed approximately the same level of return as stocks (6%–8% per year average) and were superior to bonds (–.4% per year) and Treasury bills (1.1% per year). Variability in returns was higher than for stocks and bonds (standard deviation for futures funds was 21.2% versus 14.9% for stocks and 15.6% for bonds). Correlation with stocks was –.633, and for bonds –.529. Correlation with the Consumer Price Index was +.606.

Adding public futures funds to financial asset portfolios (bills, bonds and stocks) was shown to reduce risk. As the rate of inflation increased, futures funds' returns tended to rise while returns on bills, bonds, and stocks tended to fall, and vice versa.

Public Futures Funds*

Scott H. Irwin
B. Wade Brorsen

Futures funds pool investor's money to speculate in futures markets. Due to favorable tax treatment, futures funds are usually organized as limited partnerships within the United States.[1] Typically, an affiliate or subsidiary of a brokerage company acts as general partner. If limited partnership interests are sold in a public offering, the Securities and Exchange Commission (SEC) classifies a futures fund as public and requires its registration. Private futures funds must meet a series of tests to be exempted from SEC registration. As a rule-of-thumb, private funds have 35 or fewer investors.

The first public futures fund began trading in the fall of 1948 and was active until the mid-1960s (Donchian, 1984). Several other public funds were started in the early 1970s, but they were unsuccessful and ceased trading within one or two years (Hultgren, 1975). The first multimillion dollar public futures fund began trading in January 1975. Thereafter, the number of active public funds increased swiftly to a peak of 77 at the end of the first quarter of 1984 (Figure 6-1). During the fastest period of growth, 1980 through 1982, 50 public funds were established.

Issues of interest to investors, regulators, and futures market researchers have been raised by the rapid expansion of public futures funds. Aggregate information on returns, costs, balance sheet accounts, and concentration of public futures funds have been unavailable. In addition, the role of public funds in portfolios of financial assets is uncertain. The purpose of this article

*The Journal of Futures Markets, Vol. 5, No. 2, 149–171 (1985)

Figure 6-1   Active Public Futures Funds, 1971I – 1984I

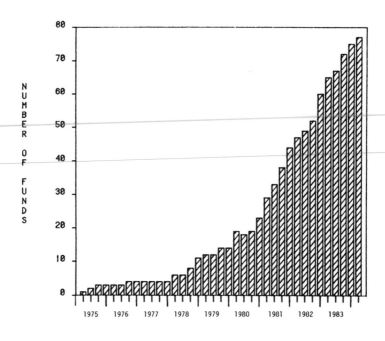

is to present the needed aggregate information and analyze the role of public futures funds in financial asset portfolios.

Data sources and classifications are described in the first section of the article. Returns and costs of public funds are presented in the second section. Aggregate balance sheet accounts are shown in the third section. Market shares of general partners and trading advisors are presented in the fourth section. Risk-return trade-offs of a portfolio of Treasury bills, Treasury bonds, common stocks, and public futures funds are analyzed in the last section.

I. Data

The basic data encompassed the 1975I through 1984I period, included 84 public futures funds, and consisted of quarterly ending equity, net asset value per unit, and cash distribution data.[2] To the best knowledge of the authors and individuals monitoring futures fund performance, the 84 funds represent all public futures funds active over the study period (Baratz, 1984; Klopfenstein, 1984). One fund was active for the entire 1975I through 1984I period. Seven public funds ceased operations due to trading losses; statistics on these seven funds are included in the data set.

Data from four different sources were used to construct the entire data set. The first source was prospectuses of new public funds, which contained audited records of other funds managed by the trading advisor(s) and general partner. The second source was data from quarterly surveys of futures fund managers conducted by *Managed Accounts Reports* since the beginning of 1983. The third source comprised data obtained directly from futures fund managers. The fourth source was quarterly and annual financial reports most public funds have filed with the SEC since 1979.[3] Constructing continuous series entailed using the audited prospectus data to the extent possible; then utilizing data obtained from *Managed Accounts Reports* surveys, fund managers, and quarterly and annual financial reports filed with the SEC.

A key distinguishing factor among public futures funds was whether the trading advisor relied on technical analysis, fundamental analysis, or some combination of the two.[4] Accordingly, the 84 public futures funds were classified into two groups. Public funds in the first group had trading advisors who relied entirely on technical analysis. Public funds in the second group had either advisors who relied on a combination of technical and fundamental analysis, or employed both technical and fundamental advisors. Based on information in prospectuses. 70 funds (83%) were classified as technical and 14 (17%) were classified as combination.

II. Returns and Costs

Information regarding aggregate returns and costs is critical to assessing the performance of public futures funds. Aggregate net returns have been reported in *Futures* magazine since May 1982, but the method used to calculate returns is questionable. Widely varying cost estimates have appeared in the popular press. Also, gross trading return estimates have been unavailable. Therefore, the purpose of the following section is to present an improved measure of aggregate net returns, estimates of costs based on a survey of 20 funds, and estimates of gross trading returns.

A. Aggregate Net Returns

One method of measuring aggregate public futures fund returns is a simple average of each fund's change in net asset value.[5] The only public source of aggregate returns, Futures magazine's "Funds Review," uses simple averages. However, giving each fund's return the same weight should be questioned in light of the size disparity among public funds; the largest fund's equity exceeded $100 million, the smallest fund's equity was under $200,000.

A value-weighted measure of aggregate returns improves upon the simple average measure by weighting each fund's change in net asset value by the total value of the fund.[4] Another improvement is to calculate returns in natural logarithmic form, which assumes continuous compounding and continuous time. Annual returns are simply the sum of quarterly returns when continuous compounding is assumed.

The log weighted-average measure of aggregate public futures fund quarterly net returns is calculated:

$$Pj = LOG \frac{N_{i=1} \left((ENAVj_i + DISTj_,) \times BUNITj_, \right)}{N_{i=1} \left(BNAVj_i \times BUNITj_, \right)} \times 100.0 \tag{1}$$

where Pj is the natural logarithmic, value-weighted, aggregate percent net return to public funds; $ENAVj_i$ is the ending net asset value per unit for the ith fund during the jth quarter; $DISTj_i$ is the cash distribution per unit made by the ith fund for the jth quarter; $BUNITj_i$ is the beginning number of outstanding units for the ith fund during the jth quarter; $BNAVj_i$ is the beginning net asset value per unit for the ith fund during the jth quarter; and N is the number of funds actively traded during the jth quarter.

Both simple-average and log weighted-average measures of public fund net returns were calculated for the 1975 through 1983 period (Table 6-1).[6] In all but two years, 1982 and 1983, the measures were different by more than 6%. Also, the simple average apparently understated returns from 1976 through 1981, due to the above-average returns of the largest fund. The series did exhibit the same pattern, losses in 1976, 1982, and 1983, and profits in the remaining years. Nevertheless, the log weighted-average measure appears to have been a more accurate measure of aggregate public futures fund returns.

Aggregate net returns for all public futures funds averaged 15.2% per year from 1975 through 1983 (log weighted-average, Table 6-1). Except for 1976, returns were positive from 1975 through 1981. During 1982 and 1983 returns were negative, which may explain why investors have recently been more cautious about investing in futures funds (Zaslow and MacKay-Smith,

**Table 6-1   Aggregate Net Returns for Public Futures Funds,
1975 – 1983***

Year	Log Weighted-Average for All Funds (%)	Simple-Average for All Funds (%)	Log Weighted-Average for Technical Funds (%)	Log Weighted-Average for Combination Funds (%)
1975	10.2	17.4	28.6	21.3
1976	− 24.9	− 32.4	− 118.3	24.9
1977	50.6	44.0	28.9	56.1
1978	26.3	17.5	− 33.8	40.4
1979	46.8	35.3	33.1	52.5
1980	24.3	12.1	40.6	19.1
1981	16.0	6.2	14.6	18.8
1982	− 0.9	− 1.9	7.0	− 12.5
1983	− 11.1	− 9.8	− 15.8	− 0.4
Mean	15.2	9.8	− 1.7	24.5
Standard Deviation	25.1	23.1	50.0	22.6

[a]Net Returns = Gross Realized Trading Profits – Commissions + Unrealized Trading Profits + Interest Earnings – Management and Incentives Fees – Administrative Cost.

1984). In addition, recent returns may be more relevant because an average return weights each year's return equally, regardless of the number of active funds. Thus, returns in early years may not have been as representative as later year returns when more funds were active.

Differences in the aggregate net returns of technical and combination funds were striking (Table 6-1). Combination funds had a mean annual return of 24.5%, whereas technical funds averaged an annual return of –1.7%. Furthermore, the standard deviation of technical funds was twice that of combination funds. Again, these results should be viewed cautiously since only three technical funds and one combination fund were active

**Figure 6-2   Frequency Distribution of Average Public Futures Fund
              Returns, 1975I – 1984I**

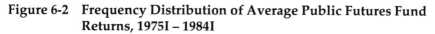

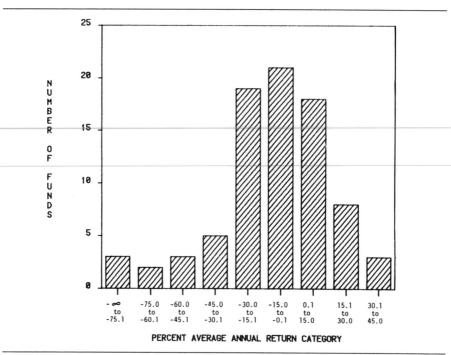

PERCENT AVERAGE ANNUAL RETURN CATEGORY

previous to 1978. If only the 1978 through 1983 period was considered,
technical funds averaged a return of 7.6% and combination funds averaged
a return of 19.6%.

A different view of returns was provided by the frequency distribution
of average annual net returns for public funds (Figure 6-2). Overall, 65% of
the funds had negative returns and 35% had positive returns. The distribution was centered on the 0.0% to –15.0% category, which contained 21 of the
82 returns. The distribution was not symmetric; the highest profit category
was 30.1 to 45.0%, while the lowest was –75.1% to ∞. (The negative infinity
results from one fund losing all its equity.)

Although the frequency distribution seems to imply an average return for
all funds of less than zero, it does not. The distribution gives equal weight
to a return regardless of the time a fund has been actively traded or its size.
The distribution does point to an important anomaly. If an investor randomly selected any fund, the probability of selecting a profitable one was

0.35. However, the aggregate net return averaged over 15% per year (Table 6-1). Thus, a few public funds were extremely profitable, whereas the majority were unprofitable. For example, if the four most profitable funds were excluded from profit calculations, aggregate net returns for the remaining 80 funds averaged −14.3% per year.[7]

B. Costs

Public futures funds are perceived to be relatively high cost enterprises. Estimates of costs published in the popular press range from 10 to 35% of average annual equity (Zaslow and MacKay-Smith, 1984). However, the accuracy of these estimates is uncertain. To gain a more accurate estimate, cost data from a sample of 20 funds were examined. The data were obtained from audited prospectuses and included at least one year of observations.

Two categories were formed: commission costs and management, and incentive and administrative costs. Each was expressed as a percent of average annual equity (Table 6-2). Commission costs for the 20 public funds averaged 10.7% per year, with a range of 6.0 to 27.8%. The relatively high level of commission costs was primarily due to the 20 funds paying 70 to 80% of retail commission rates. Given the volume of trading which a futures fund generates, and thus the potential for reduced commission rates, general partners may be subject to conflict of interest. In fact, the prospectus for every new public fund has a section which discusses such a potential conflict. For example, the prospectus for Thompson Commodity Partners I (1981, p. 14) states:

> "Because the General Partner is an affiliate of TMSI (Thomson McKinnon Securities, Inc.), the General Partner has a conflict of interest between its responsibility to the Partnership to limit or reduce the cost of brokerage commissions and its interest in the generation of brokerage commissions which would benefit TMSI as the partnership's futures broker...Because the General Partner is an affiliate of TMSI, there has been no negotiation of brokerage commission rates and the Partnership will pay 75% of TMSI's standard commission rates charged to public customer accounts from time to time. The General Partner believes this arrangement is fair to the partnership, and it does not presently intend to negotiate for lower commission rates with other brokerage firms."

Management, incentive, and administrative costs averaged 8.5% of average annual equity, with a range of 0.7 to 23.8% (Table 6-2). When reported

Table 6-2   Public Futures Fund Annual Costs

Public Futures Fund	Average Annual Commission Cost (% of Average Equity)	Average Annual Management, Incentive, and Administrative Cost (% of Average Equity)	Total
1	27.8	3.6	31.4
2	7.0	4.1	11.1
3	18.7	5.9	24.6
4	12.1	10.1	22.2
5	10.7	8.4	19.1
6	6.0	23.8	29.8
7	6.9	15.5	20.4
8	6.3	10.1	16.4
9	10.3	11.4	21.7
10	13.3	0.7[a]	14.0
11	11.4	2.3[a]	13.7
12	7.7	13.3	21.0
13	9.6	7.7	17.3
14	8.5	4.4	12.9
15	9.6	9.2	18.8
16	11.9	6.1	18.0
17	11.8	5.4	17.2
18	7.2	11.9	19.1
19	8.9	4.2	13.1
20	8.4	12.6	21.0
Mean	10.7	8.5	19.2

[a]Management and incentive fees were paid as a percent of commissions.

separately, administrative costs were less than 2% per year. Generalizations were elusive due to the variety of arrangements concerning management and administrative fees. Eighteen of the 20 funds paid trading advisors 4 to 6% of average equity with an incentive fee of 12 to 15% of gross trading profits. Funds 10 and 11, however, paid the advisor based on a percent of commissions. Fund 6's administrative costs included a 7% per year payment which covered both yearly administrative costs and initial sales commissions.

Total average costs of 19.2% per year indicate public futures funds had to overcome a major hurdle to generate competitive rates of return. Furthermore, the sample cost data did not account for the initial sales commission, which typically increases costs 8 to 10% the first year of trading.

The poor performance of public futures funds during 1982 and 1983 increases the importance of costs. More specifically, if public futures funds had negotiated for 10 to 15% of retail commission rates and halved all other costs, aggregate returns would have been at least 10% in 1982 and near the breakeven level in 1983, rather than –0.1 and –11.1%, respectively. If recent trends continue, future profitability and expansion opportunities of public futures funds may depend on lowering costs.

C. Gross Trading Returns

Gross trading returns equal net returns minus interest earnings plus total costs. An estimate of aggregate gross trading returns for public futures funds was calculated utilizing the previous net return and cost information (Table 6-3). Interest earnings were calculated as 80% of US Treasury bill rates because fund managers keep approximately 20% of the Treasury bill rate) was a further cost to investors in futures funds.

Aggregate gross trading returns were estimated to average 27.4% over 1975 through 1983. The highest gross return was 65.7% in 1977 and the lowest was –9.8% in 1976, the only negative year. Interest earnings averaged 7.0% per year, nearly 50% of average net returns. The impact of total costs on returns is evidenced by the fact that average gross trading returns were nearly twice the level of average net returns. Significantly, 50% lower costs would have increased average net returns to 24.8%.

Return and cost data indicate public futures funds averaged an aggregate net return of 15.2% per year. However, net returns were negative in the two most recent years, 1982 and 1983, and nearly 50% of net returns were interest earnings. The distribution of aggregate returns across individual funds was skewed, with 65% of funds earning an average annual net loss. Costs were estimated to average 19.2% per year. Commission costs accounted for 10.7%, and management, incentive, and administrative costs accounted for 8.5%. Fifty percent lower total costs would have increased the average net returns of public futures funds to nearly 25%. Finally, aggregate gross trading returns were estimated to average 27.4%.

Table 6-3   Aggregate Gross Trading Profits for Public Futures Funds, 1975 – 1983

Year	Net Return[a] (%)	Interest Earnings[b] (%)	Total Cost[c] (%)	Gross Trading Return[d] (%)
1975	10.2	4.6	19.2	24.8
1976	− 24.9	4.1	19.2	− 9.8
1977	50.6	4.1	19.2	65.7
1978	26.3	5.7	19.2	39.8
1979	46.8	8.3	19.2	57.7
1980	24.3	9.0	19.2	34.5
1981	16.0	11.8	19.2	23.4
1982	− 0.9	8.4	19.2	9.9
1983	-- 11.1	7.1	19.2	1.0
Mean	15.2	7.0	19.2	27.4

[a]Column one of Table I.
[b]Eighty percent of the US Treasury bill rate (Ibbotsen and Sinquefield, 1982).
[c]Average total cost from Table II.
[d]Gross Trading Return = Net Return–Interest Earnings + Total Costs.

III. Balance Sheet Accounts

Aggregate balance sheet accounts register in nominal dollars the investment, withdrawals (redemptions of outstanding units), cash distributions, profits, and equity of public futures funds. Such information is useful because it shows the total value of public funds and sources of the value.

The flow of money in and out of public futures funds from 1975I through 1984I is summarized by the ending aggregate balance sheet (Table 6-4). Three categories—investment, cash distributions, and withdrawals—were approximated due to data limitations. A complete record of each fund's starting equity was not available, so investment was approximated by summing each fund's ending equity for the first quarter of active trading.[8] Actual cash distributions are made monthly and based on the number of outstanding units at the end of a month. Since available data were quarterly, cash distributions were calculated using the outstanding number of units at the end of the quarter. Withdrawals were calculated as the residual of ending

Table 6-4   Aggregate Public Futures Fund Balance Sheet

Investment (1975I–1984I)	$680,699,433
− Withdrawals (1975I–1984I)	(320,389,898)
− Cash Distributions (1975I–1984I)	(29,584,436)
+ Net Profits (1975I–1984I)	104,368,424
= Ending Equity (1984I)	$435,093,523

equity minus beginning equity and cash distributions plus net profits. Ending equity equals investment minus net withdrawals and cash distributions plus net profits.

Investment in public futures funds totaled approximately $680.7 million from 1975I through 1984I. Withdrawals were $320.4 million for the same period. Thus, nearly 50% of the money placed in public funds was subsequently withdrawn. Cash distributions, similar to dividends paid on an irregular basis, totaled approximately $29.6 million.

Total net profits from 1975I through 1984I were $104.4 million. Overall, combination and technical funds earned total profits of $84.4 million and $20.0 million, respectively. In addition, the four most profitable public funds earned $155.7 million over the period, while the remaining 80 funds had a combined net loss of $51.3 million.[9] At the end of the first quarter of 1984, total equity for all public funds was $435.1 million.

The pattern of ending equity, net profits, and net investment (investment minus withdrawals and cash distributions) over 1975I through 1984I indicates the public futures fund industry has gone through three phases (Figure 6-3). The first phase, from 1975I through 1977IV, was a startup period. Aggregate equity was relatively small, averaging $17.0 million. Net investment and net profits moved erratically. Net investment was the source of all equity growth during the first two years because net profits were negative. Just the opposite occurred during 1977, when equity growth came from net profits because no new funds were started.

The second phase, from 1978I through 1982IV, was a period of accelerated growth and high profits. Aggregate equity shot from $38.4 million to $504.9 million, a 13-fold increase in five years. Net profits for the period were $146.6 million, or 31% of the growth in equity. Net investment of $319.9 million was the source of the remaining 69% of equity growth.

**Figure 6-3   Aggregate Public Futures Fund Balance Sheet Accounts,
             1975I – 1984I**

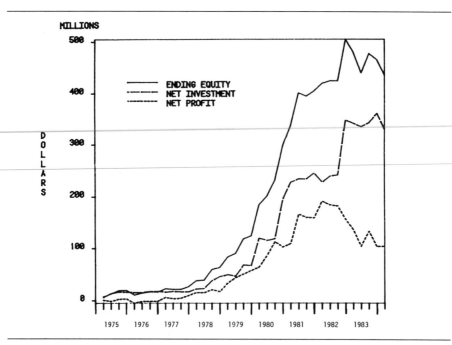

The third phase, from 1983I through 1984I, was a period of contraction, with ending equity decreasing by nearly $70 million. Net losses for the period totaled $52.3 million, or 75% of the decline in equity. In addition, net investment declined over the five-quarter period. Withdrawals of $136.0 million, or 43% of total withdrawals over the entire 1975I through 1984I period, exceeded the $122.4 million invested.

Combination fund equity exceeded technical fund equity 19 of the 20 quarters from 1975I through 1979IV (Figure 6-4). After 1979, though, technical fund equity grew at a much faster rate. For example, at the end of 1984I technical fund equity was nearly $200 million more than combination fund equity. In light of one combination fund's averaging 75% of total combination equity for the period, the pre-1979 comparison should be interpreted cautiously because the number of technical funds was greater than the number of combination funds for the entire 1975I to 1984I period. Total investment in public futures funds was approximately $680.7 million from 1975I through 1984I. Nearly 50% of the investment was subsequently with-

Figure 6-4   Technical and Combination Fund Ending Equity, 1975I – 1984I

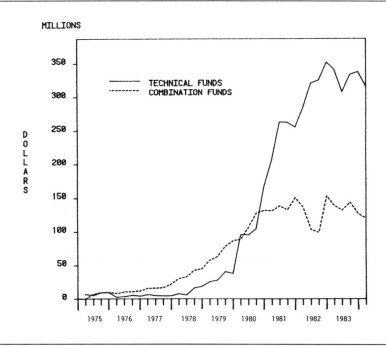

drawn. Net profits for the period totaled $104.4 million, but the four most profitable funds earned $155.7 million while the remaining 80 funds had a combined loss of $51.3 million. Ending equity increased from $7.2 million at the end of 1975I to $435.1 million at the end of 1984I.

IV. Market Shares Of General Partners And Trading Advisors

The level of market shares of leading general partners and trading advisors provide information on competition in the public futures fund industry. By combining share, the degree of market concentration is revealed. The structure-conduct-performance paradigm of industrial organization suggests concentration is positively related to profits (Scherer, 1980). General partner and trading advisor profits are directly related to the costs of public futures

Table 6-5   Market Shares of Leading Public Futures Fund General Partners, 1975 – 1983[a]

	General Partner					
Year	A	B	C	D	E	Total
1975	51.0[b]	49.0	0.0	0.0	0.0	100.0
1976	73.3	15.1	11.6	0.0	0.0	100.0
1977	81.7	12.7	5.6	0.0	0.0	100.0
1978	57.5	26.5	5.9	0.0	0.0	89.9
1979	40.5	43.5	9.7	0.0	0.0	93.7
1980	29.0	33.8	0.4	11.1	9.2	83.5
1981	25.5	25.4	0.9	13.2	4.1	69.1
1982	11.9	30.6	1.6	19.2	11.7	75.0
1983	9.4	26.7	2.8	17.9	8.5	65.3

[a]A general partner's market share series was reported if market share exceeded 10% in any quarter.
[b]Market share was calculated as the percent of total futures fund equity in the general partner's funds at the end of the year.

funds. Thus, high levels of market concentration may lead to noncompetitive costs.

The general partner of a public futures fund manages all aspects of the fund's business including selection of the trading advisor and futures commission merchant. The combined market share of five leading general partners averaged 86% from 1975 through 1983 (Table 6-5). Concentration was highest during the first three years when the combined market share of general partners A, B, and C averaged 100%. After 1977, market concentration with respect to the five general partners declined, but was no lower than 65%.

The two largest general partners (A and B) have had varying market shares. General partner A reached a market share of 81.7% in 1977, but then declined to a low of 9.4% in 1983. General partner B peaked at a market share of 49.0% in 1975, declined to 12.7% share in 1977, and then rose to a 43.5% share by 1979. The other three general partners also experienced changes in market share, but not as large in magnitude as A or B.

The trading advisor for a futures fund has sole responsibility for the selection of futures market transactions. The combined market share of five

Table 6-6   Market Shares of Leading Public Futures Fund Trading
              Advisors, 1975 – 1983[a]

			Trading Advisors			
Year	A	B	C	D	E	Total
1975	51.0[b]	0.0	49.0	0.0	0.0	100.0
1976	73.3	0.0	15.1	0.0	0.0	88.4
1977	81.7	0.0	12.7	0.0	0.0	94.4
1978	57.5	14.6	0.0	8.9	0.0	81.0
1979	40.5	22.2	0.0	19.5	0.0	82.2
1980	29.0	25.1	0.0	7.8	5.9	67.8
1981	25.5	19.1	0.0	3.6	3.9	52.1
1982	11.9	24.5	0.0	2.7	9.5	48.6
1983	9.4	20.4	0.0	3.4	7.3	40.5

[a]A trading advisor's market share series was reported if market share exceeded 10% in any quarter.
[b]Market share was calculated as the percent of total public futures fund equity in funds managed by the trading advisor at the end of the year.

leading trading advisors averaged 73% from 1975 to 1983 (Table 6-6). Similar to general partners, concentration was highest during the first three years when the combined market shares of advisors A and C averaged 94%. Unlike the five general partners, concentration declined relatively quickly, reaching a low of 40% in 1983.

Individual market shares of the trading advisors were variable. For example, trading advisor C started out in 1975 with a 49.0% share, which declined to zero by 1978. Advisor A peaked at a share of 81.7% in 1977 and then declined to 9.4% in 1983. The declines in market share, with the exception of advisor C, were not due to net losses, but to the fact that total equity in public funds grew faster than the equity in funds managed by the particular advisor.

The combined market shares of five leading general partners and trading advisors averaged 86 and 72%, respectively, from 1975 through 1983. Scherer (1980, p. 67) suggests noncompetitive conditions are present when the leading four firms control 40% or more of the market. The minimum concentration of four general partners and trading advisors was 63 and 40%, respectively. Thus, Scherer's threshold was equaled or surpassed, for both general partner and trading advisor concentration, every year from 1975 through 1983. The costs estimated previously (Table 6-2) tend to reinforce a conclusion that noncompetitive behavior was present in the public futures fund industry; approximately $175 million in commissions and $130 million in management and incentive fees were paid by public funds over 1975 through 1983.[10] Two cautions are necessary. First, Scherer's threshold is only a rule of thumb. The precise level of market concentration where noncompetitive behavior begins is open to debate. Second, a broader market definition, including private futures funds, may be more relevant.

V. Portfolio Effects

Financial assets are commonly held as parts of diversified portfolios. An important question relating to public futures funds is their potential role in portfolios of financial assets. Lintner (1983) showed that overall risk- return tradeoffs of a stocks and bonds portfolio could be improved with the possibility of investing in public futures funds. The conclusions, however, were based on only 3 1/2 years of data on eight public funds. Utilizing a much larger sample of 84 public funds, the portfolio question will be examined.

The framework used to investigate the portfolio question is known as mean- variance analysis. The basic premise of the mean-variance model is that investors are risk averse; given the choice between two assets with the same expected return (reward), the investor will choose the one with a lower variance (risk). Importantly, this premise assumes either that the investors utility function is a quadratic function of returns, or that returns are normally distributed.

Mean-variance models employ a two-stage decision making process to derive optimal portfolios (Markowitz, 1952). The first stage involves finding the efficient, or minimum-variance, portfolios. Initially, an investor finds the minimum risk portfolio, determines the reward associated with it, and then successively derives other portfolios offering the highest reward with the least possible risk. More formally, deriving the efficient set of portfolios requires solving the following quadratic programing problem:

Minimize

$$V(z) = \sum_{i=1}^{n} \sum_{j=1}^{n} \sigma_{ij} X_i X_j \qquad (2)$$

Subject to

$$\sum_{j=1}^{n} X_j = 1.0 \qquad (3)$$

$$\sum_{j=1}^{n} E(c_j)X_j = \beta \qquad \beta = 0 \rightarrow Emax \qquad (4)$$

where $V(z)$ is the variance of portfolio returns; σ_{ij} is the covariance of the expected returns between assets i and j; X_j is the proportion of the portfolio held in asset j; $E(c_j)$ is the expected return on asset j; and β is the portfolio expected return, which is varied parametrically from zero to the highest expected return of the j assets.

The second stage of deriving an optimal portfolio involves maximizing utility subject to the set of efficient portfolios generated in stage one. Optimal choices depend critically on each investor's preferred tradeoff of mean and variance. For this reason, the second stage is usually not presented when reporting research on portfolios (Anderson, Dillon, and Hardaker, 1977). Instead, investors can individually identify the optimal portfolio by inspection of the efficient set, which is the same for all investors.

Deriving an efficient set of portfolios requires the expected returns, variances, and covariances of the assets being considered for inclusion. How should the required statistics be estimated? Given the multitude of expectations individual investors may hold, it is reasonable to use historical estimates as the best approximation. It is important to remember, however, that any portfolios derived are based on historical relationships which may or may not continue in the future.

The investments considered for inclusion in the portfolio were Treasury bills, Treasury bonds, common stocks, and public futures funds (Table 6-7). Since investors are concerned with real purchasing power, all returns were adjusted for changes in the general price level by the Consumer Price Index. Returns were not adjusted for taxes. Average real returns were 1.1% for bills, −0.4% for bonds, 8.3% for stocks, and 6.6% for public funds. Bills were the least volatile over the nine-year period. Bonds, stocks and public funds were much more volatile, with public funds having the largest standard deviation of returns.[11] Correlation coefficients of the series point to some interesting relationships.[12] Bills, bonds, and stocks were all negatively correlated with inflation, while public funds were positively correlated with inflation. Additionally, public funds were negatively correlated with the other three investments.

**Table 6-7   Annual Real Rates of Return for Financial Assets,
              1975 – 1983**

Year	US Treasury Bills[a]	Long-Term Treasury Bonds[b]	Common Stocks[c]	All Futures Funds[d]	Rate of Inflation[e]
1975	-1.1	2.0	28.2	3.0	7.0
1976	0.3	11.4	18.2	-28.3	4.8
1977	1.6	-6.9	-13.1	41.0	6.8
1978	-1.8	-7.3	-2.4	15.9	9.0
1979	-2.6	-12.8	4.5	29.6	13.3
1980	-1.8	-15.8	17.4	10.6	12.4
1981	4.4	-6.5	-12.7	6.5	8.9
1982	6.4	35.1	16.9	-4.6	3.9
1983	4.8	-3.0	18.0	-14.4	3.8
Mean	1.1	-0.4	8.3	6.6	7.8
Standard Deviation	3.3	15.6	14.9	21.2	3.5

Correlation Coefficients:

	Bonds	Stocks	Funds	Inflation
Bills	0.606	-0.075	-0.367	-0.708
Bonds		0.374	-0.529	-0.727
Stocks			-0.633	-0.270
Funds				-0.606

[a]Based on a strategy of buying and selling a bill once a month (Ibbotsen and Sinquefield, 1982).
[b]Based on a strategy of buying a 20-year bond at the beginning of the year and selling at the end (Ibbotsen and Sinquefield, 1982).
[c]Total returns from Standard and Poor's Composite Index of 500 stocks (Ibbotsen and Sinquefield, 1982).
[d]Aggregate log weighted-average return for all public funds (Table 6-1).
[e]Changes in the Consumer Price Index (Bureau of Labor Statistics).

The first step of the analysis was to estimate points along the efficient risk-return curve for portfolios consisting of bills, bonds and stocks (Table 6-8). Point A, with a mean of 2.1% and standard deviation of 3.4%, represents

Table 6-8   Efficient Risk-Return Tradeoff Curve for a Bills, Bonds, and Stocks Portfolio

Point	Mean (%)	Standard Deviation (%)	Portfolio Proportions		
			Bills	Bonds	Stocks
A	2.1	2.8	0.84	0.00	0.09	0.07
B	3.0	3.1	0.71	0.00	0.18	0.11
C	4.0	4.1	0.56	0.00	0.28	0.16
D	5.0	5.5	0.41	0.00	0.38	0.21
E	6.0	7.0	0.26	0.00	0.48	0.26
F	7.0	8.5	0.11	0.00	0.58	0.31
G	8.0	11.3	0.00	0.00	0.82	0.18
H	8.3	14.9	0.00	0.00	1.00	0.00

Figure 6-5   Efficient Risk-Return Tradeoff Curves

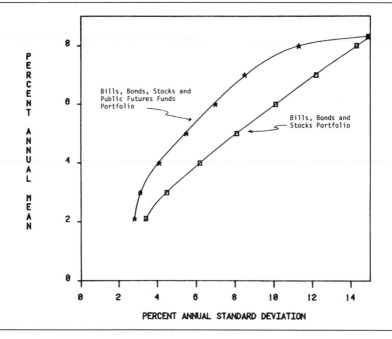

Table 6-9   Efficient Risk-Return Tradeoff Curve for a Bills, Bonds,
             Stocks, and Futures Funds Portfolio

Point	Mean (%)	Standard Deviation (%)	Portfolio Proportions			
			Bills	Bonds	Stocks	Futures Funds
A	2.1	2.8	0.84	0.00	0.09	0.07
B	3.0	3.1	0.71	0.00	0.18	0.11
C	4.0	4.1	0.56	0.00	0.28	0.16
D	5.0	5.5	0.41	0.00	0.38	0.21
E	6.0	7.0	0.26	0.00	0.48	0.26
F	7.0	8.5	0.11	0.00	0.58	0.31
G	8.0	11.3	0.00	0.00	0.82	0.18
H	8.3	14.9	0.00	0.00	1.00	0.00

the minimum-risk point of the efficient set. Points B through G are members of the efficient set with successively higher portfolio means and standard deviations. Point H, with a mean of 8.3%, is the point of maximum return. The portfolio proportions indicate bonds did not enter any efficient portfolios. Bills were a majority of the portfolio at low mean returns, and stocks an increasing majority at higher means. The second step of the analysis was to estimate points along the efficient risk-return curve for a portfolio of bills, bonds, stocks and public futures funds (Table 9). Point A, with a portfolio mean of 2.1% and standard deviation of 2.8%, represented the minimum variance point. Similar to a portfolio of only bills, bonds, and stocks, the reward of higher mean returns came at a cost of higher standard deviations (points B through G). Portfolio proportions show that 7% was held in public funds at the minimum- risk point A. The proportion of public funds rose with increasing levels of mean returns until a peak of 31% was reached at Point F. Bonds were not held at any point along the efficient risk-return curve. Inclusion of public funds meant bills and stocks were held in reduced proportions (compared to a portfolio of only bills, bonds and stocks). The largest reduction in proportions, ranging from 5% to 20%, occurred for stocks. Portfolio reductions for bills were limited between 2 and 7%.

The efficient risk-return curves indicate a risk-averse investor could have achieved a higher level of utility if public futures funds were added to a portfolio of bills, bonds and stocks, because at each level of mean returns risk was reduced from 0.6 to 3.7%. The beneficial portfolio effect of public funds was due to the correlation between inflation and public funds, bills, bonds, and stocks. Historically, when the rate of inflation increased public fund returns tended to rise while bills, bonds and stocks returns tended to fall, and vice versa. Thus, adding public funds to the portfolio smoothed real return variation by offsetting the fluctuations of returns on bills and stocks. The analysis of the effects of adding public futures funds to a bills, bonds and stocks portfolio demonstrated that public funds could have beneficial risk-reduction characteristics. However, benefits of public funds would be much lower if returns in the two most recent years, 1982 and 1983, were used as expectations. Also, any particular public futures fund may not have the same relationship with bills, bonds, and stocks as the aggregate measure of fund returns.

IV. Summary

Public futures funds grew rapidly in both numbers and size over the 1975I through 1984I period. The number of active public funds increased from one during 1975I to 77 at the end of 1984I. Aggregate equity increased from $7.2 million to $435.1 million over the same period.

Aggregate net returns of public futures funds averaged 15.2% per year. However, returns in the two most recent years, 1982 and 1983, were negative and interest earnings were nearly 50% of average net returns. In addition, the distribution of individual public fund returns was skewed, with 65% of public funds averaging annual net losses. Annual total costs were estimated to average 19.2% per year. Gross trading returns averaged an estimated 27.4% per year.

The combined market shares of five leading general partners and trading advisors averaged 86 and 72%, respectively, from 1975 through 1983. Such concentration levels suggest noncompetitive conditions were present in the public futures fund industry. Cost levels tend to reinforce the conclusion; approximately $175 million in commissions and $130 million in management and incentive fees were paid by public funds from 1975 through 1983.

Adding public futures funds to a portfolio of bills, bonds and stocks was shown to reduce real portfolio risk from 0.6 to 3.7%. The beneficial portfolio effect of public funds was due to the correlation between inflation and public funds, bills, bonds and stocks. Historically, when the rate of inflation increased public funds returns tended to rise while returns on bills, bonds, and stocks tended to fall, and vice versa. Thus, adding public funds to the portfolio smoothed real return variation by offsetting the fluctuation of returns on bills, bonds, and stocks.

Endnotes

1. The principal advantage of limited partnerships is that cash distributions are generally treated as a return of capital for Federal income tax purposes. Thus, the double taxation of corporate dividends is avoided.

2. To simplify the presentation, year and quarter were written as 1975I, 1975II, 1975III, 1975IV, etc. Also, if a prospectus was filed with the SEC, a fund was classified as public. Net asset value per unit times the number of outstanding units equals equity.

3. For the first year of operation after a public fund has registered with the SEC, quarterly and annual financial reports must be submitted regardless of the size of the fund or number of investors. However, a public fund may be exempted from further reporting if it has less than 500 investors and total equity of less than $3.0 million, or it has less than 300 investors and total equity greater than $3.0 million.

4. Technical analysis examines futures prices, trading volume, and open interest for trends or patterns to guide trading decisions. Fundamental analysis examines supply and demand for the actual commodity.

5. Adjustments for cash distributions are included in the calculations.

6. Quarterly returns are presented in Appendix A. Statistics on each public fund are shown in Appendix B.

7. The four funds contained an average of 55% of the total equity in public futures funds from 1975 through 1983.

8. Additional investment in public futures funds after the first quarter of trading was also included.

9. Two of the four most profitable public funds were technical and two were combination.

10. The estimates were calculated by multiplying the aggregate average annual equity of all public futures funds by 10.2% for commissions and 7.5% for management and incentive fees.

11. Standard deviations, rather than variances, are presented in Table 6-7 and the remainder of the portfolio section to allow easier interpretation

of results. Risk-return relationships are identical whether stated in mean-variance or mean-standard deviation terms.

12.
$$p_i = \frac{\sigma_{ij}}{\sigma_i \sigma_j}$$

where

p_{ij} = correlation coefficient for investments i and j,

σ_{ij} = covariance between investments i and j,

σ_i, σ_j = standard deviation of investments i and j.

Bibliography

Anderson, J., Dillon, J., and Hardaker, B. *Agriculture Decision Analysis*, Iowa State University Press, Ames, IA, 1977.

Baratz, M., Ed. *Managed Accounts Reports, Personal Conversations*, Columbia, MD, August 1984–December 1984.

Bodie, Z. "Commodity Futures as a Hedge Against Inflation," *Journal of Portfolio Management*, 9: 12—17, 1983.

Brorsen, B., and Irwin, S. (forthcoming): "Evaluation of Commodity Funds," *Review of Research in Futures Markets*.

Donchian, D. *Personal Conversation*, Shearson Lehman American Express, Ft. Lauderdale, FL, December, 1984.

Hultgren, R. "The Market Millionares," *Commodities*, 4: 16–22, 1975.

Ibbotsen, and Sinquefield. *Stocks, Bonds, Bills and Inflation: The Past and the Future*, Financial Analysts Federation, Charlottesville, VA, 1982.

Irwin, S., and Uhrig, J. *Statistical and Trading System Analysis of Weak Form Efficiency in U.S. Futures Markets*, Agricultural Experiment Station Bulletin No. 421, Purdue University, 1983.

Klopfenstein, J. *Personal Conversation*, Norwood Securities, Chicago, IL, December, 1984.

Lintner, J. *The Potential Role of Managed Commodity-Financial Futures Accounts (And/or Funds) in Portfolios of Stocks and Bonds*, paper presented at the annual conference of the Financial Analysts Federation, Toronto, Canada, 1983.

Mackay-Smith, A. "Commodity Funds Let Small Investors Partake with Limited Liability, but Risks are Sizable," *The Wall Street Journal*, p. 46, October, 3, 1983.

Markowitz, W. "Portfolio Selection," Journal of Finance, 7: 77–91, 1952.

Scherer, F. *Industrial Market Structures and Economic Performance, Rand McNally College Publishing Company*, Chicago, IL, 1980.

Thomson McKinnon Securities, Inc. *Thomson Commodity Partners I Prospectus*, 1981.

Zaslow, J., and Mackay-Smith, A. "Public Commodity Funds Acquire Bad Image that Won't Fade Soon," *The Wall Street Journal*, p. 31, April 24, 1984.

Appendix A   Quarterly Public Futures Fund Returns, 1975I – 1984I

Year/Quarter	Log Weighted-Average Return for Technical Funds (%)	Log Weighted-Average Return for Combination Funds (%)	Log Weighted-Average Return for All Funds (%)
75/1	10.02	—	10.02
75/2	− 30.93	. —	− 30.93
75/3	42.22	17.64	28.46
75/4	7.30	− 2.17	2.69
76/1	− 128.26	− 14.01	− 54.63
76/2	33.86	26.58	28.40
76/3	.47	3.42	2.67
76/4	− 24.34	8.87	− 1.30
77/1	51.73	30.85	36.86
77/2	− 26.84	− 7.18	− 12.64
77/3	− 6.64	8.23	4.91
77/4	10.64	24.23	21.47
78/1	− 1.45	22.95	18.90
78/2	− 27.86	6.49	.24
78/3	10.16	13.65	13.11
78/4	− 14.64	− 2.73	− 5.95
79/1	10.51	26.38	21.95
79/2	17.54	9.48	12.01
79/3	3.76	8.85	7.31
79/4	1.24	7.76	5.57
80/1	30.41	− 8.53	5.07
80/2	.73	21.43	11.22
80/3	4.58	19.10	12.51
80/4	4.85	− 12.88	− 4.48
81/1	1.14	3.46	2.17
81/2	18.49	10.95	15.63
81/3	− .79	− 3.16	− 1.60
81/4	− 4.29	7.50	− .18
82/1	14.16	− 4.55	7.62
82/2	5.85	− 19.57	− 1.71
82/3	− 1.50	2.15	− .60
82/4	− 11.51	9.45	− 6.20
83/1	− 2.27	− 8.01	− 3.97
83/2	− 8.65	− 3.23	− 7.05
83/3	3.16	13.94	6.51
83/4	− 8.04	− 3.17	− 6.55
84/1	− .06	.68	.14

Appendix B Individual Public Futures Fund Statistics

Fund[a]	Trading Period	Average Equity ($)	Annual Mean Return[b] (%)	Annual Standard Deviation[b] (%)
1. Admiral Futures Fund	81IV–84I	9,684,386	8.15	31.23
2. Commonwealth Financial Futures Fund	83II–84I	8,783,945	19.82	0.79
3. Enterprise Futures Fund Series I	81IV–84I	8,151,881	−6.72	17.13
4. E.F. Hutton Commodity Ltd. Partnership II	80IV–84I	8,898,956	1.69	26.97
5. E.F. Hutton Reserve Fund	82IV–84I	35,208,800	−15.47	10.36
6. Harvest Futures Fund I	78III–84I	11,296,588	31.21	57.31
7. Harvest Futures Fund II	80I–84I	7,774,047	12.83	57.08
8. Lake Forest Futures	80IV–84I	3,070,754	−18.96	23.72
9. LaSalle Street Futures Fund	81III–84I	3,825,026	−0.32	11.17
10. McClean Futures Fund I	78IV–80IV	4,862,428	−∞	−∞
11. McClean Futures Fund II	79III–81I	2,170,000	−89.66	101.49
12. Global Futures Fund (B)	84I–84I	3,730,300	N.A.[c]	N.A.
13. SEK Futures Fund	82III–83III	265,436	−36.00	21.70
15. Advantage Futures Fund	83IV–84I	2,163,000	−8.25	N.A.
16. Antares Futures Fund	78I–80I	2,058,462	−26.15	76.51
17. Aries Commodity Fund	80I–84I	2,283,346	7.53	21.78
18. Boston Futures Fund I	80I–84I	3,214,107	−21.06	47.12

19. Boston Futures Fund II	80III–84I	3,806,193	−25.54	49.63
20. Boston Futures Fund III	82II–84I	1,155,915	−62.17	42.01
21. Boston Futures Fund IV	82IV–84I	2,798,445	−28.95	14.14
22. Capital Fund II	83IV–84I	7,093,000	−8.60	N.A.
23. Chancellor Financial Futures I	81I–84I	6,065,613	−26.59	55.69
24. Chancellor Financial Futures II	81IV–84I	2,508,874	−14.10	23.01
25. Chancellor Financial Futures III	82I–83III	1,054,362	−65.27	50.38
26. Chancellor Futures Fund	80I–84I	2,102,738	8.08	31.10
27. Chancellor Futures Fund II	83II–84I	12,963,013	−54.54	9.52
28. Clark Street Futures Fund	82IV–84I	5,417,600	5.03	18.11
29. Columbia Futures Fund	83III–84I	22,469,500	−48.91	N.A.
30. Commodity Strategy Partners	82III–84I	11,163,384	−33.88	19.30
31. Commodity Trend Timing Fund	80I–84I	15,480,074	−1.01	22.26
32. Commodity Trend Timing Fund II	82IV–84I	28,394,399	−12.65	17.61
33. Commodity Venture Fund	80IV–84I	18,474,640	18.13	19.84
34. Commodity Venture Fund II	83IV–84I	10,673,000	31.10	N.A.
35. Commodore I Futures Fund	81IV–84I	546,651	11.52	33.80
36. Commodore II Futures Fund	83III–84I	773,230	−13.87	N.A.
37. Dean Witter Reynolds Commodity Partners	81I–84I	5,712,058	−4.98	22.98
38. Dearborn Street Futures Fund	83III–84I	2,157,000	7.38	N.A.
39. Financial Futures Fund	81III–84I	509,299	−13.53	27.17
40. The Futures Fund	79III–84I	27,210,846	27.73	24.23
41. The Futures Fund II	82II–84I	26,953,153	−7.32	11.59
42. Galileo Futures Fund	79I–84I	2,590,540	4.86	26.46

Appendix continues

Appendix B Continued

Fund[a]	Trading Period	Average Equity ($)	Annual Mean Return[b] (%)	Annual Standard Deviation[b] (%)
43. Gemini Futures Fund	83II–84I	1,492,666	−0.59	24.12
44. Global Futures Fund (A)	81III–83IV	6,514,328	−16.68	24.58
45. Hutton Commodity Partners I	80I–84I	7,995,938	1.42	15.95
46. Horizon Futures Fund	80IV–84I	27,980,507	8.69	22.97
47. Horizon World Futures Fund	83IV–84I	18,087,055	21.27	N.A.
48. Illinois Commodity Fund	78I–84I	746,593	11.95	30.09
49. Iroquois Futures	84I–84I	597,000	N.A.	N.A.
50. McCormick Fund I	82I–84I	5,465,396	3.06	34.20
51. McCormick Fund II	82IV–84I	2,684,800	6.20	31.05
52. Major Trend Futures, Ltd.	78IV–84I	503,285	9.24	39.33
53. Matterhorn Commodity Partners I	81II–84I	11,809,348	−1.54	14.08
54. Midwest Commodity Fund I	81II–84I	2,743,170	−30.56	40.00
55. Mint, Ltd.	83I–84I	3,367,311	−38.49	22.16
56. Monetary Futures	82IV–84I	6,438,500	3.19	8.36
57. Mountain View Futures Fund	76III–80I	1,209,595	−23.60	48.50
58. North American Commodity Fund I	83I–84I	1,086,256	−17.00	5.62
59. North American Commodity Fund II	83IV–84I	1,395,000	−75.43	N.A.
60. Pacific Financial Futures Fund	83IV–84I	2,646,000	31.32	N.A.
61. Peachtree Futures Fund	83III–84I	649,000	−4.01	N.A.
62. Palo Alto Futures Fund	83I–84I	7,733,250	−16.92	3.35

63. Peavey Futures Fund I	80IV–84I	3,462,691	−11.09	53.73
64. Peavey Futures Fund II	81II–84I	2,254,519	−22.66	48.02
65. Peavey Futures Fund III	82III–84I	2,192,852	−37.41	14.06
66. Princeton Futures Fund I	81I–84I	13,386,529	−17.39	22.08
67. Princeton Futures Fund II	81IV–84I	8,177,909	−15.15	11.70
68. Recovery Fund I	75I–84I	2,138,122	−0.43	64.60
69. Recovery Fund II	75III–84I	346,530	−19.22	69.46
70. The Resource Fund	78III–84I	17,905,800	−24.84	23.15
71. Saturn Commodity Fund	81I–84I	5,369,955	−4.78	19.36
72. Sceptre Futures Fund	81I–84I	545,802	−2.08	28.67
73. Sunshine Futures Fund	83I–84I	769,344	−13.67	9.04
74. Sycamore Futures Fund	82IV–84I	6,758,169	−20.71	28.81
75. Tactical Fund	81III–84I	308,424	17.14	33.51
76. Thomson Commodity Partners I	81III–84I	3,902,566	−5.50	23.48
77. Thomson Commodity Partners II	82IV–84I	4,822,400	−29.55	14.87
78. Thomson Commodity Partners III	83III–84I	744,000	−21.41	N.A.
79. Thomson McKinnon Financial Futures Partners I	82I–84I	2,625,156	−17.52	36.12
80. Thomson McKinnon Futures Fund	78IV–84I	2,939,240	10.34	20.49
81. Trendview Commodity Fund IV	81I–84I	586,808	16.33	34.12
82. Trendview Commodity Fund VI	84I–84I	983,000	N.A.	N.A.
83. Vista Futures Fund	81II–84I	3,314,909	−12.23	23.29
84. Western Capital Fund I	81IV–84I	878,290	−45.44	45.72
85. Winchester International Ltd.	80IV–84I	9,340,942	0.09	33.92

[a]Funds 1 through 14 were classified as combination funds, while funds 15 through 85 were classified as technical. In addition, fund 14 information cannot be disclosed.

[b]Means and standard deviations are calculated excluding net performance during a fund's initial quarter.

[c]N.A.: Not applicable due to insufficient data.

Chapter Seven

Management Summary

Title: "The Stock Market and the Commodity Futures Market: Diversification and Arbitrage Potential"

Publication: *Financial Analysts Journal*, July–August, 1985

Authors: Cheng F. Lee, Distinguished Professor of Finance, University of Illinois
Raymond M. Leuthold, Professor, University of Illinois
Jean E. Cordier, Professor, Institut de Gestion Internationale, France

Data: Daily prices for the time period 1/1/78 through 12/31/81 for the S & P 500 cash index and Commodity Futures Index (CFI) as constructed by the Commodity Research Bureau.

Methodology: Regression and other statistical analyses was performed on both indices in order to determine if the two price series were independent, to judge if there was potential for arbitrage between the two, or if both would complement one another in portfolios.

Results: The two indices were found to be statistically independent. The authors suggest that commodity futures contracts may be used in an equity portfolio to help reduce risks and enhance portfolio returns. Opportunities for profitable arbitrage between the two indices did not appear to be likely.

Comments: The authors examined a passive buy and hold strategy for a market basket of commodity futures contracts, as opposed to active management. The results again corroborated the findings of the majority of other researchers that passive portfolios of stocks and commodity futures are independent from stocks. This was the only study to consider *daily* data.

The Stock Market and the Commodity Futures Market: Diversification and Arbitrage Potential*

Cheng F. Lee,
Raymond M. Leuthold
Jean E. Cordier

Summary

Historical relationships between the stock market and the commodity futures market, as proxied by the S&P 500 and the Commodity Futures Index, suggest that the S&P may have slightly outperformed the CFI over the 1978-81 period. In earlier years, however, the CFI clearly outperformed the S&P. Relative performances of the stock and commodities futures markets appear to be sensitive to investment horizon.

Regression analysis indicates virtually no relationship between the rates of return of the two series. Risk and return, however, increase with horizon, whereas skewness and kurtosis are generally negatively related to horizon. Investors should be aware of these factors when selecting investment horizons.

*The authors thank Richard W. McEnally for his helpful comments.
Financial Analysts Journal, July–August, 1985. Reprinted with permission.

Investigation of the lead-lag relation between the two series confirms their independence. The S&P led the CFI by one day in 1969 and in 1972, while the two were instantaneously related in 1970. Data for 1973 through 1981 showed complete independence, regardless of evaluation technique.

These results suggest that commodity futures contracts may be used in conjunction with an equity portfolio to help reduce risks and enhance portfolio returns. Opportunities for profitable arbitrage between the two indexes are not likely, however.

Introduction

Can the commodity futures market provide diversification for the underlying stock market? Are there arbitrage possibilities between stock and commodity markets resulting from lead-lag relations? This article evaluates the distributional and causal relations between the stock and commodity futures market indexes.

Characteristics of the Market Indexes

Indexes provide a benchmark against which individual contracts and stocks can be compared. We used the Standard & Poor's 500 as the daily stock index. The daily commodity futures index is based on futures contract prices for 27 commodities and is constructed by the Commodity Research Bureau, Inc. The sample period is January 1, 1978 through December 31, 1981.[1]

The distributional characteristics of an index can be described by the first four moments.[2] These are its mean return, the standard deviation of return about the mean, skewness (a measure of the dispersion of returns about the mean) and kurtosis (a measure of the relative proportion of small or large, as compared to medium-sized, deviations from the mean). We calculated these moments using daily data for the stock market index (S&P 500) and the commodity futures market index (CFI). We computed the rates of return assuming we were on the "long" side of the market and did not adjust them for interest rates.[3]

Tables 7-1 and 7-2 show the first four moments of percentage returns from the CFI and S&P indexes. Each statistic is calculated for all horizons from one to 22 days in order to investigate in detail the impact of horizon on the four measures. The 22-day horizon approximates one month in trading days and is selected as the limit.

Table 7-1   Statistics on the Commodity Futures Index, 1978–1981

Arithmetic or Logarithmic	Horizon (Days)	Mean Return	Standard Deviation	Skewness	Kurtosis
Arithmetic	1	0.00025	0.00681	− 0.32893*	1.41077*
Logarithmic	1	0.00023	0.00682	− 0.36283*	1.45264*
Arithmetic	2	0.00051	0.00996	− 0.41229*	1.61525*
Logarithmic	2	0.00046	0.00997	− 0.46441*	1.72820*
Arithmetic	3	0.00075	0.01227	− 0.42874*	0.56471*
Logarithmic	3	0.00067	0.01229	− 0.47282*	0.62038*
Arithmetic	4	0.00103	0.01512	− 0.70900*	2.87293*
Logarithmic	4	0.00091	0.01519	− 0.81241*	3.32472*
Arithmetic	5	0.00129	0.01767	− 0.87678*	2.68768*
Logarithmic	5	0.00113	0.01779	− 0.98527*	3.14553*
Arithmetic	6	0.00151	0.01788	− 0.71355*	0.87659*
Logarithmic	6	0.00135	0.01797	− 0.77780*	1.00061*
Arithmetic	7	0.00178	0.01883	− 0.42292*	0.15598
Logarithmic	7	0.00161	0.01888	− 0.47957*	0.24912
Arithmetic	8	0.00199	0.01900	− 0.43524*	− 0.20927
Logarithmic	8	0.00181	0.01904	− 0.48125*	− 0.15106
Arithmetic	9	0.00221	0.02219	− 0.40874*	0.15658
Logarithmic	9	0.00196	0.02226	− 0.47551*	0.23374
Arithmetic	10	0.00258	0.02485	− 0.90145*	3.49222*
Logarithmic	10	0.00226	0.02511	− 1.08666*	4.27981*
Arithmetic	11	0.00283	0.02423	− 0.54730*	0.51748
Logarithmic	11	0.00253	0.02434	− 0.63067*	0.73033
Arithmetic	12	0.00303	0.02616	− 0.56036*	1.05231*
Logarithmic	12	0.00268	0.02630	− 0.67086*	1.29841*
Arithmetic	13	0.00341	0.02872	− 0.68135*	1.28291*
Logarithmic	13	0.00299	0.02895	− 0.80780*	1.63488*
Arithmetic	14	0.00353	0.02717	− 0.63135*	1.20184*
Logarithmic	14	0.00315	0.02735	− 0.74880*	1.46983*
Arithmetic	15	0.00378	0.02681	− 0.09393	− 0.37082
Logarithmic	15	0.00341	0.02677	− 0.15820	− 0.38704
Arithmetic	16	0.00409	0.02883	− 0.45864	0.60007
Logarithmic	16	0.00367	0.02894	− 0.56688*	0.89338
Arithmetic	17	0.00414	0.03256	− 0.77674*	1.68916*
Logarithmic	17	0.00387	0.03290	− 0.93436*	2.15059*
Arithmetic	18	0.00461	0.03207	0.05335	− 0.00718
Logarithmic	18	0.00514	0.03946	− 0.04042	− 0.06383
Arithmetic	19	0.00537	0.03842	− 0.23525	− 0.35501
Logarithmic	19	0.00462	0.03846	− 0.32776	− 0.27687
Arithmetic	20	0.00522	0.03693	− 0.48526	− 0.21896
Logarithmic	20	0.00452	0.03713	− 0.57376*	− 0.04815
Arithmetic	21	0.00618	0.03908	− 0.44034	0.38446
Logarithmic	21	0.00540	0.03926	− 0.57288*	0.62765
Arithmetic	22	0.00581	0.04011	− 0.07872	− 0.63015
Logarithmic	22	0.00500	0.04000	− 0.16144	− 0.58331

*Significantly different from zero at the 95% level of confidence.

Table 7-2   Statistics on the Standard & Poor's 500, 1978–1981

Arithmetic or Logarithmic	Horizon (Days)	Mean Return	Standard Deviation	Skewness	Kurtosis
Arithmetic	1	0.00033	0.01007	− 0.02364	21.23223*
Logarithmic	1	0.00028	0.01008	− 0.37624*	21.58152*
Arithmetic	2	0.00067	0.01510	− 0.10277	7.60066*
Logarithmic	2	0.00055	0.01512	− 0.32108*	7.78056*
Arithmetic	3	0.00099	0.01711	− 0.19169	3.71323*
Logarithmic	3	0.00085	0.01714	− 0.33854*	3.86467*
Arithmetic	4	0.00132	0.02049	− 0.29326*	1.79889*
Logarithmic	4	0.00111	0.02054	− 0.40908*	1.96497*
Arithmetic	5	0.00165	0.02242	− 0.22975	2.38878*
Logarithmic	5	0.00140	0.02247	− 0.37296*	2.33457*
Arithmetic	6	0.00195	0.02234	− 0.12305	− 0.01829
Logarithmic	6	0.00170	0.02234	− 0.18864	− 0.01308
Arithmetic	7	0.00242	0.02732	− 0.14658	0.85510*
Logarithmic	7	0.00204	0.02735	− 0.26187	0.86755*
Arithmetic	8	0.00266	0.02906	− 0.22630	0.05384
Logarithmic	8	0.00224	0.02911	− 0.31378	0.10447
Arithmetic	9	0.00274	0.02717	− 0.11042	− 0.04960
Logarithmic	9	0.00237	0.02716	− 0.18815	− 0.07543
Arithmetic	10	0.00339	0.03425	− 0.06042	1.28802*
Logarithmic	10	0.00280	0.03424	− 0.22272	1.13082*
Arithmetic	11	0.00364	0.02923	− 0.15070	− 0.18524
Logarithmic	11	0.00321	0.02921	− 0.22897	− 0.16450
Arithmetic	12	0.00357	0.03337	− 0.57117*	0.19989
Logarithmic	12	0.00300	0.03362	− 0.66537*	0.30827
Arithmetic	13	0.00450	0.03706	− 0.71036*	0.79513
Logarithmic	13	0.00379	0.03746	− 0.83889*	0.99016*
Arithmetic	14	0.00479	0.04212	0.04276	0.24423
Logarithmic	14	0.00389	0.04199	− 0.09492	0.15984
Arithmetic	15	0.00506	0.03914	− 0.01266	0.70404
Logarithmic	15	0.00428	0.03905	− 0.16837	0.66079
Arithmetic	16	0.00541	0.04082	− 0.54805*	0.37764
Logarithmic	16	0.00456	0.04115	− 0.67648*	0.54411
Arithmetic	17	0.00551	0.03876	− 0.44353	0.60429
Logarithmic	17	0.00474	0.03897	− 0.58344*	0.72527
Arithmetic	18	0.00593	0.03940	− 0.28725	− 0.33501
Logarithmic	18	0.00514	0.03946	− 0.38195	− 0.23979
Arithmetic	19	0.00659	0.04342	− 0.63991*	0.36831
Logarithmic	19	0.00562	0.04385	− 0.76769*	0.52355
Arithmetic	20	0.00658	0.04410	− 0.10758	− 0.79464
Logarithmic	20	0.00559	0.04399	− 0.18664	− 0.76287
Arithmetic	21	0.00722	0.04483	− 0.25652	− 0.55157
Logarithmic	21	0.00619	0.04485	− 0.34876	− 0.51392
Arithmetic	22	0.00727	0.04372	− 0.71347*	1.06147*
Logarithmic	22	0.00628	0.04422	− 0.88509*	1.39780*

*Significantly different from zero at the 95% level of confidence.

All mean returns are positive and increase proportionately with horizon.[4] They and their standard deviations are generally smaller for the CFI than for the S&P. These results differ sharply from those of previous tests based on different time periods.[5] Which market performs best appears to depend upon the sample period used.

Although both relative skewness and relative kurtosis are important statistics in evaluating rates of return of alternative investment media, commodity futures markets have heretofore been tested for neither.[6] Our results, in Table 7-1 and 7-2, show that the logarithmic transformation (i.e., proportional rather than arithmetic) generally increases negative skewness. This same transformation generally increases positive kurtosis, although not consistently.

These results imply that logarithmic transformations do not normalize the data. Furthermore, almost all the skewness statistics are negative, with a higher proportion being significant for the CFI than for the S&P.[7] That is, over this period the CFI demonstrated less upside potential than the S&P. Finally, the tables show that relative kurtosis for both indexes is significant for one-half or less of the cases, and these coefficients are generally associated with smaller horizons. The significant kurtoses imply that there is an unstable variance, meaning risk is less predictable.[8]

Finance theory suggests that investors prefer return and positive skewness and dislike risk and negative skewness. Our analysis indicates that these measures are very sensitive to the sample period. In an earlier time period, futures outperformed stocks and the former had mainly positive skewness. More recently, stocks have done slightly better than futures, although both showed positive returns, and the skewness coefficients have become predominantly negative. This indicates that the lower (negative) tail of the distribution is extended. Finally, more recent data show less kurtosis coefficients to be significant than the earlier data. This implies that the variance in the recent period has become more predictable.

Relation Between the Indexes

To test for systematic risk in the CFI, we regressed it on the S&P, using the following equation:

$$R_{cjt} = \sigma_j + \beta_j R_{mjt} + \varepsilon_{jt},$$

where

R_c = rates of return for the CFI,
R_m = rates of return for the S&P,
$j = 1, \ldots, 22$ (unit of horizon), and
$t = 1, \ldots, n$ (number of observations).

This equation relates the percentage return on the CFI to the percentage return on the S&P. The larger the β, the greater the systematic (nondiversifiable) risk. Systematic risk is the portion of total risk that hinders rather than helps diversification. Investors would require more return to induce them to include commodity futures in a stock portfolio if β is large, because futures would not have the capacity to reduce risk through diversification. A small β indicates primarily unsystematic (diversifiable) risk, or a low level of systematic risk.

Table 7-3 gives the regression results for each of 22 horizons. No β coefficient is statistically significantly different from zero; regressions on 1972–77 data showed similar results. That is, there is virtually no relation, or systematic risk, between the two indexes.[9] These results imply that commodities in the CFI can be included in an equity portfolio to reduce risk and improve performance of the portfolio, regardless of horizon. Futures contracts as a whole have no systematic risk relative to stocks, and provide diversification for a stock portfolio.[10]

When regressed against time, the first four moments are generally not independent of horizon, but the signs vary. Mean return and standard deviation of both indexes and CFI skewness are positively related to horizon, whereas S&P skewness and kurtoses of both indexes are negatively related to horizon. These results suggest that the relative risk assumed can change with investment horizon, as well as the negative impact of skewness and kurtosis. Investors should be aware of this when selecting investment horizon.

The Lead-Lag Relationship

Given that investments in commodity futures can provide diversification for equity portfolios, the fund manager now needs to know the informational linkages between the markets in order to make investments in the proper sequence. Leads and lags present arbitrage possibilities between stock and commodity markets.

We might expect that the link of causality between the S&P and CFI (called X_t and Y_t, respectively) would be revealed through their sample cross-correlations.[11] Alternatively, we might consider regressing Y_t on past and

Table 7-3   β **Coefficient from Regressing Commodity Futures Index on Stock Index over 22 Horizons, 1978 – 1981 (Standard errors in parentheses)**

Horizon (Days)	Arithmetic	Logarithmic
1	0.00497	0.00510
	(0.02136)	(0.02137)
2	0.02019	0.01948
	(0.02948)	(0.02950)
3	− 0.02990	− 0.03041
	(0.03929)	(0.03932)
4	0.00742	0.00700
	(0.04675)	(0.04686)
5	− 0.01436	− 0.01524
	(0.05600)	(0.05628)
6	− 0.01295	− 0.01333
	(0.06228)	(0.06262)
7	0.01307	0.01224
	(0.05801)	(0.05812)
8	0.01648	0.01622
	(0.05892)	(0.05898)
9	− 0.09364	− 0.09488
	(0.07775)	(0.07800)
10	− 0.01919	− 0.02183
	(0.07328)	(0.07405)
11	− 0.13403	− 0.13544
	(0.08670)	(0.08713)
12	− 0.01441	− 0.01263
	(0.08707)	(0.08691)
13	− 0.05737	− 0.05790
	(0.08925)	(0.08899)
14	− 0.01865	− 0.02386
	(0.07764)	(0.07837)
15	− 0.03113	− 0.03370
	(0.08553)	(0.08558)
16	− 0.01869	− 0.019905
	(0.09116)	(0.09077)
17	− 0.05374	− 0.05561
	(0.11104)	(0.11158)
18	− 0.14259	− 0.14184
	(0.11009)	(0.10948)
19	− 0.05815	− 0.05691
	(0.12489)	(0.12377)
20	− 0.09016	− 0.09597
	(0.12016)	(0.12101)
21	− 0.05832	− 0.06210
	(0.12968)	(0.13018)
22	− 0.03889	− 0.03875
	(0.13978)	(0.13782)

present X_t, or vice versa, and performing an F test on the appropriate set of regression coefficients.[12]

In practice, however, both these procedures (correlation and regression) can be misleading if the autocorrelation in the series is not taken into account. Ignoring autocorrelation results in overestimating the significance of the tests and asserting relations that do not exist. One solution proposed is to model the univariate series and then to analyze the relation of the residuals.[13] The appendix describes the procedure.

We expanded the two series back to 1968 and examined each calendar year of data individually, rather than as a single series. The extension of both series gives us an opportunity to examine whether the relation between the CFI and S&P has changed over time in response to structural changes in the U.S. economy in the early 1970s, specifically significantly higher energy and food prices. Table 7-4 presents the results of applying the Box-Jenkins technique to the daily S&P and CFI indexes. All but one are expressed in first differences and most contain autoregressive processes.

Table 7-5 summarizes the results from dependence tests described in the appendix. The results show a positive lead-lag relation between the CFI and S&P for three years—1969, 1970 and 1972. The indexes were independent for each of the other years. These results are consistent regardless of the number of lags.

To determine which series led the other in the three years 1969, 1970 and 1972, we computed statistics for the three-day lag. Table 7-6 gives the results, which indicate that the S&P led the CFI by one day in 1969; that in 1970 the S&P and CFI were instantaneously related within one day; and that the S&P led the CFI by one day in 1972.

The S&P had a tendency to lead the CFI prior to 1973, but the tendency was not strong. From 1973 onward, there is no relation between the two series. This suggests that structural changes in the early 1970s did affect the relation between the two indexes.

Implications for Investors

Including commodity futures contracts in an equity portfolio may help reduce risks and enhance portfolio performance. The futures contracts will not only provide diversification, which reduces overall portfolio risk, but they have the potential to outperform stock investments. However, the independence between the two indexes suggests that profitable arbitrage opportunities do not exist, although arbitrage between individual stocks in the S&P 500 and individual futures contracts in the CFI may exist.

Table 7-4   **Results of Box-Jenkins Analysis on S&P and CFI Indexes, 1968 – 1981**

Year	Index	AR Process[a]	Differences	MA Process	Coefficients[b]		
1968	CFI	1	0	0	0.99		
	S&P	1, 3	1	0	0.24	0.16	
1969	CFI	1	1	0	-0.18		
	S&P	1, 2	1	0	0.38	-0.11	
1970	CFI	1	1	0	-0.20		
	S&P	1, 2, 6	1	0	0.38	-0.08	-0.12
1971	CFI	1	1	0	-0.03		
	S&P	1	1	0	0.26		
1972	CFI	1, 2, 4	1	0	0.26	-0.09	0.20
	S&P	1	1	0	0.29		
1973	CFI	1, 2, 4	1	0	0.20	-0.18	0.16
	S&P	1, 2, 5	1	0	0.26	-0.11	-0.12
1974	CFI	1, 2, 4	1	0	0.01	-0.14	0.16
	S&P	1, 2	1	0	0.31	-0.09	
1975	CFI	1	1	0	0.03		
	S&P	1, 2, 5	1	0	0.28	-0.16	-0.00
1976	CFI	1	1	0	-0.06		
	S&P	1	1	0	0.14		
1977	CFI	1	1	0	0.12		
	S&P	1, 6	1	0	0.20	-0.15	
1977	CFI	0	1	1	-0.18		
	S&P	0	1	0			
1979	CFI	0	1	0			
	S&P	1	1	0	0.16		
1980	CFI	1	1	0	0.13		
	S&P	0	1	1	0.35		
1981	CFI	0	1	0			
	S&P	0	1	1	0.46		

[a]The numbers indicate the specific autoregressive processes in the model.
[b]The coefficients correspond to the specific autoregression or moving average element in the model.

Table 7-5   Test Results of Univariate Cross-Correlation Analysis[a]

Year	Five-Day Lag Q	vs. 19.7[b]	17.3[c]	Three-Day Lag Q	vs. 14.0[b]	12.0[c]	One-Day Lag Q	vs. 7.8[b]	6.2[c]
1968	7.1	−	−	2.1	−	−	1.3	−	−
1969	15.6	−	−	14.2	+	+	7.5	±	+
1970	19.3	±	+	13.4	±	+	7.2	±	+
1971	8.6	−	−	3.6	−	−	1.6	−	−
1972	22.6	+	+	16.8	+	+	10.2	+	+
1973	15.9	−	−	9.4	−	−	4.0	−	−
1974	13.6	−	−	9.1	−	−	1.2	−	−
1975	9.2	−	−	3.3	−	−	1.6	−	−
1976	12.3	−	−	5.8	−	−	3.8	−	−
1977	9.7	−	−	4.3	−	−	1.4	−	−
1978	4.20	−	−	2.62	−	−	0.65	−	−
1979	8.26	−	−	4.63	−	−	0.55	−	−
1980	6.90	−	−	4.87	−	−	1.44	−	−
1981	13.34	−	−	4.05	−	−	0.12	−	−

[a]Minus sign indicates that S&P and CFI are independent. Plus sign indicates dependence. Combined sign indicates supposed dependence.
[b]Ninety-five percent confidence level.
[c]Ninety percent confidence level.

Table 7-6   Direction of Causality, Three-Day Lag[a]

Year	S&P-CFI	vs. 7.8[b]	6.2[c]	CFI-S&P	vs. 7.8[b]	6.2[c]
1969	12.5	+	+	1.2	−	−
1970	5.4	−	−	1.4	−	−
1972	7.8	+	+	1.7	+	−

[a]Minus sign indicates independence. Plus sign indicates dependence.
[b]Ninety-five percent confidence level.
[c]Ninety percent confidence level.

Appendix

Lead-Lag Relation

This appendix describes the univariate residual cross-correlation procedure for determining the linear lead-lag relation between the two series.
Suppose the two series X_t and Y_t are described by the following models:

$$\hat{u}_t = F(B)X_t, \tag{A1}$$

$$\hat{v}_t = G(B)Y_t. \tag{A2}$$

The $\hat{u}_t$ and $\hat{v}_t$ are by definition constructed free from autocorrelation, so
that the defects in the use of correlation procedures on the original series
should now be removed. Thus the cross-correlation between the u's and v's
defined at lag k as:[14]

$$\rho_{uv}(k) = \frac{E(u_{t-k}, v_t)}{[E(u_t^2)E(v_t^2)]^{1/2}} \tag{A3}$$

may be used to assess lead-lag relation between X_t and Y_t.

The u's and v's of Equation (A3) are not observable. However, their
estimates, $\hat{u}_t$ and $\hat{v}_t$, are fitted in Equations (A1-A2).

Once the white noise residuals are obtained for each original time series,
statistical tests of the significance of the calculated cross-correlations between the u's and v's, denoted as the $r_{\hat{u}\hat{v}}(k)$'s, may be used to infer the
lead-lag relation between X_t and Y_t. If X_t and Y_t are independent, the $r_{\hat{u}\hat{v}}(k)$'s
are asymptotically, independently and normally distributed with zero mean
and variance N^{-1}, where N is the sample size.

The hypothesis that X_t and Y_t are independent may be rejected at significant level a if:

$$Q_{2m+1} = N \sum_{k=-m}^{+m} (r_{\hat{u}\hat{v}}(k))^2 > X_{\alpha,2m+1}^2, \tag{A4}$$

where $X_{\alpha,2m+1}^2$ is the upper α percentage point of the chi-square distribution with 2m + 1 degrees of freedom; and m is chosen so as to include all
$p_{\hat{u}\hat{v}}(k)$'s expected to differ from zero. The contention that X_t leads Y_t is
suggested at significant level α if:

$$Q_m = N \sum_{k=1}^{m} (\hat{r}_{\hat{u}\hat{v}}(k))^2 > X_{\alpha,m}^2. \tag{A5}$$

Similarly, Y_t leads X_t may be asserted at α if:

$$Q_{\overline{m}} = N \sum_{k=-1}^{-m} (\hat{r}_{\hat{u}\hat{v}}(k))^2 > X_{\alpha,m}^2. \tag{A6}$$

The significance of an individual $\hat{r}_{\hat{u}\hat{v}}(k)$ may be determined by comparison to its standard error, $N^{-1/2}$. The convention is to judge an $\hat{r}_{\hat{u}\hat{v}}(k)$ significant if it is at least twice as large as its standard error (theoretically, ± 2 (N - k)$^{-1/2}$).

To test the dependence between the two indexes CFI and S&P, we looked at three different lags—five days, three days and one day. We computed respectively Q_{11}, Q_7 and Q_3, the Q_{2m+1} statistics related to five, three and one days of lag.

We then compared the Q statistics with the value of $X_{\alpha,2m+1}^2$ with m = 5, 3 and 1 (degrees of freedom) and α = 95% or 90% of confidence. If $Q_i > X_{\alpha,i}^2$, then the S&P and CFI are dependent. If $Q_i = X_{\alpha,i}^2$, then we suppose the S&P and CFI are dependent. If $Q_i < X_{\alpha,i}^2$, then the S&P and CFI are independent.

Endnotes

1.   Bodie, Z. and Rosansky, V. ("Risk and Return in Commodity Futures," *Financial Analysts Journal*, May/June 1980, pp. 27–39) compared rates of return on commodity futures contracts with those on stocks and bonds, but examined individual contracts using quarterly data from 1950 to 1976. This article uses daily and more recent data and multiple investment horizons. Bodie and Rosansky did not use a standard commodity index, as this article does, nor did they provide statistical tests of distribution beyond the first two moments.

2.   The impact of investment horizon on the moments of a distribution of market returns is discussed in: Brenner, M., "On the Stability of the Distribution of the Market Component in Stock Price Changes," *Journal of Financial and Quantitative Analysis*, 1974, pp. 945–961; Fogler, H.K. and Radcliff, R.C., "A Note on Measurement of Skewness," *Journal of Financial and Quantitative Analysis*, 1974, pp. 485–489; and Lee, C.F.,

"Investment Horizon and the Functional Form of the Capital Asset Pricing Model," *Review of Economics and Statistics*, 1976, pp. 356–363.

3.   The relative skewness and kurtosis are defined as:

$$\text{skewness } (g_1) = \frac{\Sigma(X - \overline{X})^3/n}{[\Sigma(X - \overline{X})^2/n]^{3/2}}$$

$$\text{kurotsis } (g_2) = \frac{\Sigma(X - \overline{X})^4/n}{[\Sigma(X - \overline{X})^2/n]^2} - 3.$$

Tests for these statistics followed G.W. Snedecor and W.G. Cochran, *Statistical Methods*, 6th ed. (Ames, Iowa: Iowa State University Press, 1967). This method allows for nonnormality of distributions. Values of zero for g_1 and g_2 imply no skewness or kurtosis in the sample.

4.   Mathematically, one would expect the geometric rates of return to vary proportionately with horizon. This will not always be exactly the case, however, because of varying ending observations. For a time series of 11 observations, for example, the average geometric return for a one-day horizon is $(-\log P_1 + \log P_{11})/10$, for a two-day horizon it is $(-\log P_1 + \log P_{11})/5$, whereas for a four-day horizon it is $(-\log P_1 + \log P_9)/2$. Note that in the four-day horizon case the last observation differs from the one and two-day horizons, and that two observations are lost. Thus in our sample of 1,004 observations, the ending observation is different for most horizons, and between the 21- and 22-day horizons it can vary as much as one- half month. In empirical application it is difficult to estimate returns over several horizons without losing observations, and the actual returns will not coincide with theoretical expectations if the time series shows instability at the end.

5.   These results differ sharply from those based on 1972 through 1977 data analyzed in C.F. Lee and R.M. Leuthold, "Impact of Investment Horizon on the Determination of Risk and Return in the Commodity Futures Market" (Department of Agricultural Economics Staff Paper No. 80 E-110, University of Illinois, Urbana-Champaign, March 1980). The earlier data showed CFI rates of return increasing proportionately with horizon, but S&P rates of return were erratic and most often negative.

6. See Folger and Radcliff, "A Note on Measurement of Skewness," *op. cit.*; R.W. McEnally, "A Note on the Return Behavior of High Risk Common Stock," *Journal of Finance,* 1974, pp. 199–202; A. Kraus and R.H. Litzenberger, "Skewness Preference and the Valuation of Risky Assets," *Journal of Finance,* 1976, pp. 1084–1100; and C.F. Lee, "Functional Form, Skewness Effect, and the Risk-Return Relationship," *Journal of Financial and Quantitative Analysis,* 1977, pp. 55–72, for details.

7. This is contrary to 1972–77 results, which showed a much smaller proportion of the coefficients to be significant and most, at least for the CFI, positive. W.L. Beedles ("On the Asymmetry of Market Returns," *Journal of Financial and Quantitative Analysis,* 1979, pp. 653–660) found some skewness for stock market rates of return in both logarithmic and arithmetic cases, but he did not investigate the effect of horizon.

8. Since the variance is a function of kurtosis, as shown by Snedecor and Cochran, Statistical Methods, op. cit., and C.F. Lee and C. Wu, "The Impacts of Skewness and Kurtosis on Risk Estimation and Determination" (Faculty Working Paper No. 888, College of Commerce and Business Administration, University of Illinois, Urbana-Champaign, 1982).

9. The results show that most of the beta coefficients are, in fact, negative. Negative beta coefficients can be used to cancel other positive betas. The negative beta does not therefore represent systematic risk in terms of the portfolio diversification process (see M. Ben-Horim and H. Levy, "Total Risk, Diversifiable Risk and Non-Diversifiable Risk: A Pedagogic Note," *Journal of Financial and Quantitative Analysis,* 1980, pp. 289–297). Nevertheless, betas close to zero conform to individual commodity results found under different circumstances by Bodie and Rosansky, "Risk and Return," op. cit. and K. Dusak, "Futures Trading and Investor Returns: An Investigation of Commodity Market Risk Premiums" *Journal of Political Economics,* 1973, pp. 1387–1406.

10. If individual stocks and commodity returns were computed along with their correlation coefficients, portfolios could be developed as in A.A. Robichek, R.A. Cohn and J.J. Pringle, "Returns on Alternative Investment Media and Implications for Portfolio Construction," *Journal of Business,* 1972, pp. 427–443.

    Although data and method are completely different, our results are consistent with those of G.D. Gay and S. Manaster in "Hedging Against Commodity Price Inflation: Stocks and Bills as Substitutes for Futures Contracts," Journal of Business, 1982, pp. 317–343; they found that stock returns contain little information about relative commodity price changes.

11. Sample autocorrelations are found by:

$$r_{xy}(k) = \frac{\Sigma(X_{t-k} - \overline{X})(Y_t - \overline{Y})}{[\Sigma(X_t - \overline{X})^2 \, \Sigma(Y_t - \overline{Y})^2]^{1/2}} \, .$$

12. This method has been used by J.C. Francis ("Intertemporal Differences in Systematic Stock Price Movements," *Journal of Financial and Quantitative Analysis,* 1975, pp. 205–217) to investigate possible lead-lag relations between the market rates of return and individual stock rates of return.

13. This solution is proposed by L.D. Haugh in "Checking the Independence of Two Covariance-Stationary Time Series: A Univariate Residual Cross Correlation Approach," *Journal of the American Statistical Association,* 1976, pp. 378–385 and by D.A. Pierce, "Relationships—and the Lack Thereof—Between Economic Time Series, with Special References to Money and Interest Rates," *Journal of the American Statistical Association,* 1977, pp. 11–22.

14. This follows L.D. Haugh and G.E.P. Box, "Identification of Dynamic Regression (Distributed Lag) Models Connecting Two Time Series," *Journal of the American Statistical Association,* 1977, pp. 121-130.

Chapter Eight

Management Summary

Title: "Examination of Commodity Fund Performance"

Publication: *Review of Research in Futures Markets,* Vol. 4, 1985

Authors: B. Wade Brorsen, Assistant Professor, Purdue University
Scott H. Irwin, doctoral student, Purdue University

Data: Monthly returns for the period December, 1978 through May, 1983, for stocks (S & P 500), U.S. Treasury Bills, and commodity funds.

Methodology: The performance of public and private pool commodity funds as stand-alone investments was analyzed using stochastic dominance, a technique which ranks investments based on their demonstrated ability to control risk of not achieving a given minimum level of return. A procedure which analyzes dominance from a perspective of risk seeking, risk neutral and risk averse investors was applied.

Results: The results indicate that risk seeking investors would find futures funds superior to stocks and Treasury Bills. Risk-neutral to slightly risk-averse investors would prefer stocks, and highly risk averse investors would prefer Treasury Bills. The authors concluded they could not reject the hypothesis of efficient futures markets.

Examination of Commodity Fund Performance*

B. Wade Brorsen
Scott H. Irwin

Abstract

The performance of commodity funds is evaluated using Meyer's stochastic dominance procedure. Monthly returns of the funds are compared to monthly returns from stocks and Treasury bills. The results indicate risk-seeking investors would prefer the funds, risk-neutral or slightly risk-averse investors would prefer stocks, and highly risk-averse investors would prefer Treasury bills. Since most investors are not risk seeking, only a small number of investors would prefer commodity funds. Thus, the hypothesis of efficiency futures markets cannot be rejected.

Introduction

Commodity funds have grown rapidly since their introduction in 1976. Nine such funds were active in January 1979 while 64 were in existence as of June 1983. Over the same period, the dollar amount invested in these funds increased from $120 million to $400 million (Baratz [1983]).

Commodity funds, which trade commodity futures contracts, operate similarly to the mutual funds that invest in securities. Typically, a commod-

*Research support from the Columbia University Center for the Study of Futures Markets is gratefully acknowledged.
Review of Research in Futures Markets, Vol. 4, No. 1, 1985, copyright 1985 by Board of Trade of the City of Chicago. Reprinted with permission.

ity fund is organized in the following fashion: a brokerage house, acting as general partner, sets up a limited partnership registered with the Securities and Exchange Commission, and issues a prospectus. It may call, for example, for a $5 million fund, consisting of 5,000 units of $1,000 each. A minimum purchase of five units is generally required. Public commodity funds differ from private pools run by some brokers that are made up of 35 or fewer investors, each of whom invests more than most limited partners in public funds. Also, private pools are not required to be registered with the Securities and Exchange Commission.

The buying and selling of futures contracts for a commodity fund is usually carried out by an independent, outside trading advisor in return for a fee and percentage of profits. A distinguishing characteristic of fund managers is their reliance on technical analysis to guide trading decisions. The two most frequently used types are charting and trend-following "systems." Exceptions are Harvest Futures Fund I, Harvest Futures Fund II, and Lake Forest Futures Fund whose trading advisors use a combination of technical and fundamental analysis.

Commodity funds provide investors with several advantages. First, they provide a diversified futures market portfolio. Second, funds offer a chance to participate in futures trading while limiting potential losses to the size of the initial investment. Third, they provide professional management whose trading decisions may well be "better" than the decisions of most of the investing public. Finally, funds offer advantages, such as earning interest on margin deposits, otherwise available only to large traders.

Despite the advantages, commodity funds subject investors to considerable risk. For example, the front page of the prospectus for each fund reads: "The partnership will trade commodity futures contracts. Such business and these securities involve a high degree of risk. These securities are suitable for investment only by a person who can afford to lose his entire investment" (Heinold Securities, Inc.; Blyth Eastman Dillon, Inc.) Precisely because of this riskiness, investors need information concerning the ranking of commodity funds as an investment alternative. Other researchers interested in evaluating these funds as investments used inadequate techniques (*Futures Industry's Managed Account Reports*). More information can be gained by using Meyer's stochastic dominance procedure (Meyer [1977a]) to compare the performance of these funds to alternative investments.

In this chapter, the performance of commodity funds is compared to returns from common stocks (as measured by Standard & Poor's Composite Index) and U.S. Treasury bills. These results are used to draw implications concerning (1) the performance of commodity funds relative to alternative investments, and (2) the efficiency of futures markets.

The first section of the chapter examines risk-adjusted performance measures followed by market-efficiency concepts. Subsequent sections present the data and testing results. Finally, conclusions are drawn regarding the investment performance of commodity funds and futures market efficiency.

Stochastic Dominance

The search for a risk-adjusted measure of investment performance has been the focus of much research. Early efforts sought to produce a single measure that included risk (Sharpe; Treynor; Jensen). One of these, Sharpe's reward-to-variability criterion, was used by Powers to evaluate the futures funds. Unfortunately, this measure has been criticized because it is correlated with variability (Ang and Chua; Wilson and Jones).

Theoretical research on risk usually assumes investors attempt to maximize their expected utility. Empirical work has often considered only the mean and variance of probability distributions, placing unnecessary restrictions on the expected utility function. Rothschild and Stiglitz narrowed the gap between the theoretical and empirical work on risk by introducing a theoretically valid and empirically useful definition of increasing risk. This definition considers the entire probability distribution instead of just the first two moments.

The ranking of distributions can be accomplished by stochastic dominance procedures (Hadar and Russell; Hanoch and Levy). In theory, these stochastic dominance criteria are ideal methods for ranking distributions, but, in practice, they work poorly because of the large number of distributions that cannot be ranked. Furthermore, only first-degree stochastic dominance allows for risk-seeking behavior which we might expect for some investors in futures funds. These problems can be negated by using a method introduced by Meyer [1977a] that utilizes the Arrow and Pratt measure of local risk aversion, $r(X) = -U''(X)/U'(X)$, where X is either income or wealth and $U'(X)$ and $U''(X)$ are the first and second derivatives of the utility function. Any utility function can be uniquely expressed in terms of $r(X)$ (Pratt). The sign of the second derivative of the utility function, $U''(X)$, indicates whether an investor is risk averse [$U''(X) < 0$] or risk seeking [$U''(X) > 0$].

Meyer considers a group of decision-makers whose risk preferences fall in a certain interval. He defines $(U[r_1(X), r_2(X)]$ as the set of agents with preferences represented by $r(X)$ such that

$$r_1(X) \leq r(X) \leq r_2(X) \ VX \tag{1}$$

where $r_1(X)$ and $r_2(X)$ are known functions. For first-degree stochastic dominance, $r_1(X) = -\infty$ and $r_2(X) = +\infty$, while, for second-degree stochastic dominance, the range is $[0, +\infty]$.

Empirical applications of Meyer's procedure have assumed $r_1(X)$ and $r_2(X)$ to be constants, thus investigating stochastic dominance over intervals (Meyer [1977b]; Kramer and Pope; King and Robison [1981a]; King and Robison [1981b]; Martin and Petty). The difficulty in empirical application of Meyer's procedure is specifying $r_1(X)$ and $r_2(X)$. Meyer [1977b] selected several intervals from the range [0.5,6] based on the certainty equivalence rule. The most comprehensive work to date on measuring individual risk preferences is a review of studies in the agricultural economics literature by Young et al. This study was used by Kramer and Pope to select $r_1(X)$ and $r_2(X)$ as a series of intervals from the range [-.04, .03]. King and Robison [1981b] suggest the range [-.001, .01] based on their estimates of individual risk preferences.

These estimates were based on risk preferences of farmers, not on the risk preferences of investors. We might expect more extreme risk-seeking behavior for commodity fund investors and more extreme risk-averse values for investors in Treasury bills. Also $r(X)$ is sensitive to the units of measurement. Kramer and Pope adjusted their data to a mean of 20. King and Robison suggested their range for annual net income. The data used in this study have a lower mean. Thus, we will consider a slightly wider range than the one considered by Kramer and Pope and King and Robison [1981b].

Market Efficiency

Fama defined an efficient market as one that fully reflects all available information and then used this definition to develop tests of efficiency. Danthine criticized Fama's zero autocorrelation in returns tests of market efficiency as simultaneously testing (1) market efficiency, (2) perfect competition, (3) risk neutrality, (4) constant returns to scale, and the impossibility of corner optima. Danthine and Panton have offered the alternative definition that an efficient market is one that does not yield a return above a return to risk. In other words, a trader cannot earn an "above normal" return. Rausser and Carter have offered further criticism—"There is a growing awareness that much of the empirical work that has been conducted on futures market efficiency is without a sound foundation." This empirical work has concentrated on a search for a random walk or more general martingale model (e.g., Dale and Workman; Stevenson and Bear). Stein argued that efficient markets would not necessarily follow a martingale if there is feedback from the price, which equates the stock demand to the stock in existence, to the rate of change in the stock. Grossman and Stiglitz argue that Fama's definition is invalid because information is costly and, thus, prices cannot perfectly reflect the information available.

A number of researchers have evaluated efficiency with tests of the forecasting ability of futures markets (e.g., Kofi; Rausser and Carter). Rausser and Carter [p. 471] argue that "if a forecasting scheme can be discovered which generates probability distributions—which in some sense stochastically dominate the futures prices probability distributions—the necessary condition (relative accuracy) for inefficiency holds." However, Rausser and Carter base their evaluation on mean-squared error criteria. Trapp has criticized these statistical procedures because they do not necessarily select the model that would yield the highest profit. Furthermore, Rausser and Carter [p. 477] admit that, in evaluating efficiency, a relative cost/benefit analysis is most important. In order to accomplish this, they suggest evaluating forecasts on the basis of achievable speculative profits adjusted for risk.

Another method employed by researchers to investigate efficiency is to simulate returns from a technical trading strategy (e.g., Peterson and Leuthold; Taylor). These studies suffer from two deficiencies: (1) they have not accounted for risk, and (2) they represent simulated rather than actual returns. Simulated returns ignore the action of scalpers and possible lags in getting an order filled. Importantly, the commodity fund returns analyzed in this paper represent actual returns and, thus, do not suffer from the previous criticisms.

The discussion in this section points out the growing consensus that an efficient market is, as Danthine suggested, one in which a trader cannot earn profits above the *normal* returns level available in other economic sectors. In this chapter, *normal* returns are represented by returns from the two most common investments, common stocks (the S&P 500) and interest-bearing deposits (U.S. Treasury bills). Meyer's stochastic dominance procedure is an ideal tool for comparing commodity fund returns to common stock and Treasury bill returns. If the futures funds are preferred to the other *normal* investments (over a range of risk preferences expected to include most investors), then commodity funds yield *above normal* returns which are characteristic of inefficient futures markets.

Data

The data consist of monthly total percentage returns from common stocks, U.S. Treasury bills, and the commodity funds. The base for the common stock returns in Standard & Poor's (S&P) Composite Index. This index is a market-value weighted index, which means the weight of each stock in the index is proportional to its price times the number of shares outstanding. The S&P Composite Index includes 500 of the largest stocks in terms of value of outstanding shares.

Ibbotson and Sinquefield's method of calculating monthly common stock returns is used. Their results are published annually and updates through May 1983 were also obtained. In their method, the monthly returns are calculated as

$$R_{m,t} = [(P_{m,\ t} + D_{m,\ t})/P_{m,\ t-1}] - 1 \qquad (2)$$

where $R_{m,\ t}$ is the common stock total return during month t; $P_{m,t}$ is the value of the S&P Composite Index at the end of month t; and $D_{m,t}$ is the estimated dividends received during month t. The series runs from December 1978 to May 1983.

The source for monthly U.S. Treasury bill returns was the same as for common stocks (Ibbotson and Sinquefield). To reflect achievable returns, rather than yields, the returns measure the gain for a one-month holding period of a one-bill portfolio. U.S. Treasury bill monthly returns are designated as

$$R_{f,\ t} = [P_{f,\ t}/P_{f,\ t-1}] - 1 \qquad (3)$$

where $R_{f,t}$ is the U.S. Treasury bill total return during month t; and $P_{f,t}$ is end-of-calendar-month-t discount bill prices. Prices used are the average of bid and ask. The series runs from December 1978 to May 1983.

Monthly commodity fund returns were obtained from Klopfenstein previous to April 1982. Thereafter, returns were taken from the monthly "Funds Review" published in *Commodities*. The total monthly return for commodity fund i during month t, $R^i_{c,\ t}$ is calculated as

$$R^i_{c,\ t} = [(NAV^i_{c,t} + D^i_{c,t})/NAV^i_{c,t-1}] - 1 \qquad (4)$$

where $NAV^i_{c,t}$ is the net asset value per unit of commodity fund i at the end of month t; and $D^i_{c,t}$ is the cash distribution received during month t.

Two sample periods were considered. The first sample, December 1978 to May 1983, contains six funds. Nine funds were in existence at the beginning of this sample period. However, one ceased trading due to the death of the trading advisor and two others were dissolved after losing over 50 percent of their capital. The bankrupt funds are not included because they have no continuous series of monthly returns and rational investors would prefer other investment alternatives to the bankrupt funds. The second sample, January 1981–May 1983, includes the six funds from the first sample plus 14 funds which started trading later than December 1979.

The mean and standard deviation of monthly returns for the funds, common stocks, and Treasury bills are presented in Table 8-1. Three funds had a mean return greater than both common stocks and Treasury bills over the 1978–1983 period. The remaining funds had positive means which were greater than the mean return to Treasury bills. All six funds had standard deviations higher than that of either common stocks or Treasury bills. When the shorter 1981–1983 period is considered, nine of the 20 funds examined had mean monthly returns greater than common stocks. Also, six funds had mean returns which were negative. Similar to the longer period, no fund had a standard deviation over 1981–1983 which was lower than common stocks or Treasury bills.

The previous information illustrates the need to analyze commodity fund returns in a framework which incorporates risk. Many funds had higher mean returns than either common stocks or Treasury bills, but this must be weighed against the substantially higher risk associated with the funds.

Results

The range of risk preferences used to compare the monthly returns of commodity funds, common stocks, and Treasury bills was [–0.1, 0.1]. This range is expected to include the majority of investors. For the period 1978–1983, all six funds are preferred to Treasury bills for all risk-seeking investors (Table 8-2). None of the funds is dominated by Treasury bills for risk-neutral preferences. Treasury bills become attractive only as the level of risk aversion is increased. One fund is preferred to Treasury bills over the full range of risk preferences considered.

The comparison with stock returns for the 1978–1983 period again shows all funds are preferred by highly risk-seeking investors (Table 8-2). The S&P 500 is preferred to half of the funds by risk-neutral investors. As with Treasury bills, the S&P 500 becomes more attractive as the level of risk aversion increases and one fund is preferred to the stocks over the full range of risk preferences considered. Only this one fund can be said to exhibit *above normal* returns. Over the period 1981–1983, fund performance is less attractive. A majority of the funds are preferred to both alternatives only for highly risk-seeking preferences (Table 8-3). Risk-neutral investors slightly favor Treasury bills over the funds during this period.[1] One fund dominates

Table 8-1   Mean and Standard Deviation of Monthly Commodity
            Fund Returns[a]

Fund or Security	Dec. 1978–May 1983		Jan. 1981–May 1983	
	Mean	Std. Dev.	Mean	Std. Dev.
U.S. Treasury Bills	0.90	0.22	0.94	0.25
S&P 500	1.54	4.48	1.16	4.54
Harvest Futures Fund I	2.73	16.39	0.63	14.05
Illinois Commodity Fund	2.10	8.79	1.63	9.22
The Resource Fund	3.08	6.17	2.30	5.93
Thomson McKinnon Futures Fund	1.41	6.72	0.97	7.18
Recovery Fund I	1.26	11.15	–1.67	9.36
Recovery Fund II	1.06	11.69	–2.47	9.27
Aries Commodity Fund	—	—	1.83	8.88
Boston Futures Fund I	—	—	–0.79	12.53
Boston Futures Fund II	—	—	–1.06	12.79
Chancellor Futures	—	—	0.55	9.19
Commodity Trend Timing	—	—	1.19	6.86
Commodity Venture	—	—	2.33	5.48
Galileo Futures Fund	—	—	0.27	8.15
Harvest Futures Fund II	—	—	1.35	14.43
Horizon Futures Fund	—	—	1.68	7.05
Hutton Commodity Partners	—	—	0.66	5.93
E. F. Hutton Commodity Ltd. Partnership II	—	—	3.37	16.88
Lake Forest Futures Fund	—	—	–1.46	7.05
Peavey Fund I	—	—	–0.90	12.78
The Futures Fund	—	—	2.30	6.65

[a]Mean and standard deviation expressed as percent per month.

Treasury bills over the full range of risk preferences considered and two
funds dominate the S&P 500.

The ranking of commodity funds, common stocks, and Treasury bills for
each period depends heavily on risk preferences (Table 8-4). For example,
E.F. Hutton's Commodity Ltd. Partnership II fund is ranked first over

Table 8-2   Comparison of Commodity Funds with Stocks and Treasury Bills, December 1978 – May 1983[a]

$r_1(X)$	$r_2(X)$	Treasury Bills			S&P 500		
		Funds>Bills	Indifferent	Bills>Funds	Funds>S&P	Indifferent	S&P>Funds
-.10	-.02	6	0	0	6	0	0
-.02	-.005	6	0	0	3	3	0
-.005	.005	5	1	0	3	0	3
.005	.02	3	2	1	2	1	3
.02	.04	1	2	3	1	1	4
.04	.10	1	0	5	1	0	5

[a]Negative values of $r(X)$ represent risk-seeking preferences while positive values represent risk aversion. Risk neutrality is represented by the range [-.005, 005].

Table 8-3   Comparison of Commodity Funds with Stocks and Treasury Bills, January 1981 – May 1983[a]

$r_1(X)$	$r_2(X)$	Treasury Bills			S&P 500		
		Funds>Bills	Indifferent	Bills>Funds	Funds>S&P	Indifferent	S&P>Funds
-.10	-.02	13	6	1	11	7	2
-.02	-.005	11	2	7	9	2	9
-.005	.005	8	3	9	7	2	11
.005	.02	6	2	12	6	1	13
.02	.04	3	3	14	3	3	14
.04	.10	1	2	17	2	1	17

[a]Negative values of $r(X)$ represent risk-seeking preferences while positive values represent risk aversion. Risk neutrality is represented by the range [-.005, 005].

Table 8-4   Ranking of Commodity Funds, Common Stocks, and U.S. Treasury Bills[a]

Period	Fund or Security	Highly Risk Seeking	Risk Neutral	Highly Risk Averse
Dec. 1978– May 1981	The Resource Fund	5	1	1
	Harvest Futures Fund I	1	1	8
	Illinois Commodity Fund	4	3	5
	S&P 500	7	4	3
	Thomson McKinnon Futures Fund	6	5	4
	Recovery Fund I	3	6	6
	Recovery Fund II	2	7	7
	U.S. Treasury Bills	8	8	2
Jan. 1981– May 1983	E. F. Hutton Commodity Ltd. Partnership II	1	1	14
	Commodity Venture	12	2	1
	The Futures Fund	9	3	4
	The Resource Fund	11	3	3
	Aries Commodity Fund	4	5	9
	Horizon Futures Fund	12	6	6
	Harvest Futures Fund II	2	6	21
	Illinois Commodity Fund	7	6	11
	S&P 500	19	9	4
	Commodity Trend Timing Fund	15	9	8
	U.S. Treasury Bills	20	11	2
	Thomson McKinnon Futures Fund	16	11	10
	Chancellor Futures	9	13	13
	Hutton Commodity Partners	17	13	6
	Harvest Futures Fund I	3	13	22
	Galileo Futures Fund	14	16	12
	Boston Futures Fund I	6	17	18
	Peavey Fund I	4	18	19
	Boston Futures Fund II	7	19	20
	Lake Forest Futures Fund	22	20	14
	Recovery Fund I	18	21	16
	Recovery Fund II	20	22	17

[a]The range of risk-aversion parameters for the highly risk-seeking, risk-neutral, and highly risk-averse categories are $[-.1, -.08]$, $[-.005, .005]$, and $[.08, .1]$, respectively.

1981–1983 in the highly risk-seeking and risk-neutral categories, but drops to fourteenth in the highly risk-averse category. Similar to the earlier comparisons, the rankings of both common stocks and Treasury bills rise appreciably as the level of risk aversion increases. However, in both periods at least one fund ranked higher than either common stocks or Treasury bills for each risk category.

Conclusions

The results of this study indicate that one commodity fund yielded *above normal* returns. However, a majority of the futures funds are preferred to each of the other investments only by risk-seeking investors, probably a relatively small group. Since only a small number of investors would prefer the futures funds, the hypothesis that futures markets are efficient cannot be rejected. However, the results indicate futures markets may have been inefficient for a relatively brief period during 1980.[2] This period was characterized by structural change in financial and currency futures markets and a speculative bubble in the silver futures market. Such occurrences may have favored the technical trading schemes that guide the trading decisions of nearly all fund managers. An alternative hypothesis is that potential for large profits existed at the time of the introduction of these funds, but as more users of computer-based trading schemes entered the market, the potential for profit disappeared. More research is needed into the causes of profits to the technical trading strategies upon which the majority of these funds base their trading.

The conclusions of this study must be viewed in light of several criticisms. First, the relatively short time span of the sample period may not be adequate. Second, no portfolio or liquidity effects were considered. Third, the exclusion of the returns from bankrupt funds implies that the risk of investing in futures funds is substantially underestimated. However, this only strengthens the conclusion that commodity funds as a group have not exhibited *above normal* returns.

Endnotes

1.   For the period 1978–1983, Treasury bills were preferred to stocks for $r(X)$ greater than .07. However, for 1981–1983, Treasury bills were preferred for $r(X)$ greater than .05. This information is useful in determining the relevant range of risk-aversion parameters to use in further

research of this type. Since a large number of investors prefer Treasury bills, some investors must be more risk averse than these levels.

2.   If only 1980 is considered, all but one of the six funds dominates the other investments over the range $[-\infty, .08]$.

References

Ang, James S., and Chua, Jess H. "Composite Measures for the Evaluation of Investment Performance." *Journal of Financial and Quantitative Analysis* 14 (June 1979), pp. 361–84.

Arditti, F.D. "Another Look at Mutual Fund Performance." *Journal of Financial and Quantitative Analysis* 6 (June 1971), pp. 909–12.

Arrow, K.J. *Essay in the Theory of Risk Bearing*. Chicago: Markham, 1971.

Baratz, Morton, ed. *Managed Accounts Reports*. Personal communication. August 1983.

Blyth Eastman Dillon, Inc. "The Future Fund Prospectus." *Commodities* (March 7, 1979), and "The Funds Review," various issues.

Dale, Charles, and Workman, Rosemarie. "Patterns of Price Movement in Treasury Bill Futures." *Journal of Economics and Business* 33 (Winter 1981), pp. 81–87.

Danthine, J.P. "Martingale Market Efficiency and Commodity Prices." *European Economic Review* 10 (1977), pp. 1–17.

Fama, Eugene F. "Efficient Capital Markets: A Review of Theory and Empirical Work." *Journal of Business* 25 (May 1970), pp. 383–417.

Futures Industry's Managed Account Reports, Issue No. 51, 1983.

Grossman, Sanford J., and Stiglitz, Joseph E. "On the Impossibility of Informationally Efficient Markets." *American Economic Review* 70 (June 1980), pp. 393–408.

Hadar, J., and Russell, W.R. "Rules for Ordering Uncertain Prospects." *American Economic Review* 59 (March 1969), pp. 25–34.

Hanoch, G., and Levy, H. "Efficiency Analysis of Choices Involving Risk." *Review of Economic Studies* 38 (1969), pp. 335–46.

Heinold Securities, Inc. "Heinold Illinois Commodity Fund Prospectus." September 28, 1977.

Ibbotson, R.G., and Sinquefield, R.A. *Stocks, Bonds, Bills, and Inflation: The Past and the Future.* Charlottesville, VA: The Financial Analysts Research Foundation, 1982.

Jensen, M.C. "The Performance of Mutual Funds in the Period 1945–1964." *Journal of Finance* 23 (May 1968), pp. 389–416.

Joy, O. Maurice, and Porter, R. Burr. "Stochastic Dominance and Mutual Fund Performance." *Journal of Financial and Quantitative Analysis* (January 1974), pp. 25–31.

King, Robert P., and Robison, Lindon J. "An Interval Approach to Measuring Decision Maker Preferences." *American Journal of Agricultural Economics* 63 (August 1981a), pp. 510–20.

——."Implementation of the Interval Approach to the Measurement of Decision Maker Preferences," East Lansing, MI, Michigan State University, Agricultural Experiment Station, Research Report 418, 1981b.

Klopfenstein, Jay. Norwood Securities. Chicago, IL (unpublished data).

Kofi, T.A. "A Framework for Comparing the Efficiency of Futures Markets." *American Journal of Agricultural Economics* 55 (November 1973), pp. 584–94.

Kramer, R.A., and Pope, R.D. "Participation in Farm Commodity Programs: A Stochastic Dominance Analysis." *American Journal of Agricultural Economics* 63 (January 1981), pp. 119–28.

Martin, John D., and Petty, J. William. "An Analysis of the Performance of Publicly Traded Venture Capital Companies." *Journal of Financial and Quantitative Analysis* 18 (December 1983), pp. 401–10.

Meyer, Jack. "Choice Among Distributions." *Journal of Economic Theory* 14 (April 1977a), pp. 327–36.

——. "Further Application of Stochastic Dominance to Mutual Fund Performance." *Journal of Financial and Quantitative Analysis* 12 (June 1977b), pp. 235–42.

Panton, D.B. "A Semi-Strong Form Evaluation of the Efficiency of the Hog Futures Market: Comment." *American Journal of Agricultural Economics* 62 (1980), p. 584.

Peterson, Paul E., and Leuthold, Raymond M. "Using Mechanical Trading Systems to Evaluate the Weak-Form Efficiency of Futures Markets." *Southern Journal of Agricultural Economics* 14 (July 1982), pp. 147–52.

Powers, John G. "How Trading Advisors are Doing." *Commodities* (June 1982), pp. 54–56.

Pratt, J.W. "Risk Aversion in the Small and Large," *Econometrica* 32 (January–April 1964), pp. 122–36.

Rausser, Gordon C., and Carter, Colin. "Futures Market Efficiency in the Soybean Complex." *Review of Economics and Statistics* 65 (August 1983), pp. 469–78.

Rothschild, M., and Stiglitz, J.E. "Increasing Risk I: A Definition." *Journal of Economic Theory* 2 (1970), pp. 225–43.

Sharpe, W.F. "Mutual Fund Performance." *Journal of Business* 39 (January 1966), pp. 119–38.

Standard & Poor's. *Trade and Security Statistics, Security Price Index Record.* Orange, CT: Standard & Poor's Corporation, 1982.

Stein, Jerome L. "The Dynamics of Spot and Forward Prices in an Efficient Foreign Exchange Market." *American Economic Review* 70 (September 1980), pp. 565–83.

Stevenson, R.A., and Bear, R.M. "Commodity Futures, Trends or Random Walks." *Journal of Finance* 25 (March 1970), pp. 65–81.

Taylor, Stephen J. "Tests of the Random Walk Hypothesis Against a Price-Trend Hypothesis." *Journal of Financial and Quantitative Analysis* 17 (March 1982), pp. 37–61.

Trapp, James N. "An Alternative Parameter Estimation Approach for Risk Management Decision Models." Paper presented at annual meeting of American Agricultural Economics Association, West Lafayette, IN, August 1983.

Treynor, Jack L. "How to Rate Management of Investment Funds." *Harvard Business Review* (January–February 1965), pp. 63–75.

Wall Street Journal. "Commodity Funds Let Small Investors Partake with Limited Liability, But Risks are Sizeable." October 3, 1983, p. 46.

Wilson, Jack W., and Jones, Charles P. "The Relationship Between Performance and Risk: Whence the Bias?" *The Journal of Financial Research* 4 (Summer 1981), pp. 103–8.

Young, Douglas L., et al. "Risk Preferences of Agricultural Producers: Their Measurement and Use." *Risk Management in Agriculture: Behavioral, Manage-*

rial, and Policy Issues. Department of Agricultural Economics, University of Illinois, July 1979, AE-4478, pp. 1–28.

Chapter Nine

Management Summary

Title: "The Role of Managed Futures Accounts in an Investment Portfolio (I)"

Publisher: Managed Accounts Reports and LJR Communications, 5513 Twin Knolls, Columbia, MD 21045, July 1986

Authors: Morton S. Baratz, Ph.D., President, Managed Account Reports
Warren Eresian, Ph.D.

Data: Monthly returns for six years, 1980–1985, for 12 futures money managers, the S&P 500 Stock Index and U.S. Treasury Bonds (weighted average of all bonds with maturities of ten years or more).

Methodology: The purpose of this work was to repeat some of Lintner's earlier work on a longer time horizon (Lintner used 42 months of data between 1979–1982) as well as to see if the popularization of stock index and interest rate futures with futures money managers had changed the low to negative correlations between futures and stocks, and futures and bonds, found previously by other researchers.

Results: In all but one of the 12 trading advisors, managed futures were found to retain their low or negative correlation to stocks and bonds. Stocks and bonds were found to be highly positively correlated.

Results of the portfolio diversification analysis using managed futures were consistent with earlier research. Managed futures were found to effectively reduce risk and/or increase return in portfolios of stocks and bonds.

Comments: The authors pointed out that while Lintner's work focused in on a period when managed futures advisors did extremely well, their study dealt with a time period of choppy and trendless markets.

The Role of Managed Futures Accounts in an Investment Portfolio*

Morton S. Baratz
Warren Eresian

The hypothesis that investors can lower unsystematic risk by distributing their respective eggs among several baskets, rather than concentrating them in one place, has been in common coinage for many decades. Originally, it was a product of inductive reasoning; the idea was distilled from practical experience. But beginning in the early 1950s, the idea was developed and refined by a group of talented financial theoreticians, notably including Harry Markowitz, John K. Lintner, and William R. Sharpe. Their and others' theoretical and empirical analysis now constitute the corpus known generically as Modern Portfolio Theory, or MPT for short.

Until recently, MPT was applied primarily to portfolios of stocks and bonds. Now the analysis more or less routinely encompasses such additional forms of investment as gold, real estate and gas-and-oil ventures, among other things. Not until 1983, however, were commodity futures acknowledged by the theorists to be a legitimate component of a fully diversified investment portfolio. Two contributions along that line appeared in print within a few weeks of one another in Spring 1983. One,

*An updated study based on the work of Professor John K. Lintner, Harvard University Graduate School of Business (May 1983), and presented by the authors at the MAR Mid-Year Conference on Futures Money Management, Chicago, Illinois, July 11, 1986.
Published by Managed Account Reports, LJR Communications, Inc. Reprinted with permission from Managed Account Reports, Inc.

authored by Professor Zvi Bodie of Boston University and published in the *Journal of Portfolio Management*, addressed "Commodity Futures as a Hedge against Inflation." As the title makes clear, Bodie's central argument was that whereas common stocks are a poor hedge against inflation because their real (price-level adjusted) rate of return is—contrary to popular belief—negatively correlated with movements in the general price level, "commodities are positively correlated with unanticipated inflation [which] makes them valuable as an asset in the portfolio."

In order to arrive at this conclusion, Bodie computed annual rates of return on futures by assuming that they, like stocks, bonds and bills, were bought and held. That assumption is at odds, of course, with what futures traders almost invariably do, but its "unreality" does not vitiate the point he was bent on making. In any case, Bodie's paper was soon supplemented by one presented to the Financial Analysts' Federation by Professor John Lintner of Harvard's Graduate School of Business Administration.

Using data for 1979–82 obtained from *Managed Account Reports,* Lintner set out "to explore whether investments in managed accounts of trading advisors in the commodity and financial futures markets, and/or publicly traded futures funds, have shown risk and return characteristics which would make them a desirable means of further diversification for portfolios of stock and bond investments." In accordance with the tenets of Modern Portfolio Theory, Lintner postulated that "they will be desirable supplements to more conventional stock and bond portfolios *provided* they improve the reward-risk tradeoffs for the overall portfolios by shifting the efficient frontier of portfolio returns and portfolio risks upward and/or to the left when returns are plotted vertically and risks horizontally."

Lintner's general conclusions have by now been widely disseminated, but no harm and some good will be done by restating his chief findings:

1. "There are very large benefits from spreading funds dedicated to futures investments selectively ("efficiently") among different managers...Indeed, the improvements from holding efficiently selected portfolios of managed accounts...are so large—*and* the correlations between the returns on the futures-portfolios and those on the stock and bond portfolios so surprisingly low (sometimes even negative)—that the return/risk tradeoffs provided by *augmented portfolios,* consisting partly of funds invested with appropriate groups of futures managers...combined with funds invested in portfolios [of] stocks alone (or in mixed portfolios of stocks and bonds), clearly dominate the tradeoffs available from portfolios of stocks alone (or from portfolios of stocks and bonds). Moreover, they do so by a considerable margin." (Emphasis in original.)

2. "The combined portfolios of stocks (or stocks and bonds) *after* including judicious investments in appropriately selected sub-portfolios of investments in managed futures accounts...show substantially less risk at every possible level of expected return than portfolios of stocks (or stocks and bonds) alone." (Emphasis in original.)

3. "... [A]ll the above conclusions continue to hold when returns are measured in real as well as in nominal terms, and *also* when returns are adjusted for the risk-free rate on treasury bills." (Emphasis in original.)

As usually happens when a seminal work appears, numerous extensions or adaptations of Lintner's analysis have been undertaken. In February 1985, for example, Almer Orr (a prominent futures money manager) presented a paper to *Managed Account Reports'* Sixth Annual Conference on Commodity Money Management, in which he explained, then elaborated upon Lintner's paper. That part of Orr's work which was original covered nearly six years of futures trading, as against Lintner's three-and-a-half years; and Orr used somewhat different measures than did Lintner for representing the performance of managed futures accounts. Yet Orr came to essentially the same conclusion as Lintner, viz.: "I am familiar with no easily liquidated investment other than managed futures which, while generating positive rewards over time, lowers the volatility of more traditional investments to any significant degree. This is the reason portfolios augmented by just 20% of managed futures show such an improvement from a reward/risk standpoint over those lacking futures."

Similarly, in a short paper published in *Managed Account Reports* for March 1985 (Issue No. 73), Peter Matthews, another futures trading manager, compared rewards and risks of portfolios of futures only, stocks only, and varying combinations of stocks and futures; the futures portfolio assumed equal allocation of funds among each of the managers in the MAR/Leading Managers Index, the portfolio of stocks was assumed to be the S&P 500 Index, and the period covered was early 1979 through the end of 1984. Matthews concluded that "the updated information continues to support Lintner's conclusion that one can achieve a much better reward/risk profile by combining futures and stocks than by trading futures or stocks alone ... [T]he combined portfolio shows much smoother and steadier growth—getting higher returns for less risk is what investment management is all about." (The last statement is technically incorrect, because one cannot achieve both objectives concurrently. Rather, one has the choice either of maximizing the rate of return at any given level of risk or minimizing the degree of risk at any given rate of return.)

To round out this non-exhaustive survey of the relevant literature, we must take note of a report by Irwin Investment Research Associates, prepared in early 1986 for a major brokerage firm on the verge of marketing a large-sized public futures fund. While not literally replicating Lintner's analytical methods, IIRA followed it closely. Its central conclusion was that "The estimated efficient frontier [for portfolios combining Treasury bills, Treasury bonds, common stocks and the designated managed futures accounts] dominated the individual investment return-risk combinations and all possible combinations of subsets of the five investments. Most important, the efficient frontier dominated the returns and risk available from conventional portfolios consisting of Treasury bills, Treasury bonds, common stocks, and gold ... [O]nly small proportions of the [managed futures account] were required to produce the relatively large risk-reductions on conventional portfolios."

The Aims of This Study

For some time *Managed Account Reports* has wondered if or to what extent Lintner's conclusions would be modified, were his investigation to be repeated, using raw data that cover a longer period than three-and-a-half years. More importantly, we have wondered if the rapid growth in trading of stock-index and interest-rate futures by futures money managers has transformed the negative correlation between returns on managed futures accounts and (a) stocks, and (b) stocks and bonds, into a positive correlation. The first of these issues has been addressed in substantial part by Orr, Matthews and Irwin. All three also addressed, indirectly and partially, the second issue. In this paper, both matters are taken into full account. And in the process we put to further test other propositions that emerged from Lintner's path-breaking paper.

The Mathematics of Diversification

If investments handled by futures money managers are to be combined in a fully-diversified portfolio, each manager's trading system should have certain characteristics: a history of high monthly gains, a low standard deviation (i.e., low variability) of those gains, and—perhaps most importantly—a track record that is weakly or (better yet) negatively correlated with the performance of the others. The aim of the portfolio's owner is to combine the futures trading managers in such a fashion that, for any specified monthly rate of gain in an account that each trades, the risk involved to obtain that rate of gain is minimized. This objective is, of course, the essence of diversification, its *raison d'etre*, and is graphically illustrated by the "efficient frontier."

We construct a portfolio from N different investments, each having a compounded monthly gain of G_N. The gain of the portfolio is then the weighted average of the individual gains:

$$G_p = d_1 G_1 + d_2 G_2 + \underline{\quad} + d_N G_N \tag{3.1}$$

where the ds are the fractions of each investment contained in the portfolio. Of course,

$$d_1 + d_2 + \underline{\quad} + d_N = 1 \tag{3.2}$$

Associated with each of the monthly gains is the risk, measured by the standard deviation, σ_N. The standard deviation of the portfolio is:

$$\sigma_p = \left[\sum_{i=1}^{N} \sum_{j=1}^{N} d_i d_j \sigma_i \sigma_j \rho_{ij} \right]^{\frac{1}{2}} \tag{3.3}$$

where ρ_{ij} is the correlation coefficient between investment i and j.

The correlation coefficient describes the degree to which the variations between two changing parameters agree. Two parameters which change in the same way (say, one increases by a given amount, the other increases by the same fraction of that amount) are perfectly correlated and have a correlation coefficient of +1.000. Parameters which change in exactly the opposite way (one increases by a given amount, the other decreases by the same fraction of that amount) have a coefficient of -1.000. For purposes of assembling a diversified portfolio, the performance of the separate accounts should be as uncorrelated as possible, i.e., coefficients should be near zero or better yet, negative.

For any desired portfolio gain G_p, there are many different combinations of the investment fractions, d, which satisfy equation 3.1. Each of these combinations, when substituted into equation 3.3, will yield a value for the portfolio standard deviation, σ_p. There is only one combination, however, for which the standard deviation is a minimum. The efficient frontier is simply the locus of points which results in a minimal standard deviation for a given portfolio gain.

To illustrate how the efficient frontier "behaves," we consider a portfolio which consists of only two investments. Equations 3.1-3.3 become, respectively,

$$Gp = d_1 G_1 + d_2 G_2$$
$$d_1 + d_2 = 1$$

$$\sigma_p = \left[d_1^2 \sigma_1^2 + d_2^2 \sigma_2^2 + 2d_1 d_2\sigma_1\sigma_2\rho_{1.2} \right]^{1/2}$$

By varying d_1 and d_2, we obtain the curves shown in Figure 9-1.

Curve A results whenever the correlation coefficient between the two investments is negative. Beginning at G_2, the portfolio risk decreases as the portfolio gain increases. At some point, this behavior reverses direction and the curve proceeds toward G_1.

When the correlation coefficient between the two investments is positive, either curve A or curve B is obtained, depending on the relation between the standard deviations σ_1 and σ_2. For either curve, one simply chooses the desired gain (or risk), and that point determines the "mix" of the portfolio.

The techniques illustrated here are used in the next section of this paper, where we analyze the performance of futures money managers, with an eye toward either risk-minimization or revenue maximization.

Application of the Preceding Analysis

The data used in this study are verified performance figures for 12 futures money managers, all of whom were trading substantial sums of money on or before New Year's Day 1980.[1] Seventy-two months of trading, spanning the period January 1980 through December 1985, have been analyzed. The results are presented in the upper portion of Table 9-1.

For each of the 12 managers, the compounded monthly return and the standard deviation of the 72 monthly rates of return are shown. We have also computed the correlation coefficient of each manager with every other manager and shown the average coefficient. With only one exception, F1, the performance of the managers is positively correlated; F1's trading methods apparently differ materially from those of the other trading managers in the sample.

The lower portion of Table 9-1 shows comparable data for a "stock portfolio" (S), as measured by the S&P 500, and a "bond portfolio" (B), as measured by a weighted average of all Treasury bonds with maturities of

Figure 9-1   Efficient Frontier

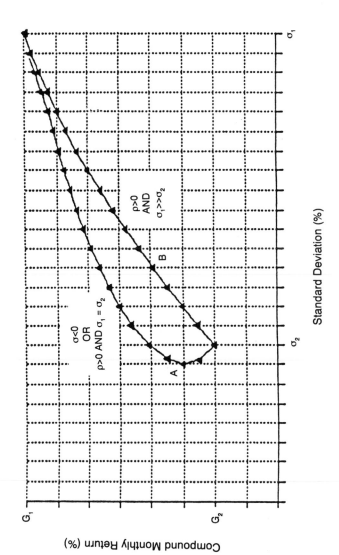

Table 9-1

Futures Money Manager	Compounded Monthly Gain (%)	Standard Deviation	Gain: Risk Ratio	Ave. Correlation With 11 Other Money Managers
F1	2.150	6.555	0.328	–0.025
F2	4.827	18.418	0.262	0.511
F3	3.604	14.391	0.250	0.501
F4	1.869	7.981	0.234	0.563
F5	2.812	12.469	0.226	0.478
F6	2.944	13.956	0.211	0.425
F7	2.271	10.963	0.207	0.544
F8	2.678	12.930	0.207	0.512
F9	1.135	5.766	0.197	0.339
F10	4.844	27.011	0.179	0.419
F11	1.831	10.766	0.170	0.542
F12	1.974	12.979	0.152	0.548
Ave. of Columns	2.745	12.849	0.219	0.446
Stocks	0.913	4.265	0.214	
Bonds	1.060	4.282	0.248	

Ave. Correlation, Stocks and 12 Managers = –0.036

Ave. Correlation, Bonds and 12 Managers = –0.101

10 years or more. Of importance is the observation that performance of both stocks and bonds is negatively correlated with that of futures money managers. Table 9-2 shows the correlation coefficients among all 12 money managers, stocks and bonds, from which the correlation data in Table 9-1 were derived. As was argued in the preceding section, futures funds (or any investment instrument) can be combined into a portfolio which results in a reduction of risk associated with any particular gain, or an increase in gain for any particular degree of risk, and this is the basis for the efficient frontier. One requirement for that result, as was also noted above, is that the components of the portfolio be randomly or negatively correlated with one another. It is clear from the data presented in Table 9-2 that the inclusion of futures into a portfolio of stocks or bonds, or both, would greatly enhance the

Table 9-2

	F_1	F_2	F_3	F_4	F_5	F_6	F_7	F_8	F_9	F_{10}	F_{11}	F_{12}	S	B
F_1	1.000	-0.013	-0.047	-0.095	-0.160	-0.113	-0.010	0.057	-0.034	0.036	-0.048	-0.037	-0.045	-0.016
F_2		1.000	0.529	0.660	0.515	0.437	0.649	0.627	0.343	0.663	0.628	0.581	-0.100	-0.116
F_3			1.000	0.689	0.522	0.389	0.629	0.637	0.512	0.365	0.641	0.648	-0.004	-0.190
F_4				1.000	0.552	0.425	0.718	0.685	0.479	0.468	0.665	0.753	0.003	-0.196
F_5					1.000	0.520	0.553	0.497	0.399	0.379	0.595	0.550	0.000	-0.051
F_6						1.000	0.571	0.400	0.444	0.420	0.584	0.598	0.048	-0.136
F_7							1.000	0.613	0.281	0.568	0.665	0.741	-0.217	-0.142
F_8								1.000	0.265	0.574	0.707	0.573	-0.132	-0.180
F_9									1.000	0.193	0.381	0.467	0.322	0.116
F_{10}										1.000	0.467	0.475	-0.197	-0.193
F_{11}											1.000	0.681	-0.023	-0.181
F_{12}												1.000	-0.094	0.071
S													1.000	0.377
B														1.000

portfolio with respect to risk-reduction, the latter deriving from the fact that stocks and bonds, on one hand, and futures, on the other, are negatively correlated.

Let's assume that there is a futures "pool" available to us, having the characteristics of the performance of the 12 money managers included in Table 9-1, i.e., a compounded average monthly rate of return of 2.745%, a standard deviation of 12.849%, and a correlation coefficient with stocks of -0.037. Using the methods described previously, we find that combination of futures and stocks which results in the same standard deviation for stocks alone, namely, 4.265%. For a combination of 21.5% futures and 78.5% stocks,[2] the standard deviation is also 4.265%. But the gain of this combination is 1.308%, a 43.3% increase over that of stocks alone—for the *same* degree of risk.

We need not, however, restrict ourselves by using all 12 of the futures money managers. Instead, let's repeat the calculation above, this time using a futures "pool," the performance of which is the average of those individual managers (F1 through F5) which have a reward/risk ratio higher than the average of the 12. The characteristics of this five-managers' subset[3] are: compounded monthly rate of return of 3.052%, standard deviation of 11.963%, and an average correlation coefficient with stocks of -0.029. Now, a combination of 23.9% futures and 76.1% stocks produces the same standard deviation as for stocks alone, but yields a monthly rate of return of 1.425%, 56.1% higher than that for stocks alone. Figure 9-2 portrays the efficient frontier for this case.

Repetition of the preceding analysis, using bonds, yields much the same story. The subset of individual managers (F1 through F5), representing 27.9% of the total portfolio, combined with the remaining 72.1% in bonds, produces a monthly rate of return of 1.616%, an increase of 52.4% over the return on bonds alone—at the same degree of risk. The results are shown in Figure 9-3.

Finally, Figure 9-4 depicts a portfolio consisting of futures, stocks and T-bonds. Again, there is a substantial increase in the monthly rate of return, with the same degree of risk associated with stocks and bonds alone.

Although our analytical method differs slightly from Lintner's, our results are consistent with his. In both cases, that is, the inclusion of a relatively small portion (20% plus or minus) of futures into a portfolio of stocks or bonds, or both, can dramatically improve—on the order of 50%—the rate of gain on the portfolio as a whole, with the same degree of risk as for a portfolio of stocks or bonds, standing alone. As Lintner points out, these results are attained because of the low correlation between futures and stocks (and bonds).

Figure 9-2   Futures and Stocks

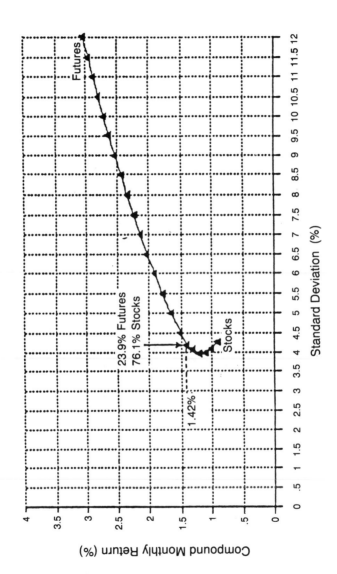

Figure 9-3   Futures and T-Bonds

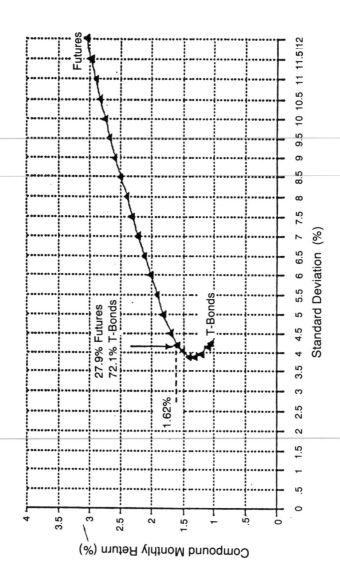

Figure 9-4   Futures, Stocks, and T-Bonds

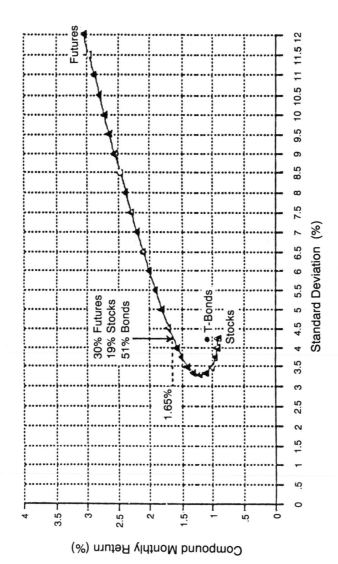

Table 9-3

Year	Ave. Correlation, S&P 500 With Futures Money Managers
1980	−.055
1981	−.057
1982	−.079
1983	−.128
1984	−.279
1985	+.261
1980–85	−.037

What about our working hypothesis that, because stock-index futures are playing a growing role in the portfolios traded by futures money managers, the performance of portfolios of stocks is becoming more positively correlated with the performance of portfolios of futures? To test the hypothesis, we recomputed the correlation between the S&P 500 and the performance of the 12 futures money managers for separate one-year periods and for the six-year period as a whole. The findings, reported in Table 9-3, give it, at most, only mild support.

Conclusion

At the close of his pioneering paper, John Lintner observed that "while all the general principles and all the *qualitative* conclusions we have stated have universal applicability, the particular numerical results we have given defend [depend?] on the particular data we have used. We have been conservative in restricting ourselves to futures funds or futures management companies which had at least forty-two months of recent data to work with. But the period from July 1979 through [the] end of 1982 may not be a fully adequate basis for forming numerical assessments of the future levels of returns and risks." (Emphasis in original.)

We echo these sentiments with respect to our own work. Whereas the data Lintner used included a period (mid-1979 through March 1980) when many futures trading managers reaped an extraordinary harvest of profits, we have focused on a six-years' period during most of which the majority of trading managers counted themselves lucky if they avoided heavy losses in futures markets that were repeatedly choppy or trendless. It is fair to say, then, that we have been even more conservative in our empirical analysis than was Lintner.

Nevertheless, our findings generally conform with, therefore confirm, his. We can do naught but endorse the dictum with which he ended his paper: "[A]lthough the specific numbers may change...*low* intercorrelations between portfolios of futures accounts and stocks and bonds are very likely to persist strongly into the future. And, in that event, all the general conclusions of the study will prove to be solid and robust." Portfolio managers, take heed!

Endnotes

1. The 12 managers constitute the large majority of all trading advisors who satisfy the stated criteria: verified track record covering 1980-85 and trading a substantial sum.

2. Interestingly enough, this combination is closely comparable with the 20% futures/80% stocks and bonds that Orr (see above) found optimal.

3. The usage of only the five "best" managers in this analysis should not be cause for concern. In reality, only the better-performing managers would be seriously considered by investors assembling a portfolio of them.

Chapter Ten

Management Summary

Title: "An Examination of the Risk/Return Characteristics of Portfolios Combining Commodity Futures Contracts with Common Stocks"

Publication: Working Paper Series, Center for the Study of Futures Markets, Columbia University, January 1986.

Authors: Anthony F. Herbst, Professor, Rollins College
Joseph P. McCormack, Professor, University of Texas at Arlington

Data: Monthly data for 48 months (exact dates unknown) of prices for individual common stocks and individual commodity futures contracts.

Methodology: The purpose of this study was to analyze the effects of diversifying stock portfolios with commodity futures. The authors created portfolios of randomly chosen individual stocks of size 8, 12, 14, 16 and 32 each. Repeated random sampling from the universe of all common stocks produced 1350 such portfolios. Next, eight commodity futures contracts were selected based upon their lack of correlation and added, one at a time, to each of the stock portfolios. Each time a future was added a randomly chosen stock in the portfolio was deleted. The effects of gradually adding commodity futures to portfolios of individual stocks were analyzed on a return-risk (standard deviation) basis.

Results: The authors found that substituting commodity future contracts for stocks in stock portfolios produced portfolios with superior risk/return performance. The beneficial effect of doing so decreased as more futures were added, up to a point where futures comprised approximately 70% of the portfolio, beyond which no further benefits were obtained.

continued

Comments: The study pointed out the beneficial effects of portfolio diversification using commodity futures. The results were based on extremely conservative assumptions: diversification was done by choosing stocks and commodity futures at random, with no active management of commodity futures.

An Examination of the Risk/Return Characteristics of Portfolios Combining Commodity Futures Contracts with Common Stocks*

Anthony F. Herbst
Joseph P. McCormack

Summary

A rational investor holding a portfolio of securities attempts to maximize return for a given level of risk, or to minimize risk for a given level of return. If successful, the portfolio will dominate other investments which lie below and to the right of it in mean-variance return space. The locus of all such portfolios, termed the efficient frontier, is located above and to the left of other feasible, but less desirable investment combinations.

The major research on diversification and the number of common stocks required to obtain a certain level of diversification was done by Evans and Archer (1968) and Wagner and Lau (1971). Their work centered on the relationship between the number of randomly selected common stocks and the level of unsystematic risk in the portfolio. They found that diversifiable

*This research was facilitated by a grant from the Futures Center, Columbia University. The authors wish to thank the many persons who contributed in various ways to the completion of this project, especially Larry Lockwood.

or unsystematic risk decreases rapidly as stocks are initially combined to form a portfolio, but that the rate of decrease diminishes after eight to ten different common stocks are combined into a portfolio.

Research on diversification of commodity futures has taken a different tack. Recently, Herbst and McCormack (1985) used principal components analysis and factor analysis on the logarithms of commodity price relatives to identify the factors generating the observed returns. And Irwin and Brorsen (1985) using value-weighted aggregate returns for 20 public commodity funds selected from 84 that were active over their period of study, found that by combining public futures fund investments with portfolios of common stocks and U.S. Treasury bills that the efficient frontier shifted upward and/or to the left, and that real portfolio risk was reduced by 0.6 to 3.7 percentage points from that of a stock and T-bills only portfolio, where such risk is measured by the percentage standard deviation of portfolio returns.

This study is among the first to examine the risk/return performance of portfolios composed of individual futures contracts and common stocks relative to the performance of stock-only portfolios. As employed in Evans and Archer (1968), and Wagner and Lau (1971), common stocks are selected randomly from the CRSP data tapes for inclusion into portfolios of different sizes. The standard deviation is averaged from a large number of portfolios of different sizes and is plotted against portfolio size and mean return. Initial portfolios of 8, 10, 12, 14, 16, and 32 randomly selected common stocks are formed and the efficient frontier is calculated using a Markowitz algorithm and 48 months of data. Then, for each of these portfolio sizes commodity futures contracts are added, one at a time, displacing a randomly chosen common stock. After each such substitution the portfolio variance is recalculated for the portfolio with the weights adjusted to the level of return corresponding to the minimum risk (i.e., variance) of the stock-only portfolio. In other words, return is held constant at the level of a minimum variance, 100% stock portfolio, and the weights adjusted to obtain a variance for the combined portfolio at the level of return obtained for the stocks-only minimum variance portfolio. The entire process is repeated 25 times and this variance calculated for each set of stocks and futures contracts: 8–0, 8–1, . . . 0–8, 10–0, 10–1, etc. Thus, portfolios of randomly selected stocks and commodity futures are formed and the number of securities and futures within the portfolios is allowed to vary so that the relative proportion of futures within the portfolios varies.

Efficient frontiers are calculated from the means obtained from the 25 replications of each common stock-commodity within each portfolio size. Analysis of 1,350 randomly selected portfolios of common stocks and commodity futures (a generic term inclusive of financial and index futures as well as physical commodities) suggests that portfolios of common stocks combined with futures can dominate stock-only portfolios. Not surprisingly, the substitution of commodity futures contracts exhibits diminishing marginal risk reduction, with the benefits from adding futures eventually disappearing when they comprise more than about 70% of the portfolio.

The findings of this study clearly indicate that combined common stock commodity portfolios, in a suitable regulatory environment, can offer superior risk/return performance to all-stock portfolios. Consequently, they suggest that portfolio managers should consider including some proportion of futures contracts in their common stock portfolios.

Research Objectives

The purpose of this research is to investigate the risk/return performance of portfolios comprised of both commodity futures contracts and common stocks relative to the performance of stock-only portfolios.

Research on the efficient frontier has been conducted using securities only[1] (most always common stock) portfolios. By adding investment in individual commodity futures, this study attempts to determine if the efficient frontier can be shifted upward and to the left. If the efficient frontier can be shifted this indicates that portfolios of commodities and stocks offer better risk/return performance than stock-only portfolios and thereby allow investors the opportunity to reach a higher utility curve. Recent relaxation by some states of laws that restrict the use of futures contracts by fiduciaries suggests the current or potential legal feasibility of such combined portfolios—if they can be justified on grounds of economic performance.

Prior Research

Finding the optimal investment portfolio has long been an objective of finance practitioners and academics alike. The first major published work in this area was conducted by Markowitz [4] whose seminal efforts resulted in the concept of the efficient frontier. By posing the existence of a risk-free asset, Sharpe [8] initiated development of the Capital Asset Pricing Model (CAPM). If the underlying assumptions of the CAPM are accepted, it follows that:

1. An investor can attain a higher utility curve than was previously attainable under the Markowitz analysis by placing some of his wealth in the risk-free asset and the remainder in the market portfolio, or by borrowing to invest more than his original wealth (i.e., to leverage himself) in the market portfolio.

2. Each investor who does not place all his money in the risk-free asset
    will purchase a portion of the *same* portfolio. This *market portfolio*
    consists of all individual assets available in the market place in the
    same proportions within the portfolio as their market values are to
    the total market value of all assets.

Although conceptually the CAPM applies to all assets, research on the
CAPM has typically been confined to a single market and that single market
has been the securities market or, more specifically, the market for common
stocks. One reason for this is that common stocks are considered to be
homogeneous—they are good substitutes for one another and there are
thousands of them. The large number of securities is very helpful in statistical studies because of the freedom it allows one in selecting alternative
samples of varying sizes for hypothesis testing or for investigating the effect
of sample size on results

Analogous construction of portfolios of commodity futures contracts has
seldom been seen. This may be because commodity futures contracts are not
considered good substitutes for one another (buying pork bellies is not the
same as buying gold). Also, not only are there far fewer different commodity
futures contracts than there are common stocks, but futures contracts have
different expiration dates, different margin requirements, different commission costs, and other differences which tend to make forming portfolios
more challenging.

The major research on diversification and the number of common stocks
required to obtain a certain level of diversification was done by Evans and
Archer [1] and Wagner and Lau [9]. Their work centered on the relationship
between the number of randomly selected common stocks and the level of
unsystematic risk in the portfolio. They found that diversifiable or unsystematic risk decreases rapidly as stocks are initially combined to form a
portfolio, but that the rate of decrease diminishes after eight to ten different
common stocks are combined into a portfolio.

Research on diversification of commodity futures has taken a different
tack. Recently, Herbst and McCormack [2] used principal components
analysis and factor analysis on the logarithms of commodity price relatives
to identify the factors generating the observed returns. The results they
obtained are intuitively plausible. Precious metals loaded on one factor
while grains loaded on another and foreign currencies loaded on a third and
so on. Variables loading highly on the same factor are highly correlated, but
since the principal components are orthogonal, variables loading highly on
different components are uncorrelated, or much less correlated.

Irwin and Brorsen [3] used value-weighted aggregate returns for 20 public commodity funds selected from 84 that were active over their period of study. They found that by combining public futures fund investments with portfolios of common stocks and U.S. Treasury bills, the efficient frontier shifted upward and/or to the left, and that real portfolio risk was reduced by 0.6 to 3.7 percentage points from that of a stock and T-bills only portfolio, where such risk is measured by the percentage standard deviation of portfolio returns.

Methodology

This study is among the first to examine the risk/return performance of portfolios composed of individual futures contracts and common stocks relative to the performance of stock-only portfolios. As employed in Evans and Archer [1], and Wagner and Lau [9], common stocks are selected randomly from the CRSP data tapes for inclusion into portfolios of different sizes. The standard deviation is averaged from a large number of portfolios of different sizes and is plotted against portfolio size and mean return.

Factors for futures contracts are obtained from a varimax rotation of a principal components analysis, following Herbst and McCormack [2]. This yields eight factors. From among those futures contracts loading heavily on each factor the one which has the highest loading is selected for use in portfolio construction. Thus, a total of eight commodities is used. These are selected randomly such that no commodity is used twice (i.e., sampling without replacement). This is similar to the methodology used by Pinches and Mingo [6] and ensures that the futures contracts chosen do not exhibit a high degree of correlation.

Initial portfolios of 8, 10, 12, 14, 16, and 32 randomly selected common stocks are formed and the efficient frontier is calculated using a Markowitz algorithm and 48 months of data. For each of these portfolio sizes eight commodity futures contracts are added, one at a time, displacing a randomly chosen common stock. After each such substitution the portfolio variance is recalculated for the portfolio *with the weights adjusted to the level of return corresponding to the minimum risk (i.e., variance) of the stock-only portfolio.* In other words, return is held constant at the level of a minimum variance, 100% stock portfolio, and the weights adjusted to obtain a variance for the combined portfolio at the level of return obtained for the stocks-only mini-mum variance portfolio. The entire process is repeated 25 times and this variance calculated for each set of stocks and futures contracts: 8-0, 8-1,...0-8, 10-0, 10-1, etc. Thus, portfolios of randomly selected stocks and commodity futures are formed and the number of securities and futures within the portfolios is allowed to vary so that the relative proportion of futures within the portfolios varies.

The standard deviation is averaged from a large number of portfolios of different sizes and relative compositions and is plotted against portfolio size, mean return, and relative composition. Equal weighting is used for all portfolios.[2]

Results

Table 10-1 contains the mean standard deviations of sets of 25 randomly selected stocks and commodities. The rows correspond to the initial number of stocks, the columns to the number of futures contracts. It is clear that addition of commodity futures contracts reduces risk for each stock portfolio, up to a point where commodities comprise more than 70% of the portfolio.

Table 10-2 contains the *incremental* changes in risk obtained from the standard deviations of Table 10-1. All are positive, except in those cases where the proportion of commodities is over 70% of the portfolio.[3]

Efficient frontiers are calculated from the means obtained from the 25 replications of each common stock-commodity combination within each portfolio size. Figure 10-1 shows the average efficient frontier for the stock-only portfolio (using portfolio size 8) and the efficient frontiers obtained with 2, 4, or 8 of the original stocks are replaced by commodities. Figures 10-2 and 10-3 are similar to Figure 10-1 for the 12 stock and 16 stock portfolios, respectively.

Conclusion

Analysis of 1350 randomly selected portfolios of common stocks and commodity futures (a generic term inclusive of financial and index futures as well as physical commodities) suggests that portfolios of common stocks combined with futures can dominate stock-only portfolios. Not surprisingly, the substitution of commodity futures contracts exhibits diminishing marginal risk reduction, with the benefits from adding futures eventually disappearing when they comprise more than about 70% of the portfolio. The results obtained in this study suggest that portfolio managers should consider including some proportion of futures contracts in their common stock portfolios.[3] The evidence clearly indicates that combined common stock-commodity portfolios, in a suitable regulatory environment, can offer superior risk:return performance to all-stock portfolios.

Table 10-1   Risk Comparison of Initial Minimum Risk Portfolios Held to Constant Return.
Numbers listed in the table represent the mean standard deviations of the portfolios.

Initial Number of Stocks[b]	Number of Commodities								
	0	1	2	3	4	5	6	7	8
8	.0431	.0359	.0366	.0359	.0377	.0430	.0450[a]	.0602[a]	.0732[a]
10	.0393	.0336	.0321	.0323	.0332	.0357	.0336	.0412[a]	.0459[a]
12	.0372	.0310	.0298	.0300	.0299	.0310	.0315	.0355	.0357
14	.0350	.0282	.0273	.0274	.0272	.0270	.0265	.0274	.0284
16	.0328	.0259	.0247	.0246	.0243	.0243	.0238	.0241	.0247
32	.0213	.0167	.0159	.0158	.0155	.0150	.0149	.0151	.0152

[a] Note that risk increases after a point at which too many commodities are included in the portfolio. For the eight commodity portfolio the efficient frontier is the same as in all 25 tries since there are only eight commodities available for inclusion.

[b] Note also that as the size of the portfolio becomes larger the proportion of commodities in it becomes smaller and it takes more commodities to get the greatest reduction in risk.

Table 10-2 Incremental Reduction (+) or Increase (−) in Risk of Initial Minimum Risk Portfolios Held to Constant Return

Initial Number of Stocks[b]	Number of Commodities							
	1	2	3	4	5	6	7	8
8	.0072	.0065	.0073	.0054	.0001	−.0019	−.0171	−.0301
10	.0057	.0072	.0065	.0060	.0036	.0027	−.0019	−.0066
12	.0062	.0075	.0073	.0074	.0062	.0057	.0038	.0015
14	.0068	.0077	.0076	.0078	.0080	.0085	.0076	.0066
16	.0068	.0081	.0082	.0085	.0085	.0090	.0087	.0081
32	.0046	.0054	.0055	.0058	.0063	.0064	.0062	.0061

Figure 10-1   Stock & Commodity Portfolios—Efficient Frontier: 8 Stock Portfolio

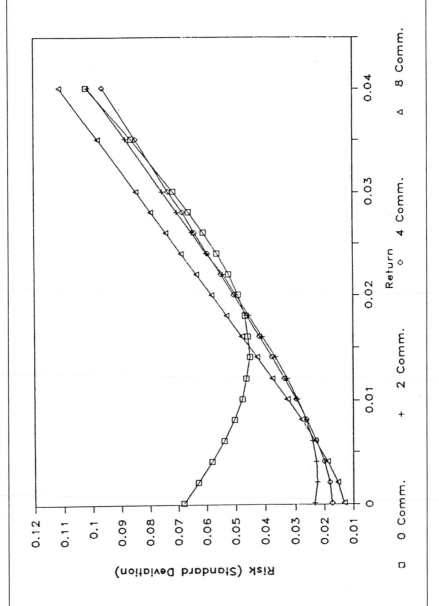

Figure 10-2   Stock & Commodity Portfolios—Efficient Frontier: 12 Stock Portfolio

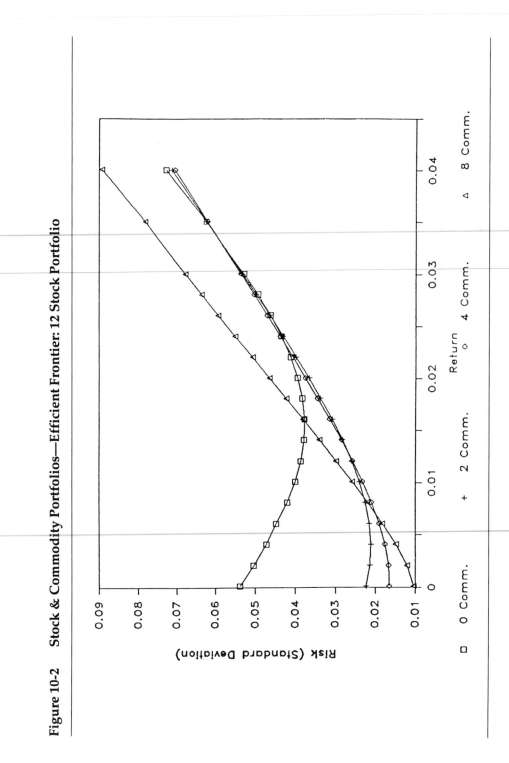

Figure 10-3   Stock & Commodity Portfolios—Efficient Frontier: 16 Stock Portfolio

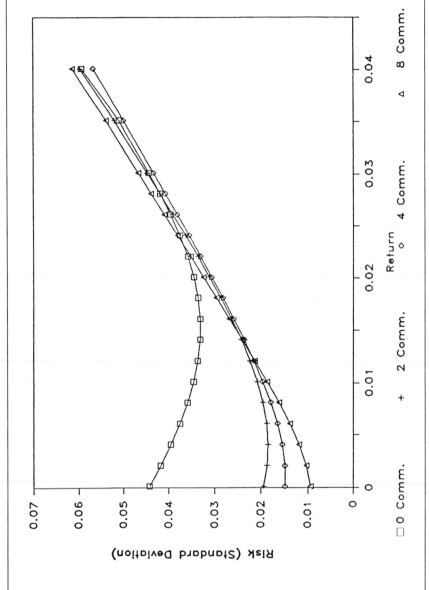

Endnotes

1   A recent paper by Irwin and Brorsen [3] provides an interesting exception. They examined the portfolio effects obtained by combining investment in public futures funds with investment portfolios composed of
stocks and U.S. Treasury securities.

2.   This convention is adopted both to avoid having to select arbitrary
weights for comparing the market values of stocks and commodity
futures and for ease of computation.

3.   Such inclusion may, as this study suggests, go beyond the limited use
of stock index futures for hedging common stock portfolios.

References

Evans, J.L. and Archer, S.H. "Diversification and the Reduction of Dispersion: An Empirical Analysis." *Journal of Finance*, (December 1968), 761–769.

Herbst, A.F. and McCormack, J.P., "An Empirical Examination of APT in
the Commodity Futures Markets." Working paper, the University of Texas
at Arlington, 1985.

Irwin, S.H. and Brorsen, B.W. "Public Futures Funds." *The Journal of Futures
Markets*, Vol. 5, No. 3 (Fall 1985), 463–485.

Markowitz, H.M. "Portfolio Selection." *Journal of Finance*, (March 1952),
77–91.

Modigliani, F. and Pogue, G.A. "An Introduction to Risk and Return:
Concepts and Evidence." *Financial Analysts Journal*, Part 1 (March/April),
Part 2 (May/June 1974).

Pinches, G.B. and Mingo, K.A. "A Multivariate Analysis of Industrial Bond
Ratings." *Journal of Finance*, Vol. 28, No. 1 (March 1973).

Roll, R. "A Critique of the Asset Pricing Theory's Tests." *Journal of Financial
Economics*, Vol. 4 (1977), 129–176.

Sharpe, W.F. "Capital Asset Prices: A Theory of Market Equilibrium Under
Conditions of Risk." *Journal of Finance*, Vol. 19, No. 4 (Sept. 1964), 425–442.

Wagner, W.H. and Lau, S. "The Effect of Diversification on Risk." *Financial
Analysts Journal*, Vol. 26 (November/December 1971), 2–7.

Chapter Eleven

Management Summary

Title: "Real Estate, Futures, and Gold as Portfolio Assets"

Publication: *The Journal of Portfolio Management,* Fall 1987

Authors: Scott H. Irwin, Associate Professor, Ohio State University
                Diego Landa, Managing Partner, Borrani, Mexico City,
                Mexico

Data: Annual rates of return for 11 years, 1975–1985, for Trea-
                sury Bills, Treasury Bonds, Common Stocks, Real Estate,
                Futures, Gold, and inflation.

Methodology: Historical rates of return for all the above assets were
                compared individually through correlation analysis, and
                from a modern portfolio theory perspective. Futures
                were analyzed two ways, as a simple buy and hold asset,
                and as managed futures using returns from actively man-
                aged futures funds.

Results: Futures under a passive buy and hold strategy were
                found to have negative correlation with Treasury Bills
                and Bonds, but positive correlation with stocks, real es-
                tate and gold. Managed futures were, in addition to being
                negatively correlated with Treasury Bills and Bonds, also
                negatively correlated with stocks but had no significant
                correlation with real estate. When combined in portfolios
                with stocks, bonds and bills, futures and real estate were
                shown to be attractive diversifiers. In the model portfolio,
                risk (for the portfolio with minimum risk) was reduced
                almost 50% and return increased 12%. Futures funds
                were part of efficient portfolios at all levels of risk and
                return in percentages ranging from 3.8% to 19.4%. Gold
                was not found to be an attractive diversifier.

                                                              continued

Comments: This research was conducted to see how traditional port-folio asset diversifiers-gold and real estate-compared to futures. Managed futures and real estate far out-per-formed gold as diversifiers.

Real Estate, Futures, and Gold as Portfolio Assets*

Real estate and commodities futures are attractive diversifiers; gold falls short.

Scott H. Irwin
Diego Landa

The purpose of this paper is to investigate the simultaneous use of real estate, futures, and gold as portfolio assets.

The search for the "best" portfolio allocation of assets has been a predominant focus of investment research for twenty-five years. Early studies focused almost exclusively on common stock and bond portfolios, but subsequent research has shown that real estate, futures, or gold may improve the real performance of conventional portfolios. As the research on each of these alternatives was conducted separately, this paper provides direct comparison across the alternative assets.

The first two sections of the paper present brief reviews of portfolio theory and previous studies. Following sections discuss historical asset returns and estimated return-risk trade-off curves, and give a summary.

*The authors wish to thank Keith Smith, Wade Brorsen, and two anonymous reviewers for their helpful comments. They also gratefully acknowledge the computer programming assistance provided by Vince Showers.

The Journal of Portfolio Management, Fall 1987, 29–34. Reprinted with permission.

Modern Portfolio Theory

Modern Portfolio Theory (MPT) is the analytical framework underlying the research we refer to in the introduction. MPT implies that a risk-averse investor should construct a set of portfolios having the minimum risk (standard deviation) for a given expected return (mean). Investors then choose the portfolio from the "efficient set" that matches their personal preference for return and risk.

An important empirical issue is the condition assets must meet to be included in an efficient portfolio. A special corollary of the general condition required is particularly useful: If a candidate asset has a positive expected return and is negatively correlated with portfolio returns, then the asset should be included in the efficient portfolio.[1] With this special corollary in mind, let us examine previous portfolio studies of real estate, futures, and gold.

Previous Portfolio Studies of Real Estate, Futures, and Gold

The potential benefit of holding real estate in portfolios has been an active field for study. Zerbst and Cambon (1984) show that nominal real estate returns from seven studies were all negatively correlated with stock returns. The same seven series either had a negative or small positive correlation with bill and bond returns. Ibbotson and Siegel (1984) find similar results comparing a composite of farm, residential, and commercial real estate returns with bill, bond, and stock returns from 1947 through 1982. As all the real estate series in the previous studies had positive means, real estate appears to meet the condition for inclusion in portfolios of bills, bonds, and stocks. Using data from 1915 through 1978, Fogler (1984) shows that real estate was included in efficient portfolios of bills, bonds, and stocks. He recommended devoting a minimum of 20% of portfolio funds to real estate.

Two strategies for using commodities futures as a portfolio asset have been analyzed. The first is a passive strategy of buying and holding a bundle of futures contracts. Bodie (1983) finds that real commodity returns from 1953 through 1981 were positively correlated with inflation and negatively correlated with real bill, bond, and stock returns. The commodity series had a positive mean, so buying and holding futures is a strategy that meets the condition for inclusion in efficient portfolios of bills, bonds, and stocks. The second strategy is to buy shares in futures funds. This approach is an active strategy, because an advisor is employed in an effort to "beat the market."[2] Lintner (1983) and Irwin and Brorsen (1985) find that futures funds improve the return-risk trade-off available from stocks alone, or stocks, bonds, and bills, and "by a considerable margin," according to Lintner. In contrast, Elton, Gruber, and Rentzler (1987) have concluded that it is "doubtful that public commodity funds should be included in an investor's portfolio," although this conclusion depends on the existence of a riskless asset.[3]

Gold traditionally has been viewed as an "inflation hedge" for conventional portfolios. McDonald and Solnik (1977) report that nominal gold returns were negatively correlated with stocks from 1948 through 1975. Herbst (1983) shows that real gold returns were negatively correlated with real stock returns from 1962 through 1976. As the previous series had non-negative means, gold also appears to meet the condition for inclusion in efficient portfolios. Simulations conducted by Renwick (1979) and Sherman (1982) show that gold would be included in efficient portfolios of bills, bonds, and stocks.[4] Sherman concludes that failure to "hold some significant fraction of gold mining stocks results in suboptimal and economically inefficient allocation of resources and, therefore, is unequivocally imprudent."

The studies we have reviewed all provide support for including real estate, futures, or gold in conventional portfolios. The similarity of the results across assets raises the question whether all three should be included in efficient portfolios. Before answering this question, we must turn to the historical record to estimate the expected returns, risks, and correlations of bills, bonds, stocks, real estate, buy-and-hold commodities futures, futures funds, and gold.

Historical Returns

Table 11-1 contains the real, pre-tax rates of return for the seven alternative assets and the inflation rate from 1975 through 1985.[5] The sample period is constrained by the futures funds return data, which are not available for years before 1975. Unfortunately, an eleven-year sample period is atypically short for estimating expected returns, volatilities, and correlations.

Column 1 of Table 11-1 presents the real returns from a policy of rolling over thirty-day U.S. Treasury bills and is representative of the returns on riskless money-market instruments. With a standard deviation of 3.5% (and this is overstated due to the non-stationarity of the mean), bills are the least volatile asset. We will assume that the most likely future scenario is that real Treasury bill returns will be 1.0%, slightly lower than the arithmetic mean from 1975 through 1985.

Table 11-1 Annual Real Rates of Return for Alternative Assets, 1975–1985[a]

Year	Treasury Bills	Treasury Bonds	Common Stocks	Real Estate	Buy-and-Hold Futures	Futures Funds	Gold	Inflation Rate
1975	-1.1	2.0	28.3	6.0	-12.5	3.5	-29.7	7.0
1976	0.3	11.4	18.2	4.7	2.2	-25.6	-8.5	4.8
1977	-1.6	-7.0	-13.1	4.0	-8.3	55.3	14.8	6.8
1978	-1.7	-9.4	-2.3	5.3	4.2	19.3	25.7	9.0
1979	-2.6	-12.9	4.5	4.7	9.1	40.9	104.6	13.3
1980	-1.0	-14.7	17.9	0.8	-2.5	13.4	0.1	12.4
1981	5.3	-6.7	-12.8	-3.7	-24.1	7.8	-37.7	8.9
1982	6.4	35.1	16.8	3.8	-11.6	-4.7	10.0	3.9
1983	4.8	-3.0	18.1	3.2	14.3	-13.9	-19.6	3.8
1984	5.7	11.1	2.2	0.7	-15.4	3.3	-22.3	4.0
1985	3.7	26.1	27.2	5.7[b]	-9.6	10.1[b]	3.0	3.9
Arithmetic Mean	1.6	2.9	9.5	3.2	-4.9	9.9	3.7	7.1
Geometric Mean	0.1	1.8	8.5	3.1	-5.6	7.8	-1.6	7.0
Standard Deviation	3.5	16.3	14.7	2.9	11.5	22.9	38.8	3.5

[a]Sources are as follows:

Bills, Bonds, Stocks, and Inflation Rate: *Stocks, Bonds, Bills, and Inflation*

Real Estate: Ibbotson and Siegel; Ibbotson Associates

Buy-and-Hold Futures: Commodity Research Bureau

Futures Funds: Irwin and Brorsen

Gold: Sherman (1984); *The Wall Street Journal*, various issues

[b]Preliminary estimate of return.

The second column of Table 11-1 presents the total real returns an investor would have earned by investing in U.S. Treasury bonds with a constant twenty-year maturity. From 1975 through 1985, total real bond returns were negative in six of the eleven years. As a result, the average real return was low relative to volatility. A reasonable expectation for the future is that bonds will yield a real return of 3.0%, approximately equal to the arithmetic mean from 1975 through 1985.

The third column presents the total real return on the value-weighted Standard & Poor's 500-stock Composite Index. The arithmetic and geometric means of stocks from 1975 through 1985 were the second highest and highest, respectively, of the seven assets. Surprisingly, only real estate volatility (which we will see was probably underestimated) and bill volatility were lower than stock return volatility. From a single asset perspective, stocks have been a relatively good investment over the last eleven years. We will assume expected real stock returns of 9.0%, slightly lower than the arithmetic mean from 1975 through 1985.

The fourth column of Table 11-1 presents the real returns on a composite of unleveraged U.S. residential, farm, and business real estate. Real returns were positive in ten out of the eleven years from 1975 through 1985. The arithmetic mean real return of real estate was 3.2%, exceeded only by stocks, futures funds, and gold, investments with much higher volatility. Nevertheless, the impressive return-risk ratio of real estate should be viewed with skepticism. Ibbotson and Siegel (1984) note that the reported series is based on appraised values that greatly smooth the true fluctuations in returns. In addition, the imperfect marketability of real estate complicates the comparison across assets. With these problems in mind, we assume expected real returns on real estate of 3.0%, slightly lower than the arithmetic mean from 1975 through 1985.

The fifth column of Table 11-1 presents the real returns from buying and holding a composite index of commodities futures contracts. The index, calculated by the Commodity Research Bureau, is a geometric average of the prices from twenty-seven non-financial futures markets. While volatility was relatively low, the arithmetic mean of –4.9% was by a wide margin the lowest of the seven assets. Furthermore, real returns were negative in seven of the eleven years. The commodity price declines of the early 1980s were especially large. We believe a reasonable expectation is that buying and holding futures will yield a real return of –3.0%, reflecting the slowing in commodity price declines in the mid-1980s.

The sixth column of Table 11-1 presents the real returns on a composite index of public commodities futures funds. The index is a value-weighted portfolio of all public futures funds active from 1975 through 1985.[6] Irwin and Brorsen found that a value-weighted index yields a more accurate measure of returns, because of the skewed size distribution of public futures funds. The return series shows that public futures funds have generated both high returns and high risks. The arithmetic mean real return of public futures funds was the highest of the seven assets. The volatility of futures funds was exceeded only by that of gold, and this estimate is probably understated. Elton, Gruber, and Rentzler note that the number of funds has increased over time, so that the common element of volatility across funds may be overstated in the last year of the sample relative to the first. The number of futures funds in the composite index increased from three in 1975 to ninety-five in 1985, suggesting that the true volatility of an "average" public futures fund over the sample period was greater than 22.9%. With this problem in mind, we will assume futures funds are expected to yield a real return of 9.0%, slightly lower than the mean from 1975 through 1985.

The seventh column of Table 11-1 presents the real returns from buying one troy ounce of gold bullion at the beginning of the year and selling it at the end. Gold had the highest volatility of the seven assets—38.9%—which was nearly twice the level of the next highest volatility. As a consequence of this extreme volatility, the arithmetic mean of 3.7% (the third highest of the seven assets) was substantially larger than the geometric mean of –1.6%. We assume expected real returns of 0% for gold.

Correlation Coefficient

As we have already seen, correlation coefficients play an important role in determining whether an asset enters an efficient portfolio. Correlation coefficients for the seven assets, shown in Table 11-2, are generally consistent with those reported in previous studies. Real estate returns have a negative correlation with bill returns and moderately positive correlations with bond and stock returns. Buy-and-hold commodities futures returns exhibit a negative correlation with bill and bond returns and a low positive correlation with stock returns. Futures funds and gold returns are negatively correlated with bill, bond, and stock returns. Buy-and-hold futures, futures funds, and gold returns are positively correlated with the inflation rate, while bill, bond, and stock returns are negatively correlated with the inflation rate.

Table 11-2 Correlation Coefficients

	Bonds	Stocks	Real Estate	Buy-and-Hold Futures	Futures Funds	Gold	Inflation Rate
Bills	0.63	0.07	−0.46	−0.42	−0.54	−0.53	−0.66
Bonds		0.46	0.25	−0.33	−0.47	−0.23	−0.77
Stocks			0.51	0.22	−0.56	−0.15	−0.29
Real Estate				0.49	0.07	0.41	−0.18
Futures					−0.03	0.52	0.18
Futures Funds						0.58	0.55
Gold							0.55

Figure 11-1 Efficient Return-Risk Frontiers

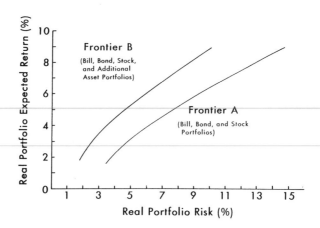

Efficient Return-Risk Frontiers

Estimated return-risk trade-off curves in this section are based on the expected returns, standard deviations, and correlations discussed so far, with the exception of the standard deviations of real estate and futures fund returns. We doubled real estate's sample standard deviation in order to approximate actual rather than appraised fluctuations in real estate returns. This results in a return-risk ratio of 0.5 for real estate, slightly lower than the ratio assumed for stocks (0.6). The sample standard deviation of futures funds is also doubled, offsetting the downward volatility bias caused by the growing number of funds in the composite index. The resulting volatility estimate is approximately three times that of common stocks and is consistent with Elton, Gruber, and Rentzler's estimate of the average volatility of futures funds.[7]

Figure 11-1 presents the estimated return-risk frontiers. Frontier A represents a benchmark strategy of holding only bills, bonds, and stocks as portfolio assets. The minimum-risk portfolio has an expected return of 1.7%, and risk of 3.5%, with all funds invested in Treasury bills and stocks. The highest return and risk is achieved at 100% stocks.

Frontier B represents strategies of holding bills, bonds, stocks, real estate, buy-and-hold futures, futures funds, and gold. A comparison of Frontier B with Frontier A shows that the additional assets reduce portfolio risk at

Table 11-3   Efficient Portfolio Proportions (Percent)

Expected Return	Risk	Proportions			
		Real Estate	Buy-and-Hold Futures	Futures Funds	Gold
1.9	1.8	19.7	3.6	3.8	0.0
2.0	1.9	19.6	3.0	4.0	0.0
3.0	2.4	12.5	0.0	6.3	0.0
4.0	3.4	0.0	0.0	9.1	0.0
5.0	4.5	0.0	0.0	11.2	0.0
6.0	5.8	0.0	0.0	13.2	0.0
7.0	7.2	0.0	0.0	15.3	0.0
8.0	8.6	0.0	0.0	17.4	0.0
9.0	10.0	0.0	0.0	19.4	0.0

every level of expected return. In fact, risk is reduced an average of 41% along Frontier B. The return-risk trade-off of the minimum-risk portfolio is improved markedly: Risk is reduced 49%, while expected return increases 12%.

These results strengthen the conclusions of earlier studies. That is, risk-averse investors can achieve substantially higher levels of satisfaction by including additional assets in their portfolios. We are, however, still left with the question of the level of additional asset holdings along the efficient frontier.

Table 11-3 presents the efficient portfolio proportions for points along Frontier B. Real estate is held in relatively substantial proportions at lower risk levels and constitutes nearly 20% of the minimum-risk portfolio. Nevertheless, the proportion of real estate declines as portfolio risk increases; real estate is not held in any of the efficient portfolios above a risk level of 3.1%. Overall, the results suggest that real estate investment has a positive and important role to play in improving the real return-risk trade-off of conventional portfolios.

Both buy-and-hold futures and futures funds are held at lower risk levels —the two futures investment strategies account for 7.4% of the minimum-risk portfolio. Buy-and-hold futures investment then diminishes rapidly as portfolio risk increases, although futures fund investment steadily increases. In fact, futures funds are held at all points along Frontier B and reduce the risk of the highest expected return portfolio by 32%. These results are not overly sensitive to the assumed expected return of futures funds. If expected returns are assumed to be 2.7% (the arithmetic mean real return of futures funds over 1980–1985), fund proportions range from 3.6% of the minimum-risk portfolio to a peak of 15.9%, and portfolio risk is reduced an average of 29%. We find similar results if the expected return of futures funds is reduced to 0%.[8]

The results above show that futures investment may be useful for improving the real return-risk trade-offs of conventional portfolios. Futures fund investment was the more predominant of the two futures investment strategies analyzed. The impressive performance of futures funds, however, must be viewed cautiously because of the short sample period. We should hesitate to draw firmer conclusions until a longer sample period is available for study.

Gold is not held in any of the efficient portfolios along Frontier B. This finding is inconsistent with the results of previous studies of gold as a portfolio asset. The explanation for gold's absence from efficient portfolios here is the extreme volatility of gold returns relative to the return volatility of the other assets (with the exception of futures funds).[9] On the other hand, we should view the results with respect to gold cautiously also, because the sample period may not be representative of gold's future volatility.

Conclusions

Research has shown real estate, futures, or gold may substantially improve the real return-risk trade-offs of bill, bond, and stock portfolios, but to date the research on each alternative has been conducted separately. This paper investigates the simultaneous use of real estate, futures, and gold as portfolio assets.

The estimated efficient frontiers show that portfolio risk was reduced an average of 41% by holding the additional assets. The return-risk trade-off of the minimum-risk portfolio was markedly improved; risk was reduced 49%, while expected return increased 12%. Real estate was held in substantial proportions at lower portfolio risk levels, making up nearly 20% of the minimum-risk portfolio. Both buy-and-hold commodities futures and futures fund investments were held at lower risk levels. Buy-and-hold futures holdings diminished rapidly as portfolio risk increased, while futures fund holdings increased steadily. Moreover, futures funds were held at all points along the efficient frontier and reduced the risk of the highest expected return portfolio by 32%. Gold was not held in any of the efficient portfolios.

Endnotes

1. Lintner (1983) has shown that the return-risk trade-off of an efficient portfolio can be improved by the inclusion of a candidate asset if and only if:

$$\frac{r_i}{\sigma_i} > \frac{r_p}{\sigma_p} \rho_{ip}$$

   where:
   r_i = expected return for candidate asset i;
   r_p = expected return for portfolio p;
   σ_i = standard deviation of returns for candidate asset i;
   σ_p = standard deviation of returns for portfolio p; and
   ρ_{ip} = correlation between candidate asset i and portfolio p.

2. The first futures fund was introduced in 1948 and continued trading until the mid-1960s. Multimillion dollar futures funds, however, were not introduced in substantial numbers until the mid-1970s. See Irwin and Brorsen for a complete description of futures funds.

3. Elton, Gruber, and Rentzler assumed the existence of a riskless asset for their break-even portfolio comparisons. If a riskless asset does not exist, which is a reasonable assertion at least in real terms, then their inequality condition is the same as that derived by Lintner (see footnote 1). Under an assumption that a riskless asset does not exist, Elton, Gruber, and Rentzler's break-even comparisons show that public futures funds enter 100% stock and stock-and-bond portfolios for the six-year scenario and have an estimated return less than 0.1% smaller than is required to enter portfolios for the twenty-five year scenario.

4. Both Renwick and Sherman analyzed buying and holding gold stocks. We assume such a strategy is equivalent to holding gold bullion.

5. Investors are concerned with the real purchasing power of their portfolio. See Bodie.

6. The composite index includes funds that were liquidated because of trading losses. Thus, we avoid a survivorship bias in the return series.

7. The reported and "transformed" (standard deviation doubled) real estate and futures funds returns are:

	Real Estate		Futures Funds	
	Reported	Transformed	Reported	Transformed
1975	6.0	8.8	3.5	−2.9
1976	4.7	6.2	−25.6	−61.1
1977	4.0	4.8	55.3	100.6
1978	5.3	7.4	19.3	28.6
1979	4.7	6.2	40.9	71.8
1980	0.8	−1.6	13.4	16.8
1981	−3.7	−10.6	7.8	5.6
1982	3.8	4.4	−4.7	−19.3
1983	3.2	3.2	−13.9	−37.7
1984	0.7	−1.8	3.3	−3.3
1985	5.7	8.2	10.1	10.2
Arithmetic Mean	3.2	3.2	9.9	9.9
Standard Deviation	2.9	5.8	22.9	45.8

The transformation leaves the arithmetic mean of the series unchanged. Thus, correlation coefficients with the other assets are unchanged, but covariances with other assets are doubled.

8. If expected returns are assumed to be 0%, futures fund proportions range from 3.5% of the minimum-risk portfolio to a peak of 13.2% (at a portfolio risk level of 9.2%), and portfolio risk is reduced an average of 26%.

9. Gold enters efficient portfolios if futures funds are omitted from the set of candidate assets. However, gold proportions do not exceed 2%.

References

Bodie, Z. "Commodity Futures as a Hedge Against Inflation." *Journal of Portfolio Management*, Spring 1983, pp. 12–17.

Elton, E. J., Gruber, M. J., and Rentzler, J. C. "Professionally Managed Publicly Traded Commodity Funds." *Journal of Business*, 1987, forthcoming.

Fogler, H. R. "20% in Real Estate: Can Theory Justify It?" *Journal of Portfolio Management,* Winter 1984, pp. 6–13.

Herbst, A. F. "Gold versus U.S. Common Stocks: Some Evidence on Inflation Hedge Performance and Cyclical Behavior." *Financial Analysts Journal,* January/February 1983, pp. 66–74.

Ibbotson, R. G., and Siegel, L. B. "Real Estate Returns: A Comparison with Other Investments." *American Real Estate and Urban Economics Association Journal,* Fall 1984, pp. 219–242.

Irwin, S. H., and Brorsen, B. W. "Public Futures Funds." *Journal of Futures Markets,* Fall 1985, pp. 463–485.

Jacob, N. L., and Pettit, R. R. *Investments.* Homewood, Ill.: Richard D. Irwin, Inc., 1984.

Lintner, J. "The Potential Role of Managed Commodity-Financial Futures Accounts (and/or Funds) in Portfolios of Stocks and Bonds." Paper presented at the annual conference of the Financial Analysts Federation, Toronto, Canada, May 16, 1983.

McDonald, J. G., and Solnik, B. H. "Valuation and Strategy for Gold Stocks." *Journal of Portfolio Management,* Spring 1977, pp. 29–33.

Markowitz, H. M. Portfolio Selection. New York: John Wiley & Sons, 1959.

Renwick, F. B. "Are Gold Mining Shares Prudent Investments? The Case of International Investors Incorporated." Salomon Brothers Center for the Study of Financial Institutions, New York University Graduate School of Business Administration, September 1979.

Sherman, E. J. "Gold: A Conservative Prudent Diversifier." *Journal of Portfolio Management,* Spring 1982, pp. 21–27.

Sherman, E. J. *Performance of Gold Versus Stocks, Bonds, and Money Markets in Six Countries, 1968–1983.* International Gold Corporation, Ltd., Gold Investment Papers, March 1984.

Stocks, Bonds, Bills, and Inflation 1985 Yearbook, Chicago: Ibbotson Associates, Inc., 1985.

Stocks, Bonds, Bills, and Inflation: Quarterly Service (Fourth Quarter 1985). Chicago: Ibbotson Associates, Inc., 1985.

The Wall Street Journal. Various issues 1984 and 1985.

"Unpublished Data." New York: Commodity Research Bureau, Inc., 1986.

"Unpublished Data." Chicago: Ibbotson Associates, Inc., September 1986.

Zerbst, R. H., and Cambon, B. R. "Real Estate Historical Returns and Risks." *Journal of Portfolio Management,* Spring 1984, pp. 5–20.

Chapter Twelve

Management Summary

Title: "Futures Fund Performance: A Test of the Effectiveness of Technical Analysis"

Publication: *The Journal of Futures Markets*, Vol. 6, No. 2, 1986

Author: J. Austin Murphy, Assistant Professor, Oakland University

Data: Returns for 60 months for the time period May 1980 through April 1985 for all purely technical futures funds as reported by *Commodities Magazine*. Eleven such funds were used in the analysis.

Methodology: Returns for each fund and the total were analyzed to determine if excess profits were generated, or if stock and bond portfolio enhancement could have been accomplished using these technical-based funds. Excess profits are defined as those above risk-free rates of return. The analysis was done for both gross returns, and for net returns assuming an expense factor of 1.5% of assets per month.

     Returns were also compared to a naive buy and hold strategy with rollovers for a marketbasket of 30 commodities which included financials, metals, foods and agriculturals. No oils were included.

Results: As a group on a gross basis the funds (2.31% per mo.) outperformed the S & P 500 (1.38% per mo.), the naive buy and hold strategy (.17% per mo.), and the risk-free rate of return (.82% per mo.). They also produced statistically significant improvement in stock and bond portfolios.

     The opposite was true on a net return basis, with the funds returning only .81% per month.

     The author concluded that technical analysis holds the potential for generating superior performance in commodity funds if expenses are reduced.

Futures Fund Performance: A Test of the Effectiveness of Technical Analysis*

J. Austin Murphy

Technical analysis is the use of past price and volume relationships to forecast price movements. This type of analysis is especially popular in the futures markets, where high leverage, high liquidity, and low brokerage costs permit quick trading profits (and losses). According to Fama (1970), however, the capital markets are characterized by the weak form of the Efficient Market Hypothesis (EMH), a hypothesis which states that the *ex ante* expected return from a technical trading system cannot be greater than that from a naive buy-and-hold strategy of equal risk.

Numerous tests of the effectiveness of technical analysis in the futures markets have been undertaken by various distinguished authors, including Smidt (1965), Stevenson and Bear (1970), Leuthold (1972), and Irwin and Uhrig (1984). Most such tests have focused on the profitability of certain mechanical trading strategies, and the evidence is mixed.

However, all such tests are subject to dispute. Research which uncovers a profitable trading system and therefore rejects the weak form of the EMH are subject to the Tomek and Querin (1984) criticism that some trading strategy is always successful *ex post*, even in a random-walk world. On the other hand, studies which reject the possibility of trading profits are subject

*The helpful comments of two anonymous reviewers are gratefully acknowledged.
The Journal of Futures Markets, Vol. 6, No. 2, 175–185 (1986)

to the technician's critique that the traditional tests employed by researchers only reject isolated technical tools, whereas most technicians use a variety of different indicators in a variety of different ways. In fact, much of technical trading is judgmental and cannot be tested mechanically. The only realistic test of the usefulness of technical analysis is to examine the public performance of professional technicians.

Previous studies have been conducted on the general performance of professional futures traders. For example, Houthakker (1957) and Rockwell (1967) have found that professional speculators do earn greater profits on futures trading than small speculators, although Chang (1985) has found the evidence on this subject to be statistically insignificant. Nevertheless, none of these studies differentiates between professionals who use technical trading systems and traders who rely on fundamental analysis.

In this article, the effectiveness of technical analysis is tested by examining the performance of publicly-offered futures funds which employ strictly technical trading systems. In Section I, the necessary background on futures funds is developed. In Section II, the method to be used in evaluating the funds is defined. In Section III, the data are described, in Section IV, the findings are interpreted, and, in Section V, the results are summarized.

I. Function and Characteristics of Futures Funds

In order to determine the usefulness of technical analysis, it is necessary to compare the performance of active technical trading systems to that of the passive alternative, a naive strategy of buying and holding futures contracts. Active technical trading systems can be evaluated by examining the performance of publicly offered futures funds which are managed by professional technicians.

Publicly offered futures funds, the first of which were introduced in 1974 according to *Business Week* (1975), are mutual funds which invest in futures contracts. The funds are generally set up as limited liability partnerships, and, although few funds are open for new investment after the initial subscription, many permit the limited partners to redeem their shares at net asset value. As partnerships, all fund income, whether distributed or not, is taxable to the individual investors, with 60% of all capital gains and losses being treated as long-term and 40% being treated as short-term. Many individuals invest in the funds through IRAs, and their share of partnership income is tax-exempt.

Futures funds provide investors with the opportunity to take diversified positions in the futures market with a small investment. In fact, because of the indivisibility and unwieldy size of most futures contracts, futures funds represent the only means of holding diversified futures positions for many investors.[1]

Futures funds can also provide investors with a specialized skill in futures trading. The previously mentioned studies by Houthakker (1957) and Rockwell (1967), as well as research by Working (1967), indicate that a specialized skill may in fact be required for futures investment.

General empirical examinations of the performance of futures mutual funds have been previously undertaken in Brorsen and Irwin (1985) and in Irwin and Brorsen (1985). Their findings indicate that futures funds can contribute positively to portfolio performance when added to holdings of stocks and bonds, but the authors did not test for the existence of abnormal returns. In addition, since the authors failed to compare the performance of the funds to that of a passive strategy, the studies failed to provide any information on the actual investment skill provided by the funds.

II. Specification of the Testing Procedure

By examining the relative performance of futures funds which use strictly technical trading systems, a direct test of the usefulness of technical analysis is possible. The basic framework for testing and evaluating mutual fund performance has been developed by several authors.

Sharpe (1966) has shown that, since investors are generally risk-averse, a useful index by which to measure the performance of mutual funds would be the ratio of reward per unit of risk. Sharpe defined the difference between the return on a risky fund and the return on a risk-free asset as an appropriate measure of reward, and defined the variance of the return on a fund as an appropriate measure of risk. According to Korkie (1983), the formula for an unbiased estimator of Sharpe's measure of reward per unit of risk is

$$\text{Sharpe's Index} = \{(\bar{r}_j - \bar{r}_f)/\sigma_j\}\,\{T/(T + .75)\}, \tag{1}$$

where $\bar{r}$ is the arithmetic average return on an asset, subscripts j and f denote fund j and the risk-free asset f, respectively, $\bar{r}_j - \bar{r}_f$ is defined as the excess return on fund j, σ_j is the estimated standard deviation of the return on fund j, and T is the number of observations. Since an alternative to investing in futures funds is the more traditional investment in equities, a relevant benchmark by which to compare fund performance using Sharpe's index is the S&P 500.

Hakansson (1971a), however, has shown that simple mean-variance analysis can sometimes lead to distorted results in the case of assets with volatile returns. For example, a futures fund which generates high returns initially but eventually loses all of the invested capital could rank favorably according to Sharpe's index. Hakansson (1971b) therefore advocated the geometric mean as a more useful measure of performance. In fact, Hakansson (1970) has shown that, if investors have log utility functions, the only relevant measure of portfolio performance is the expected geometric mean. In this case, investors require the same compounded return on risky portfolios as riskless portfolios, and the risk-free T-bill represents an appropriate benchmark by which to evaluate performance.

Both Sharpe's index and the geometric mean measure the risk-return performance of a fund in isolation, as if an individual's entire portfolio were invested in the fund. Jensen (1968) has stated that, ideally, a performance measure should take into consideration the usefulness of the fund in a portfolio context. Assuming investors to be well-diversified, Jensen hypothesized that a relevant indicator of performance would measure how the fund contributed to the risk-return tradeoffs of a well diversified portfolio, such as the market portfolio. For this purpose, Jensen developed the concept of alpha or abnormal return, which represents the additional return on a fund which is above that required by investors for its contribution to the risk of diversified portfolios.

Jensen's index can be estimated by regressing a fund's excess returns on the excess returns of the market portfolio m. The intercept from the regression equation

$$\tilde{r}_j - r_f = \alpha_j + \beta_j \, (\, \tilde{r}_m - r_f) + \tilde{e}_j \qquad\qquad (2)$$

then provides an indication of the abnormal return on the fund, while the regression coefficient, β_j, is a measure of the contribution of the fund to the riskiness of well diversified portfolios. Here, ~ denotes a random variable, and e is the error term. Using two-tailed t-tests, it is possible to determine whether the individual alphas, as well as the betas, are significant from zero.

By constructing Chi-squared statistics, it is also possible to test joint hypotheses that the parameters in Equation (2) are equal to zero for all the funds. As shown by Theil (1971), Chi-squared statistics with J degrees of freedom are calculated as $-21n\lambda \sim \chi^2_{(J)}$, where J is the number of parameter restrictions being tested, and λ is the ratio of the restricted/unrestricted likelihood functions. In order to adjust for cross-sectional correlation between fund residuals, a Seemingly Unrelated Regressions (SUR) estimator can be used to transform the residuals before calculating the log ratio.[2]

The foregoing procedures provide the basic framework for a thorough analysis of the usefulness of technical funds to investors. However, as previously mentioned, in order to determine whether technical analysis is a useful tool for futures investors, the performance of active technical trading systems must be compared to the passive alternative for investing in the futures market. Bodie and Rosansky (1980) have therefore specified that the appropriate benchmark for evaluating futures trading performance is a passive strategy of periodically rolling over long positions in a diversified portfolio of futures contracts. In order to facilitate a comparison with this benchmark, the returns to the passive strategy can be subtracted out from the returns to each technical fund. Subtracting out the returns to the passive strategy effectively separates the pure technical trading profits of the funds from returns derived from general movements in the futures market and thus permits a direct examination of the returns derived strictly from technical analysis.

Since returns to futures funds are measured on a net basis after fund expenses, evaluation of technical fund performance examines the effectiveness of technical analysis only after transaction costs and management fees. However, Irwin and Brorsen (1985) have found the annual management and brokerage expenses generated by futures funds to be enormous, with annual expenses for a sample of 20 funds averaging 19.2% of net asset value. Examination of fund performance on a gross basis would therefore also be useful, since it would provide some indication of the full potential of technical analysis if the trading systems could be operated at a lower cost.

III. The Data

Data for this study consist of 60 monthly observations from May 1980 through April 1985 on all purely technical futures funds which were listed in the first "Funds Review" section of *Commodities Magazine*. Of the original 16 funds listed in the magazine, 3 were not used in the sample because they were categorized by Irwin and Brorsen (1985) as using some fundamental analysis. In addition, full-sample data are available on only 11 of the technical funds, because 1 fund was removed from the listing by the magazine due to its small size, and 1 fund was liquidated.[3]

Although results can be analyzed on an individual basis only for the 11 surviving funds, it is possible to construct an index of the equal-weighted monthly returns on all of the originally listed technical funds, including the 2 delisted funds up through the month of delisting. Study of this index is especially useful since it eliminates any survivorship bias.[4]

In addition, although it is not feasible to calculate gross returns to each individual fund, largely because expense data are fragmented and unavailable on a monthly basis, it is possible to estimate the gross return to the index of all technical funds by using a cross-sectional average expense ratio. Examination of reports from each fund's primary advisor shows annual expenses for each of the funds to range between 12.5% and 26.7% of net asset value and to average 17.5%. Since these figures are consistent with the previously mentioned findings of Irwin and Brorsen (1985), it seems reasonable to estimate monthly expenses as 1.5% of net asset value for the index of all funds.

The naive portfolio to be used for comparison is specified as posting 100% T-bill margin on equal-dollar long positions in the "second-nearest" futures contract for each different type of commodity and financial future listed on US exchanges in *The Wall Street Journal* in 1980 and still listed through 1985. This benchmark is similar to that advocated by Bodie and Rosansky (1980) for use in evaluating futures trading strategies, and it comprises 30 contracts, including CBT Corn, CBT GNMAs, CBT Oats, CBT Soybeans, CBT Soymeal, CBT Soyoil, CBT Treasury Bonds, CBT Wheat, CME Feeder Cattle, CME Live Cattle, CME Live Hogs, CME Lumber, CME Pork Bellies, CMX Copper, CMX Gold, CMX Silver, CSCE Coffee, CSCE Cocoa, CSCE World Sugar, CTN Cotton, CTN Orange Juice, KC Wheat, IMM British pounds, IMM Canadian dollars, IMM Japanese yen, IMM Swiss francs, IMM T-Bills, IMM W. German marks, MPLS Wheat, and NYM Platinum.[5]

Returns on each futures contract position are measured by adding the percentage change in the futures price over the month to the return on one-month T-bills.[6] The second-nearest maturity is maintained by rolling over the investment at the end of each month in which the nearest contract expires. Futures prices are collected from *The Wall Street Journal*, while r_d, the ask yield on one-month T-bills listed in *The Wall Street Journal*, is converted to a monthly return using the formula

$$r_f = \{r_d/12\}/\{1 - (r_d/12)\}. \tag{3}$$

For the market proxy, two alternative portfolios are employed, with the first proxy being a simple 100% investment in corporate equities. This proxy has been used in previous investigations of the futures market by Dusak (1973) and others.

The second proxy employed is a portfolio consisting of 60% equities, 30% corporate bonds, and 10% T-bonds. This weighting has been employed in other risk-return research by Friend, Westerfield, and Granito (1978),[7] and, as shown by Galai and Masulis (1976), this proxy is theoretically more correct since, by including corporate bonds, it represents a better measure of the total return to productive business assets.[8]

For equities, the return on the S&P 500 is used, with capital gains and dividend yield being gathered from *Outlook*. For corporate bonds, returns are measured assuming equal-weighted investment in the 20 bonds of the Dow Jones composite bond index, with capital gains on the index being available from *The Wall Street Journal* and coupon income being listed in *Barron's*. For T-bonds, the return on the Treasury bond with the longest maturity at the end of each month is used, with prices and coupon income being collected from *The Wall Street Journal*.

IV. Fund Performance Evaluation

The average monthly return as well as the standard deviation of return for each fund are shown in Columns 1 and 2 of Table 12-1, with Sharpe's index being used to initially rank the funds. Although most of the funds earned positive returns, only one fund outperformed the S&P 500 on the mean-variance criterion. This finding implies that, in general, concentration of wealth in a futures fund is inferior to portfolio concentration in a group of stocks.

Funds are ranked according to the geometric mean in column 5 of Table 12-1. As shown, only five funds outperformed a risk-free strategy of rolling over one-month T-bills, and the average fund did not do as well as the riskless benchmark.

In Table 12-2, the funds are ranked by Jensen's index, which measures the average monthly alpha or abnormal return that would have occurred if the funds had been added to a portfolio of stocks. From the t-statistics, it appears that no fund exhibited statistically significant abnormal performance over the sample period. As shown by the insignificant alphas in column 3 of Table 12-2, there is also no statistical evidence that any of the futures funds would improve the performance of a diversified portfolio of stocks and bonds. These results are supported by the Chi-squared statistics, which also indicate that none of the funds generated significant abnormal returns.

In evaluating the relative merits of technical analysis versus a naive buy-and-hold strategy, the evidence is somewhat more positive although still inconclusive. As can be observed from Tables 12-1 and 12-2, the naive strategy was outperformed by the average technical fund on all three performance criteria. In fact, the naive strategy exhibited a lower rank than 11, 9, and 10 of the individual funds for the Sharpe, Hakansson, and Jensen indexes, respectively. In addition, the naive strategy generated statistically significant negative abnormal returns over the sample interval,[9] while the average abnormal return for the technical funds was approximately zero.[10]

Table 12-1   Fund Performance In Isolation, May 1980–April 1985

	(1) $\bar{r}_j^c$	(2) σ_j^d	(3) Sharpe's Index[e]	(4) EGM[f]	(5) EGM Rank
1. Future Fund	1.77%[g]	5.92%	.16[a]	1.60%	1[b]
2. Resource Fund	1.46%[g]	6.06%	.11	1.28%	2[b]
3. Illinois Commodity Fund	1.54%	8.53%	.08	1.19%	3[b]
4. Chancellor Futures Fund	1.54%	9.03%	.08	1.17%	4[b]
5. Thomson McKinnon Futures Fund	1.42%	7.50%	.08	1.15%	5[b]
6. Aries Commodity Fund	1.06%	9.93%	.02	0.60%	6
7. Galileo Futures Fund	0.68%	7.26%	−.02	0.42%	7
8. Recovery Fund I	0.48%	9.87%	−.03	0.03%	9
9. Hutton Commodity Partners	0.44%	5.89%	−.06	0.27%	8
10. Commodity Trend Timing Fund	0.13%	6.45%	−.11	−0.17%	10
11. Boston Futures Fund I	−0.76%	9.71%	−.16	−1.22%	11
Average Technical Fund[h]:					
Net	0.81%	5.92%	−.01	0.64%	
Gross[i]	2.31%	5.92%	.25	2.14%[b]	
Naive Strategy[j]	0.17%	2.76%	−.23	0.13%	
S&P 500	1.38%	4.13%	.13	1.29%[b]	
Market Proxy[k]	1.16%[g]	3.22%	.10	1.11%[b]	
One-month T-bill	0.82%	0.21%	.00	0.82%	

[a]Denotes performance superior to the S&P 500.
[b]Denotes performance superior to the T-bill.
[c]The monthly arithmetic mean return.
[d]The monthly standard deviation of return.
[e]The excess return on the fund divided by the standard deviation of return, with the appropriate adjustment made for bias.
[f]The monthly geometric mean return.
[g]Significant at the 90% confidence level.
[h]Equal-weighted investment in the 11 funds listed above plus two other technical funds which were originally listed in *Commodities* but were subsequently delisted.
[i]GROSS, before brokerage expenses and management fees. All other data for the funds are NET, after expenses.
[j]A portfolio of equal dollar long positions in the "second nearest" futures contract for each of 30 different types of commodities and financials.
[k]A portfolio of 60% equities, 30% corporate bonds, and 10% T-bonds.

Table 12- 2 Fund Performance in a Portfolio Context, May 1980– April 1985 (*t*-Statistics are Given in Parenthesis)

$$\tilde{r}_j - r_f = \alpha_j + \beta_j (\tilde{r}_m - r_f) + \tilde{e}_j$$

	Portfolios			
	Stocks[b]		Stocks and Bonds[c]	
	(1) α_j	**(2)** β_j	**(3)** α_j	**(4)** β_j
1. Chancellor Fund	0.98	−0.47[a]	0.90	−0.54
	(0.85)	(−1.72)	(0.78)	(−1.52)
2. Future Fund	0.97	−0.03	0.97	−0.06
	(1.25)	(−0.18)	(1.25)	(−0.24)
3. Illinois Commodity Fund	0.68	0.07	0.71	0.04
	(0.61)	(0.27)	(0.63)	(0.11)
4. Resource Fund	0.65	−0.02	0.66	−0.05
	(0.82)	(−0.10)	(0.83)	(−0.19)
5. Thompson McKinnon Futures Fund	0.59	0.09	0.60	0.01
	(0.61)	(0.04)	(0.61)	(0.02)
6. Aries Commodity Fund	0.17	0.13	0.15	0.26
	(0.13)	(0.41)	(0.11)	(0.67)
7. Galileo Futures Fund	−0.24	0.17	−0.25	0.33
	(−0.25)	(0.76)	(−0.27)	(1.15)
8. Hutton Commodity Fund	−0.32	−0.10	−0.35	−0.09
	(−0.42)	(−0.56)	(−0.45)	(−0.40)
9. Recovery Fund I	−0.60	0.48	−0.73	0.58
	(−0.47)	(1.57)	(−0.42)	(1.49)
10. Commodity Trend Timing Fund	−0.70	0.02	−0.73	0.13
	(−0.83)	(0.10)	(−0.87)	(0.50)
11. Boston Futures Fund I	−1.29	−0.51[a]	−1.37	−0.61
	(−1.05)	(−1.72)	(−1.11)	(−1.61)
$\chi^{2e}_{(11)}$	9.28	19.84[a]	9.90	21.28[a]
Average Technical Fund[d]: Net	−0.04	0.05	−0.04	0.07
	(−0.05)	(0.25)	(−0.05)	(0.31)
Average Technical Fund[d]: Gross[f]	1.46[a]	0.05	1.46[a]	0.07
	(1.88)	(0.25)	(1.89)	(0.31)
Naive Strategy[g]	−0.81[a]	0.28[a]	−0.76[a]	0.31[a]
	(−2.39)	(3.54)	(−2.18)	(2.93)

[a]Significant at the 90% confidence level.
[b]The S&P 500.
[c]A portfolio consisting of 60% equities, 30% corporate bonds, and 10% T-bonds.
[d]Equal-weighted investment in 13 technical funds.
[e]Test for the H_0 that the parameter for all of the funds is 0.
[f]GROSS, before brokerage expenses and management fees. All other data for the funds are NET, after expenses.
[g]A portfolio of equal dollar long positions in the "second nearest" futures contract for each of 30 different types of commodities and financials.

Table 12-3   Pure Technical Trading Profits[b] in a Portfolio Context, May 1980–April 1985   (t-Statistics are Given in Parenthesis)

$$\tilde{r}_j - r_m = \alpha_j - \beta_j (\tilde{r}_m - r_n) + \tilde{e}_j$$

	Portfolios			
	Stocks[c]		Stocks and Bonds[d]	
	(1) α_j	(2) β_j	(3) α_j	(4) β_j
1. Chancellor Fund	1.79 (1.39)	−0.76[a] (−2.47)	1.66 (1.27)	−0.85[a] (−2.13)
2. Future Fund	1.77[a] (1.93)	−0.32 (−1.45)	1.72[a] (1.87)	−0.37 (−1.31)
3. Illinois Commodity Fund	1.49 (1.17)	−0.21 (−0.71)	1.46 (1.15)	−0.27 (−0.70)
4. Resource Fund	1.46 (1.57)	−0.30 (−1.37)	1.41 (1.52)	−0.36 (−1.25)
5. Thompson McKinnon Futures Fund	1.40 (1.27)	−0.28 (−1.05)	1.35 (1.23)	−0.30 (−0.90)
6. Aries Commodity Fund	0.97 (0.72)	−0.16 (−0.49)	0.90 (0.67)	−0.05 (−0.11)
7. Galileo Futures Fund	0.57 (0.55)	−0.11 (−0.46)	0.50 (0.48)	0.02 (0.07)
8. Hutton Commodity Fund	0.49 (0.55)	−0.39[a] (−1.85)	0.41 (0.46)	−0.40 (−1.48)
9. Recovery Fund I	0.21 (0.16)	0.19 (0.60)	0.22 (0.17)	0.27 (0.67)
10. Commodity Trend Timing Fund	0.11 (0.12)	−0.26 (−1.17)	0.02 (0.03)	−0.18 (−0.63)
11. Boston Futures Fund I	−0.48 (−0.36)	−0.79[a] (−2.48)	−0.61 (−0.46)	−0.91[a] (−2.23)
$\chi^2_{(11)}$[f]	10.34	21.06[a]	10.44	21.48[a]
Average Technical Fund[e]: Net	0.77 (0.85)	−0.24 (−1.11)	0.72 (0.79)	−0.24 (−0.86)
Average Technical Fund[e]: Gross[g]	2.27[a] (2.51)	−0.24 (−1.11)	2.22[a] (2.45)	−0.24 (−0.86)

[a]Significant at the 90% confidence level.

[b]All returns are measured after subtracting out the returns on a naive portfolio n, consisting of equal dollar long positions in the "second nearest" futures contract for each of 30 different types of commodities and financials.

[c]The S&P 500.

[d]A portfolio consisting of 60% equities, 30% corporate bonds, and 10% T-bonds.

[e]Equal-weighted investment in 13 technical funds.

[f]Test for the H_0 that the parameters for all of the funds is 0.

[g]GROSS, before brokerage expenses and management fees. All other data for the funds are NET, after expenses.

Nevertheless, as shown in Table 12-3, only one technical fund was found to generate returns significantly superior to those of a passive strategy, and the Chi-squared statistics provide evidence that none of the funds can significantly outperform a naive buy-and-hold trading system.

Although the foregoing results (measured net after expenses) lack statistical significance, the full potential of technical analysis can be seen by examining the average fund performance on a gross basis before expenses. On this level, the technical funds not only generated statistically significant abnormal returns, but also outperformed the naive strategy, the S&P 500, and the T-bill on all criteria.

V. Conclusion

Measures of performance in isolation show technical funds to be inferior investment vehicles relative to the stock market and the T-bill market over the sample interval. In addition, although technical funds performed adequately in a portfolio context, there is no statistical evidence of any abnormal returns. This research also discovers no statistically significant evidence that any of the technical funds can outperform a naive buy-and-hold strategy. These findings are consistent with the hypothesis that the futures markets are technically efficient.

However, the discovery of statistically significant negative abnormal returns for the naive strategy indicates that an active technical strategy is at least as effective as the passive alternative.[11] In fact, the analysis of fund performance on a gross return basis demonstrates that the potential for abnormal technical trading profits does exist, if expenses are reduced.[12] Regardless, the findings demonstrate that it is possible to earn sufficient technical trading profits to at least cover brokerage and management fees.

Endnotes

1. Although low margin requirements permit holding large futures positions with a minimal investment, the risk associated with such leverage is prohibitive for many investors.

2. Since the independent variable is the same for each fund, however, an SUR estimator does not affect the parameter estimates (Judge, Hill, Griffiths, Luetkepohl, and Lee, 1982).

3. It should be noted that the liquidated funds merely redeemed all part-
    nership units at net asset value and did not actually go bankrupt. In fact,
    the fund earned a positive return in the final three months of operation.

4. Even for the analysis of the individual funds, it is questionable whether
    there is any survivorship bias, since the 2 delisted funds did not actually
    go bankrupt.[3] In fact, the average compounded returns for the two funds
    through their month of delisting were 2.88% and –1.11%.

5. In cases of substantially identical commodities sold on two different
    exchanges, such as CMX silver and CBT silver, only the contract with
    the greatest open interest in 1980 was used. Three different wheat
    contracts were included because the three contracts permit delivery of
    substantially different commodities with substantially different prices.

6. It is not necessary to incorporate Bodie and Rosansky's (1980) adjust-
    ment for mark-to-market effects, because the impact is negligible for
    one-month returns. Similarly, the transaction costs for the naive strategy
    would be insignificant, especially if a discount broker were employed.

7. The weights are based on the security holdings of US individuals and
    financial institutions reported in the Federal Reserve's *Flow of Funds*.

8. Justification for failure to include other assets into the market proxy,
    such as real estate, human capital, and foreign assets, can be found in
    Friend and Blume (1975), Fama and Schwert (1977), and Black (1974),
    respectively.

9. The negative abnormal returns to the naive strategy over the sample
    interval are in contrast to the findings of Bodie and Rosansky (1980), who
    discovered the abnormal returns to a passive trading system to be
    significantly positive over an earlier time interval. The difference in
    results can be at least partially explained by Murphy (1984), who dem-
    onstrated that a structural change occurred in the futures market in 1974.

10. In further tests (not shown), cross-sectional regressions revealed a pos-
    itive, albeit statistically insignificant, relationship between fund excess
    returns and betas. Although by no means conclusive, these findings
    imply that technical trading systems which generate positive systematic
    risk will, on average, generate non-negative excess returns.

11. Although not directly relevant to the focus of this study, it is also
    interesting to note in Table 12-2 that the naive strategy generated signif-
    icantly positive beta risk while the average technical fund did not
    significantly contribute to the risk of well-diversified portfolios. In fact,

two of the funds' trading strategies generated significantly negative beta risk in portfolios of stocks.

In further tests designed to determine whether any of the strategies represented good hedges against inflation, it was found (not shown) that neither the naive strategy nor any of the technical funds exhibited any meaningful correlation with monthly changes in the Consumer Price Index (CPI). In fact, the naive strategy as well as several of the funds generated slight negative correlation with the inflation rate.

12. Large-scale reductions in fund expenses are quite feasible. For example, for one of the top performing funds, the Future Fund, brokerage expenses could be cut by 2/3 just by using a discount broker, while administrative costs could be cut by 4/5 if the management fee could be reduced to a level commensurate with equity mutual funds. These two actions would reduce annual expenses from an estimated 18.9% of net asset value to approximately 3.3% (see The Future Fund Prospectus).

Bibliography

Black, F. (1974): "International Capital Market Equilibrium with Investment Barriers," *Journal of Financial Economics*, 1:337–352.

Bodie, Z. and Rosansky, V. (1980, May/June): "Risk and Return in Commodity Futures," *Financial Analysts Journal*, 36:27–39.

Brorsen, W. and Irwin, S. (1985): "Evaluation of Commodity Funds," *Review of Research in Futures Markets*, 4:84–94.

Business Week (1975, July 7): "Computer Help for Commodity Funds," pp. 57–58.

Chang, E. (1985): "Returns to Speculators and the Theory of Normal Backwardization," *Journal of Finance*, 40:193–208.

Dusak. (1973): "Futures Trading and Investor Returns: An Investigation of Commodity Market Risk Premiums," *Journal of Political Economy*, 81: 1387–1406.

Fama, E. (1970): "Efficient Capital Markets: A Review of Theory and Empirical Work," *Journal of Finance*, 25:383–417.

Friend, I. and Blume, M. (1975): "The Demand for Risky Assets," *American Economic Review*, 65:900–922.

Friend, I., Westerfield, R., and Granito, M. (1978): "New Evidence on the Capital Asset Pricing Model," *Journal of Finance,* 33:903–920.

Galai, D. and Masulis, R. (1976): "The Option Pricing Model and the Risk Factor of Stock," *Journal of Financial Economics,* 3:53–81.

Hakansson, N. (1970): "Optimal Investment and Consumption Strategies Under Risk for a Class of Utility Functions," *Econometrica,* 38:587–607.

Hakansson, N. (1971a): "Capital Growth and the Mean-Variance Approach to Portfolio Selection," *Journal of Financial and Quantitative Analysis,* 6:517–557.

Hakansson, N. (1971b): "Multiperiod Mean-Variance Analysis: Toward a General Theory of Portfolio Choice," *Journal of Finance,* 26:857–884.

Houthakker, H. (1957): "Can Speculators Forecast Prices?" *Review of Economics and Statistics,* 39:143–151.

Irwin, S. and Brorsen, W. (1985): "Public Futures Funds," *Journal of Futures Markets,* 5:149–166.

Irwin, S. and Uhrig, W. (1984): "Do Technical Analysts Have Holes in Their Shoes?" *Review of Research in Futures Markets,* 3:264–277.

Jensen, M. (1968): "The Performance of Mutual Funds in the Period 1945-1964," *Journal of Finance,* 23:389–416.

Judge, G., Hill, C., Griffiths, W., Luetkepohl, H., and Lee, T. (1982): *Introduction to the Theory and Practice of Econometrics,* New York: John Wiley, pp. 319–328.

Korkie, B. (1983, Spring): "External Versus Internal Performance Evaluation," *Journal of Portfolio Management,* 9:36–42.

Leuthold, R. (1972): "Random Walk and Price Trends: The Live Cattle Futures Market," *Journal of Finance,* 27:879–889.

Murphy, A. (1984): "Risk-Return Tradeoffs on Commodity Futures Contracts with the Second Nearest Delivery Date," Dissertation: University of Georgia, pp. 69–70.

Rockwell, N. (1967): "Normal Backwardization, Forecasting, and the Returns to Commodity Futures Traders," *Food Research Institute Supplement,* 7:107–130.

Sharpe, W. (1966): "Mutual Fund Performance," *Journal of Business Supplement,* 2:119–138.

Smidt, S. (1965): "A Test of the Serial Independence of Price Changes in Soybeans Futures," *Food Research Institute Studies,* 5:117–136.

Stevenson, R. and Bear, R. (1970): "Commodity Futures: Trends and Random Walks," *Journal of Finance,* 25:65–81.

Theil, H. (1971): *Principles of Econometrics,* New York: John Wiley, pp. 396–397.

Tomek, W. and Querin, S. (1984): "Random Processes in Prices and Technical Analysis," *Journal of Futures Markets,* 4:15–23.

Working, H. (1967): "Tests of a Theory Concerning Floor Trading on Commodity Exchanges," *Food Research Institute Supplement,* 7:5–48.

Chapter Thirteen

Management Summary

Title: "Professionally Managed, Publicly Traded Commodity Funds"

Publication: *Journal of Business,* 1987. Vol. 60, No. 2

Authors: Edwin J. Elton, Professor, New York University
Martin J. Gruber, Professor, New York University
Joel C. Rentzler, Associate Professor, Baruch College

Data: Monthly prices and returns for 72 months, from July, 1979, through June, 1985, for public commodity funds, stocks, bonds, Treasury bills, Consumer Price Index and Dow Jones Commodity Futures Index and Commodity Cash Index.

Methodology: Returns from commodity funds were compared to returns from stocks and bonds. Funds were analyzed as a stand-alone investment and in conjunction with stock and bond portfolios.

Results: The authors concluded that commodity funds were not useful stand-alone investments, that it was doubtful that they should be included in portfolios of stocks and bonds, and that it was unlikely that superior performance in returns could be predicted from past performance, although they did find predictability in standard deviation.

Comments: This study produced results which were in sharp disagreement with earlier and later research findings. Reasons for these differences include:

1. The study examined returns between July, 1979, and June, 1985—a period of two distinct environments for futures funds (and stocks and bonds). During 1979–1981, futures funds were significantly profitable (see Lintner,

continued

and Irwin and Brorsen) while stocks were marginal and bonds were poor. The reverse happened during the period 1982–1985, which is consistent with negatively correlated assets.

2. In calculating the minimum return threshold necessary for commodity funds to benefit stock portfolios, the authors averaged the minimum break-even rates of return (see Table 13-4) for overlapping six-year and twenty-five-year periods. Not only was the use of the twenty-five-year period questionable since commodity fund data was available for the six-year period only, but the averaging of overlapping intervals was also questionable. Had the authors instead compared six-year performance of commodity funds to six-year break-even rates of return, the conclusions would have been opposite. However, even in this case, commodity funds were barely above the breakeven point.

In addition, others[1] have criticized the methods of this study:

a. the lack of capitalization weighting of performance
b. their use of annual holding periods (and thus monthly geometric equivalents) rather than monthly holding periods
c. the use of nominal rather than real (adjusted for inflation) returns
d. inadequacy of statistical tests used
e. no consideration of dynamic leveraging

1."Dynamic Leveraging Strategies and the Risk/Return Profile of Professionaly Managed Futures;" Sanford J. Grossman; *Risk Management*, Vol. II, No. 2, 1991.

Professionally Managed, Publicly Traded Commodity Funds*

Edwin J. Elton
Martin J. Gruber
Joel C. Rentzler

"The best laid schemes o' mice and men
Gang aft a-gley;
An lea's us nought but grief an pain,
for promis'd joy."

[Robert Burns]

Summary

Investment in professionally managed, publicly traded commodity funds
has grown rapidly in recent years. This is the first comprehensive study of
the performance of these funds. It is found that randomly selected funds
offer neither an attractive alternative to bonds and stocks nor a profitable
addition to a portfolio of stocks and bonds. Furthermore, past performance

*We would like to thank the Institute of Quantitative Research in Finance and the Center for the
Study of Business and Government, Baruch College, and a PSC-CUNY research grant for financial
support.
Journal of Business, 1987, Vol. 60, No. 2.

of these funds offers very little information about future performance. The findings may be explained by the large transaction costs incurred by these funds and their primary reliance on technical analysis.

Introduction

The concept of a professionally managed investment portfolio composed of positions in commodity and financial futures is appealing to the investment community. One thinks of investment in commodities as a way to protect capital in times of high inflation. Perhaps this partially accounts for the tremendous growth of professionally managed public commodity funds. Prior to February 1979, there was only one fund for which monthly data existed, but by 1985, the number had grown to 94 funds, with over $600 million in assets under management.[1]

Most of the funds have the ability to trade in all available futures and commodities. These include financial instruments and futures on financial instruments, foreign currencies and futures and forward contracts on foreign currencies, and commodities and futures on commodities. Most funds do not restrict themselves to subsectors of the market but take positions across all sectors; funds can and do take both long and short positions in the futures market. A typical quote from a prospectus is as follows: "Diversification will be achieved by trading a variety of commodities...."[2]

Most commodity funds trade on the basis of technical systems. In particular, trend-following systems that assume that a trend in price will continue over time are typical. Here is a representative statement from a prospectus: "Trading decisions of the Advisor will be based primarily on technical analysis and trend-following trading strategies which seek to identify price changes and trends. The buy and sell decisions based on these strategies are not based on analysis of fundamental supply and demand factors, general economic factors or anticipated world events."[3]

Given the popularity of these funds and their probable continued growth, it seems worthwhile to examine their performance. Interest in their performance is increased because of the apparent handicaps that investors in these funds face. These handicaps are of two types. First, their management fees and transaction costs are very high compared with transaction costs and management fees for more traditional fixed-income or equity investments. Yearly management fees and transaction costs of commodity funds have been estimated to average over 19.2% of assets under management.[4] Second, most commodity fund managers appear to rely primarily on trend following and technical trading rules for decision making. These rules have been discredited in the common stock area. In fact, many of these rules were first tested (and found not to work) on commodity data (e.g., Mandelbrot 1966).

In this paper, we will examine the performance of publicly traded commodity funds. One problem encountered in the analysis is that the data sample is small since these funds have not been in existence very long. There are only 6 years of performance figures. In addition, as we will see, the standard deviation of return on these funds is extremely large relative to other investments. This makes the problem of analysis from 6 years of data even more difficult.

This paper is divided into four sections. In Section I we discuss the data we analyze in the subsequent sections. In Section II we examine the performance of publicly traded commodity funds. In particular, we consider whether it is optimal either to hold such a fund in isolation or to add it to an existing portfolio of stocks and bonds. In Section III we examine whether we can differentiate between funds that will do well and funds that will do poorly in the future. If past performance data are indicative of future performance in either an absolute or a relative sense, then performance can be improved beyond that found in Section II. Section IV contains our conclusion.

I. Data

The basic data set employed in this paper is the monthly total rate of return on each publicly traded commodity fund in existence from July 1979 to June 1985. Total return is defined as the cash distribution during any month plus the change in net asset value over the month divided by the value per unit at the beginning of the month.[5] When we performed this study, the latest data available were for the month of June 1985. Thus, we ended our last year in June 1985. We then had six years' worth of usable data. We could have started the data series one year earlier, but there were monthly data on only one fund in that year. Table 13-1 shows the number of funds in existence in June of each sample year that were publicly reporting monthly data.[6] When a fund dissolved midyear, we computed returns as if the proceeds were invested in the average commodity fund. However, dissolved funds were not included in standard deviation calculations.

In order to make some comparisons with alternative investments, we also employed indexes of monthly return performance on several other types of investments. Monthly returns on the Standard and Poor's 500 Stock Index, Treasury bills, long-term government bonds, long-term corporate bonds, and small stocks were taken from Ibbotson (1985). In addition, for our

Table 13-1   Return and Risk Data for Commodity Funds

| | | Average Monthly Return | | |
Year	No. of Funds	For Monthly Holding Period	For Annual Holding Period	Average SD
1	12	.0182	.0027	.1577
2	16	.0219	.0090	.1211
3	34	.0149	.0112	.0824
4	49	−.0191	−.0267	.1167
5	70	−.0020	−.0054	.0793
6	85	.0097	.0048	.0943
Average	. . .	.0073	−.0007	.1130*

*Not simply an average of the six yearly numbers. Rather, it is an average arrived at using the technique discussed in the text.

six-year sample period the Shearson Bond Index was employed. Finally, to get some idea of how a long market position in commodities and futures might perform, monthly rates of return were calculated from the Dow Jones Spot Index and the Dow Jones Futures Index.

II. The Performance of Publicly Traded Commodity Funds

In this section, we will look at the desirability of holding a randomly selected, publicly traded commodity fund. The appropriate way to analyze this question is to examine whether such a commodity fund should be added to a bond or stock portfolio. However, before doing so, we will briefly examine whether a randomly selected commodity fund is a desirable stand-alone investment.

A. Commodity Funds as an Alternative Investment Vehicle

Assume an investor, at the beginning of each year, selected a commodity fund at random. What would the performance look like? Table 13-1 gives a partial answer. Table 13-1 lists the average monthly returns (assuming both

Table 13-2 Return and Risk Data for Comparable Assets

	June 1960–June 1985		Sample 6-Year Period	
	Average Monthly Returns (Annual Holding Period)	SD Monthly Returns*	Average Monthly Returns (Annual Holding Period)	SD Monthly Returns
Common stocks	.0074	.0414	.0131	.0399
Small stocks	.0123	.0639	.0168	.0465
Long-term corporate bonds	.0045	.0271	.0079	.0428
Long-term government bonds	.0041	.0279	.0075	.0435
Shearson Bond Index	N.A.	N.A.	.0097	.0293
Treasury bills	.0051	.0026	.0085	.0015

Source: Ibbotson (1984), except for Shearson Bond Index.
*25 years ending December 1984.

a one-month and a one-year holding period), the average standard deviation of returns, and the number of funds in our study at the beginning of each year. To provide points of comparison, Table 13-2 shows some data for stocks and bonds. All of this data was also computed using a one-year holding period.

The data shown for common stocks, small stocks, and the Shearson Bond Index can be considered typical of the performance of a widely diversified passive investment in each type of security. The common stock data are for the Standard and Poor's 500 Index and would be reflective of the results for most index funds before management fees. The small stock data are for the 20% of the stocks with the lowest capitalization on the NYSE. The amount invested in each stock is directly proportional to the stock's capitalization. Finally, the Shearson index is an index of all government and corporate bonds. Like the stock indexes described above, it is a capitalization-weighted index with the weights directly proportional to the bond's capitalization. Government bonds constitute about 75% of the Shearson Bond Index, and the index is dominated by bonds of intermediate maturity. The Shearson Bond Index is not used over the entire twenty-five-year period because it has only been computed for recent years.

The Ibbotson and Sinquefield indexes (Ibbotson 1985) are indexes for single twenty-year bonds. These indexes, which have become a standard for the industry, are employed here because, unlike the Shearson Bond Index, they exist over a long time period. The disadvantage of the Ibbotson and Sinquefield data for our purpose is that they may not be an accurate representation of a typical bond portfolio. The typical bond portfolio contains many bonds and has a shorter duration. The latter will surely cause differences in return. We would expect a bond portfolio to have less risk than the Ibbotson and Sinquefield data both because of the diversification effect of multiple bonds and because of shorter duration. This is reflected in our sample period. The standard deviation of the Shearson Bond Index is .0293 compared with .0435 for the Ibbotson and Sinquefield government bond index over the same time period.

Before examining commodity funds as an investment vehicle, one other issue needs to be discussed. We are using a mean-variance framework. On the surface it might seem that commodity funds could serve as a hedge against shifts in the prices of consumption goods or inflation. If this were true, then a more general framework such as Long's (1974) or Breeden's (1979) equilibrium model might be necessary to examine their relative value. However, a little reflection shows that this is an inaccurate perspective. As discussed before, commodity funds do not specialize in a commodity or group of commodities. They can hold commodities, commodity futures, financial instruments, financial futures, currencies, and currency futures long or short. Some months a fund can be long a commodity position, and the next period it may be short the same commodity position. Funds allow all these possibilities in their prospectuses. Thus an investor could not analyze a prospectus and determine that a particular commodity fund was a potential hedge against a price rise in any commodity or inflation in general. Further, as we discuss later, the actual return data does not allow an investor to determine which funds might serve as a hedge against inflation. The rank correlation between funds from one period to the next ranked on correlation with inflation is insignificant and sometimes positive and sometimes negative. The correlations of the average fund with inflation is close to zero. Thus an investor could not use an existing commodity fund as a potential inflation hedge, and therefore, a general mean-variance framework is appropriate. The most striking characteristic of commodity funds relative to bonds and stocks is their high standard deviation. The standard deviation of the typical commodity fund is more than three times as high as that of the bond index and more than twice as high as the stock index for most years.

There are two different monthly returns displayed in Table 13-1. The monthly return labeled "monthly holding period" literally applies only if an investor has a one-month holding period. The average monthly return with an annual holding period is the twelfth root of the annual return minus one. Why the difference in the two numbers? To get an annual return, one compounds the monthly returns. The average monthly return for the one-year holding period is the twelfth root of this annual rate. This is, of course, a geometric average, while the figures shown in Table 13-1 under the heading "monthly holding period return" are an arithmetic average. To see what a difference a change in holding period can make, let us examine one of the 12 firms in year 1. It had an arithmetic average return of 9.6% per month, or a 200% annualized return. The actual yearly return was 35%, or 2.53% per month. One reason for this difference was a decline in one month of 43% followed by a rise of 85%. The arithmetic mean of this is 21% while the geometric mean is 2.7%. We feel the assumption of an annual holding period is likely to be more relevant. Few, if any, investors have an investment horizon of only one month. In addition, the sales fees (for purchase of commodity funds) would virtually ensure a negative return on a one-month holding period basis. The same kind of considerations hold, of course, for bonds and stocks. We calculated these returns on the same annual holding period basis.[7]

How do publicly traded commodity funds compare as an investment alternative to bonds or stocks? As discussed earlier, the risk for commodity funds is two to three times larger than for stock or bond funds. While six years is a short period to generalize from, an examination of Table 13-1 shows that returns on commodity funds were poor relative to actual performance on stocks and bonds over the sample period and relative to our expectations concerning stock and bond returns in the long run. The average return on commodity funds was negative in two of the six years and negative overall.[8] For the 266 fund years in our sample, 130 were negative and 136 were positive. These numbers assume that each fund year is equally likely to be picked. Since we have more funds in later years, it emphasizes performance in these years. If we assume that each year is equally likely to be picked and then randomly select a fund within that year, then the probability of picking a fund with a positive return is .56. Commodity funds use Treasury bills as collateral for their futures contracts. With zero selection ability and no management fees or transaction costs we should observe a return equal to that on Treasury bills. We found that, of the 266 fund years in our sample, 162 funds had returns below this benchmark and 104 had returns above. The average probability over the six years of selecting a fund at random with a return above the riskless rate was .42. Over our sample period, the probability that the mean return on commodity funds was equal to or greater than the mean return of either the stock fund or the bond fund was about 5%.[9] Thus both risk and return considerations would suggest that commodity funds are not a useful stand-alone investment.

While commodity funds do not seem to be an attractive alternative to a portfolio of bonds or stocks, it is still possible that they are an appropriate addition to a portfolio of bonds and/or stocks. This depends not only on the expected value and standard deviation of fund returns but also on how these returns are correlated with bond and stock returns. It is to this issue that we now turn.

B. Commodity Funds as Part of an Overall Portfolio

In this section we will examine whether a commodity fund selected at random should be added to a portfolio of stocks and bonds. In Appendix A, we show that a commodity fund should be added as long as[10]

$$\frac{\overline{R}_c - \overline{R}_f}{\sigma_c} > \left(\frac{\overline{R}_p - \overline{R}_f}{\sigma_p}\right) \rho_{cp}.$$

where $\overline{R}_c$ is the expected return of commodity fund c, $\overline{R}_f$ is the riskless rate, σ_c is the standard deviation of the commodity fund c, $\overline{R}_p$ is the expected return of portfolio p, σ_p is the standard deviation of portfolio p, and ρ_{cp} is the correlation between commodity fund c and portfolio p.

The left side of equation (1) should be familiar to most readers as the Sharpe ratio for evaluating mutual funds. Whether or not a commodity fund enters a portfolio depends on estimates of the expected return and standard deviation of return on commodity funds, the expected return and the standard deviation of the bond-stock portfolio, and the correlation between commodity funds and the portfolio.

We now examine each of these in turn. We will start with correlations and then examine standard deviations. We will save expected return for last since this is the most difficult quantity to estimate.

1.   *Correlation coefficients.* In this section of the paper, we examine the correlation of commodity funds with other investments. Our primary concern is how highly correlated these funds are with stock and bond indexes. However, some interesting insights can be gained into the performance of these funds by examining their correlation with some other indexes.

  The arithmetic average of the funds' correlations with seven indexes are presented in Table 13-3. A correlation coefficient for each year is reported along with two average correlation coefficients. The simple

Table 13-3 Correlation Coefficients

Year	Stocks	Bonds	Treasury Bills	Consumer Price Index	Commodity Futures Index	Commodity Cash Index	Average Fund
1	.183	-.021	-.127	.180	.267	.236	.504
2	-.044	-.050	-.065	-.194	-.260	-.114	.541
3	-.003	.228	-.165	-.024	-.402	-.073	.705
4	.050	-.067	-.218	.067	.435	.365	.743
5	-.186	-.203	.194	-.024	.091	.119	.503
6	-.214	.114	.009	-.092	-.543	-.538	.676
Overall average*	-.121	-.003	.010	.009	-.021	-.018	.617
Simple average	-.036	.007	-.062	-.015	-.069	-.001	.612

*The overall average is not an average of the six yearly numbers but rather an average across funds of the correlation of each fund with the respective index for the entire time period over which we have data for the fund.

average is just the arithmetic average of the six yearly correlation coefficients, one for each year. The overall average is computed by finding the correlation coefficient of each fund with the relevant index using data over the full history of that fund and then averaging across funds.

In order to see if the typical commodity fund should be added to a portfolio of stocks and bonds, we need estimates of the correlation of funds with both stocks and bonds. Note that the correlation with both stocks and bonds is close to zero. The maximum association (coefficient of determination) between commodity funds and stocks is less than 5%. This correlation coefficient is positive in two years and negative in four years. The simple average of their correlation coefficients is –.036, while the overall average is –.121.

The correlation coefficients are on average close to and not statistically different from zero. We will use the overall average as our best estimate of the correlation coefficient in later sections. Since this is the smaller value, it gives the maximum chance for commodity funds to enter the portfolio.

When we turn to bonds, we find a parallel case. The largest value for the coefficient of determination is just over 5%. The two estimates of the average correlation are .007 and –.003. We will use –.003, the overall average, in later analysis.

The other numbers in Table 13-3 are not directly related to the analysis in later sections, but they do shed some light on the characteristics of commodity funds. Commodity funds are often thought of as a hedge against inflation. Note that the correlation with the consumer price index is close to zero. Commodity funds do not exhibit the strong tendency to move with inflation usually attributed to them. Instead they show returns that are almost independent of inflation. The correlation of commodity funds with inflation is less than one-fifth of the correlation of Treasury bills with inflation. As a further test, we ranked funds by correlation with inflation in each of the 6 periods. A Spearmen rank correlation was calculated between adjacent periods. While this averaged .10, it was insignificant in each case and sometimes positive and sometimes negative. Thus, commodity funds as a group or individually do not serve as a hedge against inflation.

Another interesting point to note from Table 13-3 is that the return on commodity funds is not consistently correlated with the return on either a commodity cash index or a commodity futures index. The two correlations with each index are small, on average, and positive half the time. This indicates that the typical commodity fund does not

consistently resemble either of those indexes. The major factor accounting for this probably is the tendency of the funds to sometimes sell and
sometimes buy futures contracts, although the tendency of the funds
to weight their long positions in futures differently from the indexes is
also a contributing factor.

The last column in Table 13-3 shows the average correlation of each
fund with an equally weighted index of all funds. This is the only index
with which the funds have consistently high correlation. However, if
the same analysis were performed for mutual funds, the correlation
would be much higher. For example, Sharpe (1966) reports an average
correlation of close to .90 between mutual funds and a market index.
Thus commodity fund managers do make decisions that lead to similar
patterns of returns but not nearly to the extent of managers of common
stock mutual funds.

2. *Standard deviation of commodity funds.* Table 13-1 can be used to estimate
    the anticipated standard deviation for a randomly selected commodity
    fund. As noted above, the standard deviation of the typical commodity
    fund is two to three times the standard deviation of a bond or stock
    index.

    Although there is year-to-year variability in the average standard
    deviation across funds, it is not so large as to suggest that the future
    will be much different from the past. What is our best estimate of the
    standard deviation of the average commodity fund? From the high
    correlation of returns on individual funds with the fund index, we see
    that fund returns exhibit strong cross-sectional dependence. If this
    dependence were reasonably stable and there were an equal number
    of funds each year, then an arithmetic average of the standard deviation
    across all funds and all years would be appropriate.

    However, the number of funds varies dramatically over time from
    12 in the first year to 85 in the sixth. To use a simple average of the
    variance on all funds does not take into account this change in the
    number of funds. This would overemphasize the common element
    across funds in the sixth year relative to the first year. To adjust for this
    change in number, we regressed each fund's return against the return
    on an index of all funds. This divided the total variance into the
    systematic component and a component unique to each fund for each
    year. We then calculated an average unique variance by averaging
    across all funds and all years (266 fund-years). This variance was added
    to our best estimate of the systematic variance to produce an overall

estimate. The details are discussed in Appendix B and the estimate is reported in Table 13-1.

Although the estimate of the average standard deviation of monthly returns from the six years of data is likely to be a good estimate of the future standard deviation, it is hard to look at Table 13-1 and feel very comfortable about any estimate of the mean return. It would be nice to have a longer history. Unfortunately, this does not exist. Instead of using Table 13-1 to get an estimate of expected return, we will solve equation (1) for the break-even expected return and then use the data in table 1 to analyze whether or not commodity funds are likely to have returns higher than this break-even point.

3. *Break-even analysis.* The other inputs we need in order to apply equation (1) are the expected return and standard deviation of the optimum bond-stock mix. What values might an investor expect for returns on stocks and bonds and for the covariance structure between them? We used two sets of data for stocks and bonds to estimate these: the last six years and the last twenty-five years of data. Both are shown in Table 13-2. For the twenty-five-year bond index we used an average of long-term government and corporate bonds. This gave us an expected return of .0043 and a standard deviation of .0275. For the six-year bond index we used the numbers shown in Table 13-2 for the Shearson Bond Index.

    If one compares the return on bonds to the Treasury bill rate over the last six years and last twenty-five years, the Treasury bill rate is higher. Unless bond returns are negatively correlated with stock returns (and there is no evidence that they are), bonds will never enter the optimum portfolio. Thus the relevant question is, Should a commodity fund be added to a stock fund? For the six-year data the inequality is

$$\frac{\overline{R}_c - .0085}{.1130} > \left(\frac{.0131 - .0085}{.0399}\right)(-.121).$$

Solving for $\overline{R}_c$ gives the minimum expected return that a commodity fund must earn to enter the optimum portfolio. This result and a similar calculation for twenty-five years of data are shown in the first two rows of Table 13-4.

We used a second set of stock and bond return forecasts to obtain break-even returns for commodity funds. The optimal bond-stock split

Table 13-4   Break-Even Rates of Return

Scenario	% Stock	Excess Return $(\bar{R}_p - R_F)$*	SD (σ)*	Correlation with Portfolio ρ (cp)†‡	Break-even Rate of Return $(\bar{R}_c)$‡
6 year	100	.0046	.0399	−.121	.0069
25 year	100	.0023	.0414	−.121	.0077
6 year	63	.0033	.0309	−.099	.0073
25 year§	63	.0012	.0289	−.110	.0080

*Entries from Table 13-2.

†The covariance of a commodity fund with a portfolio is the sum of the proportion in each asset in the portfolio times the correlation of the commodity fund with the asset times the product of the standard deviation of commodity funds times the standard deviation of the asset. For example, the covariance for the third entry is .63(−.121)(.1130)(.0399) + .37(−.003)(.1130)(.0293).

‡Assumes standard deviation of commodity funds of .1130 (see Table 13-1).

§Assumes a correlation of .10 between stocks and bonds, which is the average correlation between corporate and government bonds and the stock index, as shown in Ibbotson (1985).

using the full 1926–85 Ibbotson and Sinquefield data is 63% stock and 37% bonds.[11] We took these optimum proportions and applied these proportions to the six-year and twenty-five-year data shown in Table 13-2. We again solved for the expected return on commodity funds that would just cause commodity funds to enter the optimum portfolio. These results are shown in the last two rows of Table 13-4.

The expected return that would have commodity funds enter is very similar across the four sets of assumptions. It varies between .0069 and .0080 across the four scenarios examined with an average of .0075.

Examining Tables 13-1 and 13-4 shows that, if a monthly holding period is used, and if we take the six years of actual return data as a reasonable estimate of expected returns, then the average return of .0073 is below the average number in Table 13-4 and commodity funds should not enter. If an annual holding period is used and the six-year average return of −.0007 is used as the expected return, the evidence is even stronger that commodity funds should not enter. As discussed earlier, we feel that an annual holding period is the more reasonable assumption. For our sample of 266 fund years, 163 had returns below and 103 had returns above .0075. The average probability of the return on a commodity fund being above .0075 over the six years is .42. The odds of the mean return on commodity funds being .0075 or better when the average return over the six years is −.0007 and the standard deviation of the mean return across the six years is .0052 are less than 6%.

An alternative way of examining expected returns for commodity funds is to utilize economic theory to examine what we might logically expect for returns. Commodity managers frequently go short as well as long in the futures contracts. Table 13-3 shows correlation coefficients of fund returns with futures and spot indexes of −.021 and −.018, respectively. Only 1% of the return of commodity funds can be explained by index movements. The average correlation is sometimes positive and sometimes negative. These results provide no evidence of a consistent pattern of long or short purchases. If managers were equally likely to be long or short, the expected return before transaction costs, management fees, and management forecasting ability would be zero. This is in contrast to stock and bond funds that have substantial positive expected returns before transaction costs and management fees, even with no management forecasting ability.

Transaction costs should not be taken lightly. Even though costs per transaction are low, transactions are frequent. Irwin and Brorsen (1985) find commissions averaging 10.7% for the 20 firms they sample. In addition, the management fee on commodity funds is substantially higher than the management fee on stock or bond funds. There are two types of management fees on commodity funds: a fee related to asset size and a fee related to performance. For the funds in our sample, asset fees ranged 3%–6% per year. This is in contrast to stock and bond funds where one-half of 1% is usual. In addition, there is an incentive fee. Examining Table 13-1 might suggest that incentive fees are unimportant. However, given the tremendous variability of monthly returns and the basing of incentive fees on shorter-term performance, incentive fees can be high even with poor long-term performance. Irwin and Brorsen (1985) find that management and incentive fees average 8.5%. Thus total yearly fees of 19.2% can be expected. In contrast, Sharpe (1981) reports that total fees for mutual funds average about 1% per year.

Examining Table 13-4 shows that commodity managers must earn a return of about 9% per year to be attractive investments. Adding this to transaction costs and management fees of above 19% and an expected return that is close to zero without forecasting ability suggests that a return to forecasting ability of over 28% is necessary for commodity funds to be attractive. Evidence from other security markets should lead to a healthy degree of skepticism.

Thus, actual returns of commodity funds as well as the more general evidence of financial economics suggest that a randomly selected commodity fund should not be held. In the next section we will examine whether there are characteristics of commodity funds that allow funds that will have above- average performance to be selected.

III. Prediction of Superior Performing Funds

Ex post, there is always a commodity fund that did best. Given the high variance in fund performance (both over time for any fund and cross sectionally among funds), it is not at all surprising that at any point of time or over any short period of time there always exists a fund that did well. The relevant question for an investor is, Can he or she identify, ex ante, the funds that will do well? In this section, we shall examine whether any of several attributes of fund performance is predictive of future performance. The degree of consistency and predictability of performance is interesting in its own right. It also has major implications for the inclusion of commodity funds in optimal portfolios.

This section is divided into two parts. In the first part, we discuss the tests of consistency and predictability we use as well as the performance series we look at. In the second part, we discuss empirical results.

A. Consistency and Predictability

The majority of our analysis in this section is based on two types of tests. The first type is a test of consistency. That is, do funds that have high values on a measure in one period tend to have high values in the subsequent period? Two separate tests of consistency will be used. The first measures consistency across all funds, while the second examines consistency only for those funds that have done extremely well or extremely poorly. The second type is a test of predictability, namely, whether past values of a performance measure forecast better than a naive model.

1.   *Consistency.* To test consistency we examined performance both across all funds and for the tails. In order to judge whether overall perfor-

mance in one year was associated with performance in the next year, Spearman's rank correlation was computed between all adjacent years for all funds that were present in both of the paired years.[12] These results are contained in Table 13-5.

For example, all funds that existed in the first year of our sample period were ranked by return from high to low in that year. The return of each of these funds was computed for the second year of our sample, and funds were again ranked from best to worst. The Spearman correlations were computed between the ranks for the first and second years. In the case of the first and second set of paired years, small sample tests of Spearman's coefficient were used.[13] For the third, fourth, and fifth paired sample years, Kendall's large sample test was used to compute the adjusted correlation coefficient, which is distributed as Student's t.[14]

A second set of tests were performed to examine consistency. That is, if we selected the funds that had unusually high (or low) values on a performance characteristic in one period, would we get unusually high or low values for that or another important characteristic in the next period? For example, the return from purchasing the three funds that had the highest return and holding them for one year was compared with the return from purchasing and holding the three funds with the lowest return. Similarly, the return from purchasing and holding the top third, middle third, and bottom third of funds in each period was computed and compared. Even if there is no consistency across the population of funds from period to period, it is possible that there is consistency in the very best and worst performing funds.

2.   *Predictability.* While a measure of association is interesting in itself, perhaps the more important set of tests for our purposes is whether past values of a performance measure can be used to predict future performance. To test this, we examine whether past values of a performance measure are better predictors than the most naive possible prediction (see Tables 13-6 through 13-9). In all cases (except for one noted in the next section), the naive prediction used is that the best estimate for all funds is zero. For example, in the case of predicting returns, we compare the prediction that next period's return equals this period's return with the prediction that next period's return equals zero. If past return is a better predictor than zero, then past return allows one to differentiate between funds.

Table 13-5 Spearman Rank Correlations

	10 Observations: Year 1 vs. Year 2		15 Observations: Year 2 vs. Year 3		34 Observations: Year 3 vs. Year 4		49 Observations: Year 4 vs. Year 5		67 Observations: Year 5 vs. Year 6	
	Correlation	t-Value[a]	Correlation	t-Value[a]	Correlation	t-Value[b]	Correlation	t-Value[b]	Correlation	t-Value[b]
Sharpe ratio: Year t vs. year t + 1[c]	.2242	…	.4393	**	.0591	.335	−.1008	−.695	.2886	2.43*
Returns: Year t vs. year t + 1	.0667	…	.4679	**	.1499	.858*	.1023	.705	.3068	2.600*
SD: Year t vs. year t + 1	.9152	*	.4464	**	.1704	.978	.6543	5.932*	.3357	2.873*
SD: Year t vs. Sharpe ratio year t + 1	−.6485	**	−.4429	**	−.4460	−2.819*	−.0548	−.376	−.1923	−1.580

[a]For small samples (under 30), the statistical significance of any correlation was arived at using small sample tests based on the number of permutations possible. For a discussion of the tests, see Siegel (1956, pp. 210, 211); and for critical values, see Siegel (1956, Table P, p. 284).

[b]For large samples (over 30), t-values were computed using Kendall's procedure. See Siegel (1956, p. 212) for a discussion of the procedure

[c]These tests are conducted in terms of monthly returns assuming an annual holding period. The tests were also run on monthly returns assuming a monthly holding period. The results are very similar, and, in the interest of brevity, the second set of results have not been reported.

*Statistically significant at the 1% level.

**Statistically significant at the 5% level.

Table 13-6 Values of Sharpe at t + 1 from Ranking by Sharpe Ratio in t

	Period 2		Period 3		Period 4		Period 5		Period 6		Avg. Ratio	Avg. Rank
	Sharpe Ratio	Rank	Sharpe Ratio	Rank	Sharpe Ratio	Rank	Sharpe Ratio	Rank	Sharpe Ratio	Rank		
Top 3	.3279	1	.1031	1	-.1834	2	-.0933	2	.3392	2	.0987	1.4
Bottom 3	.2898	2	-.1966	2	-.1032	1	.1262	1	.0770	1	.0386	1.6
Top ⅓*	.3279	1	.0569	1	-.2427	1	-.1903	2	.0622	2	.0028	1.2
Middle ⅓	-.1154	3	-.0567	2	-.4090	3	-.2308	3	-.0488	3	-.1495	2.6
Bottom ⅓	.2898	2	-.1685	3	-.2691	2	-.1115	1	-.1613	1	-.0841	2.2

*In forming the three groups, if the total number of firms was not divisible by 3, the extra one or two firms were placed in the middle group.

Table 13-7 Value of Return at t + 1 for Ranking of Return at t

	Period 2		Period 3		Period 4		Period 5		Period 6		Avg. Return	Avg. Rank
	Return	Rank	Return	Rank	Return	Rank	Return	Rank	Return	Rank		
Top 3	.0167	1	.0170	1	-.0229	1	-.0109	2	.0044	2	-.0009	1.4
Bottom 3	.0149	2	-.0054	2	-.0285	2	.0249	1	.0136	1	.0039	1.6
Top ⅓*	.0167	1	.0127	1	-.0162	1	-.0009	2	.0152	1	.0059	1.2
Middle ⅓	.0050	3	.0118	2	-.0351	3	.0035	1	.0003	3	-.0029	2.4
Bottom ⅓	.0149	2	.0045	3	-.0275	2	-.0127	3	.0018	2	-.0038	2.4

*In forming the three groups, if the total number of firms was not divisible by 3, the extra one or two firms were placed in the middle group.

Table 13-8 Value of Standard Deviation at $t+1$ for Ranking of Standard Deviation at t

	Period 2		Period 3		Period 4		Period 5		Period 6		Avg. SD	Avg. Rank
	SD	Rank	SD	Rank	SD	Rank	SD	Rank	SD	Rank		
Top 3	.2300	1	.1131	1	.1795	2	.1599	1	.0364	2	.1438	1.4
Bottom 3	.0637	2	.0639	2	.1955	1	.0346	2	.0639	1	.0843	1.6
Top ⅓*	.2300	1	.0934	1	.1244	1	.1077	1	.1326	1	.1376	1.0
Middle ⅓	.1183	2	.0749	2	.1074	3	.0880	2	.0915	2	.0960	2.2
Bottom ⅓	.0637	3	.0648	3	.1127	2	.0525	3	.0678	3	.0723	2.8

*In forming the three groups, if the total number of firms was not divisible by 3, the extra one or two firms were placed in the middle group.

Table 13-9 Values of Sharpe Ratio at $t+1$ for Ranking of Standard Deviation at t

	Period 2		Period 3		Period 4		Period 5		Period 6		Avg. Ratio	Avg. Rank
	Sharpe Ratio	Rank	Sharpe Ratio	Rank	Sharpe Ratio	Rank	Sharpe Ratio	Rank	Sharpe Ratio	Rank		
Top 3	-.1312	2	.0520	2	-.3518	2	-.0765	1	-.5559	2	-.2127	1.8
Bottom 3	.5380	1	.1335	1	-.1032	1	-.3483	2	.1481	1	.0736	1.2
Top ⅓*	-.1312	3	-.0992	3	-.3722	3	-.2768	3	-.1229	2	-.2005	3.0
Middle ⅓	.0420	2	-.0697	2	-.3637	2	-.0552	1	.0077	3	-.0878	1.6
Bottom ⅓	.5380	1	.1160	1	-.1890	1	-.2116	2	-.0353	1	.0436	1.4

*In forming the three groups, if the total number of firms was not divisible by 3, the extra one or two firms were placed in the middle group.

For each fund present in a particular year, we predict performance in the subsequent year. We examined five pairs of adjacent years. For each fund, we computed the squared forecast error under each of our two forecasts. Since we have related samples (two forecasts for each fund), the properties of the mean difference in squared forecast error were examined. The average difference in squared forecast error and the standard deviation of the mean difference in squared forecast error was computed and the associated t-value of the difference is reported in Table 13-10.

A positive value in this table indicates that the naive model led to lower forecast errors. For the later three pairs of years, the samples are large enough that, by the central limit theorem, the statistic should be normally distributed. A one-tailed test is used to see if past performance predicts better than the naive model. Statistical significance is indicated in Table 13-10. For the first two pairs of years, the sample is too small to resort to the central limit theorem. Here, the Wilcoxon Matched Pairs Signed-Ranks Test was used to judge statistical significance.[15] In Table 13-10, t-values are reported to show how many standard deviations away from zero the mean is, even though they are not used to test significance.

B. The Empirical Results

Examining equation (1) shows that the condition for commodity funds to enter into an optimal portfolio is the Sharpe performance index. In this section, we first examine the Sharpe ratio itself to see if its value across funds is consistent and predictable over time. We then examine each of its components, return and standard deviation, in turn. If either of these shows predictability, we will then examine whether it can be used to better differentiate between funds with respect to their Sharpe ratios. In all cases, we will use monthly returns based on an annual holding period. Results for a monthly holding period were very similar.

1. *The Sharpe ratio.* The first question examined was, Do funds that have a high value for the Sharpe ratio in one period tend to have a high value for the Sharpe ratio in the subsequent period?

    From Table 13-5, the average of the five rank correlations for the Sharpe index for adjacent years is 0.182. While it is statistically different from zero at the 1% level in one out of five years, it is negative in one year and the average association is less than 4%.

Table 13-10 *t*-Values of Squared Error of Forecast Model Minus Naive Forecast

	10 Observations: Years 1 and 2	15 Observations: Years 2 and 3	34 Observations: Years 3 and 4	49 Observations: Years 4 and 5	67 Observations: Years 5 and 6
Sharpe ratio at t as forecaster of Sharpe ratio at $t + 1$*	-.05	1.48	-1.72	.81	2.18
Returns at t as forecaster of return at $t + 1$*	.49	2.04	4.94	2.36	2.57
SD at t as forecaster at SD at $t + 1$†	-1.03	.89	1.02	-.60	.25

*These tests were conducted in terms of monthly returns assuming a yearly holding period. Similar results were obtained when monthly returns assuming a monthly holding period were used. The naive model was zero for all funds.

†The naive model was the average (across all funds) SD for the previous year. The values used were .1577, .1211, .0824, .1167, and .0793, respectively.

When we examine the tails of the distribution (Table 13-6), we find a slight amount of information in the Sharpe coefficients. On average, the top three funds (and the top third of funds) ranked by the Sharpe ratio have higher values for their Sharpe ratio than the bottom three funds (or bottom third of funds). Lest we place too much emphasis on these results, we should remark that, while the top three funds do better than the bottom three on average, they do worse in two of the five years. Furthermore, while the top third of funds does better than the bottom third on average, the bottom third does better than the middle third on average. Based on these results, it appears unlikely that using the Sharpe ratio to select funds will lead to improvement.

When we examine (Table 13-10) whether this period's Sharpe ratio is a better predictor of next period's ratio than is zero, we get ambiguous results. Past Sharpe ratios forecast better in one year and worse in four years. They never forecast better at a statistically significant level, while the naive model performs best in one year at a statistically significant level.

We now turn to the components of the Sharpe ratio, return and standard deviation, to see if they show consistency and predictability over time.

2.   *Returns.* From Table 13-5 we see that the average of the five rank correlation coefficients in monthly returns assuming an annual holding period is 0.219. The correlation is positive in each sample case and is significantly different from zero at the 5% level in two of the five samples. While the association is always positive, the extent of association (less than 5%) is relatively small.

Table 13-7 shows that, if an investor bought the three funds that performed the worst and held them for one year, on average the investor would do very slightly better than buying the three funds that performed best. One would have done better in two years and worse in three years. If the sample is divided into three groups according to returns, the best performance, on average, would have been obtained by buying the third of the funds that performed best. The consistency of the return measure appears to be marginally better than the consistency of the Sharpe index. However, the change in ranking according to how the tails are defined warns us not to place undue reliance on this criterion. When we examine predictability of past returns (Table 13-10), we find that the naive forecast of zero return for each fund is a better forecast of next year's average monthly return than assuming that next year's return equals last year's return. In fact, if a two-tailed test were used, the naive model would produce lower error at the 5% significant level in four out of five cases. Clearly, past returns of any fund provide no information for predicting future returns.

3. *Risk.* While past return might not tell the potential investor anything about the kind of returns he or she should expect to receive in the future, the past would still be useful if it could allow the investor to differentiate between funds in terms of riskiness. The measure of riskiness we examined was the standard deviation of fund returns.[16]

There does seem to be consistency in standard deviation. The average rank correlation (across the five sets of paired years) between standard deviation in one period and standard deviation in the next (Table 13-5) was .0514. This is the highest value for any of our measures of performance. Furthermore, the average rank correlation across funds in each of the paired years is always positive, and it is statistically significantly different from zero on average and in four of the five paired years.

Turning now to an examination of the tails (Table 13-8) of the distribution, we see evidence that past ordering by risk provides information about future ordering by risk. When we examine the top three and bottom three funds, the top three have the highest risk on average and in three out of five years. When we look at the three equally sized groups, the top third of the funds has the biggest risk on average and in each of the five years. There seems to be information about the future risk contained in past risk for firms with very high or low standard deviations.

In examining prediction for the other variables, we have used zero as the naive forecasting model. However, this seems inappropriate (too naive) in the case of standard deviation, since we know that all values have to be greater than or equal to zero. Instead of zero, we used as the naive forecast of next year's standard deviation for each fund the average standard deviation (across funds) for the prior year. Thus the naive model forecasts all standard deviations as identical and the naive model should perform better if differences in the standard deviation of funds from the mean in the past contain no information about future differences. The results do not allow us to conclude that past standard deviations are a useful predictive tool. However, past standard deviations do outperform the naive model in three of our five paired years. While past risk does not seem to be a good predictor of future risk, there is fairly strong evidence that past values of risk can be used to identify those funds that will be most (or least) risky in future periods.

4.   *Risk as a predictor of desirability.* We have seen that, while there is at best weak evidence of return or the Sharpe ratio being able to rank funds according to future values of these measures, there is reasonably strong evidence of persistence in the relative riskiness of funds. The purpose of this section is to see whether selecting funds on the basis of standard deviation leads to improvements in the Sharpe ratio.

Table 13-5 shows the rank correlation of the standard deviation of funds in each year with the Sharpe ratio for funds in the next year. The relationship is negative in five of five paired years. It is statistically significantly different from zero (and negative) in three years. Thus, low standard deviation funds are associated with higher Sharpe ratios. The average rank correlation is –.357, which is considerably larger in absolute magnitude than the rank correlation between the Sharpe ratio in successive periods.

In Table 13-9, we present the results (in terms of the Sharpe ratio obtained one year later) of purchasing the top three funds, the bottom three funds, and the top third, middle third, and bottom third of funds ranked by their standard deviation. On average and in four out of five years, the best Sharpe ratio is obtained by purchasing the funds with the lowest standard deviation. There does appear to be information present in these rankings.

Both the association of standard deviation in one period with standard deviation in the next and the association of standard deviation and the Sharpe ratio in the next period suggest that standard deviation might be useful in picking good commodity funds. Examining Table 13-8 suggests that standard deviations of .07–.14 might be possible by selecting a low or high standard deviation fund in the prior period. Substituting this range into equation (1) gives the break-even return necessary to include a commodity fund ranging from .0067 to .0075 for the six-year 100% stock case with similar results for the other scenarios. Thus, the predictability of standard deviations results in almost no change in the break-even rate.

Furthermore, it is ambiguous whether a high or low standard deviation fund is desirable. Examining equation (1) shows that, for returns below the risk- free rate, a high standard deviation is desirable.

An investor can probably select a fund with a standard deviation different from the average. Furthermore, low standard deviations have some association with higher Sharpe ratios. However, given the minimal impact on the break-even rate and the ambiguity whether small or large standard deviations are desirable, the predictability of standard deviation is unlikely to affect the basic decision whether commodity funds should be selected in the first place.

IV. Conclusion

This paper is the first comprehensive review of publicly traded commodity funds.[17] The returns on these funds are highly variable, with a standard deviation two to three times that of bonds or common equity indexes. This variability was fairly consistent from year to year, and we expect that estimates from our six-year period will be sustained in the future. The correlation structure is also fairly stable from year to year. Calculating a break-even expected return and comparing it with actual returns make it doubtful that public commodity funds should be included in an investor's portfolio.

When we examined whether we could select a superior commodity fund on the basis of past performance the answer was probably not. Using the past value of the Sharpe ratio as a predictor led to almost no improvement in performance. This was true whether we used the full set of funds or just the extremes. A similar result was obtained with returns. However, there is predictability in standard deviation. A fund with a lower or higher standard deviation than the average can probably be selected on the basis of past values. However, this has minimal impact on the break-even rate and hence has little impact on the desirability of commodity funds.

Appendix A

The condition for a security to enter an optimal portfolio is easy to derive using the simple rules of Elton, Gruber, and Padberg (1976). Consider an asset and a portfolio. Since there is a single portfolio and a single asset, there is a single correlation coefficient of interest. Thus the assumption of a constant correlation coefficient can be made without loss in generality. As Elton, et al. (1976), have shown, a security will enter in a positive amount if

$$\frac{\overline{R}_i - R_F}{\sigma_i} - \frac{\rho}{1 - \rho + N_k\rho} \sum_{j\varepsilon k} \frac{\overline{R}_j - R_F}{\sigma_j} > 0,$$

where $\overline{R}_i$ is the expected return on asset i, R_F is the riskless rate of interest, ρ is the correlation coefficient, N_k is the number of securities, and k is the set of included securities. With a single asset and a single portfolio, N_k and k are both one and the condition becomes

$$\frac{\overline{R}_i - R_F}{\sigma_i} - \rho\left(\frac{\overline{R}_\rho - R_F}{\sigma_p}\right) > 0.$$

This is equation (1) above. The same condition can be derived in a more cumbersome fashion using first-order conditions.

Appendix B

To estimate the variance, we ran the following single-index model for each year y:

$$R_{ity} = \alpha_{iy} + \beta_{iy}I_{yt} + \varepsilon_{ity},$$

where R_{ity} is the return in month t of year y for commodity fund i; I_{yt} is the value of the index in month t of year y, in which the index is an equally weighted index of all commodity funds; β_{iy} is the responsiveness of commodity fund i to changes in the index in year y; ε_{ity} is a random variable for fund i in month t of year y and represents unsystematic return; and α_{iy} is a constant in year y for fund i.

The total variance of fund i in year y is given by

$$\sigma_{iy}^2 = \beta_{iy}^2\sigma_{Iy}^2 + \sigma_{\varepsilon iy}^2,$$

where σ_{Iy}^2 is the variance of the index in year y and $\sigma_{\varepsilon iy}^2$ is the residual variance for fund i in year y.

Since the residuals are independent over time and the removal of the average fund performance makes them very close to cross-sectionally independent, the best estimate of the average variance of the residuals is

$$\sigma_\varepsilon^2 = \frac{\sum\limits_{y}\sum\limits_{i}\sigma_{\varepsilon iy}^2}{266}.$$

Similarly, the best estimate of the market index variance is an average across the six years:

$$\sigma_f^2 = \frac{\sum_{y} \sigma_{Iy}^2}{6}.$$

Our best estimate of the yearly variance for an average fund is the sum of the average beta squared times the variance plus the average unique variance:

$$\overline{\beta_i^2}\sigma_f^2 + \sigma_\varepsilon^2.$$

Endnotes

1. Managed Accounts Report (1979-85). We would like to thank Morton Baratz for helpful comments and information.

2. Prospectus of Dean Witter Reynolds Commodity Partners (April 1985), p. 33.

3. Prospectus of Matterhorn Commodity Partners (April 9, 1981), p. 11.

4. See Elton and Gruber (1987, ch. 20) for a discussion of transaction costs on futures and commodity funds, and see Irwin and Brorsen (1985).

5. Generally, publicly traded commodity funds allow investors to liquidate their holdings on the last day of any month at their net asset value. Risk from these funds is in reality higher relative to other investments than the numbers in subsequent tables indicate because the alternative investments can be liquidated at any time during the month.

6. Eight funds dissolved due to poor performance during our sample period. One more dissolved during the period but was not included in our sample because it did not exist during any June. Three more went bankrupt shortly after our period. Dissolution values were not obtainable for three funds. For these funds we assumed dissolutions at their prior months' asset value. This overstates returns.

7. Actually, the difference in return for these instruments is so small that it makes much less difference whether a one-month or one-year holding period is assumed.

8. We computed both Sharpe and Jensen performance measures. For the Jensen performance measures, we used both an index of bonds and an index of stocks. All performance measures had negative values, indicating that commodity funds should not be held. Actually, this result could

have been anticipated from the numbers presented in Tables 13-1 and 13-2.

9. The standard deviation of mean returns across the six years is .0052.

10. An equivalent condition is presented in Blume (1984)

11. This was obtained by solving standard first-order conditions. The calculations are available from the authors.

12. Correlation coefficients were also computed on the unranked (raw) data. The results were so similar to the rank correlations that we have not bothered to report them or to discuss them further in this paper.

13. See Siegel (1956, pp. 211, 212, and Table P).

14. See Siegel (1956, pp. 212, 213).

15 See Siegel (1956, pp. 75–83, and Table G).

16. In addition, the rank correlations and naive predictions were examined for betas and correlations of the funds with the common stock index, the bond index, and an index of commodity bond performance. No association or predictive power was found.

17. Lintner (1983) discussed results for eight publicly traded funds that existed over a 3 1/2-year period.

References

Blume, Marshall. "The use of alphas to improve performance." *Journal of Portfolio Management* 11 (Fall 1984): 86–92.

Breeden, Douglas. "An intertemporal asset pricing model with stochastic consumption and investment opportunities." *Journal of Financial Economics* 6 (September 1979): 265–96.

Elton, Edwin J. and Gruber, Martin J. *Modern Portfolio Theory and Investment Analysis.* 3d ed. New York: Wiley, 1987.

Elton, Edwin J., Gruber, Martin J., and Padberg, Manfred. Simple criteria for optimal portfolio selection. *Journal of Finance* 31 (December 1976): 1341–57.

Ibbotson, Roger. *Stocks, Bonds, Bills and Inflation 1985 Yearbook.* Chicago: Ibbotson, 1985.

Irwin, Scott H., and Brorsen, Wade B. Public futures funds. *Journal of Futures Markets* 5 (Summer 1985): 149–71.

Lintner, J. The potential role of managed commodity—financial futures accounts (and/or funds) in portfolios of stocks and bonds. Paper presented at the annual conference of the Financial Analysts Federation, Toronto, 1983.

Long, John. Stock prices, inflation, and the term structure of interest rates. *Journal of Financial Economics* 1 (July 1974): 131–79.

Managed Accounts Report. Columbia, Md.: L.J.R. Communications, 1979–85.

Mandelbrot, Benoit. Forecasts of futures prices, unbiased markets and Martingale models. *Journal of Business* 39, no. 4, pt. 2:242–55, 1966.

Sharpe, William. Mutual fund performance. *Journal of Business* 39, no. 4, pt. 2:119–39, 1966.

Sharpe, William. *Investments.* 2d ed. Englewood Cliffs, N.J.: Prentice-Hall, 1981.

Siegel, Sidney. *Nonparametric Statistics for the Behavioral Sciences.* New York: McGraw-Hill, 1956.

Chapter Fourteen

Management Summary

Title: "A Further Examination of the Risk/Return Characteristics of Portfolios Combining Commodity Futures Contracts with Common Stocks"

Publication: Working Paper Series, Center for the Study of Futures Markets, Columbia University, February 1988.

Authors: Anthony F. Herbst, Professor, University of Texas at El Paso
Joseph P. McCormack, Professor, Texas Christian University

Data: Monthly data for 58 months (January, 1980 through November, 1984) of prices for individual common stocks and individual commodity contracts.

Methodology: This is an updated version of their earlier work which dealt with 48 months of data. The methodology is modified slightly from the previous study in that two portfolios are constructed consisting of ten and fifteen randomly selected common stocks each (as opposed to the five portfolios of eight, twelve, fourteen, sixteen and thirty-two stocks each used in their earlier study). As before, randomly selected commodity futures contracts are added to the stock portfolios, one at a time, replacing randomly chosen individual stocks. The effects of such diversification were measured on a return-risk basis.

Results: Adding commodity futures to common stock portfolios was shown to significantly reduce the variability (standard deviation) of the portfolio. The reduction was most significant in portfolios which had lower levels of return before diversification. Portfolios containing 25%–30% commodity futures tended to dominate others consisting of common stock only, and combinations of commodity futures and common stocks with less than 25% futures.

A Further Examination of the Risk/Return Characteristics of Portfolios Combining Commodity Futures Contracts with Common Stocks

Anthony F. Herbst
Joseph P. McCormack

Summary

There has been a great deal of research on diversification and the benefits of diversification. Indeed, diversification is a well accepted tenet of investing.

Two of the most often quoted studies on diversification, Evans and Archer (1968) and Wagner and Lau (1971) showed that the total risk (defined as variability of returns) of a portfolio decreased rapidly of stocks were initially combined to form a portfolio. As more and more stocks were combined into the portfolio, the risk continued to decrease but at a slower and slower rate until all possible stocks were combined into the portfolio and the risk of the portfolio reached a non-zero minimum. The risk that remained was called nondiversifiable risk or systematic risk and the risk that was eliminated or

This research was aided by a grant from the Center for the Study of Futures Markets, Columbia University. The authors wish also to acknowledge the assistance of the Commodity Futures Trading Commission in obtaining some of the data used in this study.

289

diversified away by combining stocks into a portfolio was called diversifiable risk or unsystematic risk.

Through the seventies, diversification research was limited primarily to common stocks. The research that was done tended to look at correlations between a portfolio of U.S. common stocks and a portfolio of foreign stocks (or some other alternative investment vehicle) to determine how these two portfolios moved relative to one another. The emphasis was on portfolios of U.S. stocks or portfolios of foreign stocks, not on adding individual foreign or alternative investments to an already existing portfolio of U.S. common stocks.

It was not until the 1980s that researchers started to consider empirically the possibility of adding other investments to diversify an existing portfolio. Bodie and Rosansky (1980) started the decade of the eighties by using the older technique of examining a portfolio consisting of two component portfolios—one being a portfolio of common stocks and the other being a portfolio of commodities. This was followed by Irwin and Brorsen (1985) who examined a portfolio consisting of three component portfolios—one being a portfolio of common stocks, one a portfolio of commodities, and one being a portfolio of U.S. Treasury bills.

This study extends the earlier studies of Bodie and Rosansky (1980) and Irwin and Brorsen (1985) by examining the influence of commodities on a portfolio of common stocks on a stepwise basis. In this study commodities are added one at a time to an already existing portfolio of common stocks such that the commodity added replaces one of the common stocks. Different size portfolios are also examined to determine the effect of portfolio size.

The common stocks selected for the portfolios were chosen randomly from the Center for Research of Securities Prices (CRSP) data tapes. The commodities selected were those that had the highest loading from a varimax rotation of a principal components analysis, following Herbst and McCormack (1985). The selection of the commodities was done to insure that each of the eight commodities selected had very little correlation with any of the other commodities. For example, if an investor added a soybean futures contract to his portfolio, he would not also add a soybean meal or a soybean oil contract because these contracts would not offer as much diversification benefit than if the investor had chosen another unrelated futures contract such as gold. Also, if gold was added to a portfolio, platinum or silver would not also be added because they would not enhance diversification.

Initial portfolios of ten and fifteen common stocks were used and the efficient (mean-variance) frontier was constructed using a Markowitz algorithm. One common stock was randomly selected to be replaced with one commodity which was also randomly selected (from the eight commodities considered) and the efficient frontier was again constructed. Another common stock would then be selected and replaced with a commodity and the efficient frontier constructed until eight stocks had been deleted and eight commodities added. This resulted in the creation of nine efficient frontiers— one for the all common stock portfolio and one each for the various combined stock/commodity portfolios.

The above process was repeated one hundred times. The efficient frontiers were examined at eleven specific, evenly spaced points along their return axis. The level of variance of these eleven points was measured and averaged. These average levels of variance were compared to one another over the different portfolio compositions.

The evidence obtained in this research indicates that the addition of commodities to an initial all common stock portfolio reduces the risk of the portfolio over a portion of the efficient frontier. This means that the efficient frontier is not entirely shifted, but only a portion.

The portion of the efficient frontier that is shifted upward or to the left is the low and moderate return portion. This tends to indicate that commodity futures contracts may be appropriate for investors who are more risk averse. Interestingly, the evidence seems to indicate that combined portfolios would be less attractive to risk loving investors (unless they like investing in commodities because they like the thrill of the game).

The evidence also indicates that the benefit of diversification decreases as the concentration of commodities increases. In other words, concentrations of commodities in excess of 30% tend to increase rather than decrease the risk of the portfolio.

Finally, there is a high probability that a combined portfolio will routinely dominate (have a higher return for a given level of risk or a lower risk for a given level of return) a common stock only portfolio at relative low levels of return. But, as the level of return is increased it becomes less probable that the combined portfolio will dominate the common-stock-only portfolio.

Introduction

A rational investor will attempt to hold a portfolio of securities that maximizes return for a given level of risk, or minimizes risk for a given level or return. In short, the investor attempts to hold a portfolio of securities that lie on the efficient frontier. These portfolios are said to *dominate* the other portfolios in mean-variance space which are located below and to the right of the efficient frontier. The precise location of the investor on the efficient frontier is going to be a function of the particular investor's utility function.

I. Research Objectives

The purpose of this research is to extend the investigation of the risk: return performance of portfolios comprised of both commodity futures contracts and common stocks relative to the performance of stock-only portfolios begun by Herbst and McCormack (1986).

Prior to the papers by Bodie and Rosansky (1980), and Irwin and Brorsen (1985), virtually all research on the Markowitz (1952) efficient frontier was conducted using common stock portfolios only. This study attempts to determine the extent to which the efficient frontier is shifted as commodity futures replace, one by one, common stocks in an initial common-stock-only portfolio. If the efficient frontier is shifted leftward and upward, all investors will be given the opportunity to reach a higher utility curve. However, if the efficient frontier is shifted leftward and/or upward, but only over a certain portion rather than its entirety, then only a subset of investors will be able to reach a higher utility curve. Furthermore, if the efficient frontier is shifted leftward but only over a certain portion rather than its entirety, this would tend to argue for the existence of two points of tangency between these efficient frontiers (with and without commodities) and the capital market line drawn from the vertical axis. One point of tangency would occur if the risk-free rate was low while a separate point of tangency would exist when interest rates were higher. The portfolios at these points of tangency would not be perfectly correlated.

In the current study, however, the fact that the efficient frontier shifts only over a portion rather than in its entirety is due to the sample of commodities selected. The eight commodities used were selected because of their low degree of correlation. Thus, the fact that the efficient frontier shifted leftward over its lower portion was anticipated. It is quite possible that by using additional commodities the efficient frontier would be seen to shift leftward over its entirety.

Recent relaxation by some states of laws that restrict the use of futures contracts by fiduciaries suggests the current or potential legal feasibility of such combined portfolios—if they can be justified on grounds of economic performance.

II. Prior Research

Finding the optimal investment portfolio has long been an objective of finance practitioners and academics alike. The first major published work in this area was conducted by Markowitz (1952) whose seminal efforts resulted in the concept of the efficient frontier. By posing the existence of a risk-free asset, Sharpe (1964) initiated development of the Capital Asset Pricing Model (CAPM). If the underlying assumptions of the CAPM are accepted, it follows that:

1) An investor can attain a higher utility curve than was previously attainable under the Markowitz analysis by placing some of his wealth in the risk-free asset and the remainder in the market portfolio, or by borrowing to invest more than his original wealth (i.e., to leverage himself) in the market portfolio.

2) Each investor who does not place all his money in the risk-free asset will purchase a portion of the *same* portfolio. This *market portfolio* consists of all individual assets available in the market place in the same proportions within the portfolio as their market values are to the total market value of all assets.

Although conceptually, the CAPM applies to all assets, research on the CAPM has typically been confined to a single market and that single market has been the securities market or, more specifically, the market for common stocks. One reason for this is that common stocks are considered to be homogeneous—they are good substitutes for one another and there are thousands of them. The large number of securities is very helpful in statistical studies because of the freedom it allows one in selecting alternative samples of varying sizes for hypothesis testing or for investigating the effect of sample size on results.

Analogous construction of portfolios of commodity futures contracts has seldom been seen. This may be because commodity futures contracts are not considered good substitutes for one another (buying soybeans is not the same as buying Treasury bonds). Also, not only are there far fewer different commodity futures contracts than there are common stocks, but futures contracts have different expiration dates, different margin requirements, different commission costs, and other differences which tend to make forming portfolios more challenging.

Pioneering research on diversification was done by Evans and Archer (1968) and Wagner and Lau (1971). They investigated the relationship between the total risk of the portfolio and the diversifiable (or unsystematic) risk of the portfolio versus the number of securities in the portfolio. They found that diversifiable risk decreases rapidly as stocks are initially combined to form a portfolio, but that this rate of decrease diminishes rapidly after eight to ten different common stocks are randomly combined into a portfolio.

Robichek, Cohn, and Pringle (1972) examined the returns and correlations between various investment media. They noted that the three commodity futures (Cotton, Wheat, and Copper) employed in their investment universe of 13 types of investments had the highest coefficients of variation but that they had low or negative correlations with most of the other investments such as farm real estate, Treasury bills, S & P Industrials, S & P Utilities, Japanese Stocks, Australian Stocks, Canadian Pacific Perpetual Bonds and U.S. Government bonds.

Recently, the research on diversification has expanded to include commodities. Bodie and Rosansky examined quarterly returns on 23 commodity futures over the period 1950 to 1976. They found that the returns on commodity futures had low to negative correlations with the other investment media examined (Treasury bills, U.S. Government bonds, and common stocks). They also found that a portfolio consisting of 60% common stocks and 40% commodity futures had about the same mean rate of return as a common-stock-only portfolio, but that the standard deviation of the combined portfolio was one-third less.

Herbst and McCormack (1985) used principal components analysis and factor analysis on the logarithms of commodity price relatives to identify the factors generating the observed returns. The results they obtained are intuitively plausible. Precious metals are loaded on one factor while grains are loaded on another and foreign currencies are loaded on a third and so on. Commodity futures loading highly on the same factor are highly correlated, but since the principal components are orthogonal, commodities loading highly on different factors are uncorrelated, or much less correlated.

Irwin and Brorsen (1985) examined portfolios obtained by combining investment in public futures funds, common stocks, and U.S. Treasury bills, and found that the efficient frontier shifted upward and/or to the left, and that real portfolio risk was reduced by 0.6 to 3.7 percentage points from that of a stock and T-bills only portfolio. Herbst and McCormack (1986) found that at low levels of return, combined portfolios of commodity futures and common stocks tended to have lower risk than common-stock-only portfolios until the percentage of commodity futures exceeds 70%.

The question that remains unanswered from the previous research is: Does the entire efficient frontier shift upward and to the left for a combined commodity futures and common stock portfolio relative to a common-stock-only portfolio, or does only a portion of the efficient frontier shift? This is the question the present research addresses.

If the entire efficient frontier shifts, every investor is better off. If, however, only a portion of the efficient frontier shifts, then only a subset of investors will be able to reach a higher level of utility. Additionally, if only a portion of the efficient frontier shifts then an appropriate goal would be to determine that proportion of commodities within the total portfolio that is most likely to give this shift.

III. Methodology

As employed by Evans and Archer (1968) and Wagner and Lau (1971), common stocks are selected randomly from the CRSP data tapes for inclusion into portfolios of different sizes. Eight significant factors from thirty-five futures contracts were obtained from a varimax rotation of a principal components analysis, following Herbst and McCormack (1985). From among those futures contracts loading heavily on each factor the one which had the highest loading was selected for use in portfolio construction. Thus a total of eight commodities were used. Having been selected from a varimax rotation of a principal components analysis insures that these commodities possess low levels of correlation with one another.

These commodity futures are added to the portfolio randomly such that no commodity is used twice (i.e., sampling without replacement). This procedure is similar to the methodology used by Pinches and Mingo (1973).

Initial portfolios of ten and fifteen randomly selected common stocks are formed, and the efficient frontier is calculated using a Markowitz algorithm and 58 months of data from January 1980 through November 1984. For each of these portfolio sizes the eight commodity futures contracts are added randomly, one at a time, displacing a randomly chosen common stock. After each such substitution, the efficient frontier is recalculated for the portfolio. Therefore, nine efficient frontiers are obtained, one for each portfolio size.

For example, using the initial portfolio of size 10, one efficient frontier is obtained for the common-stock-only portfolio, then one for the portfolio consisting on nine stocks and one commodity, etc. This continues until an efficient frontier is obtained for the portfolio consisting of two stocks and eight commodity futures.

The process of creating randomly chosen common stock portfolios of size ten and fifteen is repeated one hundred times each. Efficient frontiers are calculated, then one randomly chosen commodity replaces one of the stocks in the portfolio and the efficient frontier is recalculated. In all, 1800 efficient frontiers are created—900 for portfolio size 10 and 900 for portfolio size fifteen.

Since it is literally impossible to tabulate the data for every point on these efficient frontiers, eleven mean monthly return levels are used (.0001, .0041, .0081,...., .0401) and the standard deviations are calculated for each efficient frontier at these points.

IV. Results

Tables 14-1 and 14-2 contain the mean levels of risk for the 100 replications of the random portfolios of common stocks and commodity futures for the ten and the fifteen security portfolios respectively. There is a significant reduction in risk at low levels of return as commodity futures are added to the portfolio. However, as the level of return increases, the reduction of risk diminishes until the point is reached where the addition of commodity futures actually increases the risk of the portfolio.

To examine the risk reduction potential of adding commodity futures to a portfolio of common stocks the standard deviation of the combined portfolio was subtracted from the standard deviation of the common-stock-only portfolio to obtain the incremental risk associated with the combined portfolio. The differences were then averaged over the 100 replications for both the ten and fifteen security portfolios. The results of this analysis appear in Tables 14-3 and 14-4.

Note again the significant reduction in risk of the combined portfolio versus the common-stock-only portfolio at low levels of return. Now, however, only the combined portfolio consisting of three commodities with the remainder consisting of common stocks has a level of risk that is consistently below that of a common-stock-only portfolio. Thus, it is only for this combination of securities that the *average* efficient frontier is above and to the left of the efficient frontier for the common-stock-only portfolio. This means that the results obtained in this study are slightly different from the results obtained by Bodie and Rosansky (1980). They implied that the appropriate percentage was 40% commodity futures and 60% common stocks. Our results tend to indicate that the proper percentage of commodity futures to incorporate into a common stock portfolio is closer to 25% to 30% in order to obtain a portfolio that completely dominates a common-stock-only portfolio. It must be remembered, however, that Bodie and Rosansky did not use individual commodities, as was done in this study, and this could contribute to the difference in findings.

Tables 14-5 and 14-6 give the probability of the combined portfolio having a lower standard deviation than the stock-only portfolio. Again, one is able to notice the very high probability of having lower risk with a combined

Table 14-1   **Average Standard Deviations at Specified Levels of Return for Different Stock/Commodity Portfolio Compositions (10 Security Case)**

Level of Return	Stock/Commodity Composition of Portfolio								
	10/0	9/1	8/2	7/3	6/4	5/5	4/6	3/7	2/8
.0001	.0484	.0199	.0190	.0179	.0155	.0119	.0112	.0113	.0101
.0041	.0434	.0199	.0189	.0187	.0169	.0149	.0142	.0146	.0148
.0081	.0398	.0222	.0214	.0215	.0206	.0198	.0194	.0204	.0220
.0121	.0378	.0262	.0256	.0257	.0255	.0257	.0255	.0271	.0300
.0161	.0380	.0311	.0310	.0307	.0311	.0319	.0320	.0343	.0383
.0201	.0402	.0367	.0370	.0361	.0371	.0384	.0388	.0415	.0467
.0241	.0441	.0430	.0434	.0419	.0433	.0450	.0457	.0490	.0552
.0281	.0492	.0494	.0501	.0479	.0496	.0516	.0527	.0564	.0637
.0321	.0553	.0559	.0569	.0539	.0560	.0583	.0596	.0640	.0723
.0361	.0620	.0626	.0637	.0601	.0625	.0650	.0667	.0716	.0809
.0401	.0692	.0694	.0707	.0663	.0690	.0718	.0737	.0792	.0895

Table 14-2   Average Standard Deviations at Specified Levels of Return for Different Stock/Commodity Portfolio Combinations (15 Security Case)

Level of Return	Stock/Commodity Composition of Portfolio								
	15/0	14/1	13/2	12/3	11/4	10/5	9/6	8/7	7/8
.0001	.0434	.0187	.0180	.0171	.0149	.0115	.0109	.0110	.0097
.0041	.0394	.0185	.0177	.0176	.0160	.0139	.0130	.0133	.0128
.0081	.0364	.0203	.0195	.0199	.0190	.0180	.0172	.0177	.0179
.0121	.0348	.0235	.0229	.0234	.0231	.0230	.0223	.0230	.0238
.0161	.0348	.0277	.0273	.0276	.0279	.0284	.0278	.0288	.0299
.0201	.0365	.0324	.0323	.0324	.0331	.0340	.0335	.0348	.0363
.0241	.0396	.0376	.0377	.0375	.0385	.0398	.0393	.0409	.0427
.0281	.0437	.0430	.0433	.0427	.0441	.0456	.0453	.0471	.0492
.0321	.0487	.0486	.0491	.0481	.0497	.0515	.0512	.0533	.0557
.0361	.0542	.0543	.0550	.0535	.0554	.0574	.0572	.0595	.0622
.0401	.0602	.0601	.0610	.0591	.0612	.0633	.0633	.0658	.0688

Table 14-3 Incremental Reduction (+) or Increase (−) at Specified Levels of Return for Different Stock/Commodity Portfolio Compositions Relative to the Stock-Only Portfolio (10 Security Case)

Level of Return	Stock/Commodity Composition of Portfolio							
	9/1	8/2	7/3	6/4	5/5	4/6	3/7	2/8
.0001	.0285	.0294	.0305	.0329	.0365	.0371	.0370	.0383
.0041	.0235	.0245	.0247	.0264	.0285	.0292	.0287	.0286
.0081	.0176	.0184	.0183	.0192	.0199	.0204	.0193	.0177
.0121	.0117	.0122	.0122	.0123	.0121	.0123	.0107	.0079
.0161	.0068	.0070	.0073	.0069	.0061	.0060	.0037	-.0003
.0201	.0034	.0032	.0040	.0031	.0018	.0013	-.0013	-.0065
.0241	.0011	.0006	.0022	.0008	-.0009	-.0017	-.0050	-.0111
.0281	-.0001	-.0009	.0014	-.0004	-.0024	-.0034	-.0072	-.0145
.0321	-.0006	-.0016	.0014	-.0007	-.0030	-.0043	-.0087	-.0170
.0361	-.0006	-.0017	.0019	-.0005	-.0030	-.0047	-.0096	-.0189
.0401	-.0002	-.0015	.0029	.0002	-.0026	-.0045	-.0100	-.0203

Table 14-4 Incremental Reduction (+) or Increase (−) at Specified Levels of Return for Different Stock/Commodity Portfolio Compositions Relative to the Stock-Only Portfolio (15 Security Case)

Level of Return	Stock/Commodity Composition of Portfolio							
	14/1	13/2	12/3	11/4	10/5	9/6	8/7	7/8
.0001	.0248	.0254	.0263	.0285	.0319	.0326	.0325	.0337
.0041	.0209	.0217	.0218	.0234	.0255	.0263	.0261	.0266
.0081	.0161	.0169	.0165	.0174	.0184	.0192	.0187	.0185
.0121	.0113	.0119	.0114	.0117	.0118	.0125	.0118	.0111
.0161	.0072	.0075	.0072	.0069	.0064	.0070	.0060	.0049
.0201	.0040	.0042	.0041	.0034	.0025	.0030	.0017	.0002
.0241	.0019	.0018	.0021	.0010	-.0002	.0002	-.0013	-.0031
.0281	.0007	.0004	.0010	-.0003	-.0019	-.0015	-.0034	-.0054
.0321	.0001	-.0005	.0006	-.0010	-.0028	-.0026	-.0046	-.0070
.0361	-.0001	-.0008	.0007	-.0012	-.0032	-.0030	-.0053	-.0080
.0401	.0000	-.0008	.0011	-.0010	-.0032	-.0031	-.0057	-.0086

Table 14-5 Probability of the Combined Portfolio Having a Lower Standard Deviation Than a Stock-Only Portfolio (10 Security Case)

	Stock/Commodity Composition of Combined Portfolio								
Level of Return	9/1	8/2	7/3	6/4	5/5	4/6	3/7	2/8
.0001	96	100	100	100	100	100	100	100
.0041	97	100	100	100	100	100	100	100
.0081	98	100	100	100	100	100	100	99
.0121	97	99	98	98	98	96	95	84
.0161	95	95	93	90	87	85	74	84
.0201	81	79	81	70	62	64	53	62
.0241	58	58	66	53	45	45	33	40
.0281	42	47	63	50	41	40	28	23
.0321	44	39	61	47	37	38	30	19
.0361	43	38	61	49	41	41	34	18
.0401	42	41	60	50	42	43	36	23

Table 14-6 Probability of the Combined Portfolio Having a Lower Standard Deviation Than a Stock-Only Portfolio (15 Security Case)

Level of Return	Stock/Commodity Composition of Combined Portfolio								
	14/1	13/2	12/3	11/4	10/5	9/6	8/7	7/8
.0001	98	100	100	100	100	100	100	100
.0041	98	100	100	100	100	100	100	100
.0081	98	100	100	100	100	100	100	100
.0121	98	99	99	100	100	99	98	98
.0161	97	95	94	92	90	89	84	76
.0201	91	90	90	82	71	68	62	56
.0241	70	71	71	59	46	55	47	41
.0281	52	57	61	52	40	46	34	29
.0321	49	51	58	41	36	45	34	24
.0361	48	47	59	44	34	39	34	25
.0401	48	46	60	44	34	42	36	25

portfolio at low rates of return. Tables 14-3 and 14-4 show the level of risk reduction while Tables 14-5 and 14-6 show the probability of attaining that lower level of risk. For monthly rates of return of 1.21% or less both the amount of risk reduction afforded by commodities and the probability of attaining that risk reduction is great.

As the level of return increases, the reduction of risk diminishes and the probability of attaining that risk reduction is reduced. Only a portfolio composition of between 25% and 30% commodity futures had an approximately 60% or better chance of reducing the risk of this portfolio below that of an all-stock portfolio over all levels of return examined.

Conclusion

Randomly selected portfolios of common stocks and commodity futures were analyzed to investigate the risk/return performance of combined portfolios versus common-stock-only portfolios. The results indicate that, at lower levels of return, the addition of commodity futures to a common stock portfolio can significantly reduce the standard deviation of the portfolio. At higher levels of return the risk reduction potential of commodity futures is much less.

Portfolios consisting of 25% to 30% commodity futures (and thus, 75% to 70% common stocks) tended to dominate all other portfolios consisting of common stocks only, or a combination of commodity futures and common stocks, over the levels of returns and the time period examined in this study. At low levels of return there is a very high probability that the combined portfolio will have a lower standard deviation than the stock-only portfolio. However, at monthly levels of return in excess of 1.21% the standard deviation of the combined portfolio increased rapidly relative to the stock-only portfolio.

References

Bodie, Z. and Rosansky, V. "Risk and Return in Commodity Futures," *Financial Analysts Journal,* Vol 36, No. 3 (May/June 1980).

Evans, J.L. and Archer, S.H. "Diversification and the Reduction of Dispersion: An Empirical Analysis," *Journal of Finance,* (December 1968), 761–769.

Herbst, A.F. and McCormack, J.P. "An Empirical Examination of APT in the Commodity Futures Markets," Working paper, The University of Texas at Arlington, 1985.

Herbst, A.F. and McCormack, J.P. "An Examination of the Risk/Return Characteristics of Portfolios Combining Commodity Futures Contracts with Common Stocks," Working Paper #CSFM-125, The Center for the Study of Futures Markets, Columbia Business School, 1986.

Irwin, S.H. and Brorsen, B.W. "Public Futures Funds." *The Journal of Futures Markets*, Vol. 5, No. 3 (Fall 1985), 463–485.

Markowitz, H.M. "Portfolio Selection," *Journal of Finance*, (March 1952), 77–91.

Modigliani, F. and Pogue, G.A. "An Introduction to Risk and Return: Concepts and Evidence." *Financial Analysts Journal*, Part 1 (March/April 1974), Part 2 (May/June 1974).

Pinches, G.B. and Mingo, K.A. "A Multivariate Analysis of Industrial Bond Ratings." *Journal of Finance*, Vol. 28, No. 1, (March 1973).

Robichek, A.A., Cohn, R.A., and Pringle, J.A. "Returns on Alternative Investment Media and Implications for Portfolio Construction." *Journal of Business*, Vol. 45, No. 3 (July 1972).

Roll, R. "A Critique of the Asset Pricing Theory's Tests." *Journal of Financial Economics*, Vol. 4, (1977), 129–176.

Sharpe, W.F. "Capital Asset Prices: A Theory of Market Equilibrium Under Conditions of Risk." *Journal of Finance*, Vol. 19, No. 4 (September 1964), 425–442.

Wagner, W.H. and Lau, S. "The Effect of Diversification on Risk." *Financial Analysts Journal*, Vol. 26 (November/December 1971), 2–7.

Chapter Fifteen

Management Summary

Title: "A Comparative Analysis of Portfolio Diversification Criteria Using Managed Futures"

Publication: Proceedings of the Fourth Annual Convention of the Pennsylvania Economic Association, Millersville University, 1989

Author: Carl C. Peters, Executive Vice President, A. O. Management and Research Associate, Center for the Study of Futures Markets, Columbia University

Data: Monthly returns for 108 months, 1980-88, for the S & P 500 (with dividends reinvested), Salomon Bros. Broad Investment Grade Bond Index, and a composite of a representative commodity trading advisor. While it may be argued that returns from one advisor do not represent industry performance, it is unrealistic to use a composite of returns from the industry because volatility could be significantly understated, and that investment in industry indexes is not possible. The advisor used is a conservative institutional-oriented CTA with returns near the industry average.

Methodology: Managed futures' performance in combination with stocks and bonds was examined using a variety of risk-reward models. Modern portfolio theory results were contrasted to measures that included probability of loss criteria, stochastic dominance, cost/benefit analysis, and other empirical measures of performance including maximum drawdown and sequential moving windows.

Results: Managed futures as represented by the trading advisor composite were found to have low to negative correlation with stocks and bonds, and when used in diversifying equity portfolios reduced volatility as measured by variance and/or increased return. It was also found that diversifying with managed futures: (1) Lowered the

continued

probability of not achieving a given minimum level of return; (2) Raised the minimum level of return expected for a given probability of failure; (3) Raised the average return for given levels of risk control; (4) Decreased downside risk and increased upside return consistency as measured by 12-month moving windows; (5) Reduced maximum drawdown; (6) Produced portfolios that were probabilistically superior to all equity portfolios for the lower end of the return range; and (7) Produced long term portfolio-like insurance effects.

Comments: The purpose of the paper was to show how managed futures affects other measures of risk besides traditional Markowitz analysis. The results are specific to one trading advisor only.

A Comparative Analysis of Portfolio Diversification Criteria Using Managed Futures

Paper Presented at the Fourth Annual Convention
Pennsylvania Economic Association
Millersville University, May 26, 1989

Carl C. Peters

Investors, particularly large institutional investors, have used Modern Port-folio Theory as initially developed by Markowitz [11] to help design and manage their portfolios. Studies by Lintner [10], Orr [12], Baratz and Eresian [1], and Brorsen [2], among others, using the Markowitz approach have shown that diversifying equity portfolios through the use of managed futures can reduce portfolio volatility and/or increase return.

Risk is measured by variance (or standard deviation) by the Markowitz model. Variance is a measure of volatility or fluctuation around the average return. As such, variance is a measure of the dispersion of returns about the average; the larger the variance the more the uncertainty there is that the average return will occur, and therefore the greater the "risk."

The use of variance as the measure of risk has drawn its share of criticism from academia. For example, Strahm [15] points out that positive correlation in returns might result in greater equity retracements than expected by considering variance alone, and that downside skewness of return distributions might likewise present more risk than variance would indicate. Zeleny [16] points out that most executives perceive risk as a probability of failure to achieve a minimum level of return. Despite these criticisms the Markowitz model continues to find wide acceptance, perhaps in part because it was the first to offer a relatively simple, easy to calculate solution to what can be a very complex problem.

The purpose of this paper is not to criticize the Markowitz model, but to compare various risk criteria for portfolio diversification. We begin by applying traditional Markowitz analysis to monthly data for returns from stocks, bonds, and managed futures, and then extend the analysis to other measures of risk.

I. Historical Performance of Stocks, Bonds, and Managed Futures

Data used in this paper are monthly returns for stocks (S&P 500 with dividends), bonds (Salomon Brothers Broad Investment-Grade Bond Index) and managed futures (account performance of a representative commodity trading advisor[1]) for the time period January, 1980, through December, 1988.

Table 15-1 shows the performance of all three categories of assets. As has been typical of many such studies, bonds show the lowest mean return and standard deviation, and managed futures the highest.

As earlier work has shown [1], [2], [7], [10], [12], and what continues to hold, is that stocks and bonds have a relatively high correlation, and that managed futures have low or slightly negative correlation with stocks and bonds.

II. Markowitz Analysis

Figure 15-1 shows the effect of adding managed futures to a portfolio of stocks using the Markowitz mean-variance approach. As the percentage of managed futures is increased from 0% (Portfolio A) to approximately 20% (Portfolio B), return is increased *and* standard deviation is decreased. Increasing managed futures beyond 20% continues to increase return but with an increase in standard deviation. Portfolio C, approximately 42.5% man-

Table 15-1

	Monthly Average	Standard Deviation	Correlation Coefficients		
			Stocks	Bonds	Futures
Stocks	1.37%	4.82%	1.000	+.310	−.081
Bonds	1.02%	3.67%		1.000	−.109
Futures	2.44%	9.80%			1.000

aged futures, has approximately the same standard deviation as that of stocks alone (Portfolio A) but has one-third greater return.

The lower part of the curve from Portfolio A to Portfolio B is "dominated" by the upper portion; that is, a rational investor[2] would always prefer a portfolio with higher return given a choice between two portfolios with the same standard deviation. The upper portion of the curve, from Portfolio B and beyond, is the Markowitz efficient frontier. Portfolio theory usually only deals with the top portion of the curve under the assumption that the bottom part would not interest a rational investor. But it is *precisely this bottom portion* with which today's institutional investors are dealing as pilot programs at the level of 1% to 5% managed futures are being initiated.[3]

Theorists have further extended the Markowitz analysis to include the use of risk-free assets such as guaranteed money market instruments. It can be shown that any combination of such risk-free assets and a portfolio on the Markowitz efficient frontier (or any portfolio for that matter) lies on a straight line connecting the risk-free rate of return on the vertical axis. (Reilly [13]) Of all possible straight lines emanating from the risk-free rate of return and connecting to portfolios in the Markowitz efficient frontier, the "best" line is one tangent to the Markowitz frontier. See Figure 15-2. This point of tangency defines a portfolio with an important characteristic: in combination with a risk-free asset it is dominant over any other portfolio to its left and/or below it on the Markowitz curve. Assuming a risk-free monthly rate of return of .5%, line R-M represents a combination of risk-free assets *and* Portfolio M that have a higher return for a given standard deviation, or a smaller standard deviation for a given level of return, than any portfolio in the Markowitz efficient frontier to the left of, or below, M. Thus, the most efficient portfolios lie on the line connecting R and M and on the Markowitz frontier to the right of M. While prudent use of cash in risk-free assets is not the subject of this paper, Portfolio M defines another point of interest for investors on the Markowitz curve.

Before summarizing the results of Markowitz analysis for the data it should be pointed out that a weakness of using this type of analysis is the need to specify an investor's utility function before a final portfolio is selected. The optimal portfolio lies at the point of tangency between the efficient frontier and the highest utility curve for a given investor. (Reilly [13]) This necessitates definition, in mathematical terms, of an investors' utility function. But, as Elton and Gruber [4] point out, a number of brokerage firms and banks have tried to develop programs to "extract" the utility functions of through questionnaires, but have found little success. Many investors do not obey all of the rationality postulates when faced with a series of decisions regarding investment related risk and reward, particularly under complex situations as found in real-world markets. Other models for risk, reward and expectation are needed, and this is the subject of the remaining sections of this paper.

Summarizing, the Markowitz analysis produced the following:

Table 15-2

		Jan. 1980–Dec. 1988 Total Return	Average Monthly Return	Monthly Standard Deviation
Portfolio A	(0% Futures)	281.3%	1.37%	4.82%
Portfolio B	(20% Futures)	395.8%	1.58%	4.19%
Portfolio M	(30% Futures)	453.8%	1.69%	4.30%
Portfolio C	(42.5% Futures)	524.2%	1.82%	4.82%

Thus, we can see that diversification with managed futures would have considerably enhanced return and/or reduced variance (standard deviation).

III. Other Measures of Performance

This section addresses other measures which can be used to judge the effectiveness of portfolio diversification using managed futures as the diversifying asset class.

A. Probability of Loss

An appealing and realistic criterion for most investors is to avoid loss. Lerner [9] perhaps sums up the issue best in saying "...some financial writers, unfortunately, have come to look upon the standard deviation of the distribution of returns as a measure not only of the variability (which it is) but of the risk inherent in a project (which it is not). In every day usage, risk means the probability of a loss or the probability that a return will be lower than some target level."

For purposes of discussion assume that the distribution of portfolio returns can be represented by a Normal distribution,[4] as in Figure 15-3. The probability of a monthly return below some specified level, say RL, is the shaded area of distribution below RL, and will be called $\propto$ in this paper.

Now consider what happens to the return distribution for various portfolios as managed futures are increased. As Figure 15-4 indicates, increasing managed futures up to 20% has the effect of shrinking due to *both* a shift to the right in the mean *and* a reduction in variance. Beyond 20% there *may* be a further reduction in $\propto$, but the variance begins to increase along with the mean rate of return. The point of minimum $\propto$ can be computed as the point of tangency a line from RL to the Markowitz efficient line frontier. (Roy [14]) For the data used in this analysis:

Table 15-3*

Portfolio	Probability ($\propto$) of an Annual Return less than			
	−20%	−10%	0%	+6%
A (0% Futures)	1.5%	5.7%	16.3%	26.8%
B (20% Futures)	.4%	2.3%	9.1%	18.7%
C (42.5% Futures)	.6%	2.8%	9.2%	17.1%

*Annual returns are derived assuming independence of monthly returns.

Note the substantial decrease in risk as futures are added from 0% (Portfolio A) to 20% (Portfolio B). The level and pattern of risk reduction depends not only on the percentage of futures, but on the decision-makers' criterion for minimum annual return.

B. Increasing Minimum Returns

Another way of looking at how diversification benefits a portfolio is to consider the effect of increasing the minimum level of return for a given probability of failure, $\propto$. As futures are added to a portfolio the minimum return, RL, corresponding to a given $\propto$ probability of failure progressively increases to some point, and then decreases. Elton and Gruber [5] show that the point of maximum RL for a given $\propto$ is the point of tangency of a line beginning at RL, emanating upward at a slope K$\propto$, where K$\propto$ is the difference between the average portfolio return and RL, expressed in multiples of its standard deviation.[5]

The following table illustrates how the minimum return, RL, benefits from diversification.

Table 15-4*

	Minimum Level of Annual Return for $\propto$:			
Portfolio	1%	5%	10%	20%
A (0% Futures)	–22.6%	–11.1%	–5.0%	2.3%
B (20% Futures)	–14.8%	–4.9%	.4%	6.8%
C (42.5% Futures)	–17.0%	–5.6%	.5%	7.9%

*See previous section

One can see that the effect of adding futures is to increase the minimum level of return possible for a given probability of failure, $\propto$.

C. Maximizing Portfolio Return while Controlling the Probability of Failure $\propto$ at a given Level of Minimum Return, RL.

Yet another way to measure the effects of diversification is to determine the portfolio with the largest average return possible while controlling the probability of failure $\propto$ to be no more than a given amount. For example, one might ask what the maximum average portfolio return would be if returns of 0% or less were controlled to happen 5% of the time, or less.

Elton and Gruber [6] show that portfolios satisfying these conditions lie at the intersection of a straight line emanating from the given minimum

Table 15-5

Risk Level	Risk Control		Annual Returns of Portfolios With Same Risk Control Limits	
	Minimum Return, RL	Max. Prob. of Failure, α	Portfolio A	Other Portfolios
I	–10%	5.7%	16.4% (0% Futures)	22.3% (46% Futures)
II	0%	16.3%	16.4% (0% Futures)	22.6% (48% Futures)
III	+6%	26.8%	16.4% (0% Futures)	22.9% (51% Futures)

return level, RL, at a slope $K\alpha$ (see previous section) and the Markowitz efficient frontier.

As an example consider controlling risk to the three levels shown in Table 15-5. All three risk levels are controlled by Portfolio A (0% futures). Each risk level is also controlled by a portfolio diversified with futures, with significantly higher rates of return than Portfolio A:

These portfolios each control risk at the same level as Portfolio A. Markowitz analysis, on the other hand, might lead us to believe that Portfolios A and C have the same risk since they have the same standard deviation. Portfolio C uses 42.5% managed futures. It can be shown[6] that Markowitz analysis will always underestimate the amount of diversification necessary to achieve the same level of risk.

D. Stochastic Dominance

This criteria has the advantage of not necessitating detailed assumptions about an investor's utility function, or the shape of the distributions of returns in a portfolio. The basis upon which stochastic dominance rests is that investors who are reasonable will always prefer one investment over another if, for every possible level of return, the probability of failing to achieve a given level of return is less.

Fischmar and Peters [7] have shown that diversifying with managed futures can lead to a predictable degree of stochastic dominance, with portfolios diversified with managed futures dominating those less diversified up to some limit. While research is still being conducted in this area [8], the empirical evidence as shown in Figure 15-5, for example, indicates that adding managed futures can produce portfolios which are stochastically dominant and that should be preferred by reasonable investors.

E. Portfolio Insurance

A popular method of assessing the potential effect of portfolio hedging strategies is that of portfolio insurance. Figure 15-4 illustrates the general approach offered by a portfolio insuror.[7] The light line indicates performance of the S&P 500 with dividends, while the dark line shows performance of a portfolio 100% hedged against losses. The "cost" of such "insurance" is about 25% of market returns on the upside while the benefits are 100% savings of losses on the downside.

Figure 15-5 is an equivalent way of showing the "hedging" or insurance effect of managed futures in portfolio diversification. Regression lines were fitted to a scatter plot of Portfolio A and the S&P 500 with dividends. The 45 degree diagonal line on the graph is equivalent to the S&P 500 market line on Figure 15-6. One can see that Portfolio B produced "some" loss protection at very little cost when the stock market was up. Figures 15-7 – 15-9 show the effect of increasing futures to 50%. Portfolios B and C add further protection with little additional cost. For not too much more "cost" to the upside, the average protection on the downside is substantial.

This demonstrates the long-term average effect of diversifying with managed futures on the "hedging" capability of resulting portfolios. For our portfolios we have calculated:

Table 15-6

	Portfolio Hedging Effectiveness	
	Cost on the Upside*	Benefit in the Downside**
"Pure" Portfolio Hedge Strategy	25%	100%***
Portfolio A (0% Futures)	0%	0%
Portfolio B (20% Futures)	3%	26%
Portfolio C (42.5% Futures)	6%	55%
(50% Futures)	7%	127%

*Average decrease from stock market returns during up markets
**Average increase to stock market returns during down markets
***Questionable during "fast" markets such as October 19, 1987.

Obviously, *increasing* managed futures gave protection to investors on the downside, at relatively small cost. Whether this effect has statistical validity and robustness is the subject of future research.

IV. Summary and Conclusions

The purpose of this paper was to compare alternative ways for analyzing and describing risk and the effects of diversifying portfolios using managed futures. Traditional analysis using Modern Portfolio Theory and the Markowitz model was also done for comparison.

Data used for this analysis included returns for the 108-month period from January, 1980, through December, 1988. Stocks were represented by the S&P 500 Index (with dividends), bonds by the Salomon Brothers Broad Investment Grade Bond Index, and managed futures by a large institutional commodity trading advisor.

Analysis using the Markowitz approach showed the same results found by much of the earlier research: managed futures had low to negative correlation with stocks and bonds, and when used for diversifying equity portfolios, reduced variability as measured by standard deviation, and/or increased return.

The effects of diversification were analyzed using a probability of loss criterion, which is defined as the probability of failure of achieving a given minimum level of return. Managed futures were shown to lower the probability of failure for given levels of minimum return, or to raise the minimum level of return for a given probability of failure. Most importantly, it was shown that significantly greater risk reduction can occur than implied by the Markowitz approach.

Portfolio diversification with managed futures was also shown to produce partial stochastic dominance in the lower return ranges.

A final criterion was introduced—portfolio insurance as a fourth class of diversification criteria. It was shown that managed futures produced long term effects similar to insurance: reduction to upside performance (cost) with protection on the downside (benefit) with a net result of increased overall performance.

A comparison of the approaches shows that the Markowitz model may understate potential benefits of diversification, and other models should be used in performing portfolio diversification analysis.

Figure 15-1 Portfolio Return/Risk Tradeoffs—Stocks and Varying % Futures

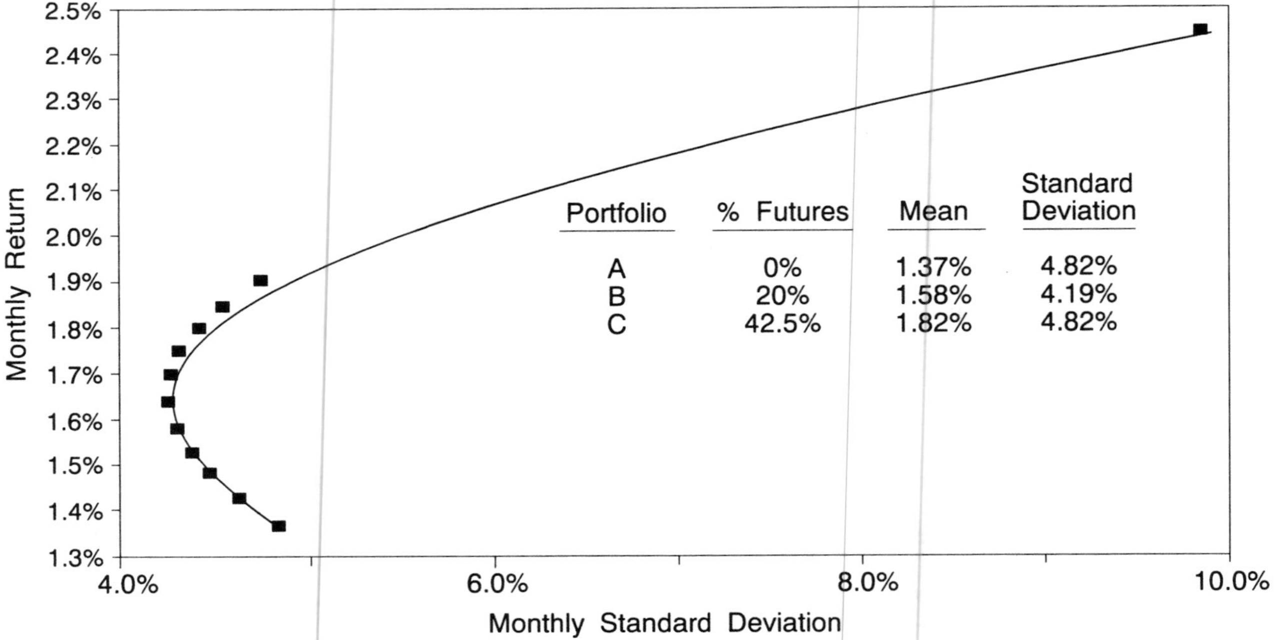

Monthly Return
2.5%
2.4%
2.3%
2.2%
2.1%
2.0%
1.9%
1.8%
1.7%
1.6%
1.5%
1.4%
1.3%
4.0%
6.0%
8.0%
10.0%
Monthly Standard Deviation
Portfolio
% Futures
Mean
Standard Deviation
A 0% 1.37% 4.82%
B 20% 1.58% 4.19%
C 42.5% 1.82% 4.82%

Figure 15-2 Portfolio Return/Risk Tradeoffs—Stocks and Varying % Futures

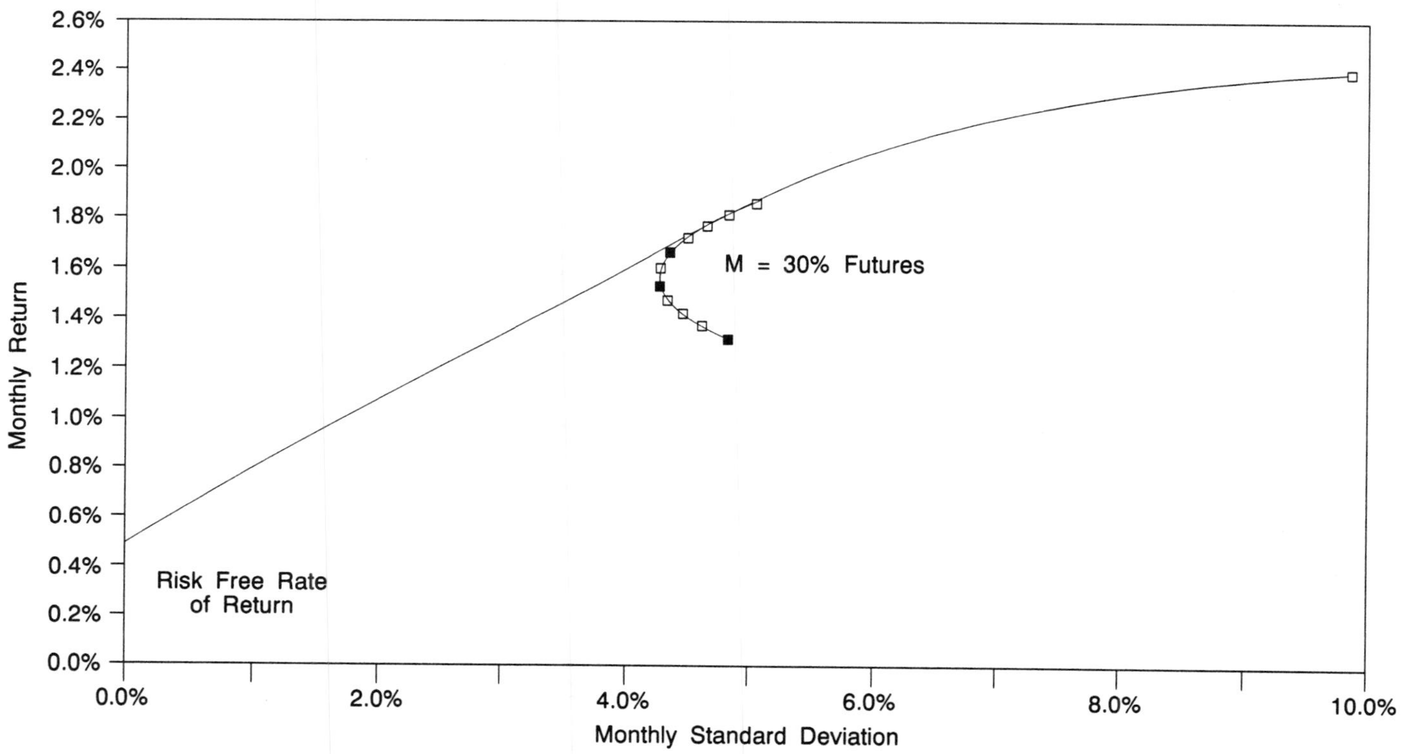

Figure 15-3

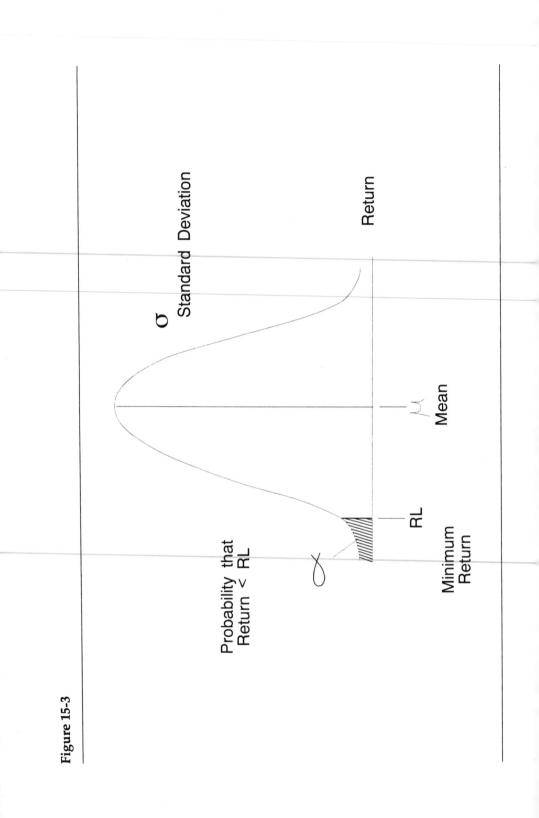

Figure 15-4

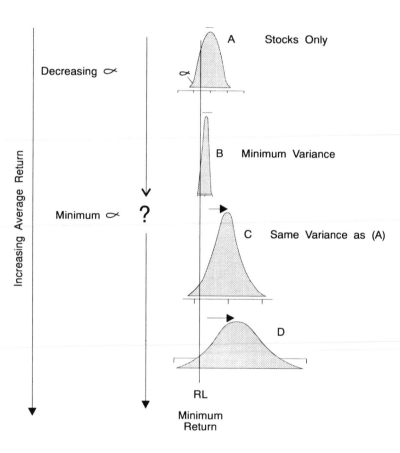

Figure 15-5 Risk of Not Achieving a Minimum Return—Stocks and ____ % Futures

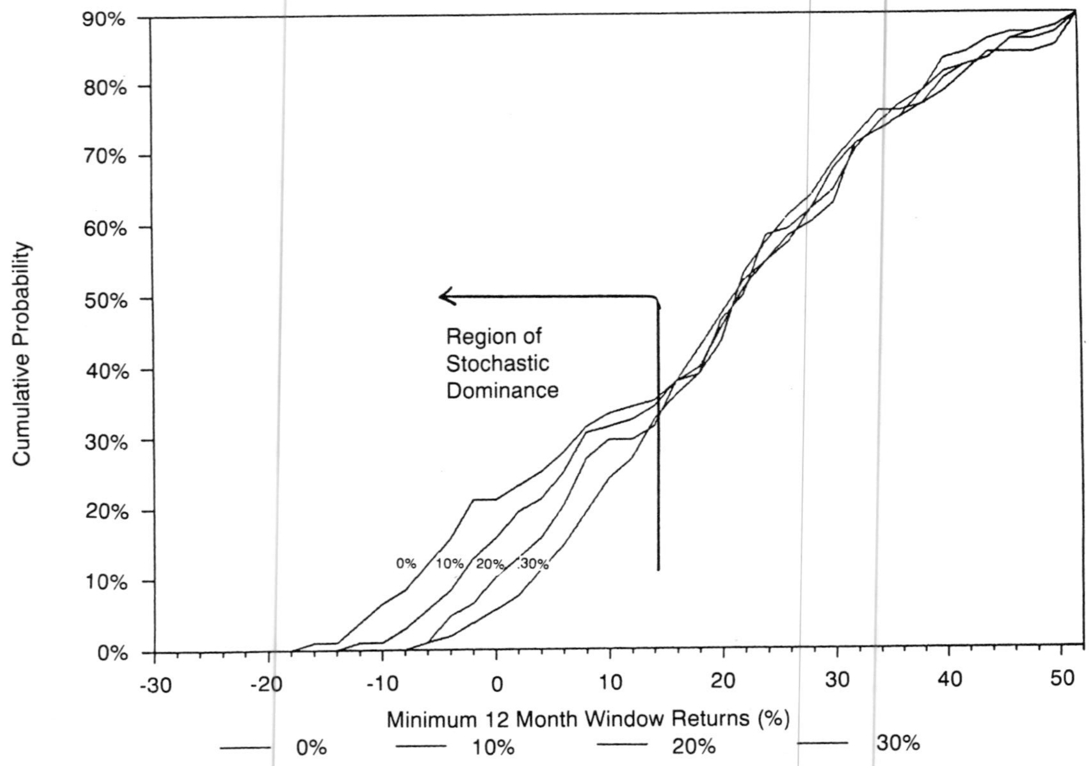

Figure 15-6   Portfolio Insurance—Minimum Return Strategy (0%, 12 month)

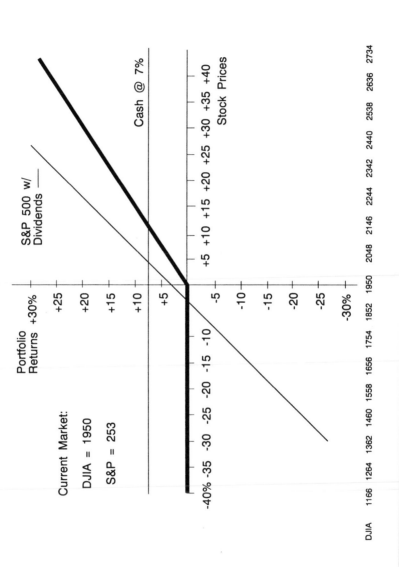

Figure 15-7   Portfolio Insurance Analysis—January, 1980–December, 1988

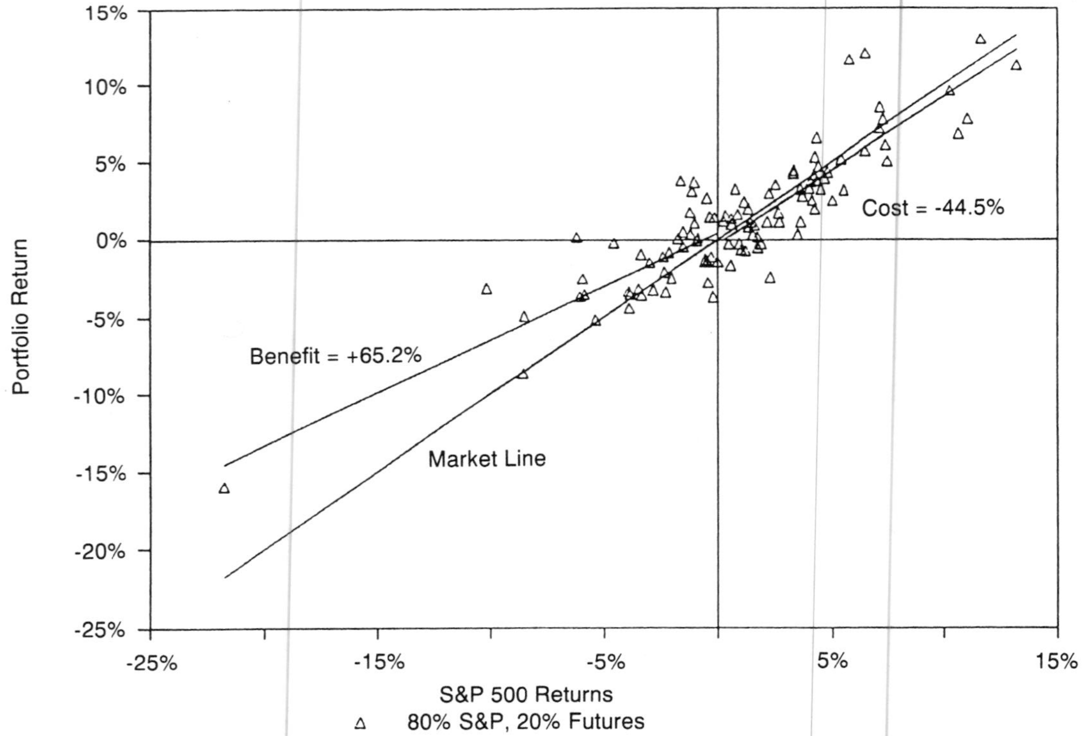

Figure 15-8 Portfolio Insurance Analysis—January, 1980–August, 1988

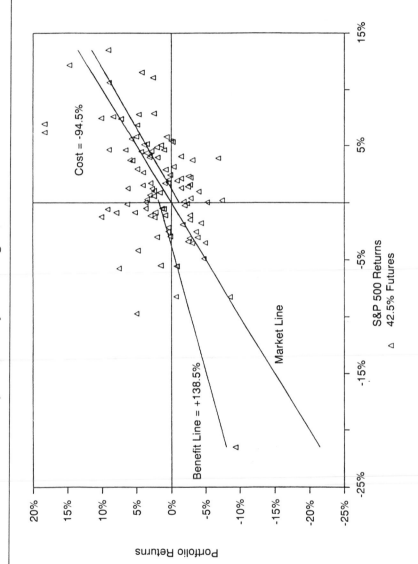

Figure 15-9 Portfolio Insurance Analysis—January, 1980–December, 1988

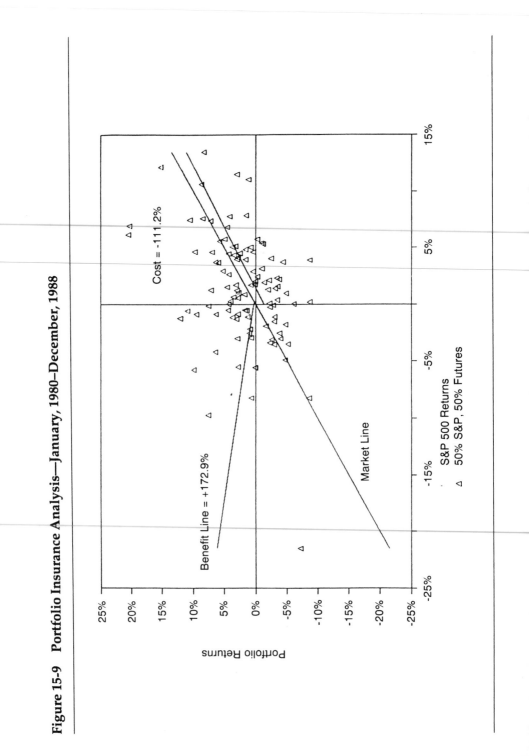

Endnotes

1   While it may be argued that returns from one advisor do not represent industry performance, it is unrealistic to use composite returns from the industry since volatility could be significantly understated. The advisor used is a conservative institutional-oriented CTA with returns near the industry average. On the other hand, use of indexes for stock and bond portfolios is appropriate since it is possible, in fact, to invest in such indices through mutual funds. Such is not the case for managed futures.

2   A rational investor is defined here as one who prefers more to less, and is risk averse.

3   Of course one could argue that a commitment of 1% to diversification represents a "reasonable" diversification for only 5% of assets, if 20% managed futures is deemed "reasonable."

4   In practicality this is not a bad assumption since the distribution of returns for a portfolio is the weighted combination of return distributions of each asset class. The larger the number of classes the more likely the resulting portfolio distribution will be Normal, according to the Central Limit Theorem.

5   Mathematically $K_\alpha = (RL-Rp)/6p$ where Rp is portfolio average return, RL is the minimum return, and 6p is portfolio standard deviation.

6   This follows from the fact that portfolios with the same standard deviation lie on a vertical line in mean-variance space with no intercept.

7   Special thanks to Advanced Investment Management, Inc., for use of this graph.

Bibliography

1. Baratz, Morton and Eresian, Warren. "The Role of Managed Futures Accounts in an Investment Portfolio." Managed Accounts Reports, Columbia, Md., July 1986.

2. Brorsen, B. Wade and Irwin, Scott. "Public Futures Funds." *Journal of the Futures Markets,* Vol. 5, No. 2, 1985.

3. Elton, Edwin J. and Gruber, Martin. *Modern Portfolio Theory and Investment Analysis,* (3rd Edition), Wiley, 1987.

4. Ibid, pp. 184-185.

5. Ibid, p. 212.

6. Ibid, pp. 213-214.

7. Fischmar, Daniel and Peters, Carl. "A Stochastic Dominance Approach to Portfolio Diversification." *Proceedings of the Annual Conference of the Pennsylvania Economic Association,* Pennsylvania State University, May 1988.

8. Fischmar, Daniel and Peters, Carl. "Risk Controlled Portfolio Models," (research and paper in progress sponsored by the Center for the Study of Futures Markets, Columbia University).

9. Lerner, E. *Managerial Finance,* Harcourt Brace Jovanovich, 1971 (p. 328).

10. Lintner, John. "The Potential Role of Managed Commodity - Financial Futures Accounts (and/or Funds) in Portfolios of Stocks and Bonds," Annual Conference of the Financial Analysts Federation, May 1983.

11. Markowitz, Harry. *Portfolio Selection: Efficient Diversification of Investments,* Wiley, 1959.

12. Orr III, Almer. "John Lintner and the Theory of Portfolio Management," Sixth Annual Managed Account Reports Conference, February 1985.

13. Reilly, Frank. *Investment Analysis and Portfolio Management,* (2nd Edition), Dryden Press, 1985 (p. 233).

14. Roy, A. D. "Safety First and the Holding of Assets." *Econometrica,* 20, July 1959 (pp. 441-449).

15. Strahm, Norman. "Preferance Space Evaluation of Trading System Performance." *Journal of the Futures Markets,* Vol. 3, No. 3, 1983.

16. Zeleny, M. *Multiple Criteria Decision Making,. McGraw Hill, 1982 (pp. 385-40)*

Chapter Sixteen

Management Summary

Title: "How to Diversify Portfolios of Euro-Stocks and Bonds with Hedged U.S. Managed Futures"

Presentation: First International Conference on Futures Money Management Geneva, Switzerland, 1990

Author: Richard E. Oberuc, President, Burlington Hall Asset Management, Inc.

Data: Monthly returns for 130 months, March 1979 through December, 1989 for stocks, bonds and cash instruments for the United Kingdom, Germany, France and Switzerland, and CTA performance as measured by the MAR Equally Weighted CTA Index. CTA performance was measured on both an unhedged and hedged basis. Hedging was assumed to be done monthly using one month forward cash contracts denominated for each country under consideration. Hedges were renewed monthly as they expired. Correlation analysis and comparisons between returns and variability were analyzed.

Methodology: Portfolios of stocks, bonds and cash were compared with and without hedged and unhedged managed futures.

Results: Portfolios using hedged and unhedged CTAs always performed better, at the same level of risk, than those not using managed futures. Correlation analysis showed that CTA performance had low to negative correlation with stock and bond performance of the various countries. Optimal portfolio allocation percentages were essentially the same for hedged and nonhedged managed futures accounts.

Comments: This study was the first to consider managed futures from a global portfolio perspective.

How to Diversify Portfolios of Euro-Stocks and Bonds with Hedged U.S. Managed Futures*

Richard E. Oberuc

Investment Selection

After the stock market crash of October 1987, investors realized that pinning their hopes of portfolio protection on stock selection methodologies was not successful. Indeed, it was found that diversifying a portfolio across equities from multiple countries provided very little protection since most countries' stock markets crashed at the same time.

If stock selection did not provide the key to protection against portfolio drawdowns, then just what is the answer? Investment theory tells us that diversification across multiple investments that are not fundamentally linked with each other is the key. Unfortunately, all stocks are tied together through their linkage to something often referred to as the "market line." This means that as the stock market goes down (as measured by any of a number of market indexes), most individual stocks also tend to go down at the same time. Therefore, stock diversification is of little value against portfolio loss.

*The opinions expressed in this report are those of Burlington Hall Asset Management, Inc. Readers are cautioned that futures products are not for all investors and that past performance of any investment can never guarantee future performance.
Copyright 1990 by Burlington Hall Asset Management, Inc. Reprinted with permission.

So, the answer must lie in selecting other kinds of investments which have price movements uncorrelated with stock market movements. Simply exhausting a list of all investment types and investigating those having sufficiently high rates of return and yet not being strongly correlated with the stock market might be a pragmatic approach.

Creating such a list of alternate investments and proposing them to investors for consideration will raise other important issues. Certain investments can only be purchased in very large parcels. This feature can be referred to as *size*. And for others there may not always be a ready market for their resale. This feature is known as *liquidity*. And for other investments there can be a problem in determining if one parcel is qualitatively the same as another. This feature involves the concept of *fungibility*.

Most investors are only interested in investments that can be purchased in small quantities, are easily sold at any time and are of a well-known quality. This eliminates many otherwise interesting and potentially profitable investments. Examples of investments having difficulty with these features are:

> Collectibles such as paintings, gems or coins.
> Real estate limited partnerships.
> Land.

Investments that generally meet all of the desired features include:

> Stocks including mutual funds and unit trusts.
> Bonds, both governmental and corporate.
> Interest-bearing cash equivalents.
> Commodities and futures products.

Because a broad range of investors will not consider collectibles and real estate for their portfolios, these items will not be considered for this investigation. Because all of the other four items meet the requirements of small *size*, good *liquidity* and acceptable *fungibility*, they will all be considered.

Constructing Portfolios

In order to find optimum combinations of investments, a whole body of knowledge is employed termed *Modern Portfolio Theory*. This theory employs the following assumptions:

- We have identified the investments we want to consider.

- The only performance measures required for each investment are expected return, standard deviation and correlation coefficients.

- We know how to form these expectations. This is normally done by looking at recent history.

- Each month of future performance is a random draw from these expectations. There is no correlation between the performance of successive months.

- All profits are reinvested.

- There is a planning horizon of known length, usually determined to be one year.

- At any level of risk there is some optimum combination of the investments that produces the highest return.

- The investor has a personal risk tolerance level whereby he demands an increased return for any increase in risk.

Several well-known portfolio evaluations of stocks, bonds and managed futures products have been conducted from the U.S. point of view. Research on portfolios employing these investments has been conducted by John Lintner and by Morton Baratz and Warren Eresian. In a nutshell, the results have indicated that mixing managed futures products with U.S. stocks and bonds produces portfolios having demonstrably higher returns at every level of risk.

The basic reasons for these results are that managed futures products as represented by the performance of commodity trading advisors have higher historical average performance than either stocks or bonds (albeit higher volatility). And managed futures products are essentially uncorrelated with stocks or bonds.

Objectives of this Report

While the benefit of using managed futures in an investment portfolio is well-known in the case of the U.S. investor, no definitive study seems to have been undertaken from the European point of view. The basic objective is to discover whether there are similar benefits to the European investor by including managed futures in a portfolio as found in the U.S. case.

Marketing a portfolio containing managed futures products must be done in terms of products that are regularly available. In the case of European investors, this means that local stocks, bonds and cash equivalents must be employed for each country. It would be desirable to show the performance of an index of managed futures products currently available in an investor's own currency. Unfortunately, there is not a sufficient number of European CTAs having a long enough track record to form the necessary indices. So we must be content with using U.S.-based CTAs and take into account any inherent currency risk by doing so.

The four largest European countries were selected for evaluation based on the size of their stock market capitalizations. The countries in order are the UK, Germany, France and Switzerland according to Morgan Stanley Capital International.

The basic questions that will be asked for each of these countries are:

- Are investors better off with or without managed futures in their portfolios?

- How do we handle the problems of currency risk?

- What are the optimum combinations of investments at various levels of risk?

Sources of Data Employed

Data series for each country were obtained for the interval of March 1979 to December of 1989. The beginning date coincides with the beginning of monthly records maintained by MAR for trading advisors. The major requirement for each investment type was to obtain an index which fairly represents the total rate of return that an investor would have received for a typical investment of that type. The monthly stock, bond and cash performance indices for each country are expressed in local terms and are on a total return basis.

Stock Data

The source for the stock data is the Morgan Stanley Capital International Perspective database. The monthly performance index for each country has gross dividends reinvested and has no adjustment for withholding taxes. Total returns do not include any commissions. The stocks are selected so that each industry sector is proportionately represented. Only stocks with sufficient liquidity for the general investor are included. The index typically represents 60% of the country's total market valuation.

Bond Data

The source for the bond data is Salomon Brothers. The indexes represent portfolios of institutionally traded fixed-rate government bonds with remaining maturities of at least five years. The monthly rate of return is determined by the ratio of successive month ending market valuations of the bond portfolio. This total return measure does not include any commissions.

Cash Equivalent Data

The source for the cash data is also Salomon Brothers. The data represent the local money market rates.

Managed Futures Data

The source for the managed futures data is *Managed Account Reports*. The index represents the equally-weighted performance of commodity trading advisors selected to be in the top 25% of CTAs based on money under management for the previous year. Managed Account Reports adjusts the data reported by CTAs by assuming that all additions and withdrawals take place at the beginning of a month instead of month end. The month end method is the current requirement of the CFTC for reporting performance. Total returns include all fees and commissions actually paid.

Dealing with Foreign Exchange Risk

European investors placing funds with a U.S.-based CTA would typically open an account in dollars. This implies that they will have a foreign exchange exposure until they repatriate their funds. Any number of hedging methodologies could be employed to reduce the risk of this exposure. For the purposes of this study, only two hedging scenarios were employed: a one-month forward interbank hedge and no hedging at all. Other hedging methods could have been employed, but the results would probably not have been much different from the one-month forward method.

One-Month Interbank Hedging

At the beginning of each month, the investor sells dollars (buys his own currency) one month forward in the amount of the value of his managed account at the beginning of the month. At the end of the month, his currency hedge from the beginning of the month is evaluated at the spot rate. No attempt is made to hedge any intra-month profits. All hedging is done using "bid" interbank rates since it is assumed that no money is actually added to or withdrawn from the U.S.-managed account arising from the hedging operation. The hedging profits or losses are simply added to the CTA performance as a bookkeeping entry to obtain an adjusted rate of return.

No Hedging

When no hedging is employed, the investor passively accepts the results of exchange rate fluctuations. No attempt is made to avoid foreign exchange risk.

As it turns out, over the 11 years used for this study, the long-term effect of the no-hedging strategy would have been roughly the same as the fully hedged strategy. This occurred because the exchange rates at the beginning and the end of the 11 year interval were nearly the same, with the exception of the French Franc. But the difference between hedged and non-hedged CTA performance was substantial for individual years. Figure 16-1 demonstrates this point graphically. Whether the hedged CTA performance was better than the un-hedged performance depends strictly on the timing of exchange rate movements and on spot/forward exchange rate ratios. Table 16-1 shows the statistical difference between the un-hedged and hedged CTA performance. Note that the volatility of the un-hedged annual performance was always larger than the hedged performance. The fact that the hedged returns were slightly lower for this interval should be treated as an accident of history and not as a justification for using or avoiding any hedging mechanism. The decision to hedge or not should be based on operational desires to reduce or accept risk.

An even more compelling reason for ignoring the difference between the un-hedged and hedged CTA averages can be shown if we split the history into two intervals, 1979-1984 and 1985-1989. The first interval was charac-

Figure 16-1   Hedged and Un-Hedged CTA Performance (By Year)

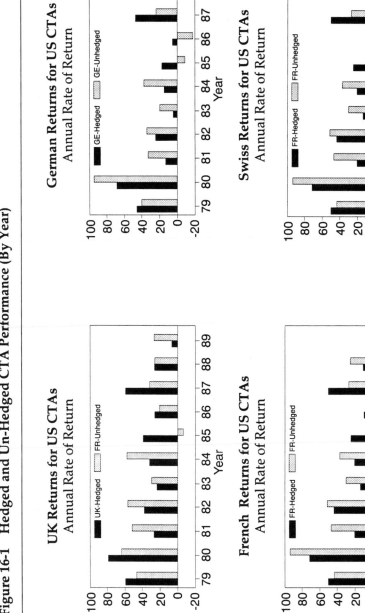

Table 16-1 1979–1989 Average Annual CTA Returns and Standard
            Deviations

	Annual Return Un-Hedged	Annual Return Hedged	Annual Std-Dev Un-Hedged	Annual Std-Dev Hedged
UK	27.2%	27.5%	37.7%	33.7%
Germany	23.6%	20.5%	38.1%	31.8%
France	28.1%	27.9%	38.8%	33.8%
Switzerland	23.9%	18.2%	38.0%	31.1%

terized by general dollar strengthening and the second by dollar weakening. The average performance for the two intervals is shown in Table 16-2.

Comparative Performance of Investment Types

Temporarily adopting the hedged CTA performance to represent managed futures, the annual historical performance statistics for stocks, bonds, cash and CTAs for the years 1979-1989 are shown in Table 16-3. Note that the CTA indexes for each country always have the highest average return, the largest standard deviation and correlation coefficients near zero. Also, note that government bonds were inefficient investments compared to cash for both France and Switzerland.

Figure 16-2 presents the performance of stocks, bonds, cash and hedged CTAs on a graphical basis. Each investment is given 1,000 units of the local currency in March of 1979. The compounded growth of each investment

Table 16-2 1979–1984 and 1985–1989 Average Annual CTA Returns

	1979–1984 Return Un-Hedged	1979–1984 Return Hedged	1985–1989 Return Un-Hedged	1985–1989 Return Hedged
UK	45.4%	33.1%	8.9%	21.1%
Germany	44.8%	27.2%	2.7%	13.1%
France	51.8%	36.9%	5.1%	18.1%
Switzerland	43.4%	23.3%	4.8%	12.6%

Table 16-3   Historical Averages, Standard Deviations and Correlation Coefficients

			Correlation Coefficients			
UK	**Return**	**Std-Dev**	**Stock**	**Bond**	**Cash**	**CTA**
UK-Stock	21.50	24.30	1.0	.32	.04	.04
UK-Bond	13.00	11.70	.32	1.0	.15	.06
UK-Cash	12.70	0.80	.04	.15	1.0	.14
UK-CTA-Hedged	27.50	33.70	.04	.06	.14	1.0
Germany	**Return**	**Std-Dev**	**Stock**	**Bond**	**Cash**	**CTA**
GE-Stock	13.90	22.30	1.0	.20	−.03	−.08
GE-Bond	7.50	6.10	.20	1.0	.09	−.02
GE-Cash	6.80	0.80	−.03	.09	1.0	.08
GE-CTA-Hedged	20.50	31.80	−.08	−.02	.08	1.0
France	**Return**	**Std-Dev**	**Stock**	**Bond**	**Cash**	**CTA**
FR-Stock	23.60	27.90	1.0	.30	.02	.04
FR-Bond	10.80	6.70	.30	1.0	.23	.10
FR-Cash	13.00	1.40	.02	.23	1.0	.08
FR-CTA-Hedged	27.90	33.80	.04	.10	.08	1.0
Switzerland	**Return**	**Std-Dev**	**Stock**	**Bond**	**Cash**	**CTA**
SW-Stock	11.00	17.80	1.0	.18	−.03	−.04
SW-Bond	2.80	3.90	.18	1.0	.09	−.03
SW-Cash	5.10	0.60	−.03	.09	1.0	.02
SW-CTA-Hedged	18.20	31.10	−.04	−.03	.02	1.0

Figure 16-2

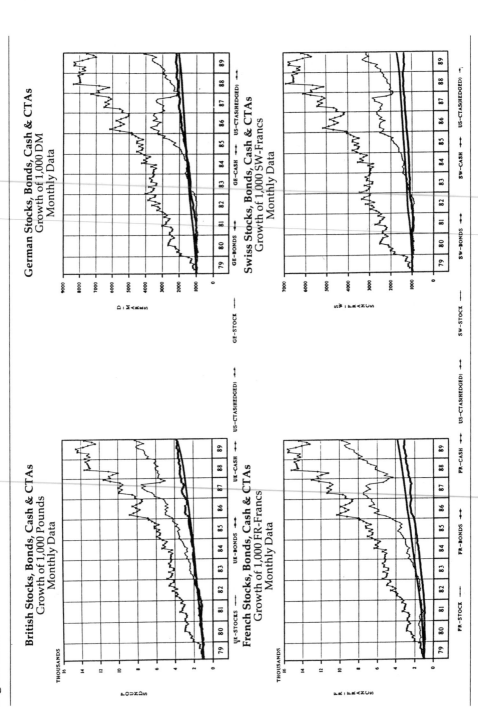

demonstrates both the growth potential and relative volatility of each investment type.

Resulting Efficient Frontiers

Based on modern portfolio theory, the efficient frontiers for portfolios containing stocks, bonds, cash and hedged CTAs are displayed in Figure 16-3 for each country. The set of lines marked 5, 10, 15, 20 indicate risk tolerance curves of losses acceptable to the investor. If the portfolio represented by the point where the 15% risk tolerance curve intersects the efficient frontier is accepted, there should be no more than a 10-percent chance in the future of exceeding a 15% loss of his initial investment. And so forth for the other curves. For example, if a UK investor can accept a 10% chance of losing more than 15% of his initial investment, then the recommended portfolio would have a 21.6% expected return and a 16.0% standard deviation. If the UK investor wanted to have a portfolio with a 23.6% expected return, he must accept a 19.5% standard deviation and a 10% chance of losing more than 20% of initial equity.

Optimal Allocations

Similar efficient frontiers can be constructed for portfolios containing no CTA component and for portfolios using the un-hedged CTA performance. Tables 16-4 – 16-7 show the optimal allocations required to achieve the acceptable levels of risk for all three CTA treatments. The expected future returns based on these allocations is also shown. This, of course, assumes that the investments will perform in the future statistically as they have in the past, which of course cannot be guaranteed.

Historical Performance of Portfolios

In order to appreciate the differences among the portfolios at the four different levels of risk, the historical growth of each portfolio is presented for each country in Figure 16-4. Increasing the allowed maximum loss gives rise to portfolios with higher growth rates and higher volatility.

Figure 16-3 Portfolio Efficient Frontier

For UK Investors Using Case Name UK-Hedged
Risk of Capital Loss, Risk Probability = .1,
Various Capital Losses

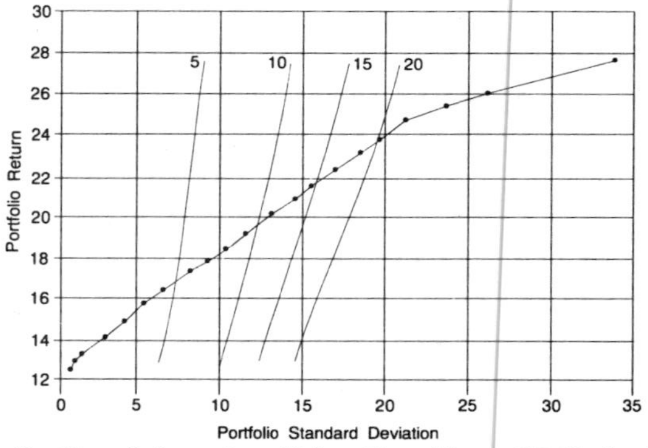

For German Investors Using Case Name GE-Hedged
Risk of Capital Loss, Risk Probability = .1,
Various Capital Losses

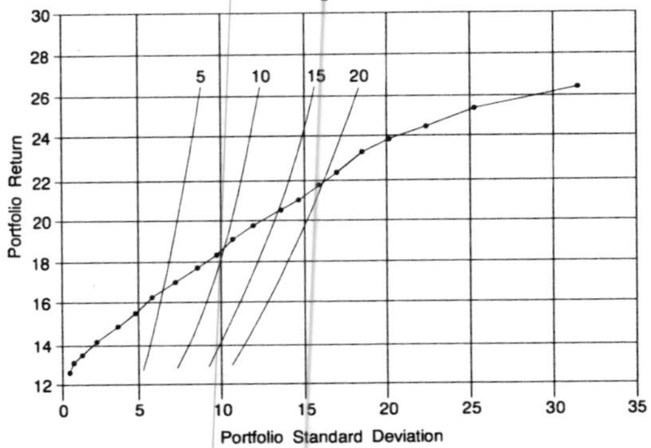

For French Investors Using Case Name FR-Hedged
Risk of Capital Loss, Risk Probability = .1,
Various Capital Losses

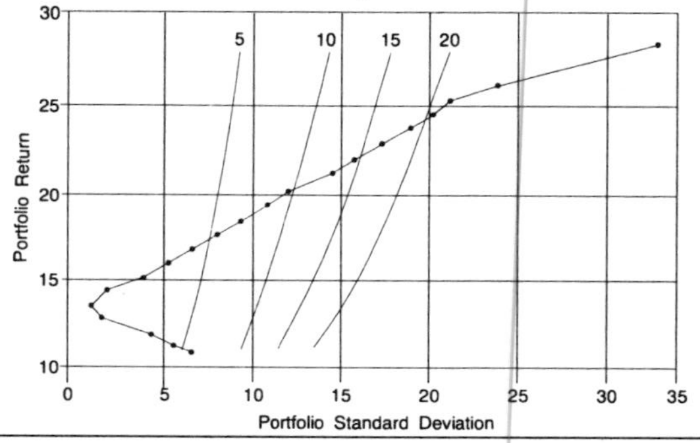

For Swiss Investors Using Case Name SW-Hedged
Risk of Capital Loss, Risk Probability = .1,
Various Capital Losses

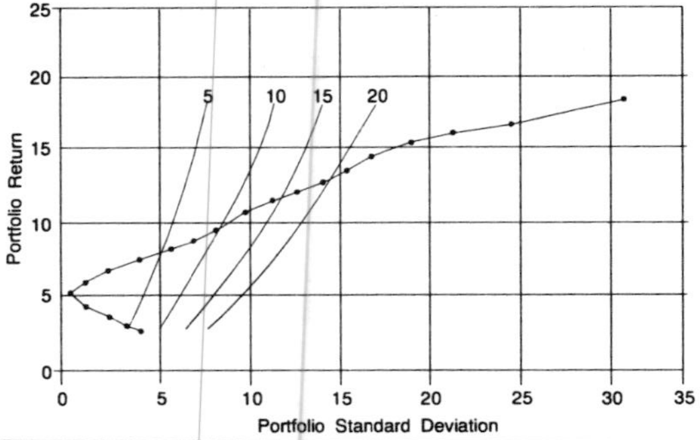

Table 16-4   Optimum Allocations for UK Investors

5% Maximum Loss	Stocks	Bonds	Cash	CTAs	Expected Return
Without CTAs	30.1	0.0	69.9	——	15.4%
Hedged CTAs	19.4	0.0	63.6	17.0	16.9%
Unhedged CTAs	20.8	0.0	65.0	14.2	16.6%
10% Maximum Loss					
Without CTAs	47.0	0.0	53.0	——	16.8%
Hedged CTAs	31.1	0.0	41.5	27.4	19.5%
Unhedged CTAs	33.2	0.0	44.1	22.7	18.9%
15% Maximum Loss					
Without CTAs	60.6	0.0	39.4	——	18.0%
Hedged CTAs	40.9	0.0	23.0	36.1	21.6%
Unhedged CTAs	43.5	0.0	26.7	29.8	20.9%
20% Maximum Loss					
Without CTAs	72.6	0.0	27.4	——	19.1%
Hedged CTAs	49.7	0.0	6.3	44.0	23.6%
Unhedged CTAs	52.7	0.0	11.0	36.2	22.6%

Conclusions

Using CTAs vs Not Using CTAs

Portfolios using hedged or un-hedged CTAs always performed better at the same level of risk than those not using CTAs. The optimal allocations to CTAs are at least 10% even at the lowest level of risk evaluated. In fact, since the CTA index includes fees and commissions while the stock and bond indices do not, then the optimal allocations to CTAs would be even higher than those shown if the stock and bond indices were charged commissions.

Hedging vs Not Hedging

Over the 11 years studied, the difference between hedging and no hedging on a risk-adjusted basis was negligible. See Tables 16-4 – 16-7.

Table 16-5 Optimum Allocations for German Investors

5% Maximum Loss	Stocks	Bonds	Cash	CTAs	Expected Return
Without CTAs	24.7	15.9	59.4	——	8.7%
Hedged CTAs	17.1	11.2	55.8	15.9	10.3%
Unhedged CTAs	15.3	28.3	42.6	13.8	10.4%
10% Maximum Loss					
Without CTAs	38.0	24.2	37.8	——	9.7%
Hedged CTAs	27.3	17.8	29.4	25.5	12.4%
Unhedged CTAs	24.6	45.4	7.7	22.3	12.6%
15% Maximum Loss					
Without CTAs	48.9	31.0	20.1	——	10.5%
Hedged CTAs	36.2	23.4	6.5	33.9	14.2%
Unhedged CTAs	33.9	36.3	0.0	29.8	14.5%
20% Maximum Loss					
Without CTAs	58.7	37.2	4.1	——	11.2%
Hedged CTAs	45.0	13.0	0.0	42.0	15.8%
Unhedged CTAs	42.5	21.2	0.0	36.3	16.1%

On an absolute basis, the un-hedged performance of CTAs was marginally better for the full 11 years. However, the performance of the un-hedged CTA performance was substantially better for the first six years when the dollar was strengthening. But the hedged CTA performance was better for the last five years when the dollar was weakening. See Tables 16-1 and 16-2.

Portfolios allocations generated for hedged vs un-hedged CTA data were not materially different.

Differences Among 4 European Countries

For the 11 years studied, government bonds were not efficient in France and Switzerland. Using the cash equivalent had a higher return and lower volatility.

Table 16-6   Optimum Allocations for French Investors

5% Maximum Loss	Stocks	Bonds	Cash	CTAs	Expected Return
Without CTAs	26.3	0.0	73.7	——	15.8%
Hedged CTAs	17.4	0.0	65.9	16.7	17.3%
Unhedged CTAs	19.0	0.0	67.2	13.7	17.1%
10% Maximum Loss					
Without CTAs	41.4	0.0	58.6	——	17.4%
Hedged CTAs	28.1	0.0	44.9	27.0	20.0%
Unhedged CTAs	30.6	0.0	47.1	22.3	19.6%
15% Maximum Loss					
Without CTAs	53.6	0.0	46.4	——	18.7%
Hedged CTAs	37.0	0.0	27.4	35.7	22.2%
Unhedged CTAs	40.2	0.0	30.4	29.4	21.7%
20% Maximum Loss					
Without CTAs	64.3	0.0	35.7	——	19.8%
Hedged CTAs	45.0	0.0	11.5	43.5	24.3%
Unhedged CTAs	48.8	0.0	15.4	35.8	23.6%

Portfolio returns were always increased by using hedged CTAs compared to portfolios at the same level of risk when not using CTAs by the amounts shown in Table 16-8.

Table 16-7   Optimum Allocations for Swiss Investors

5% Maximum Loss	Stocks	Bonds	Cash	CTAs	Expected Return
Without CTAs	29.2	0.0	70.8	——	6.8%
Hedged CTAs	20.3	0.0	65.3	14.4	8.2%
Unhedged CTAs	17.9	0.0	69.7	12.4	8.5%
10% Maximum Loss					
Without CTAs	45.0	0.0	55.0	——	7.8%
Hedged CTAs	32.5	0.0	44.4	23.1	10.1%
Unhedged CTAs	28.8	0.0	51.0	20.2	10.6%
15% Maximum Loss					
Without CTAs	58.2	0.0	41.8	——	8.5%
Hedged CTAs	43.3	0.0	25.9	30.8	11.7%
Unhedged CTAs	38.5	0.0	34.5	27.0	12.5%
20% Maximum Loss					
Without CTAs	70.1	0.0	29.9	——	9.2%
Hedged CTAs	53.3	0.0	8.7	38.0	13.2%
Unhedged CTAs	47.6	0.0	18.9	33.5	14.2%

Table 16-8   Increase in Return by Using Hedged CTAs over Using No CTAs

Country	5% Max Loss	10% Max Loss	15% Max Loss	20% Max Loss
UK	1.5%	2.7%	3.6%	4.5%
Germany	1.6%	2.7%	3.7%	4.6%
France	1.5%	2.6%	3.5%	4.5%
Switzerland	1.4%	2.3%	3.2%	4.0%

Figure 16-4 Performance of Portfolios

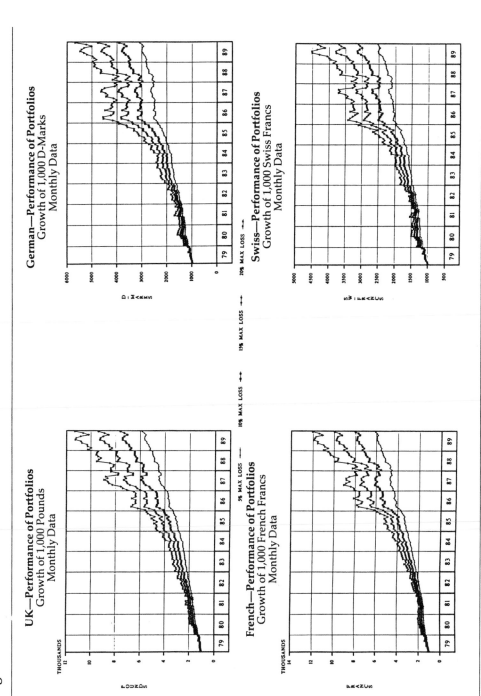

Chapter Seventeen

Management Summary

Title:	"The Role of Managed Futures Accounts in an Investment Portfolio"
Publisher:	Managed Account Reports, LJR Communications, Inc., 5513 Twin Knolls, Columbia, Maryland 21045
Authors:	Morton S. Baratz, Ph.D. Warren Eresian, Ph.D.
Data:	Monthly returns for the period January, 1984 through December, 1988 for 25 futures money managers, the S&P 500 Stock Index and U.S. Treasury Bonds (durations of five years and 20 years).
Methodology:	The purpose of this project was to compare results of an earlier study (based on data from 1980 through 1985) to more recent data, as well as to examine if the performance of futures money managers was becoming more positively correlated with stocks and bonds. The performance of each of the 25 futures money managers in terms of return, standard deviation, and correlation were examined in comparison to stocks and bonds. A subset of top 10 performing CTAs (with risk/reward ratios better than the average) were averaged together and compared to stocks and bonds in a similar manner. Efficient portfolios of stocks, bonds and managed futures (using the top 10 CTAs to represent managed futures) were constructed.
Results:	The authors note that the correlation between performance of the 25 futures managers and stocks and bonds has become more positively correlated since their last study, but that the change was small and not significant. The standard deviation of the subset of 10 was smaller than their earlier study which had a subset of five (see comments below). The addition of managed futures had a beneficial effect to portfolios of stocks and bonds. Com-

continued

pared to results of a study made four years earlier, the amount of managed futures necessary to achieve the same improvement had approximately doubled, thereby showing less effectiveness.

Comments: While the basic conclusions of this study are valid (managed futures accounts remain generally uncorrelated with stocks and bonds, and adding managed futures enhances portfolio performance), the selection of the top ten managers to represent the average CTA should be viewed with caution. As shown by Elton, Gruber and Rentzler[1] and Edwards and Ma[2], there is very little if any predictability in identifying the above average trading manager (or commodity fund) from one period to the next.

1. See Chapters 13 and 19.

2. Edwards, Franklin R. and Cindy Ma, "Commodity Pool Performance: Is the Information Contained in Pool Perspectuses Useful?"; CSFM #66, Center for the Study of Futures Markets, Columbia University, January, 1988.

The Role of Managed Futures Accounts in an Investment Portfolio*

Morton S. Baratz
Warren J. Eresian

The hypothesis that investors can lower unsystematic risk by distributing their respective eggs among several baskets, rather than concentrating them in one place, has been in common coinage for many decades. Originally, it was a product of inductive reasoning; the idea was distilled from practical experience. But beginning in the early 1950s, the idea was developed and refined by a group of talented financial theoreticians, notably including Harry Markowitz, John K. Lintner, and William R. Sharpe. Their and others' theoretical and empirical analysis now constitute the corpus known generally as Modern Portfolio Theory, or MPT for short.

Until recently, MPT was applied primarily to portfolios of stocks and bonds. Now the analysis more or less routinely encompasses such additional forms of investment as gold, real estate and gas-and-oil ventures, among other things. Not until 1983, however, were commodity futures considered by the theorists to be a legitimate component of a broadly diversified investment portfolio. Two contributions along that line ap-

*An updated study based on the work of Professor John K. Lintner, Harvard University Graduate School of Business (May 1983), and presented by the authors at the MAR Conference on Futures Money Management, Las Vegas, Nevada, January 1990.

Published by Managed Account Reports, LJR Communications, Inc. Reprinted with permission by Managed Account Reports, Inc.

peared in print within a few weeks of one another in Spring 1983. One, authored by Professor Zvi Bodie of Boston University and published in the Journal of Portfolio Management, addressed "Commodity Futures as a Hedge Against Inflation." As the title makes clear, Bodie's central argument was that whereas common stocks are a poor hedge against inflation because their real (price-level adjusted) rate of return is—contrary to popular belief—negatively correlated with movements in the general price level, "commodities are positively correlated with unanticipated inflation (which) makes them valuable as an asset in the portfolio."

In order to arrive at this conclusion, Bodie computed annual rates of return on futures by assuming that they, like stocks, bonds and bills, were bought and held. That assumption is at odds, of course, with what futures traders almost invariably do, but its "unreality" does not vitiate the point he was bent on making. In any case, Bodie's paper was soon supplemented by one presented to the Financial Analysts' Federation by Professor John Lintner of Harvard's Graduate School of Business Administration.

Using data for 1979-1982 obtained from Managed Account Reports, Lintner set out "to explore whether investments in managed accounts of trading advisors on the commodity and financial futures markets, and/or publicly traded futures funds, have shown risk and return characteristics which would make them a desirable means of further diversification for portfolios of stock and bond investments. In accordance with the tenets of Modern Portfolio Theory, Lintner postulated that "they will be desirable supplements to more conventional stock and bond portfolios provided they improve the reward-risk tradeoffs for the overall portfolios by shifting the efficient frontier of portfolio returns and portfolio risks upward and/or to the left when returns are plotted vertically and risks horizontally."

Lintner's general conclusions have by now been widely disseminated, but no harm and some good will be done by restating his chief findings:

1. "There are very large benefits from spreading funds dedicated to futures investments selectively ("efficiently") among different managers...Indeed, the improvements from holding efficiently selected portfolios of managed accounts...are so large—and the correlations between the returns on the futures portfolios and those on the stock and bond portfolios so surprisingly low (sometimes even negative)—that the return/risk tradeoffs provided by augmented portfolios, consisting partly of funds invested with appropriate groups of futures managers...combined with funds invested in portfolios (of) stocks alone (or in mixed portfolios of stocks and bonds), clearly dominate the tradeoffs available from portfolios of stocks alone (or from portfolios

of stocks and bonds). Moreover, they do so by a considerable margin."

2. "The combined portfolios of stocks (or stocks and bonds) after including judicious investments in appropriately selected sub-portfolios of investments in managed futures accounts...show substantially less risk at every possible level of expected return than portfolios of stocks (or stocks and bonds) alone."

3. "...[A]ll the above conclusions continue to hold when returns are measured in real as well as in nominal terms, and also when returns are adjusted for the risk-free rate on treasury bills."

As usually happens when a seminal work appears, numerous extensions or adaptations of Lintner's analysis have been undertaken. In February 1985, for example, Almer Orr (a prominent futures money manager) presented a paper to Managed Account Reports' Sixth Annual Conference on Commodity Money Management, in which he explained, then elaborated upon Lintner's paper. That part of Orr's work, which was original, covered nearly six years of futures trading, as against Lintner's three-and-a-half years; and Orr used somewhat different measures than did Lintner for representing the performance of managed futures accounts. Yet Orr came to essentially the same conclusion as Lintner, viz.: "I am familiar with no easily liquidated investment other than managed futures which, while generating positive rewards over time, lowers the volatility of more traditional investments to any significant degree. This is the reason portfolios augmented by just 20% of managed futures show such an improvement from a reward/risk standpoint over those lacking futures."

Similarly, in a short paper published in *Managed Account Reports* for March 1985 (Issue No. 73), Peter Matthews, another futures trading manager, compared rewards and risks of portfolios of futures only, stocks only, and varying combinations of stocks and futures; the futures portfolio assumed equal allocation of funds among each of the managers in the MAR/Leading Managers Index, the portfolio of stocks was assumed to be the S&P500 Index, and the period covered was early 1979 through the end of 1984. Matthews concluded that "the updated information continues to support Lintner's conclusion that one can achieve a much better reward/risk profile by combining futures and stocks than by trading futures or stocks alone...(T)he combined portfolio shows much smoother and steadier growth—getting higher returns for less risk is what investment management is all about."

To round out this non-exhaustive survey of the relevant literature, we must take note of an article by Scott H. Irwin and Diego Landa in the scholarly Journal of Portfolio Management (Fall 1987). Titled "The Use of Real Estate, Futures and Gold as Portfolio Assets," the paper concluded that (among other things) the performance of futures funds is negatively correlated with that of Treasury bills, bonds, and stocks, and has a low degree of positive correlation with the performance of real-estate investments; and, therefore, "futures investment (and futures-fund investment, in particular) may be useful for improving the real return-risk tradeoffs of conventional portfolios." Even more to the point, Irwin and Landa found that "futures funds were held at all points along the efficient frontier and reduced the risk of the highest expected-return portfolio by 32 percent."

The Aims of the Study

"In economics," a well-known economist once said, "the questions are always the same. It's the answers that change." This essay has been written in the same spirit. What we aim to accomplish here is just what we sought to do in an earlier version, published in 1986: confirm or refute, by resorting to empirical evidence, the findings and inferences in John Lintner's pioneering paper on the subject. As we'll make more clear at a later stage, our procedures this time differed only slightly from those employed previously, and we applied those methods to data of more recent vintage. In most respects, then, this study is a reprise of its immediate precursor.

The Mathematics of Diversification

If investments handled by futures money managers are to be combined in a fully-diversified portfolio, each manager's trading system should have certain characteristics: a history of high monthly gains, a low standard deviation (i.e., low variability) of those gains, and a track record that is weakly correlated with the performance of the others. The aim of the portfolio owner is to combine the futures trading managers in such a fashion that, for any specified monthly rate of gain for the portfolio, the risk involved to obtain that gain is minimized. This objective is, of course, the essence of diversification, its raison d'etre, and is graphically illustrated by the "efficient frontier."

We construct a portfolio from N different investments, each having a compounded monthly gain of G_i. The gain of the portfolio is then the weighted average of the individual gains:

$$G_p = d_1G_1 + d_2G_{n2} + \text{---} + d_NG_N \ldots . 3.1$$

where the d's are the fractions of each investment contained in the portfolio. Of course,

$$d_1 + d_2 + \text{---} + d_N = 1 \ldots . 3.2$$

Associated with each of the monthly gains is the risk, measured by the standard deviation S_i. The standard deviation of the portfolio is

$$S_p = \left[\sum_{i=1}^{N} \sum_{j=1}^{N} d_i d_j S_i S_j R_{ij} \right] \ldots . 3.3$$

where R_{ij} is the correlation coefficient between investment i and j.

The correlation coefficient describes the degree to which the variations between two changing parameters agree. Two parameters which change in the same way (say, one increases by a given amount, the other increases by the same fraction of that amount) are perfectly correlated and have a correlation coefficient of +1.000. Parameters which change in exactly the opposite way (one increases by a given amount, the other decreases by the same fraction of the amount) have a coefficient of -1.000. For purposes of assembling a diversified portfolio, the performance of the separate investments should be as uncorrelated as possible. As a practical matter, coefficients should be near zero.

For any desired portfolio gain G_p, there are many different combinations of the investment fractions, d_i, which satisfy equation 3.1. Each of these combinations, when substituted into equation 3.3, will yield a value for the portfolio standard deviation S_p. There is only one combination, however, for which the portfolio standard deviation is a minimum. The efficient frontier is simply the locus of points which results in a minimal standard deviation for a given portfolio gain.

To illustrate how the efficient frontier "behaves," we consider a portfolio which consists of only two investments. Equations 3.1-3.3 become respectively:

$$G_p = d_1G_1 + d_2G_2$$

$$d_1 + d_2 = 1$$
$$S_p = [\, d_1^2 S_1^2 + d_2^2 S_2^2 + 2 d_1 d_2 S_1 S_2 R_{12} \,]^{1/2}$$

By varying d_1 and d_2 we obtain the curves shown in Figure 17-1.

Curve A results whenever the correlation coefficient between the two investments is negative. Beginning at G_1, the portfolio risk decreases as the portfolio gain increases. At some point, this behavior reverses direction and the curve proceeds toward G_2.

When the correlation coefficient between the two investments is positive, either curve A or curve B is obtained, depending on the relative values of the individual return-risk ratios, R_1 and R_2, where the return-risk ratio is the compounded monthly return divided by the standard deviation of monthly returns. If they are comparable, curve A results. If R_1 is significantly greater than R_2, curve B results. From, the standpoint of enhancement of portfolio performance, curve A is the more desirable of the two, since it is possible to find a point where the portfolio risk is the same as that of the lower-risk investment, while the portfolio return is increased. (See point "1").

Application of the Theoretical Model: 1980-1985 Data

The data used in the earlier version of this study were verified performance figures for 12 futures money managers, all of whom were trading substantial sums of money on or before New Year's Day 1980.[1] Seventy-two months of trading, spanning the period January 1980 through December 1985, were analyzed. The results are presented in the upper portion of Table 17-1.

For each of the twelve managers, the compounded monthly return and the standard deviation of 72 monthly rates of return are shown. We also computed the correlation coefficient of each manager with every other manager and show the average coefficient. With only one exception, F1, the performance of the managers was positively correlated; F1's trading method apparently differed materially from those of the other trading managers in the sample.

The lower portion of Table 17-1 shows comparable data for a "stock portfolio" (S), as measured by the S&P500, and a "bond portfolio" (B), as measured by a weighted average of all Treasury bonds with maturities of 10 years or more. Of importance is the observation that performance of both stocks and bonds is weakly negatively correlated with that of futures money managers. On this basis, it is clear that the inclusion of futures into a portfolio of stocks or bonds, or both, would greatly enhance the portfolio performance.

Table 17-1

Futures Money Manager	Compounded Monthly Return (%)	Standard Deviation (%)	Return-Risk Ratio	Ave. Correlation With 11 Other Money Managers
F1	2.150	6.555	0.328	−0.025
F2	4.827	18.418	0.262	0.511
F3	3.604	14.391	0.250	0.501
F4	1.869	7.981	0.234	0.563
F5	2.812	12.469	0.226	0.478
F6	2.944	13.956	0.211	0.425
F7	2.271	10.963	0.207	0.544
F8	2.678	12.930	0.207	0.512
F9	1.135	5.766	0.197	0.339
F10	4.844	27.011	0.179	0.419
F11	1.831	10.766	0.170	0.542
F12	1.974	12.979	0.152	0.548
Ave. of Columns	2.745	12.849	0.219	0.446
Stocks	0.913	4.265	0.214	
Bonds	1.060	4.282	0.248	

Average Correlation, Stocks and 12 Managers = −0.036
Average Correlation, Bonds and 12 Managers = −0.101

We then assumed that there was a futures "pool" available to us, having the characteristics of the performance of the 12 money managers included in Table 17-1, i.e., a compounded average monthly rate of return of 2.745%, a standard deviation of 12.849%, and a correlation coefficient with stocks of -0.036. Using the methods described previously, we found that combination of futures and stocks which resulted in the same standard deviation for stocks alone, namely, 4.265%. For a combination of 21.5% futures and 78.5% stocks,[2] the standard deviation was also 4.265%. But the compounded monthly return of this combination was 1.308%, a 43.3% increase over that of stocks alone—for the same degree of risk.

We did not, however, restrict ourselves by using all 12 of the futures money managers. Instead, we repeated the calculation above, this time using a futures "pool," the performance of which was the average of those individual managers (F1 through F5) which had a return-risk ratio higher than the average of the 12. The characteristics of this five-managers' subset[3] were: compounded monthly rate of return of 3.052%, standard deviation of 11.963%, and an average correlation coefficient with stocks of -0.029. Now, a combination of 23.9% futures and 76.1% stocks produced the same standard deviation as for stocks alone, but yielded a monthly rate of return of 1.4235%, which is 56.1% higher than that of stocks alone. Figure 2 portrays the efficient frontier for this case.

Repetition of the preceding analysis, using bonds, yielded much the same story. The subset of individual managers (F1 through F5), representing 27.9% of the total portfolio, combined with the remaining 72.1% in bonds, produced a monthly rate of return of 1.616%, an increase of 52.4% over the return on bonds alone—at the same degree of risk. The results are shown in Figure 17-3.

Finally, Figure 17-4 depicts a portfolio consisting of futures, stocks and bonds. Again, there was a substantial increase in the monthly rate of return, with approximately the same degree of risk associated with stocks and bonds alone.

Although our analytical method differed slightly from Lintner's, our results were consistent with his. In both cases, that is, the inclusion of a relatively small portion (25% plus or minus) of futures into a portfolio of stocks or bonds, or both, dramatically improved—on the order of 50%—the rate of gain on the portfolio as a whole, with the same degree of risk as for a portfolio of stocks or bonds, standing alone. As Lintner points out, these results are attained because of the low correlation between futures and stocks (and bonds).

What about our working hypothesis that, because stock-index futures are playing a growing role in the portfolios traded by futures money managers, the performance of portfolios of stocks is becoming more positively correlated with the performance of portfolios of futures? To test the hypothesis, we recomputed the correlation between the S&P500 and the performance of the 12 futures money managers for separate one-year periods and for the six-year period as a whole. The findings, reported in Table 17-2, gave the hypothesis, at most, only mild support.

Application of the Theoretical Model: 1984-1988 Data

For purposes of our second iteration, we selected the period January 1984 through December 1988. One obvious advantage of using this span was that it was contemporaneous, thus could not be easily dismissed as of merely historical interest. Beyond that, its recency assured us that our data would

Figure 17-1 Efficient Frontier

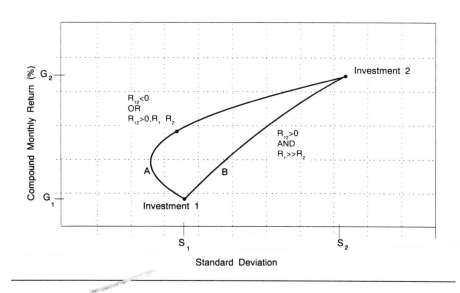

Figure 17-2 Futures vs. Stocks (1980–1985 Data)

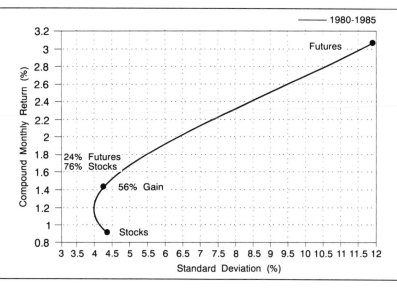

Figure 17-3 Futures vs. T-Bonds (1980–1985 Data)

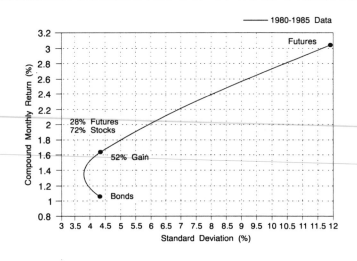

Figure 17-4 Futures Stocks and Bonds (1980–1985 Data)

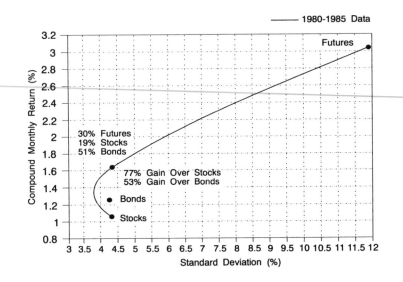

Table 17-2

Correlation Coefficient Average of 12 CTAs versus S&P500	
1980	−0.055
1981	−0.057
1982	−0.079
1983	−0.128
1984	−0.279
1985	+0.261

accurately reflect any further change that might have occurred in the degree of correlation between managed futures, on the one hand, and stocks and bonds, on the other. Most importantly of all, advancing the study's beginning date enabled us to double the size of the sample of CTAs. Where previously we had been able to identify only a dozen who satisfied our selection criteria, we now had no trouble finding 25 who did so. The two criteria were uninterrupted trading of customers' money during 1984-1988, inclusive; and no fewer than $10 million under management as of December 31, 1988.

As before, we calculated the return-risk ratio (defined as average monthly compounded rate of return divided by the standard deviation of monthly rates of return) for each of the 25 managers and the average (arithmetic mean) ratio for the group. Those results are shown in Table 17-3. Next, using the same method as before and for the same reason, we selected a subset of ten advisors, each of whose return-risk ratio exceeded the average for the 25. And, once again, we constructed an "average" or "representative" trading manager by calculating for the subset of 10 the average compounded monthly rate of return, average standard deviation of monthly rates of return, and average return-risk ratio (see Table 17-4). Of more than passing interest is that, while the average monthly gain of the subset of 10 managers was markedly lower than the gain of the earlier study's subset of five managers, and the ten's average monthly standard deviation was also lower than the earlier study, the average return-risk ratios for the two subsets were nearly identical, 0.256 vs. 0.255. On the other hand, the monthly gain and the standard deviation for stocks increased appreciably over the earlier study, while the return-risk ratio remained substantially the same. This suggests that futures and stocks are becoming increasingly similar in market behavior. In less cautious language, the efficient frontier for stocks and managed futures has shrunk.

Table 17-3

Commodity Trading Advisor	Compound Monthly Return	St. Dev. of Monthly Returns	Return-Risk Ratio
*F1	4.27	16.44	0.260
*F2	2.59	12.05	0.215
*F3	2.56	12.85	0.199
F4	2.49	16.61	0.150
*F5	2.37	6.95	0.341
*F6	2.30	11.67	0.197
F7	2.20	18.87	0.117
*F8	2.15	6.42	0.335
F9	2.03	13.48	0.151
F10	2.03	11.02	0.184
*F11	1.90	7.70	0.247
F12	1.73	12.00	0.144
*F13	1.73	3.09	0.560
F14	1.67	10.73	0.156
*F15	1.57	7.22	0.217
F16	1.52	10.43	0.146
F17	1.27	9.25	0.137
F18	1.11	8.00	0.139
F19	1.11	6.70	0.166
*F20	1.09	3.54	0.308
F21	1.06	16.09	0.066
F22	1.06	7.91	0.134
F23	0.99	12.40	0.080
F24	0.88	8.49	0.104
F25	0.63	12.87	0.049
S&P 500	1.20	5.40	0.222
5YR Bond	0.91	1.60	.569
20YR Bond	1.29	3.66	.352

Average return-risk ratio of 25 CTAs = 0.192

* = CTAs used in study, whose return-risk ratio is > than 0.192

Table 17-4

Subset of CTAs	1980–1985 (5 CTAs)	1984–1988 (10 CTAs)
Correlation with S&P500	−0.029	0.057
Correlation with 5 Year Bond	*−0.114	0.059
Correlation with 20 Year Bond		0.087
Average Monthly Return (%)	3.052	2.253
Average Monthly Stnd. Deviation (%)	11.963	8.793
Average Return-Risk Ratio	0.255	0.256
Return-Risk Ratio of S&P500	0.214	0.222
Return-Risk Ratio of 5 Year Bond	*0.248	0.569
Return-Risk Ratio of 20 Year Bond		0.352

*1980–1985 study used weighted average of bonds with maturity > ten years.

Table 17-4 reports, as well, the correlation coefficients for the "average" trading manager and for stocks, measured by the S&P500 Index, and bonds, measured by returns for instruments of 5 and 20 years maturity. As can be seen, the later coefficients were all slightly positive, whereas the earlier coefficients were slightly negative. While the changeover was measurable, it strikes us as statistically insignificant, which is simply to say that both studies provide support for Lintner's original proposition that managed futures are uncorrelated with stocks and bonds.

We also retested the proposition that increased trading of stock-index futures has raised the degree of positive correlation between futures and stocks. As can be seen in Table 17-5, the proposition has some basis in fact: the coefficient for the average of 25 trading advisors and the S&P500 changed from negative to positive in 1985 and has remained positive ever since. Notice, however, that the value of the coefficient has stayed well below +.30, a figure indicative of weak positive correlation.

Figure 17-5 depicts efficient frontiers for futures and stocks, derived from both our earlier and current studies. The figure should be self-explanatory, but two closely related points deserve to be underscored. One is that, according to the 1984-1988 data, addition of futures to the tune of 52% of the overall portfolio is required to increase the portfolio's return by 46% over that from holding stocks alone—without any increase in the degree of risk. In the earlier study, it took an injection of only 24% futures to produce, with no rise in risk, a portfolio gain of 56% over holdings of stocks alone. The

Table 17-5

Correlation Coefficient Average of 25 CTAs versus S&P500	
1980	−0.006
1981	−0.027
1982	−0.071
1983	−0.103
1984	−0.271
1985	+0.322
1986	+0.204
1987	+0.130
1988	+0.255

Figure 17-5 Futures vs. Stocks

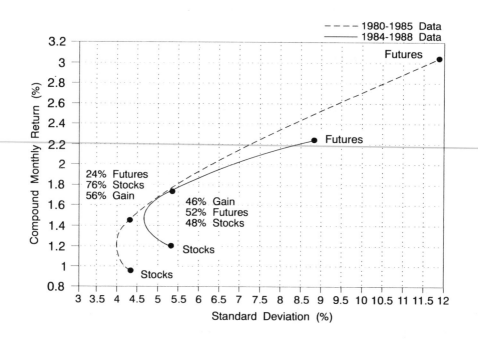

Figure 17-6 Futures vs. T-Bonds

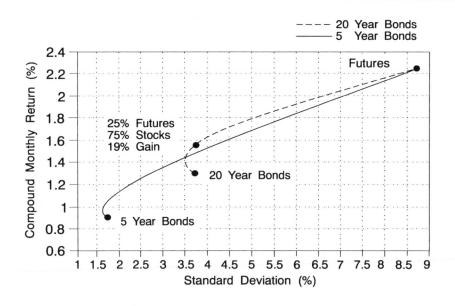

second point, a close corollary of the first, has already been mentioned: because the performance of futures has become more similar to that of stocks, the efficient frontier has "shrunk," that is, it required more than twice as much futures in the 1984–1988 portfolio to generate an increment to portfolio return comparable with that generated in 1980-1985. In other words, futures have become less effective.

In the earlier version of this study, we constructed an efficient frontier for a portfolio of futures and long-term bonds (the bonds being measured by an index of obligations with terms of ten years or more). It proved impossible to replicate that procedure, so we created efficient frontiers for futures and 5-year bonds, and futures and 20-year bonds. The results are displayed in Figure 17-6. As can be seen, the addition of futures to holdings of bonds maturing in five years would have a negligible effect on the ability of the portfolio to produce a significantly higher return at the same risk as that of bonds alone. This is due to the fact that the return-risk ratio of the bonds is 2.22 times higher than that of the futures managers, i.e., the bonds dominate the portfolio. There is little advantage to adding futures. (See curve B of Figure 17-1).

The benefits of diversification are somewhat more obvious when the yardstick for debt instruments was the 20-year bonds. As is denoted in Figure 17-6, the combination of 25% futures and 75% long-term bonds would yield a return about 19% larger than a portfolio of the bonds alone, at the same risk as the bonds alone.

The combination of futures, stocks and bonds is shown in Figure 17-7. The upper panel repeats the efficient frontier derived in our earlier study, while the lower panel shows the result of our recent work. In both cases, the addition of managed futures materially raises the portfolio rate of return at the same risk as that of stocks or bonds alone. The main difference is in the "dosage" of futures required to achieve this result, 58% of the portfolio now versus 30% of the portfolio then. The reason for this development has already been remarked, namely, that futures have become less "effective" with respect to stocks and bonds, and so it requires more futures to attain the same enhancement of portfolio performance.

Conclusion

At the close of his pioneering paper, John Lintner observed that "while all the general principles and all the qualitative conclusions we have stated have universal applicability, the particular numerical results we have given depend on the particular data we have used. We have been conservative in restricting ourselves to futures funds or futures management companies which had at least forty-two months of recent data to work with. But the period from July 1979 through [the] end of 1982 may not be a fully adequate basis for forming numerical assessments of the future levels of returns and risks."

We echo these sentiments with respect to our own work. Whereas the data Lintner used included a period (mid-1979 through March 1980) when many futures trading managers reaped an extraordinary harvest of profits, we have focused on two periods during much of each of which the majority of trading managers counted themselves lucky if they avoided heavy losses in futures markets that were repeatedly choppy or trendless. It is fair to say, then, that we have been even more conservative in our empirical analysis than was Lintner.

Nevertheless, our findings generally conform with, therefore confirm, his. We can do naught but endorse the dictum with which he ended his paper: "(A)lthough the specific numbers may change...low correlations between portfolios of futures accounts and stocks and bonds are very likely to persist

Figure 17-7 Futures, Stocks, and Bonds

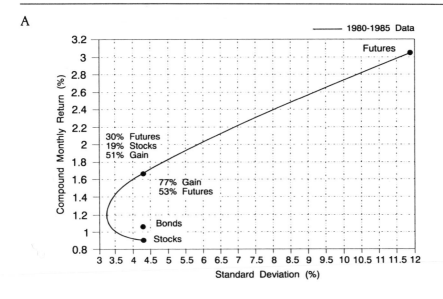

A

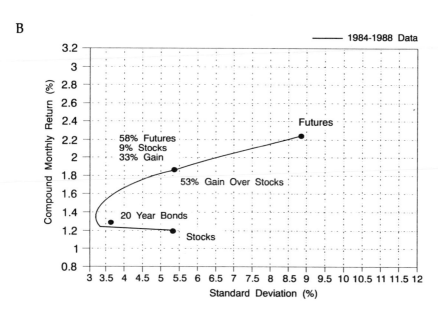

B

strongly into the future. And, in that event, all the general conclusions of the study will prove to be solid and robust." Portfolio managers, take heed!

Endnotes

1   The 12 managers constituted the large majority of all trading advisors who satisfied the stated criteria: verified track record covering 1980-1985 and trading a substantial sum.

2   Interestingly enough, this combination is comparable with the 20% futures/80% stocks and bonds that Orr found optimal.

3   The usage of only the five "best" managers in this analysis should not be cause for concern. In reality, only the better-performing managers would be seriously considered by investors assembling a portfolio of them.

Chapter 18

Management Summary

Title: "Portfolio Analysis of Stocks, Bonds, and Managed Futures Using Compromise Stochastic Dominance"

Publication: *The Journal of Futures Markets*, Vol. 11, No. 3, June 1991

Authors: Daniel Fischmar, Professor, Westminster College
                Carl C. Peters, A. O. Management Corporation

Data: Monthly returns for period January, 1980 through December, 1988 for stocks, bonds and managed futures as represented by the Managed Accounts Report Capital Weighted Index of CTA Performance.

Methodology: Stochastic dominance was used in lieu of modern portfolio theory to analyze the effect of diversifying stock and bond portfolios with managed futures. In this type of model, risk is measured as the probability of failure of a portfolio to achieve a given minimum level of return. Finding one optimum portfolio for all minimum levels of return rarely, if ever, occurs in practical application. This paper developed a method of finding the best *compromise* portfolio, i.e., one which comes the closest to a theoretically ideal optimal portfolio.

Results: It was found that the best compromise portfolios contained allocations to managed futures. In contrast to results from modern portfolio theory which provides for incremental benefits to a portfolio for increasing allocations to an asset class with beneficial properties, compromise stochastic dominance identified minimum allocation thresholds below which portfolio improvement would not occur. For the time period studied, such minimum threshold allocations appeared to be on the order of 20%. Using probability of failure as the measure of risk (as opposed to variance) it was also found that some so-called inefficient Markowitz portfolios offered a better compromise alternative than portfolios on the efficient frontier.

Portfolio Analysis of Stocks, Bonds, and Managed Futures Using Compromise Stochastic Dominance*

Daniel Fischmar
Carl C. Peters

Introduction

Investors, particularly large institutional investors, use the mean-variance (MV) approach of modern portfolio theory (Markowitz, 1959) to design and manage their portfolios. Many researchers use this technique to analyze the effectiveness of managed futures in diversifying equity portfolios with favorable results (Lintner, (1983), Baratz and Eresian (1986, 1990), Orr (1985, 1987), Brorsen and Irwin (1985), Irwin and Landa (1987), Fischmar and Peters (1988, 1990), although the conclusions are not unanimous Murphy (1987), Elton, Gruber, and Rentzler (1987, 1990).

MV methodology is criticized for a number of reasons. Variance is not an intuitively appealing measure of risk because most executives and institu-

*The authors thank the Center for the Study of Futures Markets at the Columbia Business School for its support of this study.

The Journal of Futures Markets, Vol. 11, No. 3, 259–270 (1991)

tional investors perceive risk as the probability of not achieving a minimum level of return (Zeleny, 1982). Variance is shown to overstate the true extent of tradeoff between risk and return (Fischmar and Peters, 1988), although significantly greater risk reduction can occur than implied by the MV model (Peters, 1989). The presence of outliers can have a disproportionate effect on variance, and autocorrelation can also cause significant problems in estimation (Strahm, 1983). In addition to the difficulties inherent to variance, the MV approach requires an investor's utility function to be quadratic to determine an optimal portfolio (Hadar and Russell, 1965). In reality, most investors have no idea about the shape of their utility function (Elton and Gruber, 1987). Finally, it has been shown that some portfolios in the MV-efficient set may, in fact, be inferior to others because of a nonoverlap in the probability distribution of returns (Baumol, 1963).

Stochastic dominance (Hadar and Russell, 1969), Hanoch and Levy (1965) has been proposed as a methodology for ordering uncertain outcomes and as an alternative to MV analysis in measuring the effectiveness of investment portfolios (Levy and Sarnet, 1972). Its advantage is that it accounts for the entire distribution of returns instead of only the mean and variance, thereby giving a broader measure of portfolio risk and return. If some portfolios are found to be dominant over others, then no assumptions are necessary regarding investor utility functions, except that more wealth is preferred to less. However, stochastic dominance does not perform well in actual practice, where complete and distinct dominance is seldom, if ever, found.

Some attempts have been made to overcome this difficulty (Meyer, 1983); but, in so doing, the need for specifying an investor's utility function is reintroduced (Irwin and Brorsen, 1984). Other approaches utilize a concept of partial stochastic dominance (Peters, 1989), but thereby limit the measures of effectiveness to a subset of returns. This article develops the concept of compromise stochastic dominance as a practical method of applying stochastic dominance criteria without the limitations described above.

Methodology

Stochastic dominance is an intuitively appealing criterion for ranking portfolios. Its principal advantage is that it attempts to account for the entire distribution of returns, producing a multidimensional measure of portfolio performance. First degree stochastic dominance is defined by the condition:

$$F_\alpha(r) < F_\beta(r) \qquad \text{for all } r, \text{ provided that } F_\alpha(r) < F_\beta(r)$$
$$\text{for at least one value of return, } r, \qquad (1)$$

where F_α and F_β are the cumulative probability distributions for portfolios α and β. The above condition implies that portfolio α is preferred (dominates) portfolio β if the cumulative distribution of α lies below and to the right of β, for all possible levels of return, r. Portfolios having first degree stochastic dominance provide the greatest probability of exceeding an investor's target level of return; they also provide the smallest risk of failure of achieving some minimum return. Thus, any investor, regardless of attitude toward risk, will prefer portfolios having first degree stochastic dominance (as long as more wealth is preferred to less).[1]

As mentioned above, several studies find that a pure stochastic dominance criterion does not work well in practice for stocks, bonds, or T-bills (Porter and Gaumitz, 1982), for ranking mutual funds (Meyer, 1983), for managed futures (Irwin and Brorsen, 1984), or for equity portfolios diversified with managed futures (Peters, 1989). The primary reason is that very large losses and gains are experienced occasionally in the real world by all types of investments (except perhaps T-bills), causing empirical cumulative probability distributions to overlap at one or more levels of return. Stochastic dominance is far too severe a criterion to reasonably apply to empirical distributions where this occurs.

One path of this dilemma is to use a multicriteria measure of risk that is derived from elements of stochastic dominance criteria (Colson and Zeleny, 1980). This technique makes use of a prospect-ranking vector (PRV) which includes information about three measures of performance: average return, the probability of achieving a given minimum level of return, and the probability of exceeding a given maximum level of return. The PRV criteria are limited to cases where only the first two moments of the distribution in returns are known and where a particular type of distribution can be assumed. The PRV approach has the limitation of confining itself to three measures of performance, but is suggestive of ways in which stochastic dominance-like criteria can be practically applied.

Since clear stochastic dominance is generally impossible to find, an alternative approach is to find the best compromise—i.e., that portfolio which comes closest to satisfying the conditions for stochastic dominance. Compromise programming is proposed as a technique for identifying such a portfolio. It proceeds by first identifying the ideal solution (which is unattainable), and then uses performance measures to identify those attainable portfolios which are closest to the ideal.

   The ideal portfolio is defined as one whose performance is comprised of the lower envelope of cumulative probability distributions of portfolios in the efficient MV set:

$$F* = \underset{i}{\text{Min}}\{F_i(r)\}$$

(2)

where F^* is the stochastically dominating (first degree) portfolio for every return, r.
   This ideal portfolio has the lowest probability of failure to achieve any given minimum level of return, and the maximum probability of exceeding some target level of return for any minimum or target return level specified by an investor. If first degree dominance exists among any of the efficient portfolios being considered, the ideal would coincide with it. If such dominance does not exist, then the ideal becomes the goal.
   Compromise programming identifies the portfolio which comes closest to minimizing the difference in performance between itself and the ideal. A measure of this difference is defined to be:

$$L_i = \left[\sum_r p_r^s \, (F(r_i) - F*)^s \right]^{1/s}$$

(3)

where:

$F(r_i)$ = probability distribution function of the ith portfolio in the efficient set,
F^* = probability distribution function of the ideal portfolio,
p_r = weight given to the rth level of return, and
s = parameter chosen to reflect the importance of the relative size of deviations from the ideal. (For $s = 1$ all deviations have equal weight; for $s > 1$ larger deviations have more weight, and vice-versa.)

The compromise stochastic dominance procedure is defined as:

$$\underset{i}{\text{Min } L} = \left[\sum_r p_r^s \, (F(r_i) - F*)^s \right]^{1/s}$$

(4)

Figure 18-1 Portfolios with and without futures

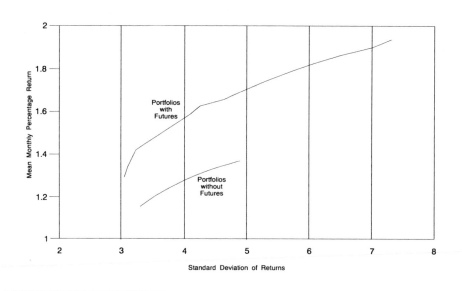

where:

$F(r_i)$ = portfolio in the MV efficient set,
  $s > 1$ (small deviations have low priority),
  $p = 1$ (all levels of return equally important).

Data

Data used for this analysis are monthly returns for the period 1980–88. Stocks are represented by the S&P 500 with dividends reinvested, bonds by the Salomon Brothers Broad Investment Grade Bond Index, and managed futures by the Managed Accounts Report Capital Weighted Index of CTA performance. See Appendix for a detailed description of managed futures data.

Table 18-1 MV-Efficient Frontiers

Portfolio	Stocks (%)	Bonds (%)	Managed Futures (%)	Average Mo. Return (%)	Monthly Std. Dev. (%)	Minimum Mo. Return (%)
1	28.3	49.5	22.2	1.32	3.03	−4.82
2	31.2	42.9	25.9	1.36	3.10	−4.72
3	34.5	35.6	29.9	1.41	3.23	−4.60
4	36.7	30.5	32.8	1.44	3.35	−4.62
5	38.9	25.4	35.7	1.48	3.49	−5.09
6	41.8	18.9	39.3	1.52	3.69	−5.71
7	43.4	15.2	41.4	1.54	3.81	−6.06
8	46.3	8.6	45.1	1.59	4.05	−6.68
9	47.8	5.1	47.0	1.61	4.18	−7.00
10	48.2	0	51.8	1.65	4.46	−6.96
11	42.2	0	57.8	1.68	4.71	−7.20
12	36.2	0	63.8	1.72	5.00	−7.76
13	30.1	0	69.9	1.75	5.33	−8.33
14	24.1	0	75.9	1.78	5.69	−8.89
15	18.1	0	81.9	1.82	6.08	−9.45
16	12.0	0	88.0	1.85	6.49	−10.03
17	5.9	0	94.0	1.88	6.91	−10.59
18	0	0	100.0	1.92	7.34	−11.15
19	38.9	61.0	0	1.16	3.35	−6.14
20	51.4	48.6	0	1.20	3.49	−9.29
21	61.6	38.4	0	1.23	3.69	−11.86
22	66.8	33.2	0	1.25	3.81	−13.17
23	75.8	24.2	0	1.28	4.05	−15.43
24	80.3	19.7	0	1.30	4.18	−16.57
25	89.0	11.0	0	1.33	4.46	−18.76
26	96.3	3.7	0	1.35	4.71	−20.60
27	100.0	0	0	1.37	4.85	−21.53

Mean-Variance (MV) Analysis

Markowitz efficient portfolio frontiers are constructed in the traditional fashion (Markowitz, 1959) with and without managed futures. The results are shown graphically in Figure 18-1. The efficient frontier of portfolios *including* managed futures lie substantially to the left (lower variance) and/or above (higher return for same variance) the attainable frontier with stocks and bonds alone. These results clearly indicate the benefits of using

Figure 18-2 Cumulative Distributions—Actual and Ideal Portfolios

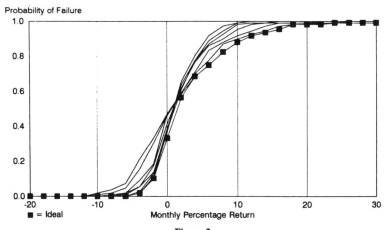

Figure 2
Cumulative Distributions—Actual and Ideal Portfolios

managed futures from an MV perspective, but many issues remain unanswered. Which portfolio is best? If risk is more appropriately measured as the probability of failure to achieve a given minimum level of return, then which would be the best portfolio? Would it still contain managed futures?

Table 18-1 describes in detail the MV-efficient frontiers for stocks and bonds, with and without managed futures. It is the basis upon which compromise stochastic dominance is applied. Portfolios 1–18 are derived considering stocks, bonds, and managed futures, while portfolios 19–27 include only stocks and bonds.

Stochastic Dominance

To test for pure stochastic dominance in the first 18 efficient portfolios of Table 18-1, cumulative probability distributions are constructed from the empirical data for each portfolio, and are shown in Figure 18-2. A pair-wise comparison is made between the cumulative distributions. In each case they cross at least once, thereby ruling out first degree stochastic dominance.

The reason for this inability of the stochastic dominance criteria to establish any preferred ordering of the efficient set can be seen in Table 18-1. In general, as the mean return of a portfolio increases, the lowest return for that portfolio becomes more extreme. The behavior of these extreme points in the cumulative distribution makes any single dominance criterion incapable of ordering the efficient set. Stochastic dominance (first degree), as a criterion for ordering efficient portfolios, is hampered by the fact that extreme returns, however small their probability, can cause an overlap in the cumulative distributions.

Compromise Stochastic Dominance

Compromise stochastic dominance identifies the portfolio that comes closest to the ideal. The ideal portfolio is defined as the lower envelope of cumulative probability distribution functions of all portfolios in the efficient frontier, as is shown in Figure 18-2.

Monthly returns in the efficient portfolios vary between the extremes of -20.8% to +34.4%. This range is arbitrarily divided into intervals of .4%, yielding 139 separate points of comparison between the ideal and actual portfolios considered. The procedure defined by eq. (4) is applied with $p = 1$ and $s > 1$. The justification for setting $p = 1$ is that, in the absence of any other information about the decision-maker, first degree stochastic dominance regards every level of return as equally important. (Potentially, this technique could be tailored to the preferences of the decision-maker by adjusting the values of p). Regarding s, large deviations are considered usually to be more critical than small deviations. Therefore, $s > 1$ is used for the analysis. Table 18-2 shows the values of L for the portfolios for varying levels of s. Portfolios 10 and 11 represent the best compromise between the ideal and actual. These portfolios contain *no bonds*, between 42% and 48% stocks, and 52% to 58% managed futures.

Figure 18-3 illustrates the cumulative distributions of portfolio 10 compared to the ideal. According to the stated definition, no other portfolio is better at approaching the ideal.

The compromise stochastic dominance procedure is applied also to the stock- and bond-efficient frontier. The results are presented in Table 18-3. One can now further appreciate the benefits of the stochastic dominance approach by the insight it brings to the tradeoff between risk and reward. Portfolio 27 (containing all stocks) is the best compromise solution from this efficient set; but it is inferior to the best compromise from the set containing managed futures, portfolio 10 (48.2% stocks, 51.8% managed futures). How-

Table 18-2   Values of *L* for the Stock, Bond and Managed Futures MV-Efficient Frontier

	L		
Portfolio	*S* = 2	*S* = 10	*S* = ∞
1	.7353	.2041	.1753
2	.7026	.1929	.1667
3	.6832	.1853	.1574
4	.6557	.1731	.1481
5	.6248	.1644	.1389
6	.6082	.1572	.1296
7	.5869	.1526	.1296
8	.5634	.1471	.1296
9	.5526	.1463	.1296
10	.5283	.1270*	.1111*
11	.5231*	.1358	.1204
12	.5358	.1643	.1574
13	.5478	.1913	.1759
14	.5697	.2071	.1819
15	.6082	.2324	.2130
16	.6541	.2434	.2222
17	.6991	.2520	.2222
18	.7638	.2704	.2315

* = Minimum *L*.

Figure 18-3 Cumulative Distributions—Compromise and Ideal Portfolios

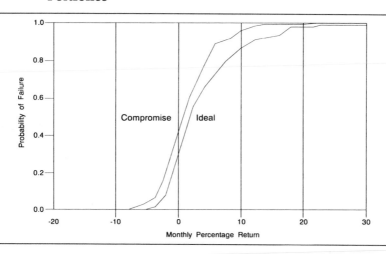

Table 18-3   Values of *L* for the Stock and Bond MV-Efficient Frontier

| | *L* | | |
Portfolio	*S* = 2	*S* = 10	*S* = ∞
19	.7422	.2115	.1852
20	.7230	.2022	.1852
21	.6904	.1826	.1481
22	.6774	.1806	.1481
23	.6470	.1715	.1481
24	.6341	.1687	.1389
25	.6068	.1626	.1389
26	.5926	.1573	.1389
27	.5817*	.1529*	.1296*

* = Minimum *L*.

ever, note that portfolios 1–6 (using between 22% and 39% managed futures) are inferior to portfolio 27 (all stocks). This result is different from what one would conclude from the MV approach (shown in Table 18-1) where portfolios 1–6 clearly are preferable to portfolio 27.

The approach shown herein indicates the possibility that under some realistic circumstances (e.g., $p = 1$, $s > 0$), some *inefficient* portfolios may be a better compromise alternative than portfolios on the efficient frontier for the assets considered here.

Another conclusion, which is different from others using an MV approach, is that the stochastic dominance framework reveals the possibility that a candidate asset class for diversification may have a minimum threshold allocation before improved performance can be realized for the portfolio. For example, portfolio 21 (approximately 62% stocks, 38% bonds—an optimal portfolio based on returns since 1926 (Elton, Gruber, and Rentzler, 1987) dominates portfolios 1–4 (stocks, bonds, and managed futures) until the managed futures component reaches approximately 35%. Other calculations done by the authors (not shown here) indicate that approximately 20% managed futures are needed as a minimum threshold to dominate the worst of stock-bond portfolios. The MV approach, on the other hand, dictates only that the ratio of excess return to variance of the candidate asset class for diversification exceed the same ratio for the portfolio multiplied by the correlation between the two (Elton, Gruber, and Rentzler, 1987). There is no minimum threshold requirement in the MV approach.

Table 18-4

Portfolio	Stocks (%)	Bonds (%)	Managed Futures (%)	L for S = ∞	Prob. of Return Less Than: 0%	.4%	−2.8%
1	28.3	49.5	22.2	.1753	.3704	.4722	.0833
2	31.2	42.9	25.9	.1667	.3704	.4537	.0648
3	34.5	35.6	29.9	.1574	.3796	.4352	.0741
4	36.7	30.5	32.8	.1481	.3889	.4537	.0741
5	38.9	25.4	35.7	.1389	.3704	.4537	.0833
6	41.8	18.9	39.3	.1296	.3796	.4722	.0648
7	43.4	15.2	41.4	.1296	.3796	.4537	.0741
8	46.3	8.6	45.1	.1296	.3889	.4630	.0741
9	47.8	5.1	47.0	.1296	.3981	.4630	.0741
10	48.2	0	51.8	.1111	.4167	.4815	.0926
11	42.2	0	57.8	.1204	.4352	.4815	.1111
12	36.2	0	63.8	.1574	.4444	.5185	.1389
13	30.1	0	69.9	.1759	.4722	.5278	.1389
14	24.1	0	75.9	.1819	.4537	.5093	.1481
15	18.1	0	81.9	.2130	.4630	.5093	.2037
16	12.0	0	88.0	.2222	.4630	.5093	.2593
17	5.9	0	94.0	.2222	.4722	.5000	.2778
18	0	0	100.0	.2315	.4722	.5000	.2870
19	38.9	61.0	0	.1852	.3704	.4259	.1111
20	51.4	48.6	0	.1852	.3519	.4167	.1204
21	61.6	38.4	0	.1481	.3333	.3889	.1204
22	66.8	33.2	0	.1481	.3426	.3889	.1204
23	75.8	24.2	0	.1481	.3519	.3889	.1296
24	80.3	19.7	0	.1389	.3519	.3889	.1389
25	89.0	11.0	0	.1389	.3704	.3981	.1389
26	96.3	3.7	0	.1389	.3611	.3981	.1574
27	100.0	0	0	.1296	.3611	.4167	.1574

Table 18-4 compares all 27 portfolios with respect to various measures of risk.

In contrast to the Markowitz criteria, not all the portfolios that exclude futures are dominated by portfolios that include futures. The column labeled $s = \infty$ reveals that the "nonfutures" portfolios 21–27 perform reasonably well when compared with portfolios 1–4 and 12–18.

The reason for this result can be seen in the columns that give the probability of returns below 0% and 0.4%. Examination of those columns reveals that the nonfutures portfolios perform well in terms of these relatively limited set of criteria. In fact, if one adopts the single criterion of minimizing the probability of returns below 0%, the nonfutures portfolio 21 becomes optimal. And, if one adopts the single criterion of minimizing the probability of returns below 0.4%, "nonfutures portfolios" 21–24 are the preferred choices to portfolios 1–18 with managed futures.

The problem with such single-dimension criteria can be understood by examining of the last column in Table 18-4. Although portfolios 21–24 minimize the probability of missing a very small return, they are inferior in their ability to prevent larger losses. For example: from the last column of Table 18-4, it is evident that portfolio 10 yields a .0926 chance of losing 2.8% or more. In contrast, portfolio 21 increases that risk to .1204, an increase of 30% compared with portfolio 10.

Similarly, the "nonfutures" portfolios perform poorly at the upper ends of the return distribution. For example: The probability of a return in excess of 8% is .037 for portfolio 21 and .1019 for portfolio 10. (This calculation is not presented in Table 18-4.) Thus, the futures portfolio 10 increases the chance of returns in excess of 8% by 175% compared with portfolio 21.

Generally, the "nonfutures" portfolios only provide better performance over a very limited range of the return distribution. "Nonfutures" portfolios 20–25 generally perform better than the "futures" portfolios over the range from 0–2% return, but are dominated by the "futures" portfolios at every other point in the distribution of returns. Portfolios that include futures do a better job of maximizing the probability of achieving any given target return and minimizing the probability of loss, except for the narrow range between 0–2%.

In summary, the evidence provided suggests that the proper way to evaluate portfolios is through a methodology that takes into account all possible levels of return. Risk is inherently a multidimensional concept that should be evaluated with multicriteria decision techniques. Since the risk of large losses as well as the failure to achieve large returns are as significant in the risk calculus as failure to achieve a single target such as the risk-free return, a multidimensional method, one that utilizes the techniques presented in this report, appears to be warranted.

A limitation of this technique is that there are an infinite number of possible portfolios, whereas only a discrete subset of empirical distributions can be used to define the ideal and compromise portfolios. However, this limitation is not unique to compromise dominance; stochastic dominance itself operates in the same way and requires an investor to partition the infinite set into a manageable and practical subset of alternative portfolios.

Conclusions

Compromise dominance provides a method for selecting from among a set of portfolios one that comes closest to dominating the others according to first degree stochastic dominance criteria. It allows the ordering of portfolios when complete stochastic dominance is impossible, as it usually is in real-world applications. It offers an alternative to other stochastic dominance ranking techniques that use modifications which often damage the nearly assumption-free nature of the original criteria.

Portfolios consisting of stocks and/or bonds and/or managed futures are analyzed based on monthly returns for the period 1980–88. Portfolios consisting of approximately one-half stocks and one-half managed futures dominate all other portfolios, based on the compromise dominance criteria. It is found that minimum thresholds of managed futures are needed to produce beneficial results, in contrast to the conclusions of modern portfolio theory, which does not imply thresholds. The analysis also shows that, under some realistic circumstances, inefficient Markowitz portfolios offer a better compromise alternative than portfolios on the efficient frontier.

Endnote

1. Second degree stochastic dominance has been proposed also as a criterion (Levy and Sarnet, 1972). It is defined by $\sum_r F_\alpha(r) = \sum_r F_\beta(r)$ for all r, with the strict inequality holding for at least one value of return, r. This report uses first degree dominance since first degree dominance implies second degree (Hadar and Russell, 1969).

Bibliography

Baratz, M., and Eresian, W. (1986): "The Role of Managed Futures Accounts in an Investment Portfolio," Managed Accounts Report Mid-Year Conference on Futures Money Management, July, Chicago, IL.

Baratz, M.S., and Eresian, W. (1990): "The Role of Managed Futures Accounts in an Investment Portfolio," *MAR Conference on Futures Money Management,* January.

Baumol, W. J. (1963): "An Expected Gain—Confidence Limit Criterion for Portfolio Selection," *Management Science,* 10(1).

Brorsen, B. W., and Irwin, S. (1985): "Public Futures Funds," *Journal of the Futures Markets,* 5(2).

Colson, G., and Zeleny, M. (1980): "Multicriterion Concept of Risk Under Incomplete Information," *Computers and Operations Research,* 7.

Elton, E.J., and Gruber, M. (1987): *Modern Portfolio Theory and Investment Analysis,* (3rd Ed.), New York: Wiley.

Elton, E.J., Gruber, M.J., and Rentzler, J.C. (1987): "Professionally Managed, Publicly Traded Commodity Funds," *Journal of Business,* 60(2).

Fischmar, D., and Peters, C. (1988): "A Stochastic Dominance Approach to Portfolio Diversification," *Proceedings of the Pennsylvania Economic Association Annual Meeting,* Pennsylvania State University, May.

Goicoechea, A., Hansen, D., and Duckstein, L. (1982): *Multiobjective Decision Analysis with Engineering and Business Applications,* New York: Wiley.

Hadar, J., and Russell, W. (1969): "Rules for Ordering Uncertain Prospects," *American Economic Review,* 59.

Hanoch, G., and Levy, H. (1969): "Efficiency Analysis of Choices Involving Risk," *Review of Economic Studies,* 38.

Irwin, S., and Brorsen, B.W. (1984): "Evaluation of Public Futures Funds," Center for the Study of Futures Markets Working Paper #CSFM-77, April.

Irwin, S., and Landa, D. (1987): "Real Estate, Futures, and Gold as Portfolio Assets," *The Journal of Portfolio Management,* Fall.

Levy, H., and Sarnet, M. (1972): *Investment and Portfolio Analysis,* New York: Wiley.

Lintner, J. (1983): "The Potential Role of Managed Commodity—Financial Futures Accounts (and/or Funds) in Portfolios of Stocks and Bonds," Annual Conference of the Financial Analysts Federation, Toronto, May.

Markowitz, H. (1959): *Portfolio Selection: Efficient Diversification of Investments,* New York: Wiley.

Meyer, J. (1977a): "Choice Among Distributions," *Journal of Economic Theory*, 14.

Meyer, J. (1983): "Further Application of Stochastic Dominance to Mutual Fund Performance," *Journal of Financial and Quantitive Analysis*, 18.

Murphy, J. (1986): "Futures Fund Performance: A Test of the Effectiveness of Technical Analysis," *Journal of Futures Markets*, 6(2).

Orr, A.H. (1985): "John Lintner and the Theory of Portfolio Management," Sixth Annual Managed Accounts Report Conference, February, Chicago, IL.

Peters, C.C. (1989): "A Comparative Analysis of Portfolio Diversification Criteria using Managed Futures," *Proceedings of the Fourth Annual Convention of the Pennsylvania Economic Association*, May.

Peters, C.C., and Fischmar, D. (1988): "A Stochastic Dominance Approach to Portfolio Selection," *Proceedings of the Third Annual Convention of the Pennsylvania Economic Association*, May.

Peters, C.C., and Fischmar, D. (1990): "Portfolio Analysis of Stocks, Bonds and Managed Futures Using Compromise Stochastic Dominance," Working Paper #208 Series Center for the Study of Futures Markets, Columbia University.

Porter, R.B., and Gaumitz, J.E. (1982): "Stochastic Dominance vs. Mean-Variance Portfolio Analysis: An Empirical Evaluation," *American Economic Review*, LXII.

Strahm, N. (1983): "Preference Space Evaluation of Trading System Performance," *Journal of the Futures Markets*, 3(3).

Zeleny, M. (1982): *Multiple Criteria Decision Making*, New York: McGraw-Hill.

Appendix

Data Source for Managed Futures Returns

The data used for performance of managed futures is the Managed Accounts Report (MAR) Commodity Trading Advisor (CTA) Index (dollar weighted), compiled by Managed Accounts Report, Inc., of Columbia, MD. The MAR CTA Index consists of equity-weighted performance of a representative group of CTAs monitored by Managed Accounts Report, Inc. Returns for each advisor are subject to audit by the National Futures Association (NFA) and Commodity Futures Trading Commission (CFTC). In 1988, the Index consisted of returns from 25 advisors, which at that time represented approximately 80% of all the equity managed by advisors tracked by Managed Accounts Report. Advisors are selected on the basis of equity under management in the preceeding year, and are kept in the Index for the following year regardless of their performance. Testing done by Managed Accounts Report, Inc., indicates no significant difference between performance of the Index and its universe.

Chapter Nineteen

Management Summary

Title:
: "The Performance of Publicly Offered Commodity Funds"

Publisher:
: *Financial Analysts Journal*, July-August, 1990

Authors:
: Edwin J. Elton, Professor, New York University
Martin J. Gruber, Professor, New York University
Joel C. Rentzler, Associate Professor, Baruch College

Data:
: Monthly returns for public commodity funds from January, 1980 through December, 1988, as well as returns for the same period for common stocks, long-term corporate and government bonds, the Shearson Lehman Bond Index, and Treasury Bills.

Methodology:
: Performance of public commodity funds was compared to alternative assets on a risk/return basis. Commodity funds as a potential hedge against inflation were examined using correlation analysis with the Consumer Price Index. Distributions of monthly returns were analyzed to determine if positive skewness existed. Predictability of returns was examined using rank-order correlation analysis.

Results:
: Performance of public commodity funds over the nine-year period generally improved, but returns were less than for alternative assets (stocks, bonds, Treasury bills) while standard deviations were higher. Probability of dissolution of funds was high; from 23% in five years to 49% over ten years. The low return from public commodity funds over the time period analyzed made them unattractive as diversification assets for stock and bond portfolios, despite their non-correlation to other asset classes. A correlation analysis of monthly returns for these funds to changes in the Consumer Price Index showed essentially non-correlation, and the authors concluded there was no value in inflation hedging. No evidence of positive skewness was found; in fact, the presence of negative skewness was detected. Size, expe-
continued

rience of general partners and past performance of funds managed by the general partners were examined as possible predictors of fund success. Size and overall experience had no clear effect on success, but funds managed by general partners with above average prior experience outperformed those managed by general partners with below average prior experience.

| Comments: | This study overcame some limitations of their earlier research, (see Chapter 13) dealing with nine years of data instead of six years, and substantially more funds. Their results were consistent with the findings of others (see Chapter 12). Fees and transaction costs must come down if public commodity funds as a group are to be a competitive and attractive investment. |

It was noted that performance had improved over time. It is a well-known fact that the fees have, in fact, come down since the early eighties, and that the trend to lower fees continues. By looking at all funds together, the effect of lower fees on performance of more recently formed funds is diluted.

Findings that public futures funds are not an effective hedge against inflation should be viewed with some caution. The authors' technique of analysis, applying correlation analysis to month-to-month returns and changes in the Consumer Price Index, may be inadequate in accounting for the lead-lag relationship between consumer and commodity prices, and the subsequent returns to commodity funds. Other studies (see Chapter 11) which using longer time periods for analysis (year-to-year changes) overcame the shortcomings of the shorter time frame lead/lag problems, and found significant inflation-hedging potential.

The Performance of Publicly
Offered Commodity Funds*

Edwin J. Elton
Martin J. Gruber
Joel C. Rentzler

Summary

Publicly offered commodity funds are limited partnerships that buy and sell
futures contracts. There were over 130 such funds in existence in 1988. An
examination of their performance over the 1980–88 period indicates that
their returns generally improved over the period, but not by enough to make
them attractive investments. Furthermore, these funds are risky. Not only
does the time pattern of their returns show an extremely high variance, but
the probability of a fund dissolving within five years is just under 25%, while
the probability of its dissolving within ten years is almost 50%.

Commodity funds might nevertheless offer attractive investment opportunities if they provided (as some have thought) positively skewed returns,
or if it were possible to pick the superior funds. The data indicate, however,
that the degree of positive skewness is too small to provide a good reason
for investing in these funds. Furthermore, the history of the funds does not
seem to offer much, if any, evidence that prediction of superior performance
is possible. If commodity funds are to be attractive investments, either their
mangement fees and transaction costs must come down, or new ways of
identifying the winners must be developed.

*Financial Analysts Journal, July–August 1990, 23–30. Reprinted with permission.

Introduction

Publicly offered commodity funds are professionally managed limited partnerships, offered to investors by prospectus, that buy and sell futures contracts. While individual funds may differ, the typical fund has the following characteristics.

(1)   Most funds have the ability to trade (and do trade) in many futures and forward contracts on financial instruments, foreign currencies and commodities. In addition, they frequently hold financial instruments directly (using them for margin against their futures transactions). Most fund prospectuses stress diversification and the ability to take long as well as short positions in commodities (i.e., to buy or sell futures contracts).

(2)   Most funds can only be purchased for a short time after the initial prospectus, but allow investors to liquidate their position at net asset value at monthly (sometimes quarterly) intervals. A monthly rate of return can, however, be computed.

(3)   Most funds use technical and trend-following systems to decide whether to take a long or short position with respect to any commodity (futures contract).

(4)   Most funds incur high management fees and transaction costs relative to other types of asset management such as mutual funds. Management fees usually exceed 5% of capital a year, while the sum of management fees and transaction costs exceeds 19% of capital per year.

(5)   Most fund prospectuses contain a clause that calls for the fund to dissolve if either the net asset value per share falls below a predetermined level (most often 25 to 30% of the initial capital an investor pays in) or the total size of the fund (assets under management) falls below a specific level.

Prior to 1978, there were only three publicly offered commodity funds, but their number has grown rapidly in recent years—from 94 funds with $600 million under management in 1985 to 130 funds with over $2 billion under management in 1988. Their popularity has continued despite two apparent handicaps—*extremely high management fees and transaction costs, and almost exclusive reliance on technical analysis.* Furthermore, an earlier study of commodity funds in existence from June 1979 through June 1985 found that these funds, on average, experienced relatively low returns and very high risk.

Prior and Current Research

We analyzed the performance of publicly offered commodity funds in an earlier paper published in 1987.[1] That study represented the first comprehensive analysis of what was at the time, and has continued to be, a fast-growing industry. Enough years have passed since that initial study that it is worthwhile examining whether our initial conclusions still hold.

Our initial study used only six years of data—all that were available at that time—and the results of several of those years were dominated by the performance of a few funds. We now have nine years of data to look at, as well as a substantially larger number of funds.

Several criticisms were directed toward our earlier paper, and we have attempted to respond to them here. One was that we looked at investment from June to June. That period was selected because, at the time, it allowed us to use the longest possible set of data. It has been suggested that if we had used the calendar year as the holding period, our results would have been different. With the luxury of more data, we have switched to a calendar year for analysis.

In the original study, when a fund dissolved during a year, we made the assumption that the funds received by investors were reinvested across all remaining funds. Because funds are not in general open for new investment, this procedure is not possible in practice. In this article we make the more conservative assumption that the proceeds from fund dissolution are placed in Treasury bills for the remainder of the year. Because the average return on funds is below the Treasury bill rate, this assumption should improve measured fund performance.

The original paper employed the geometric mean return over a one-year holding period. Objections were raised to our use of one-year returns. This article uses the continuously compounded rate of return (the log of price relatives). The log price relative is the return measure used by most investigators of return distributions. This measure has additive properties that are desirable and approximates long-term returns.

Finally, we have added some analysis, largely in response to comments received from the industry. It had been suggested, for example, that commodity funds might be desirable because, despite poor mean return and high variances, they have attractive skewness (i.e., offer investors the chance of large payoffs). We examine this explicitly.

In addition, we received a number of suggestions about how to select superior funds. In our earlier study we looked at performance year-by-year and found that funds that performed well in one year did not necessarily perform well the next year. It was suggested that superior funds could be selected by analyzing performance over longer time periods (an analysis now possible, given the longer time frame). It was also suggested that superior funds could be selected by looking at the size of the fund or looking at the past record of the general partner. We examine each of these suggestions below.

Data

The basic data consist of monthly returns on all publicly offered commodity funds listed in the MAR reports for the period January 1980 to December 1988. If a fund dissolved, we collected dissolution values, primarily from the final reports to shareholders, obtained from the Commodity Futures Trading Commission. When final reports did not exist in the CFTC files, we contacted sponsoring firms, trading advisers and accounting firms. In a few cases, we relied upon verbal statements from brokerage firms, trading advisers or MAR.

There are three sources of potential inaccuracies in our data. First, although MAR is considered all-inclusive, there may be publicly traded commodity funds that are not included in its reports. Second, in the small number of cases where dissolved values were obtained verbally, inaccuracies may exist.[2] Third, our analyses of the impact of size and the identity of general partners on future returns relied on prospectus data, and prospectuses could be obtained for only 79 out of the 91 funds in our original sample.[3]

Performance

Table 19-1 presents the returns and risks for publicly traded commodity funds for each year 1980 through 1988. We calculated return in two ways. First, we assumed that an investor is equally likely to hold any fund while it exists, hence we included data for all firms that existed at any point in time in the year.[4] This averaging method, which we term "all," is equivalent to assuming that an investor reallocates (for the remainder of the year) any funds he or she obtains from a fund dissolution to the rest of the funds in existence. Second, we assumed a fund was included in a portfolio only if it existed at the beginning of the year. If a fund dissolved during the year, we assumed that the proceeds received by the investor were placed in T-bills. This approach, which we term "beginning year," resulted in slightly higher returns, because commodity fund returns were well below the T-bill rate.

Table 19-1   The Returns and Risks of Commodity Funds, 1980-1988

| | | Annual Return (per cent) | |
Year	Monthly Standard Deviation[a]	All[b]	Beginning Year
1980	12.6[c]	5.8980	2.0748
1981	10.0	0.5452	4.0716
1982	10.1	0.4944	-0.0864
1983	11.7	-16.1568	-15.0768
1984	10.6	7.0620	7.6656
1985	8.7	10.5096	10.8840
1986	10.4	-17.3916	-17.1588
1987	8.7	27.8676	28.3200
1988	10.4	0.4962	0.5568
	10.4	2.2565	2.3612

[a]The standard deviation for non-log returns is almost identical.

[b]Simple average annual return was 4.4%.

[c]This number excludes the firm with the highest standard deviation. This firm existed for only a few months in 1980. Including this firm would result in a value of 24.3 for 1980.

Table 19-2 presents the risks and returns for a broad group of competing investments. A comparison of Tables 19-1 and 19-2 makes clear the low return and high risk associated with investment in commodity funds. The return of 2.3% per year is clearly lower than that offered by competitive

Table 19-2   Returns and Risks of Comparable Assets, 1980-1988

	Yearly Return (per cent)	Standard Deviation of Monthly Return
Common Stocks	14.88	4.91
Long-Term Corporate Bonds	11.80	3.84
Long-Term Government Bonds	11.40	4.17
Shearson Lehman Bond Index	11.40	2.38
Treasury Bills	8.64	0.25

Sources: Common stock and long-term corporate and government bond returns from R. Ibbotson, *Stocks, Bonds, Bills, and Inflation 1989 Yearbook* (Chicago: Ibbotson Associates, 1989). Shearson Lehman Bond Index data supplied by Shearson American Express.

Table 19-3   Year-by-Year Performance of Commodity Funds

Starting Year	Percentage Return in Year								Lifetime Return (per cent per year)
	1	*2*	*3*	*4*	*5*	*6*	*7*	*8*	
1980	9.45	8.72	−7.43	−6.32	−3.34	−1.19	−5.50	16.24	1.47
1981	−1.74	−7.90	−12.34	7.14	10.40	−9.67	21.16		−1.86
1982	−25.32	−23.74	9.10	23.02	16.18	15.28			−7.17
1983	−6.20	3.67	11.76	−18.38	18.01				−0.54
1984	2.26	19.60	−12.30	8.92					2.73
1985	8.24	−24.66	25.12						−0.08
1986	1.31	21.52							6.31
1987	−0.18								−0.26

investments, and the standard deviation of 10.4% per month is clearly much higher.

Despite our changed definition of return and the longer time period, the results of this more recent study do not differ substantially from the findings of our earlier study. The earlier study ended in June 1985, hence the later study includes three complete years of data not analyzed earlier. The average return during these three years was 3.64%. For the six years that overlap with our previous study, the return was 1.56%. Commodity funds have clearly enjoyed a higher rate of return over the last three years. However, the return during this time was still considerably lower than the return from Treasury bills (8.64%) and not sufficiently high to make investment in commodity funds seem worthwhile.

Table 19-3 shows the lifetime performances of the funds. The lifetime returns varied from −7.2 to +6.3%, depending on the year the fund was introduced. This table also shows the average performance in the first year of existence, the second year and so forth. There is no discernible time pattern. The diagonals represent approximately the same calendar time. Note the similarity in returns along diagonals. This shows that overall market performance, and not number of years in existence, is the more important influence on fund returns.

Given the large risk associated with commodity fund returns and the low average level of returns, we should expect to see numerous funds dissolving over time. We examine below the dissolution pattern in the industry.

Dissolution

A large number of publicly traded funds dissolved over our nine-year sample period. Almost all the dissolutions took place for one of two reasons.

Table 19-4 Dissolution Experience

	New Entrants[b]	Total Dissolved	Per Cent Dissolved	Number of Funds Dissolved in Their Year								
				1	2	3	4	5	6	7	8	9
Before 1980[a]	13	6	46									
1980	12	4	$33\frac{1}{3}$					1		1	1	1
1981	22	11	50				3	3	2		3	
1982	16	4	25		2	1	1					
1983	18	6	$33\frac{1}{3}$		1		2	1	2			
1984	12	3	25			1	2					
1985	14	2	14		2							
1986	16	2	13		1	1						
1987	21	2	10	1	1							
1988	14	0	0									
	158	40	25	1	7	3	8	5	4	1	4	1

[a]We do not show this year of existence in which these funds dissolved because they were started in very different years and the data we have simply tell us they existed as of June 1979.

[b]Funds are classified as new funds by the year for which we have the first return data. Thus a fund that started in December would have its first return in January and be classified as a new entrant in January.

First, most funds have a clause in their partnership agreement that causes automatic dissolution if the net asset value per share falls to some predetermined level. For example, a fund with an initial asset value of $1,000 might automatically dissolve if net asset value per share drops to $300. This automatic dissolution allows the seller to guarantee that investors will never lose 100% of their investment. The second major reason for dissolution is a decline of total funds under management. Many publicly traded commodity funds have as part of their partnership agreement a clause that results in dissolution if fund size becomes sufficiently small, whether as a result of withdrawals or poor performance. Because withdrawals are likely to be correlated with poor performance, poor performance is the main cause of dissolution. In our sample, only three funds dissolved at a value above their initial issuance price; the average dissolved fund had a rate of return over its lifetime of –19.99% per annum.

Table 19-4 shows in more detail the dissolution experience over our sample period. Over this period, 40 funds dissolved—25% of all funds in existence. The columns in the table show the detailed experience by year of entrance. Note that the percentage of dissolution is very high for firms that entered before 1984, ranging from 25 to 50%. For firms that entered after 1984, the percentage of funds dissolving declined substantially. However,

Table 19-5   Probability of Dissolution

i^{th} Year of Existence	Number of Firms at Beginning	Number Dissolved in Year	Probability of Dissolving in Year i	Probability of Dissolving in or Before Year i*
1	145	1	0.7%	0.7%
2	130	7	5.4	6.0
3	104	3	2.9	8.7
4	87	8	9.2	17.1
5	67	5	7.5	23.3
6	53	4	7.5	29.1
7	37	1	2.7	31.0
8	24	4	16.7	42.5
9	9	1	11.1	48.8

*The probability of dissolving in a before year i is not simply the cumulative distribution of the previous column but is adjusted for the probability that a fund may already have dissolved before it reached year i.

an examination of the columns under year of dissolution shows that funds tend to dissolve after they have been around a while. The lower dissolution rate of funds that entered in later years can thus be explained in part by their limited amount of time in existence.

Table 19-5 explores in more detail the dissolution experience as a function of number of years of existence. Consider the fifth year. There were 67 firms in our sample that had returns in the fifth year of their existence. Of these, five (7.5%) dissolved in that year. The odds of a firm dissolving by the end of its fifth year of existence are 23.3%. The probability of it dissolving by the end of the ninth year of existence is 48.8%. If the past is indicative of the future, an investor purchasing a publicly traded commodity fund has close to a 50% chance of having it dissolve within ten years.

The reader should not be surprised by the large number of funds dissolving each year. Given the low return earned by commodity funds and the high standard deviation of their returns, we would expect a large percentage of the funds to experience performances poor enough to trigger their dissolution clauses.

Arguments for Investing in Commodity Funds

Three arguments can be advanced for placing some money in commodity funds, despite their poor performance. First, while commodity funds are not appropriate as a stand-alone investment, they might be held as part of a portfolio of stocks and bonds. Second, they might be held as a hedge against inflation. Third, they may be attractive because they offer a chance of a very high return (i.e., the returns are positively skewed). We address each of these points in turn.

We developed in great detail in our earlier paper the necessary conditions for commodity funds to be included in a portfolio of stocks and bonds. We showed that, for inclusion, commodity funds must offer a higher return than Treasury bills if the correlation between commodity funds and stocks and bonds is zero or positive. In fact, over our sample period the correlation between commodity funds and stocks and bonds was positive but close to zero and, as already discussed, the return on commodity funds was considerably lower than that on Treasury bills.[5] This evidence would not support the addition of commodity funds to a portfolio of bonds and stocks.

If commodity funds are to provide a hedge against inflation, their returns would need to be highly positively correlated with inflation. That is, commodity fund returns would have to increase when inflation rose. One might initially expect positive correlation, because there tends to be some positive correlation between futures returns and inflation.[6] But commodity funds both buy and sell futures.[7] The average correlation between our commodity funds and the Consumer Price Index was -0.0337. The correlation was also negative over the shorter period of our earlier study. The data indicate that commodity funds do not provide an attractive hedge against inflation.

Finally, publicly traded commodity funds may be good investments if their payoffs are positively skewed. There are two versions of this argument. The one that has always made more sense to us proceeds as follows. On average, returns on commodity funds are low. Occasionally, however, there is a very large return. Just as people purchase lottery tickets for the opportunity to get a very good return, even though the return on average is negative, they could use commodity funds for the same purpose. This argument would be supported if we observe that the cross-sectional distribution of commodity fund returns was positively skewed. Consider, for

Table 19-6   Cross-Sectional Skewness of Commodity Fund Returns

Year	Skewness
1980	−1.0470
1981	−0.4564
1982	−1.0988
1983	−1.2860
1984	−0.3882
1985	−0.5407
1986	−0.4160
1987	0.3231
1988	2.5071

example, 1985 returns. The distribution of returns for this year comprises the annual return for each firm. An unusual opportunity for occasional high returns would be signalled by a positively skewed distribution.

To test this, we formed nine different distributions, one for each of our sample years. The entries in the distribution were the continuously compounded annual rates of return. We included all firms that existed at the beginning of the year. If a firm dissolved during the year, the proceeds were assumed to be invested in T-bills. Table 19-6 gives the results. For most years, the distribution is negatively skewed, primarily because of the extremely poor returns for the firms that dissolved in that year. Thus, empirical evidence is exactly opposite to the contention of those who defend publicly traded commodity funds on the basis of skewness.

The skewness argument as generally made is really incomplete, however. Even if the returns on publicly traded commodity funds were positively skewed, commodity funds would have to offer this pattern of returns at more attractive rates than alternative investments. One obvious alternative is common stock; Lorie and Fisher have shown that the cross-section of returns on common stock held individually and in portfolios is positively skewed in each and every year.[8]

Lorie and Fisher defined return as ending wealth divided by beginning wealth. Applying this definition of returns to our commodity funds, we found the skewness measures were positive in six years and negative in three years. Over our nine-year sample, three skewness measures were statistically significant at the 5% level, one positive and two negative. Thus, common stocks have much more desirable skewness properties, along with higher average returns and lower standard deviations. Empirical evidence rejects cross-sectional skewness as an incentive for investing in publicly traded commodity funds.

A second argument based on skewness assumes that the utility functions of some investors exhibit a preference for positive skewness. Thus, an investment that exhibits positive skewness of returns over time is desirable. To test this argument, we looked at the time series of returns for each of the 155 funds with more than six months of data. Of these, 99 were positively skewed (44 significant) and 56 negative (29 significant), with the average skewness slightly negative. This is mild evidence that some funds occasionally have high-return months and exhibit a small degree of positive skewness in the time series of returns.

Predictability of Returns

Can an investor find a way of selecting a fund with above-average performance? If so, what would the return on these funds be? We examined the predictability for two types of data.

Prior Returns

Our earlier paper showed that this year's return for a commodity fund cannot be predicted on the basis of the prior year's return. This should not be surprising in light of studies done on mutual funds. It is nevertheless possible that longer-term performance can be predicted by longer-term past performance. While we still do not have much history, a preliminary examination of this question is possible.

We calculated average continuously compounded returns for all funds with three years of history as of December 1985. We then calculated a rank-order correlation coefficient between the past three-year return and the subsequent three-year return. (If a fund dissolved before three years, we used data through its dissolution.) The rank-order correlation for the 51 firms in the sample was 0.053, which is insignificant at any normal level.

We also divided the sample into three groups on the basis of past performance. The subsequent performance of the one-third with the highest past performance was 8.5%. The middle group returned 2.76%, while the average subsequent performance of the bottom one-third was 7.7%. Both the best- and worst-performing funds did considerably better than the funds with average performance. The difference between the best and the worst groups was small.

Prospectus Data

Publicly traded commodity funds are offered by prospectus, and new investment is generally possible only for a few months around the time a fund is offered. Thus, an investor desiring returns above the average for all funds needs to base his or her selection on material available at the time of the initial offering. In a prior paper, we showed that the past performance figures contained in the prospectus could not be used to select a fund that would have superior subsequent performance.[9]

For this study, we examined whether there are other items contained in a prospectus that might be useful in selecting a superior fund. We looked at three variables—the offering size for a fund and both the amount of experience and past investment performance (with publicly traded funds) of the fund's general partner.

Size could be related to subsequent performance for several reasons. First, one could argue that funds that attempt to raise more money are run by managers that underwriters have more faith in; this is tantamount to assuming that underwriters can successfully select managers. Also, one could argue that the larger funds can hire better managers.

Most prospectuses contain two measures of size—the minimum needed to start the partnership and the maximum that will be raised. We had prospectuses for most funds for the years 1980 to 1984. For each year, we ranked funds on three measures of size—minimum to start the fund, maximum to be raised and the average of the minimum and maximum. We then calculated for each size measure for each year the Spearman rank-order correlation coefficient with the lifetime return of each fund. None of the correlations was significant on any of the three size measures, and they were all close to zero. With maximum size as the measure, the correlations were −0.11, 0.03, −0.02, −0.05 and 0.11 for the years 1980 to 1984, respectively.[10]

The second variable we analyzed was experience. The logic underlying this variable is as follows. New funds are often managed by general partners who are also general partners in existing publicly traded commodity funds. The ability to issue new partnerships can be seen as an endorsement of their prior performance and might be predictive of superior performance for their new funds. Similarly, general partners with more experience might have superior performance.[11]

We examined three years—1983, 1984 and 1985—for which we had a minimum of three years of subsequent performance. (We could have used earlier years, but there were not enough funds in existence to give meaningful experience measures.) For each year, we counted the number of publicly traded commodity funds a general partner was already managing. We then

Table 19-7   Predictability of Return from Partners' Experience

	Annual Percentage Return to Funds Managed by Partners with Prior Experience in		
	4+ Funds	1–3 Funds	0 Funds
1983	−10.04	12.51	−1.96
1984	−1.5	10.19	−7.93
1985	−	4.51	−8.35

Table 19-8   Predictability of Return from Partners' Past Performance in Public Funds

	Annual Percentage Return to Funds Managed by Partners with	
	Above-Average Prior Performance	Below-Average Prior Performance
1983	10.14	−7.67
1984	10.83	0.78
1984	7.57	6.38

divided the funds issued in each year into three groups according to whether the general partner (1) had no prior experience with publicly traded commodity funds, (2) managed one to three funds, or (3) managed four or more.[12] We then examined the average lifetime performance in each of these three categories.

Table 19-7 gives the results. No clear pattern is evident. The only interesting conclusion to be drawn is to avoid funds whose general partners have zero experience. However, the reader should be cautioned that the samples were small. A further caution on the future predictability of these results is that the second-worst-performing group was general partners with a lot of experience. The final variable we looked at was past performance of other funds managed by the same general partner. We divided newly issued funds into those with general partners whose prior public funds had above-average returns and those whose prior public funds had below-average returns; Table 19-8 gives the results. Here the results were consistent: Funds managed by partners with above-average prior experience outperformed those managed by partners with below-average prior experience.

The reader should be cautioned that the sample sizes were small. Requiring that the general partner have prior experience resulted in sample sizes of eight or nine in the three years examined. Several funds had returns very close to the average. A small change in past return could have reversed the results. Nevertheless, this is one of the few areas where we found any indication of predictability, and it may be worth pursuing as more data become available in the future.

Endnotes

1. Elton, E. J., Gruber, J. J., and Rentzler, J. "Professonally Managed Publicly Traded Commodity Funds." *Journal of Business*, April 1987.

2. Because there is no incentive for firms to understate dissolution value, using verbal statements of dissolution value might bias our results upward.

3. See Elton, Gruber, and Rentzler, "New Public Offerings, Information, and Investor Rationality: the Case of Publicly Offered Commodity Funds," *Journal of Business*, January 1989, for a more detailed discussion of our sample of prospectuses.

4. We averaged across all firms that existed in a month and then across all months. We also averaged all fund months. This later average differed in a minor way in the first years and is not reported.

5. The correlation with the S&P index was 0.08, while it was 0.05 with the Shearson Lehman Corporate Government Bond Index and 0.07 with the Ibbotson indexes for both corporate bonds and government bonds.

6. Bodie, Z. "Commodity Futures as a Hedge Against Inflation." *Journal of Portfolio Management*, Spring 1983.

7. The correlation between the percentage change in futures prices and commodity funds is positive but small.

8. Lorie, J., and Fisher, L. "Some Studies of the Variability of Returns on Investments in Common Stocks." *Journal of Business*, April 1970.

9. Elton, et al., "New Public Offerings," op. cit. 1

10. Maximums are probably the most relevant size measure. Minimums have little significant variation, lying generally between one-half million and one million, and this variation hasn't much to do with the amount they hope to raise.

11. The same argument could be used for underwriters or commodity trading advisers. The correlation between general partners and under-

writers is almost one, so no new information is contained in this analysis. Commodity trading advisers are frequently changed, and many funds have multiple advisers. There is much less continuity, so analysis here was not seen as fruitful.

12. We counted as of December of the prior year. The general partner could have had additional funds that had dissolved earlier. We wanted to use a rule an investor could potentially use. Earlier dissolved funds would be extremely difficult to trace.

Glossary

Geometric Mean Return: The average return that, when compounded, causes the beginning value to equal the ending value.

Continuously Compounded Rate of Return: The return earned when interest is assumed to be compounded continuously.

Skewness: A measure of the symmetry of a return distribution. Positive skewness would indicate a greater probability of large high returns relative to low returns.

Standard Deviation: A measure of the dispersion of the return distribution. For symmetric distributions, 19 of 20 returns should lie between the mean return minus two standard deviations and the mean return plus two standard deviations.

Chapter 20

Management Summary

Title: "Are Public Commodity Pools a Good Investment?"

Publisher: Accepted for publication (subject to revisions) by *The Journal of Futures Markets*

Authors: Scott H. Irwin, Associate Professor, Ohio State University
                Terry R. Krukemyer, Ph.D. Candidate, Ohio State University
                Carl R. Zulaf, Associate Professor, Ohio State University

Data: Monthly returns for 11 years, January, 1979 through December, 1989 for stocks, bonds, T-bills and public commodity funds.

Methodology: Returns and standard deviations for randomly selected and market portfolios of public commodity funds were compared to stocks, bonds and T-bills using Sharpe ratios. Portfolio effects of adding public commodity funds to portfolios of stocks and bonds were examined using modern portfolio theory. Correlation analysis was applied to futures funds to determine predictability, as well as correlation with inflation. Sharpe ratio and portfolio analysis was repeated using pro forma institutional costs (10% to 12% per annum) versus retail costs (18% to 20%).

Result: The market portfolio outperformed the randomly selected public commodity fund as a stand alone investment, but did not outperform stock or bonds based upon Sharpe ratios. As an addition to a stock/bond portfolio, the market public commodity fund portfolio was beneficial for the total time period selected (by inducing a favorable shift to the efficient frontier), but was not beneficial if the early year of 1979 was excluded.

                When returns were adjusted on pro forma basis for institutional fees, performance improved dramatically. Public commodity pools, under the pro forma analysis, benefited stock and bond portfolios under all time frame scenarios by increasing the return/risk tradeoff by as much as 27%.

continued

Correlation analysis of returns showed little predictability in being able to select the best performing public fund from one time period to the next, but strong potential for predicting risk (i.e. standard deviation).

Analysis of returns relative to inflation showed no correlation on a short-term, month-to-month basis but positive correlation on a longer-term, annual basis.

The authors conclude that:

(a) because conclusions regarding actual performance are sensitive to both the methodology and time period analyzed, additional years are needed to establish the long-term performance of public commodity pools.

(b) reductions in cost are important for public futures funds to be competitive investments.

Comments: The author's findings that the attractiveness of public commodity funds depends upon the methodology used and time frame analyzed explains nicely the diversity of findings from other authorities. Their pro forma analysis using institutional costs (10% to 12% per annum) which shows superior performance helps explain the current and growing interest of pension funds and other institutional investors in managed futures.

Costs of public commodity funds have been decreasing steadily since the early 1980s. The "institutional" cost structure of 10% to 12% per annum used by the authors is more the norm for public funds currently being formed.

It is not surprising that simple correlation analysis was unable to offer evidence in predictability of superior fund performance. If it had, it would be akin to finding a simple, exploitable market inefficiency. Such findings are notoriously difficult to identify and maintain. Perhaps a more sophisticated technique (such as that proposed by Elton, Gruber and Rentzler [see Chapter 19]) where general partner experience and past performance were suggested as predictors, would be more successful. The finding that risk was more predictable offers hope that fund sponsors have a tool for designing risk efficient products.

Are Public Commodity Pools a Good Investment?*

Scott H. Irwin
Terry R. Krukemyer
Carl R. Zulauf

Abstract

This study investigates performance of public commodity pools both as a single randomly selected pool and a market portfolio of pools over the 1979–1989 period. A market portfolio of public commodity pools provides superior investment performance relative to a randomly selected pool. However, in general, this study provides no evidence that even a market portfolio of commodity pools is an attractive stand-alone investment. Nevertheless, there is some evidence that public commodity pools may improve the risk-return performance of a stock-bond portfolio. This evidence is conditional on the time period analyzed. Furthermore, a portfolio analysis is conducted using the lower brokerage, management, and incentive fees paid by institutional investors in commodity pools. The analysis reveals a substantial increase in the diversification benefits of adding commodity pools to a stock-bond portfolio. This suggests that the costs of public commodity pools form a significant deterrent to wider inclusion in investment portfolios.

*The authors acknowledge the helpful comments of seminar participants at the Commodity Futures Trading Commission, Georgetown University, and the Ohio State University.

I. Introduction

Publicly traded commodity pools have grown rapidly from a total equity of $7.2 million in one pool during January, 1975, to $1.7 billion in 118 pools during December, 1988 (Irwin and Brorsen, 1985; Basso, 1989).[1] With rapid growth has come increased focus on investment performance. However, results of academic studies of investment performance differ substantially. Brorsen and Irwin (1985), Murphy (1986), and Elton, Gruber, and Rentzler (1987, 1989, 1990) concluded that public commodity pools were inferior investment vehicles compared to other financial instruments. In contrast, Lintner (1983), Irwin and Brorsen (1985), and Irwin and Landa (1987) suggested that public commodity pools produce favorable investment returns.

An important difference between the studies which found inferior performance and the studies which found favorable performance is the methodology used. Brorsen and Irwin, Murphy, and Elton, Gruber, and Rentzler measured returns for a single random pool while Lintner, Irwin and Brorsen, and Irwin and Landa measured returns for a portfolio of pools. In addition, the length of the sample period and number of pools analyzed have varied substantially among the various studies.

This study investigates performance of public commodity pools both as a single randomly selected pool and as a market portfolio of pools over the 1979–1989 period. The sample is the longest used in a study of commodity pool performance. Four aspects of investment performance are examined: 1) the attractiveness of public commodity pools as stand-alone investments, 2) the role of commodity pools in investment portfolios, 3) the predictability of commodity pools returns, and 4) the impact of costs on the portfolio performance of public commodity pools.

II. Data

Data was collected for all public commodity pools traded from January 1979 through December 1989. The pools include domestic U.S. pools which collect money predominantly from U.S. citizens, as well as off-shore commodity pools which invest in U.S. futures markets but are open only to foreign investors. The initial year was chosen because an analysis (presented in detail in the next section) revealed that ten pools are needed to approximately replicate market performance of all public commodity pools. Ten public commodity pools were traded in January 1979.[2] In contrast, during January 1978, only three public commodity pools were traded.

End of month commodity pool unit values and distributions per unit were collected for each public commodity pool. Sources included: 1) monthly reports by Norwood Securities from January 1979 to April 1982, 2) the "Funds Review" section published monthly in *Futures* (formerly *Commodities*) magazine from May 1982 through December 1989, 3) *Managed Accounts Reports* and 10-Q pools reports from the Securities and Exchange Commission, and 4) direct communication with commodity pool managers to obtain data otherwise not available.

Elton, Gruber, and Rentzler's (1987) procedures were followed for pools entering the data set and for pools that dissolved during the year.[3] A pool did not enter the calendar year's data set until its first January of trading. When a pool liquidated during the year, the dissolution value was reinvested in the market portfolio (average commodity pool) until the end of the calendar year of dissolution. This allowed the usually lower rate of return of a dissolving pool to be included in calculating average returns. Thus, an upward bias due to not including dissolved pools was avoided.

If a pool suspended trading, the unit value from the last month of trading was brought forward until trading resumed. This produced a 0% monthly rate of return for as long as trading was suspended. Once trading began again, the usual calculations were resumed.

Monthly values of a broad range of financial investments were collected to provide comparisons with public commodity pools. They included buy-and-hold portfolios of common stocks, small stocks, U.S. Treasury-bills, intermediate government bonds, long-term government bonds, and long-term corporate bonds. Data for these instruments were taken from *Stocks, Bonds, Bills, and Inflation: 1989 Yearbook* by Ibbotson Associates, Inc. In addition, using the Commodity Research Bureau Composite Index of 27 commodity futures prices, returns were calculated to a passive futures buy-and-hold strategy.[4]

III. Public Commodity Pool Returns

Consistent with earlier studies, the total monthly return of a public commodity pool is defined as the change in unit value over a month plus cash distributions per unit during the month divided by the unit value at the end of the preceding month minus one. The formula assumes cash distributions are reinvested into the pool during the month it was distributed. This is consistent with the securities industry's handling of dividends (*Stocks, Bonds, Bills and Inflation: 1989 Yearbook*).

Two different strategies for investing in public commodity pools were examined: 1) a randomly-selected pool, and 2) a market portfolio of pools. A randomly-selected pool contains both the systematic and unsystematic risk associated with holding only one pool.[5] A market portfolio of pools contains only systematic risk.

To produce the rate of return for a randomly selected commodity pool, it is assumed that funds are invested in a *single* randomly selected pool at the beginning of a year.[6] Then, all available funds at the end of the year are invested in another randomly selected commodity pool at the beginning of the following year. To produce the rate of return for a market portfolio of commodity pools, an equal amount of money is assumed to be invested in *all* pools at the beginning of a year. Available funds at the end of the year are then equally invested in all pools at the beginning of the next year.

Following Elton, Gruber, and Rentzler (1987), monthly and annual holding period investment horizons are used in this study. The two holding periods are used to reflect different time horizons which trader's may use when making investments. The average rate of return for a monthly holding period is generated by the average monthly arithmetic rate of return. The average rate of return over an annual holding period is generated by the average monthly geometric rate of return.[7]

As shown in Table 20-1, public commodity pool returns were highly variable across years for both the monthly and annual holding periods. For example, monthly holding period average returns for a random pool ranged from a high of 4.221% per month in 1979 to a low of –0.876% in 1986. Furthermore, average return over a period of years was quite sensitive to the sample period selected. For a monthly holding period, random pool returns averaged 1.125% per month over 1979–1989, but decreased to 0.599% per month over 1982–1989 and 0.751% per month over 1985–1989.

Average return of the random pool and market portfolio diverged when considering annual holding period returns. Over the entire 1979–1989 sample period and the 1982–1989 and 1985–1989 sub-periods, the market portfolio outperformed the randomly selected pool. This divergence is expected due to the fact that a geometric average will always be less than an arithmetic average, assuming the variance of the series is greater than zero (Grossman, 1987).

Standard deviation of a random pool is calculated as the standard deviation of monthly returns of a pool for a given year, averaged across all pools included in the sample year. A dissolved pool, which ended trading any month other than December was not included in calculating that year's standard deviation of a randomly selected pool. The reason is that lack of trading during part of the year could bias the standard deviation calculation

Table 20-1   Rates of Return and Standard Deviation for Public Commodity Pools, 1979–1989

Year	Number of Pools	Randomly-selected Commodity Pool			Market Portfolio of Commodity Pools		
		Average Return		Standard Deviation	Average Return		Standard Deviation
		MHP[1]	AHP[2]		MHP	AHP	
		- percent per month -			- percent per month -		
1979	10	4.221	3.138	13.713	4.221	3.912	8.352
1980	15	2.520	1.716	15.015	2.520	2.284	7.320
1981	22	0.838	0.399	8.845	0.838	0.670	6.124
1982	43	0.518	0.053	9.436	0.518	0.327	6.450
1983	62	-0.577	-1.177	10.155	-0.577	-0.818	7.303
1984	78	1.098	0.585	9.741	1.098	0.863	7.381
1985	94	1.358	1.006	8.154	1.358	1.212	5.672
1986	98	-0.876	-1.350	9.299	-0.876	-1.066	6.498
1987	111	2.854	2.495	8.441	2.854	2.696	6.038
1988	128	0.715	0.202	9.482	0.715	0.481	7.415
1989	149	-0.297	-0.622	7.413	-0.297	-0.428	5.360
Average:[3]							
1979-89		1.125	0.586	9.972	1.125	0.911	6.678
1982-89		0.599	0.149	9.015	0.599	0.402	6.413
1985-89		0.751	0.346	8.558	0.751	0.571	6.166

[1]Monthly holding period.
[2]Annual holding period.
[3]The average return and standard deviation for a randomly selected commodity pool are calculated as the averages of the individual year statistics. The aveage return and standard deviation for the market portfolio of commodity pools are calculated over the entire period.

downward. For the market portfolio, its standard deviation is calculated by first averaging the monthly returns of all pools which traded during the month, and then calculating the standard deviation of the 12 monthly portfolio returns.

A randomly selected commodity pool's monthly standard deviation ranged from 15.015% per month in 1980 to 7.413% per month in 1989 (Table 20-1). Over the entire 1979–1989 period, average monthly standard deviation was 9.972%. As expected, standard deviation for the market portfolio of commodity pools was substantially smaller. Its standard deviation for 1979–1989 averaged 6.678% per month, a one-third reduction in risk compared to holding a single randomly selected commodity pool. The smaller standard deviation reflects the less than perfect positive correlation between the various commodity pools in the market portfolio.

The standard deviation comparisons suggest that the relationship between the number of pools held and portfolio risk may be valuable information. To investigate this relationship, note that portfolio variance may be expressed as follows if equal-weighting of pools is assumed (Elton and Gruber, 1987, p.30),

$$\sigma_P^2 = \frac{1}{N} \overline{\sigma_j^2} + \frac{N-1}{N} \overline{\sigma_{jk}} \tag{1}$$

where

σ_P^2 = portfolio variance,

$\overline{\sigma_j^2}$ = average variance of the j pools (j=1,..,N),

$\overline{\sigma_{jk}}$ = average covariance between the j pools (j=1,..,N, k=1,..,N, j≠k),

N   = number of pools.

Further, note that as N becomes large in equation (1), portfolio variance approaches the average covariance between the j pools. Thus, for an equally weighted market portfolio of commodity pools, variance of the market portfolio approximately equals average covariance of the individual pools, assuming a sufficiently large N.

In order to analyze the relationship between number of pools held and portfolio risk, 1989 was selected as the base year for calculations. The 149 pools active in 1989 is a sufficiently large sample to ensure that the average covariance of individual pools can be accurately approximated by the variance of the market portfolio. Hence, average variance of the individual pools in (1) was assumed to equal variance of a random pool in 1989 (54.952% squared). Further, average covariance between the individual pools in (1) was assumed to equal variance of the market portfolio in 1989 (28.730% squared). With these inputs, N was varied between 1 and 100, and the resulting portfolio variance calculated.

As shown in Table 20-1, portfolio standard deviation dropped quickly as the number of pools increased. Compared to a single pool, combining two pools reduced portfolio standard deviation from 7.413 to 6.460%. Combining five pools reduced the standard deviation to 5.820%, a decrease of 21.5%. Most of the risk reduction was achieved by holding ten pools, and risk of the market portfolio was closely replicated by holding 30 pools.

IV. Stand-Alone Performance

For comparative purposes, average returns and standard deviations of the alternative investments over 1979–1989 are reported in Table 20-2. Several observations are noteworthy. First, the standard deviation of commodity pool returns was greater than the standard deviation of returns for alternative investments. This was especially true for a randomly selected pool. Second, returns for commodity pools were not favorable relative to alternative stock and bond investments over both 1982–1989 and 1985–1989. In contrast, over the entire 1979–1989 period, monthly and annual holding period returns for the market portfolio of pools, as well as the monthly holding period returns for a randomly selected pool, exceed returns for bills and bonds, but not for common and small stocks. Third, over none of the sample periods did the annual holding period return of a randomly selected commodity pool exceed the return of treasury bills or of the buy-and-hold futures strategy.

Given the well-known tradeoff between the return and risk of investments, a more formal test of stand-alone investment performance is needed. A widely used method of ranking individual investment alternatives is the Sharpe ratio,

$$\frac{R_c - R_f}{\sigma_c} \qquad (2)$$

where

R_c = the expected return of commodity pool c,

R_f = the risk-free return,

σ_c = the standard deviation of commodity pool c.

Table 20-2   Rates of Return and Standard Deviation for Alternative Investments, 1979–1989

Investment[1]	1979-1989			1982-1989			1985-1989		
	Average Return		Standard Deviation	Average Return		Standard Deviation	Average Return		Standard Deviation
	MHP[2]	AHP[3]		MHP	AHP		MHP	AHP	
	- percent per month -			- percent per month -			- percent per month -		
RS Comm. Pool	1.125	.586	9.972	.599	.149	9.015	.751	.346	8.558
MP Comm. Pools	1.125	.911	6.678	.599	.402	6.413	.751	.571	6.166
B&H Futures	.786	.732	3.291	.572	.529	2.983	.489	.412	2.792
Common Stocks	1.471	1.362	4.652	1.569	1.455	4.766	1.694	1.559	5.107
Small Stocks	1.564	1.396	5.671	1.195	1.051	5.209	.989	.823	5.491
T-Bills	.723	.723	.230	.635	.635	.163	.551	.551	.108
IT Gov't Bonds	.911	.887	2.249	1.057	1.043	1.681	.913	.901	1.548
LT Gov't Bonds	.973	.894	4.023	1.324	1.267	3.401	1.265	1.207	3.467
LT Corp. Bonds	.966	.899	3.704	1.365	1.322	2.980	1.205	1.173	2.544

[1]RS Comm. Pool: Randomly Selected Commodity Pool; MP Comm. Pools: Market Portfolio of Commodity Pools; B&H Futures: Buy-and-Hold Futures; T-Bills: Treasury Bills; IT Gov't Bonds: Intermediate-term Government Bonds; LT Gov't Bonds: Long-term Government Bonds; LT Corp. Bonds: Long-term Corporate Bonds.

[2]Monthly holding period.

[3]Annual holding period.

Sharpe ratios and the corresponding rankings of investments for the three sample periods are presented in Table 20-3. The most striking result is that under no scenario did a futures investment outrank a stock or bond investment, even for the longest time period. Among the alternative futures investments, except for the monthly holding period over 1982–1989, the market portfolio of commodity pools was either the highest ranked investment or tied for the highest rank.

V. Portfolio Performance: Breakeven Analysis

Elton, Gruber, and Rentzler (1987) show that a commodity pool should be added to a portfolio as long as,

$$\frac{R_c - R_f}{\sigma_c} > \frac{R_p - R_f}{\sigma_p} \cdot \rho_{cp} \qquad (3)$$

where

R_c = the expected return of commodity pool c,
R_f = the risk-free return,
σ_c = the standard deviation of commodity pool c,
R_p = the expected return of portfolio p,
σ_p = the standard deviation of portfolio p,
ρ_{cp} = the correlation coefficient between commodity pool c and portfolio p.

Solving (3) for R_c yields the required, or breakeven, rate of return that a commodity pool must generate to enter the portfolio. If commodity pool returns exceed the breakeven return, then addition of commodity pools to the portfolio will improve the return-risk tradeoff of the portfolio.

A key component of the breakeven condition is the correlation between commodity pool returns and portfolio returns. Correlation coefficients between a random commodity pool and the alternative investments are shown in Table 20-4.[8] The correlation between commodity pool returns and stock and bond returns was near zero on average, as was the correlation between commodity pools and buy-and-hold futures. The average correlation coefficient of 0.643 between random pool returns and market portfolio returns indicates that the degree of co-movement in individual commodity

**Table 20-3   Sharpe Ratio and Rank for Alternative Investments,
1979–1989**

Investment[1]	Sample Period					
	1979-1989		1982-1989		1985-1989	
	MHP[2]	AHP[3]	MHP	AHP	MHP	AHP
	- Sharpe ratio -					
RS Comm. Pool	.040	-.014	-.004	-.054	.023	-.024
MP Comm. Pools	.060	.028	-.006	-.036	.032	.003
B&H Futures	.019	.003	-.021	-.036	-.022	-.050
Common Stocks	.161	.137	.196	.172	.224	.197
Small Stocks	.148	.119	.108	.080	.080	.050
IT Gov't Bonds	.084	.073	.251	.243	.234	.226
LT Gov't Bonds	.062	.043	.203	.186	.206	.189
LT Corp. Bonds	.066	.048	.245	.231	.256	.244
	- Sharpe ratio rank -					
RS Comm. Pool	7	8	6	8	7	7
MP Comm. Pools	6	6	7	6	6	6
B&H Futures	8	7	8	6	8	8
Common Stocks	1	1	4	4	3	3
Small Stocks	2	2	5	5	5	5
IT Gov't Bonds	3	3	1	1	2	2
LT Gov't Bonds	5	5	3	3	4	4
LT Corp. Bonds	4	4	2	2	1	1

[1]RS Comm. Pool: Randomly Selected Commodity Pool; MP Comm. Pools: Market Portfolio of Commodity Pools; B&H Futures: Buy-and-Hold Futures; IT Gov't Bonds: Intermediate-term Government Bonds; LT Gov't Bonds: Long-term Government Bonds; LT Corp. Bonds: Long-term Corporate Bonds.
[2]Monthly holding period.
[3]Annual holding period.

pool returns was relatively high. In addition, monthly commodity pool returns did not show any evidence of correlation with the rate of inflation.[9]

For this study, public commodity pools were considered candidates to enter two common securities portfolios: one consisting of 100% common stocks and a second consisting of 60% common stocks and 40% long-term corporate bonds. Breakeven returns are presented in Table 20-5. Over the

Table 20-4 Correlation Between a Randomly Selected Commodity Pool and Other Financial Investments, 1979–1989[1]

Year	Number of Pools	Investment[2]								
		MP of Comm. Pools	B&H Futures	Common Stocks	Small Stocks	T-bills	IT Gov't Bonds	LT Gov't Bonds	LT Corp. Bonds	Inflation
		- correlation coefficient -								
1979	10	.641	.395	.086	.139	-.144	.319	.379	.357	.094
1980	13	.389	.121	.098	.137	-.217	-.105	-.265	-.229	-.056
1981	22	.624	-.359	-.056	-.066	.161	.092	.154	.204	.091
1982	43	.676	-.287	-.115	-.228	-.027	-.261	-.067	-.130	.145
1983	60	.708	.389	-.120	-.093	.334	-.193	-.363	-.257	.176
1984	77	.672	-.425	-.320	-.324	-.073	.153	.140	.203	-.110
1985	88	.635	-.155	.299	.404	.127	-.120	-.033	.008	-.255
1986	94	.655	-.195	.310	.305	.343	.385	.462	.485	-.378
1987	106	.705	.496	.143	.134	-.309	-.221	-.192	-.174	.008
1988	124	.744	.486	.240	.071	.085	.156	.172	.239	.019
1989	144	.622	-.334	.383	.368	.111	.162	.205	.240	.143
Average:										
1979-89		.643	.012	.086	.052	.036	.033	.054	.086	-.011
1982-89		.677	-.003	.103	.046	.074	.008	.041	.077	-.032
1985-89		.672	.060	.275	.202	.072	.072	.123	.160	-.093

[1] All correlations are based on the monthly returns of the investments.
[2] MP of Comm. Pools: Market Portfolio of Commodity Pools; B&H Futures: Buy-and-Hold Futures; IT Gov't Bonds: Intermediate-term Government Bonds; LT Gov't Bonds: Long-term Government Bonds; LT Corp. Bonds: Long-term Corporate Bonds.

Table 20-5   Portfolio Breakeven Analysis for Public Commodity Pools, 1979–1989

Sample Period Investment Portfolio	Randomly-selected Commodity Pool				Market Portfolio of Commodity Pools			
	Monthly Holding Period		Annual Holding Period		Monthly Holding Period		Annual Holding Period	
	Breakeven Return	Average Return	Breakeven Return	Average Return	Breakeven Return	Average Return	Breakeven Return	Average Return
	- percent per month -				- percent per month -			
1979-1989:								
100% Stock[1]	0.861	1.125*	0.841	0.586	0.872	1.125*	0.850	0.911*
60% Stock, 40% Bonds[2]	0.878	1.125*	0.861	0.586	0.867	1.125*	0.850	0.911*
1982-1989:								
100% Stock	0.817	0.599	0.795	0.149	0.757	0.599	0.743	0.402
60% Stock, 40% Bonds	0.880	0.599	0.864	0.599	0.796	0.599	0.785	0.402
1985-1989:								
100% Stock	1.078	0.751	1.016	0.346	0.974	0.751	0.924	0.571
60% Stock, 40% Bonds	1.196	0.751	1.156	0.346	1.093	0.751	1.059	0.571

Note: A star indicates that the average return of public commodity pools exceeds the breakeven return necessary for entry into an investment portfolio.
[1] 100% common stocks.
[2] 60% common stocks and 40% long-term corporate bonds.

1979–1989 sample period, returns for a randomly selected pool exceeded breakeven returns for the monthly holding period, but not for the annual holding period. Average returns for the market portfolio of pools were greater than breakeven returns for both the monthly and annual holding periods. In contrast, when the sample is limited to 1982–1989 or 1985–1989, pool returns were substantially less than breakeven returns for all scenarios. These results are consistent with the conclusions of earlier studies, which find positive portfolio results only when data from the high return years of the late 1970s are included.

VI. Portfolio Performance: Optimal Portfolios

The breakeven analysis presented in the previous section showed that public commodity pools were beneficial additions to securities portfolios, if the analysis was based on the full 1979–1989 sample. However, the breakeven analysis did not generate the magnitude of improvement in portfolio return-risk that resulted from including commodity pools. To generate this information, optimal portfolios with and without commodity pools were estimated for the 1979–1989 period.[10]

Elton and Gruber (1987, p.71) show that optimal portfolio proportions can be obtained by solving the following constrained optimization problem:[11]

$$\text{Maximize } \gamma_p = \frac{R_p - R_f}{\sigma_p} \tag{4}$$

Subject to

$$\sum_{i=1}^{N} X_i = 1$$

$$X_i \geq 0 \text{ for all } i$$

where

γ_p = Sharpe Ratio of optimal portfolio p,
R_p = the expected return of optimal portfolio p,
σ_p = the standard deviation of optimal portfolio p,
R_f = the risk-free return,
X_i = the proportion of asset i in optimal portfolio p.

Since the objective function of (4) is non-linear, the optimization problem must be solved using numerical techniques. For this study, solutions were obtained using a numerical algorithm in the GAMS software package.

Recent research suggests that constraining portfolio proportions reduces estimation error when solving optimal portfolio problems (Frost and Savarino, 1988). Hence, optimal portfolios are found under an unconstrained and a constrained scenario. In the constrained scenario, the minimum and maximum portfolio proportions for stocks and bonds are set to equal the minimum and maximum U.S. capital market value weights over 1970–1984 (Ibbotson, Siegel and Love), while public commodity pool proportions may range from zero to ten percent.[12]

Results of the portfolio optimization for 1979–1989 are presented in Tables 20-6 and 20-7. A randomly selected commodity pool is held only under the monthly holding period and no constraint scenario. In this case, pools represent five percent of the optimal portfolio, but the addition of pools improves the optimal portfolio's Sharpe Ratio a modest 1.18%. The market portfolio of pools is added to the portfolio under all four scenarios, including the maximum allowable proportion of 10% for the monthly holding period and constrained portfolio. Addition of the market portfolio of pools improves the optimal portfolio's Sharpe Ratio a maximum of 2.45%.

VII. Predictability of Returns

If returns and risks can be predicted, then this information can be used to improve the investment performance of public commodity pools. The tests proposed by Elton, Gruber, and Rentzler (1987) are employed in the analysis. The first test determines whether pools that have high returns or risks in one period also tend to have high values in the following period. This is accomplished by calculating correlation coefficients between average returns or risks for all adjacent years for all commodity pools that are present in the paired years. The second test is similar to the first, except that the population of pools is stratified into those with high, low, or average returns or risks for a given year.

Results of the correlation analysis are similar to those reported in previous studies (Table 20-8). If all pools are considered, only the correlation for the standard deviation, 0.45, appears to be large enough to be economically meaningful. The other correlations are between –0.10 and +0.10, levels not suggestive of the possibility of selecting better performing pools. The correlations are slightly larger if the sample is stratified into top, middle, and bottom thirds for a given year. However, given the small magnitude of

Table 20-6   Optimal Portfolio Results for a Randomly Selected Public Commodity Pool, 1979–1989

Optimal Portfolio	Unconstrained Portfolio[1]		Constrained Portfolio[2]	
	MHP[3]	AHP[4]	MHP	AHP
Proportions:[5]				
RS Commodity Pool	0.050	0.000	0.000	0.000
Common Stocks	0.398	0.536	0.617	0.632
Small Stocks	0.173	0.067	0.073	0.073
IT Gov't Bonds	0.378	0.397	0.140	0.125
LT Gov't Bonds	0.000	0.000	0.071	0.071
LT Corp. Bonds	0.000	0.000	0.099	0.099
Expected Return (percent/month)	1.258	1.176	1.314	1.226
Standard Deviation (percent/month)	3.131	3.170	3.623	3.674
Sharpe Ratio of Optimal Portfolio:				
With Commodity Pools	0.171	0.143	0.163	0.137
Without Commodity Pools	0.169	0.143	0.163	0.137
Change	+ 1.18%	0.00%	0.00%	0.00%

[1]No constraints on optimal portfolio proportions.

[2]Minimum and maximum optimal portfolio proportions for stocks and bonds are set to equal the minimum and maximum U.S. capital market proportions over 1970–1984 (Ibbotson, Siegel and Love). These are: Common Stocks, 45.5 to 64.3%; Small Stocks: 4.3 to 7.3%; IT Gov't Bonds: 8.9 to 19.8%; LT Gov't Bonds: 7.1 to 19.0%; LT Corp. Bonds: 9.9 to 17.0%. Commodity Pool proportions range from 0 to 10%.

[3]Monthly holding period.

[4]Annual holding period.

[5]RS Commodity Pool: Randomly Selected Commodity Pool; IT Gov't Bonds: Intermediate-term Government Bonds; LT Gov't Bonds: Long-term Government Bonds; LT Corp. Bonds: Long-term Corporate Bonds.

Table 20-7   Optimal Portfolio Results for the Market Portfolio of Public Commodity Pools, 1979–1989

Optimal Portfolio	Unconstrained Portfolio[1]		Constrained Portfolio[2]	
	MHP[3]	AHP[4]	MHP	AHP
Proportions:[5]				
MP Commodity Pools	0.096	0.028	0.100	0.021
Common Stocks	0.397	0.524	0.544	0.617
Small Stocks	0.142	0.060	0.073	0.073
IT Gov't Bonds	0.365	0.388	0.113	0.119
LT Gov't Bonds	0.000	0.000	0.071	0.071
LT Corp. Bonds	0.000	0.000	0.099	0.099
Expected Return (percent/month)	1.247	1.167	1.295	1.219
Standard Deviation (percent/month)	3.036	3.105	3.427	3.624
Sharpe Ratio of Optimal Portfolio:				
With Commodity Pools	0.172	0.143	0.167	0.137
Without Commodity Pools	0.169	0.143	0.163	0.137
Change	+ 1.77%	0.00%	+ 2.45%	0.00%

[1]No constraints on optimal portfolio proportions.
[2]Minimum and maximum optimal portfolio proportions for stocks and bonds are set to equal the minimum and maximum U.S. capital market proportions over 1970–1984 (Ibbotson, Siegel and Love). These are: Common Stocks, 45.5 to 64.3%; Small Stocks: 4.3 to 7.3%; IT Gov't Bonds: 8.9 to 19.8%; LT Gov't Bonds: 7.1 to 19.0%; LT Corp. Bonds: 9.9 to 17.0%. Commodity Pool proportions range from 0 to 10%.
[3]Monthly holding period.
[4]Annual holding period.
[5]MP Commodity Pool: Market Portfolio of Commodity Pools; IT Gov't Bonds: Intermediate-term Government Bonds; LT Gov't Bonds: Long-term Government Bonds; LT Corp. Bonds: Long-term Corporate Bonds.

Table 20-8   Correlation of Commodity Pool Performance Between Year t and Year t-1, 1979–1989

Sample	Number of Paired Years	Average Return		Standard Deviation	Sharpe Ratio	
		MHP[1]	AHP[2]		MHP	AHP
		- correlation coefficient -				
All Pools	596	-.057	-.104	.451	.068	.056
Top 1/3 of Pools	204	-.077	-.126	.191	-.080	-.062
Middle 1/3 of Pools	194	-.202	-.240	.075	-.211	-.233
Lower 1/3 of Pools	198	-.143	-.229	.295	.098	.071

[1] Monthly holding period.
[2] Annual holding period.

the correlations, it is debatable whether any strategy to select public commodity pools can be used to obtain an economically meaningful increase in performance.

VIII. The Impact of Cost on Portfolio Performance

Performance problems of public commodity pools frequently have been attributed to high operating costs (e.g., Elton, Gruber, and, Rentzler, 1987). Estimates of the total operating costs of public commodity pools range from about 18 to 20% of annual equity (Irwin and Brorsen, 1985; Murphy, 1986; Basso, 1989).[13] By comparison, investment costs of stock mutual funds are about one percent of annual equity (Sharpe, 1981).

An analysis of the potential performance impacts of lower costs can be made using evidence from institutional pension fund investments in commodity pools, as shown in Table 20-9. Institutions have negotiated much lower commission and management costs than those paid by public investors. Costs for institutional commodity pools are 10 to 12% of annual equity, approximately eight percentage points less than costs for public commodity pools. The biggest cost reduction is in commissions, which are reduced from nine to two percent of annual equity. This reflects a much lower brokerage charge per trade.[14]

The analysis was conducted by adjusting monthly returns on the market portfolio of pools over 1979–1989 to reflect the lower costs paid by institutional investors. The adjustment required two steps. First, gross returns of public commodity pools were estimated. This entailed subtracting treasury bill returns from net public pool returns and then adding back the public pool costs. Second, the net return to institutional commodity pools was estimated by subtracting the costs of institutional investors from the estimated gross returns and adding back Treasury Bill returns. Complete details of the procedure are reported in the Appendix.

Lowering costs substantially impacted portfolio performance. As shown in Table 20-10, average returns of commodity pools after the cost adjustment exceed portfolio breakeven returns for all three sample periods. Moreover, average returns are generally considerably larger than the breakeven returns. These results stand in sharp contrast to the original breakeven results (Table 20-5), which indicated that public commodity pools were attractive additions to stock and bond portfolios only over 1979–1989.

Optimal portfolio proportions of commodity pools for 1979–1989 increased to about 30% in the unconstrained scenarios and to the maximum level of 10% in the constrained scenarios (see Table 20-11). Over 1982–1989

Table 20-9   Costs of Futures Investments

Type of Futures Investment	Cost Category			
	Commissions	Management	Incentive	Total
	(annual percent of equity)	(annual percent of equity)	(annual percent of gross trading profits)	(annual percent of equity)
Public Commodity Pools	9.3	5.0	20.0	18 to 20
Institutional Commodity Pools	2.0	2.5	25.0	10 to 12

Sources: Irwin and Brorsen (1985), Murphy (1986), Basso (1989), Hecht (1989)

Table 20-10 Portfolio Breakeven Analysis for the Market Portfolio of Public Commodity Pools after Cost Adjustment, 1979–1989

Sample Period Investment Portfolio	Monthly Holding Period		Annual Holding Period	
	Breakeven Return	Average Return	Breakeven Return	Average Return
	- percent per month -			
1979-1989:				
100% Stock[1]	0.867	1.725*	0.846	1.539*
60% Stock, 40% Bonds[2]	0.862	1.725*	0.846	1.539*
1982-1989:				
100% Stock	0.753	1.219*	0.739	1.044*
60% Stock, 40% Bonds	0.789	1.219*	0.779	1.044*
1985-1989:				
100% Stock	0.961	1.364*	0.912	1.207*
60% Stock, 40% Bonds	1.075	1.364*	0.982	1.207*

Note: A star indictes that the average return of public commodity pools exceeds the breakeven return necessary for entry into an investment portfolio.
[1] 100% common stocks.
[2] 60% common stocks and 40% long-term corporate bonds.

and 1985–1989, proportions ranged from about two to eight percent of optimal portfolios (see Tables 20-12 and 20-13). The earlier analysis found that adding pools increased the optimal portfolio's Sharpe Ratio a maximum of 2.45% (Tables 20-6 and 20-7). After adjusting for lower costs, the improvement ranged between 13.14 and 27.22% for the 1979–1989 sample period. Sharpe Ratios improved between 0.41 and 4.22% for the two sub-periods.

Table 20-11 Optimal Portfolio Results for the Market Portfolio of Public Commodity Pools after Cost Adjustment, 1979–1989

Optimal Portfolio	Unconstrained Portfolio[1]		Constrained Portfolio[2]	
	MHP[3]	AHP[4]	MHP	AHP
Proportions:[5]				
MP Commodity Pools	0.304	0.294	0.100	0.100
Common Stocks	0.323	0.405	0.459	0.472
Small Stocks	0.077	0.000	0.073	0.060
IT Gov't Bonds	0.297	0.301	0.198	0.198
LT Gov't Bonds	0.000	0.000	0.071	0.071
LT Corp. Bonds	0.000	0.000	0.099	0.099
Expected Return (percent/month)	1.388	1.271	1.306	1.209
Standard Deviation (percent/month)	3.095	3.048	3.143	3.140
Sharpe Ratio of Optimal Portfolio:				
With Commodity Pools	0.215	0.180	0.186	0.155
Without Commodity Pools	0.169	0.143	0.163	0.137
Change	+ 27.22%	+ 25.87%	+ 14.11%	+ 13.14%

[1]No constraints on optimal portfolio proportions.

[2]Minimum and maximum optimal portfolio proportions for stocks and bonds are set to equal the minimum and maximum U.S. capital market proportions over 1970–1984 (Ibbotson, Siegel and Love). These are: Common Stocks, 45.5 to 64.3%; Small Stocks: 4.3 to 7.3%; IT Gov't Bonds: 8.9 to 19.8%; LT Gov't Bonds: 7.1 to 19.0%; LT Corp. Bonds: 9.9 to 17.0%. Commodity Pool proportions range from 0 to 10%.

[3]Monthly holding period.

[4]Annual holding period.

[5]MP Commodity Pool: Market Portfolio of Commodity Pools; IT Gov't Bonds: Intermediate-term Government Bonds; LT Gov't Bonds: Long-term Government Bonds; LT Corp. Bonds: Long-term Corporate Bonds.

Table 20-12 Optimal Portfolio Results for the Market Portfolio of Public Commodity Pools after Cost Adjustment, 1982–1989

Optimal Portfolio	Unconstrained Portfolio[1]		Constrained Portfolio[2]	
	MHP[3]	AHP[4]	MHP	AHP
Proportions:[5]				
MP Commodity Pools	0.081	0.060	0.078	0.044
Common Stocks	0.158	0.141	0.455	0.455
Small Stocks	0.000	0.000	0.043	0.043
IT Gov't Bonds	0.761	0.799	0.183	0.198
LT Gov't Bonds	0.000	0.000	0.071	0.090
LT Corp. Bonds	0.000	0.000	0.170	0.170
Expected Return (percent/month)	1.151	1.101	1.380	1.298
Standard Deviation (percent/month)	1.744	1.711	2.931	2.938
Sharpe Ratio of Optimal Portfolio:				
With Commodity Pools	0.296	0.272	0.254	0.226
Without Commodity Pools	0.284	0.266	0.250	0.225
Change	+ 4.22%	+ 2.25%	+ 1.60%	+ 0.44%

[1]No constraints on optimal portfolio proportions.

[2]Minimum and maximum optimal portfolio proportions for stocks and bonds are set to equal the minimum and maximum U.S. capital market proportions over 1970–1984 (Ibbotson, Siegel and Love). These are: Common Stocks, 45.5 to 64.3%; Small Stocks: 4.3 to 7.3%; IT Gov't Bonds: 8.9 to 19.8%; LT Gov't Bonds: 7.1 to 19.0%; LT Corp. Bonds: 9.9 to 17.0%. Commodity Pool proportions range from 0 to 10%.

[3]Monthly holding period.

[4]Annual holding period.

[5]MP Commodity Pool: Market Portfolio of Commodity Pools; IT Gov't Bonds: Intermediate-term Government Bonds; LT Gov't Bonds: Long-term Government Bonds; LT Corp. Bonds: Long-term Corporate Bonds.

Table 20-13 Optimal Portfolio Results for the Market Portfolio Commodity Pools after Cost Adjustment, 1985–1989

Optimal Portfolio	Unconstrained Portfolio[1]		Constrained Portfolio[2]	
	MHP[3]	AHP[4]	MHP	AHP
Proportions:[5]				
MP Commodity Pools	0.071	0.049	0.053	0.016
Common Stocks	0.226	0.208	0.455	0.455
Small Stocks	0.000	0.000	0.043	0.043
IT Gov't Bonds	0.222	0.285	0.089	0.143
LT Gov't Bonds	0.000	0.000	0.190	0.172
LT Corp. Bonds	0.480	0.458	0.170	0.170
Expected Return (percent/month)	1.262	1.177	1.412	1.301
Standard Deviation (percent/month)	2.283	2.190	3.168	3.092
Sharpe Ratio of Optimal Portfolio:				
With Commodity Pools	0.311	0.286	0.272	0.243
Without Commodity Pools	0.307	0.284	0.270	0.242
Change	+ 1.30%	+ 0.70%	+ 0.74%	+ 0.41%

[1]No constraints on optimal portfolio proportions.

[2]Minimum and maximum optimal portfolio proportions for stocks and bonds are set to equal the minimum and maximum U.S. capital market proportions over 1970–1984 (Ibbotson, Siegel and Love). These are: Common Stocks, 45.5 to 64.3%; Small Stocks: 4.3 to 7.3%; IT Gov't Bonds: 8.9 to 19.8%; LT Gov't Bonds: 7.1 to 19.0%; LT Corp. Bonds: 9.9 to 17.0%. Commodity Pool proportions range from 0 to 10%.

[3]Monthly holding period.

[4]Annual holding period.

[5]MP Commodity Pool: Market Portfolio of Commodity Pools; IT Gov't Bonds: Intermediate-term Government Bonds; LT Gov't Bonds: Long-term Government Bonds; LT Corp. Bonds: Long-term Corporate Bonds.

In summary, these results provide strong evidence of the importance of costs on the investment performance of public commodity pools. They also suggest that reducing costs is likely to be an important consideration for the future competitiveness of public commodity pools.

IX. Summary and Conclusions

The rapid growth of commodity pools has directed attention toward their investment performance. A number of academic studies have examined their performance; however, conclusions differ substantially. One explanation for the conflicting results is the use of different methodology, notably the use of the returns to a random commodity pool in studies which have found inferior performance versus the returns to a market portfolio of commodity pools in studies which have found acceptable performance. A second explanation is the sensitivity of results to the wide variety of data periods investigated.

This study uses monthly commodity return data for all public commodity pools active over January 1979–December 1989 to compare results for both a randomly selected pool and a market portfolio of pools. The sample is the largest used in a study of commodity pools.

Public commodity pool returns were sensitive to the period examined. For a monthly holding period, pool returns averaged 1.125% per month over 1979–1989, but decreased to 0.599% per month over 1982–1989 and 0.751% per month over 1985–1989.

In general, the market portfolio of pools outperformed the randomly selected public pool as a stand-alone investment. However, under no scenario did the market portfolio of pools outrank a stock or bond investment based on Sharpe Ratios. Thus, stand-alone investment performance of public commodity pools was poor.

Not surprisingly, given the variation in public commodity pool returns over different time periods, the portfolio performance of commodity pools also was highly sensitive to the sample period considered. Over 1979–1989, returns for a randomly selected pool exceeded portfolio breakeven returns for the monthly holding period only, while average returns for the market portfolio of pools were greater than breakeven returns for both the monthly and annual holding periods. In contrast, over the 1982–1989 and 1985–1989 samples, returns for both a randomly selected pool and the market portfolio of pools were substantially less than breakeven returns.

The cost of investing in public commodity pools is often mentioned as a reason for their poor performance. When costs were reduced to the level which large institutional pension funds have been able to obtain, commodity pools entered stock and bond portfolios in all three sub-periods. Further, the return-risk tradeoff of stock-bond portfolios was improved as much as 27%. Therefore, it would appear that reductions in cost are important for the future of public commodity pools as competitive investments.

In summary, are public commodity pools a good investment? From a stand-alone perspective, no. From a portfolio perspective, maybe. While additional years of data are needed to answer the last question definitively, lowering costs clearly has the potential to substantially improve performance.

Endnotes

1. Commodity pools also are known as commodity funds and futures funds. The official term in all regulatory matters is commodity pool, and hence, will be used throughout the paper.

2. Twelve pools reported monthly public data in January 1979 to Norwood Securities. However, The Talisman Fund and The Dunn Corporation Limited Partnership ceased reporting monthly data in April 1979 and January 1981, respectively. These pools were not included in the data set.

3. Most commodity pools are created to trade for a specific length of time (e.g., *The Futures Dimension Fund II L.P., Prospectus*). However, a pool will cease trading before the specified time if the total equity or unit value falls below the prescribed minimum in the prospectus or any amount needed to trade effectively. The pool may also stop trading if performance is less than acceptable. In the eleven-year period from 1979 through 1989, 49 pools ceased trading. Dissolution net asset values were obtrained for 42 pools. The net asse value at the end of the last reported month of trading is used as the dissolution value for the remaining seven pools. For a detailed examination of commodity pool dissolution, see Elton, Gruber, and Rentzler (1990).

4. Futures margins may be deposited in the form of interest-bearing instruments. Hence, buy-and-hold futures returns are calculated as the sum of the change in the CRB Index and Treasury Bill returns (Hilliard, 1984).

5. Note that risk is defined relative to a "market" of all public commodity pools.

6.   Equity-weighted returns were also calculated and were not signifi-
     cantly different than equal-weighted returns, so the latter were used in
     this study.

7.   An attempt was made to replicate the commodity pool returns reported
     in Elton, Gruber, and Rentzler (1987). Over the period of July 1979–June
     1985, the following results were found:

	Average Returns MHP	AHP	Standard Deviation
	—percent per month—		
EGR Study	0.73	–0.07	10.86
IKZ Study	0.79	0.10	10.48

     Comparison of the above results suggest that the data and procedures
     used in this study closely replicate those of Elton, Gruber, and Rentzler.

8.   Monthly returns of the market portfolio of pools exhibited nearly
     identical correlations with the alternative investments. Hence, only
     correlations for a randomly selected pool are presented.

9.   However, if correlations are estimated using annual returns, then a
     positive relationship is found. For example, the annual correlation
     between the market portfolio of public commodity pools and the
     inflation rate over 1979–1989 is 0.712. This suggests that commodity
     pool returns are positively correlated with longer-run movements in
     inflation, but not short-run movements.

10. Optimal portfolios were not estimated for the two sub-periods because
     the breakeven analysis indicated that pools did not enter optimal
     portfolios during these periods.

11. This formulation assumes riskless borrowing and lending is possible
     at the same rate and that short sales are not allowed.

12. The actual ranges are:

Common Stocks	45.5 to 64.3%
Small Stocks	4.3 to 7.3%
Intermediate-term Gov't Bonds	8.9 to 19.8%
Long-term Gov't Bonds	7.1 to 19.0%
Long-term Corporate Bonds	9.9 to 17.0%.

Note, in calculating the proportions it was assumed that the market portfolio consisted of only the above five securities.

13. These estimates do not account for initial "load" charges, which may be as high as 12% of invested funds.

14. Irwin and Brorsen (1985) reported that investors in their sample of public commodity pools often were charged full retail commission rates. The data in Table 20-9 imply that institutional investors have negotiated for brokerage rates nearly 80% lower than that paid by public investors (assuming similar trading strategies across the two investments).

References

Basso, T.F. "A Review of Public and Private Futures Funds —1988," working paper, Trendstat Capital Management, 1989.

Brorsen, B.W. and Irwin, S.H. "Examination of Commodity Fund Performance." *Review of Research in Futures Markets,* 4(1985): 84–94.

Brorsen, B.W. and Irwin, S.H. "Futures Funds and Price Volatility." *Review of Futures Markets,* 6(1987): 119–135.

Edwards, F.R. and Ma, C. "Commodity Pool Performance: Is the Information Contained in Pool Prospectuses Useful?" *Journal of Futures Markets,* 8(1988): 589–616.

Elton, E.J. and Gruber, M.J. *Modern Portfolio Theory and Investment Analysis.* New York, NY: John Wiley and Sons, 1987.

Elton, E.J., Gruber, M.J., and Rentzler, J.C. "Professionally Managed, Publicly Traded Commodity Funds." *Journal of Business,* 60(1987): 175–199.

Elton, E.J., Gruber, M.J., and Rentzler, J.C. "New Public Offerings, Information, and Investor Rationality: The Case of Publicly Offered Commodity Funds." *Journal of Business,* 62(1989): 1–15.

Elton, E.J., Gruber, M.J., and Rentzler, J.C. "The Performance of Publicly Offered Commodity Funds." *Financial Analysts Journal,* (1990): 23–30.

Frost, P.A. and Savarino, J.E. "For Better Performance: Constrain Portfolio Weights." *Journal of Portfolio Management,* 14(1988): 29–34.

Futures Dimension Fund II L.P., Prospectus, Merrill Lynch, Pierce, Fenner and Smith, February 1989.

Grossman, S.J. "A Note on Elton, Gruber, and Rentzler's: "Professionally Managed Publicly Traded Commodity Funds," working paper, Department of Economics, Princeton University, October 1987.

Hecht, L. "The Commodities Conundrum." *Institutional Investor,* December 1989, pp. 191–195.

Hilliard, J. "Hedging Interest Rate Risk with Futures Portfolios Under Term Structure Effects." *Journal of Finance,* 39(1984): 1547–1570.

Ibbotson, R.G., Siegel, L.B., and Love, K.S. "World Wealth: U.S. and Foreign Market Values and Returns." *Journal of Portfolio Management,* 11(1985): 1–21.

Irwin, S.H. and Brorsen, B. W. "Public Futures Funds." *Journal of Futures Markets,* 5(1985): 463–485.

Irwin, S.H. and Landa, D. "Real Estate, Futures, and Gold as Portfolio Assets." *Journal of Portfolio Management,* (1987): 29–34.

Lintner, J. "The Potential Role of Managed Commodity-Financial Futures Accounts (and/or Funds) in Portfolios of Stocks and Bonds," paper presented at the annual conference of the Financial Analysts Federation, Toronto, Canada, May, 1983.

Murphy, J. A. "Futures Fund Performance: A Test of the Effectiveness of Technical Analysis." *Journal of Futures Markets,* 6(1986): 175–185.

Sharpe, W. *Investments.* Englewood Cliffs, N.J.: Prentice-Hall, 1981.

Stocks, Bonds, Bills and Inflation: 1989 Yearbook, Chicago: Ibbotson Associates, Inc., 1990.

Appendix

The adjustment of public commodity pool returns to the lower costs of institutional investors was done in two steps. First, gross public commodity pool returns for month t were calculated as follows,

$$GPCP_t = (NPCP_t - TB_t + CCPCP_t + MMPCP_t)$$

$$\text{if } (NPCP_t - TB_t + CCPCP_t + MMPCP_t) \leq 0 \quad (5a)$$

$$GPCP_t = (NPCP_t - TB_t + CCPCP_t + MMPCP_t)/(1 - (IPCP_t/100))$$

$$\text{if } (NPCP_t - TB_t + CCPCP_t + MMPCP_t) > 0 \quad (5b)$$

where

$GPCP_t$ = gross return of the market portfolio of public pools (percent per month),

$NPCP_t$ = net return of the market portfolio of institutional pools (percent per month),

TB_t = treasury bill return (percent per month),

$CCPCP_t$ = institutional pool commission cost (percent per month),

$MMPCP_t$ = institutional pool management cost (percent per month),

$IPCP_t$ = institutional pool incentive cost (percent of gross returns).

Note that calculation of the net institutional commodity pool return is conditional on gross public commodity pool returns. If the latter return is less than or equal to zero, then no incentive costs are assumed to be incurred. Fixed values for commission, management, and incentive costs were assumed, and were based on data in the first row of Table 20-9. Monthly commission (0.775% per month) and management (0.417% per month) costs were calculated by dividing the annual figures by 12. The incentive cost (20% of gross return) was applied directly.

The second step was the calculation of net commodity pool returns based on lower institutional costs. This return was calculated as follows:

$$NICP_t = GPCP_t - CCICP_t - MMICP_t + TB_t$$

$$\text{if } GPCP_t \leq 0 \tag{6a}$$

$$NICP_t = GPCP_t (1 - (IICP_t / 100)) - CCICP_t - MMICP_t + TB_t$$

$$\text{if } GPCP_t > 0 \tag{6b}$$

where

$NICP_t$ = net return of the market portfolio of institutional pools (percent per month),

$GPCP_t$ = gross return of the market portfolio of public pools (percent per month),

TB_t = treasury bill return (percent per month),

$CCICP_t$ = institutional pool commission cost (percent per month),

$MMICP_t$ = institutional pool management cost (percent per month),

$IICP_t$ = institutional pool incentive cost (percent of gross returns).

Note that calculation of the net institutional commodity pool return is conditional on gross public commodity pool returns. If the latter return is less than or equal to zero, then no incentive costs are assumed to be incurred. Again, fixed values for commission, management, and incentive costs were assumed, and were based on data in the second row of Table 20-9. Monthly commission (0.167% per month) and management (0.208% per month) costs were calculated by dividing the annual figures by 12. The incentive cost (25% of gross return) was applied directly.

An example will help illustrate the generation of the institutional commodity pool returns. Assume a net public commodity pool return and Treasury Bill return of 1.0 and 0.5%, respectively, for month t. Then, the gross public pool return is calculated as,

$$GPCP_t = (1.000 - 0.500 + 0.775 + 0.417)/(1 - (20/100))$$
$$= 2.115\%$$

and the net institutional commodity pool return is,

$$NICP_t = 2.115 (1 - (25/100)) - 0.167 - 0.208 + 0.5$$
$$= 1.711\%.$$

Index

About the Author

Dr. Carl C. Peters is Executive Vice President of A.O. Management Corporation and President of International Derivative Investments, Inc. His academic credentials include a Ph.D. in Operations Research from UCLA, an M.S. from MIT in engineering and a B.S. from Penn State University. Dr. Peters held an endowed chair in economics and business at Westminister College in Pennsylvania (1986–1988). His previous experience includes business analysis and corporate planning at Weyerhauser Company (1971–1976), and a faculty appointment in the College of Business, University of Denver (1977–1985), where he was Department Chairman and Director of the Decision Sciences Program. He has conducted research into futures markets, trading systems and portfolio analysis, developed and taught college level courses on the futures markets as well as published and lectured nationally and internationally.

About the Publisher

PROBUS PUBLISHING COMPANY

Probus Publishing Company fills the informational needs of today's business professional by publishing authoritative, quality books on timely and relevant topics, including:

- Investing
- Futures/Options Trading
- Banking
- Finance
- Marketing and Sales
- Manufacturing and Project Management
- Personal Finance, Real Estate, Insurance and Estate Planning
- Entrepreneurship
- Management

Probus books are available at quantity discounts when purchased for business, educational or sales promotional use. For more information, please call the Director, Corporate/Institutional Sales at 1-800-PROBUS-1, or write:

Director, Corporate/Institutional Sales
Probus Publishing Company
1925 N. Clybourn Avenue
Chicago, Illinois 60614
FAX (312) 868-6250